POLICE
CASUALTIES
IN IRELAND 1919—1922

POLICE CASUALTIES
IN IRELAND 1919–1922

RICHARD ABBOTT

MERCIER PRESS

MERCIER PRESS
Cork
www.mercierpress.ie

Revised edition © Richard Abbott, 2019
First published in 2000

ISBN: 978 1 78117 634 4

10 9 8 7 6 5 4 3 2 1

A CIP record for this title is available from the British Library

This book is sold subject to the condition that it shall not, by way of trade or otherwise, be lent, resold, hired out or otherwise circulated without the publisher's prior consent in any form of binding or cover other than that in which it is published and without a similar condition including this condition being imposed on the subsequent purchaser.

No part of this publication may be reproduced or transmitted in any form or by any means, electronic or mechanical, including photocopying, recording or any information or retrieval system, without the prior permission of the publisher in writing.

Printed and bound in the EU.

*To my parents Harry and Mary,
whose understanding and patience
made this book possible.*

CONTENTS

Police Casualties per Month	9
Acknowledgements	10
Foreword	11
1 Introduction	13
The Royal Irish Constabulary	15
The Police's Lack of Preparation for Conflict	17
The Dublin Metropolitan Police	20
The Irish Republican Brotherhood	22
The Irish Republican Army	26
The Political Background	34
2 1919	37
RIC Benevolent Fund	50
Conclusions for 1919	59
3 1920	63
RIC Barracks	70
Attacks on Police	73
The Constabulary Medal	75
The Black and Tans	81
Favourable Awards	105
RIC Recruitment	114
Auxiliary Division of the RIC	133
Discipline	146
Ostracism of the RIC	165
The Ulster Special Constabulary	179
Conclusion for 1920	214

4	**1921**	**217**
	Reprisals	217
	RIC Transport Division	296
	Police Duty during the Truce	339
	Early Casualties in the New Northern Police	342
	Conclusion for 1921	347
5	**1922**	**349**
	The Coming Storm	349
	Disbandment of the RIC	374
	Conclusion for 1922	383
	Alphabetical List of Men Killed	384
6	**Missing Men**	**397**
7	**Other Casualties**	**403**
8	**Databases and Detective Work**	**414**

Notes	**418**
Bibliography	**424**
Index	**427**

POLICE CASUALTIES PER MONTH

Month	1919	1920	1921	1922
January	2	3	25	-
February	-	2	37	11
March	-	7	34	18
April	1	12	27	8
May	2	12	58	18
June	1	7	42	5
July	1	15	18	-
August	2	16	-	1
September	2	24	-	-
October	2	27	-	-
November	1	37	1	-
December	1	17	5	-
Totals	**15**	**179**	**247**	**61**

Total = 502

Casualties are recorded as having happened in the months in which members suffered the attacks that resulted in their deaths, irrespective of when they died, as in some cases death occurred several months after the attack.

ACKNOWLEDGEMENTS

It is not possible to name everyone who assisted and advised me during my research for this book but their help was invaluable and a debt of gratitude is owed to each of them. Particular thanks are due to Tom, who read and commented on different stages of the book in draft. His interest and enthusiasm are gratefully appreciated.

Special thanks go also to Derek for permitting me access to his own private collection of RIC documents, and to Jim, who was able to put me in contact with the families of some of the RIC officers involved in incidents. I also acknowledge and thank Sharon and Pamela for the many hours of invaluable work and their willing assistance in typing and re-typing draft manuscripts.

Finally, I must thank Charlie and Roy for their photographic expertise and the Royal Ulster Constabulary Museum for the use of their facilities and access to the numerous archives held by them.

FOREWORD

There are no police heroes of the Irish revolution – at least, none as defined by songs, stories, statues, memorials or collective memory. At best, a few have acquired the sort of posthumous notoriety that comes with Michael Collins having ordered your death. This anonymity has been as harmful to our understanding of what happened between 1916 and 1923, as is the pantheon of martyrs and warriors of independence.

Richard Abbott's commemorative project is thus both necessary and overdue. He does not try to raise up new heroes but rather performs the vital task of naming forgotten men who, whatever they might have been or done, ended as victims. And it is these names, appearing on nearly every page, which compel our attention. The names of the dead have a focusing and individualising power, while the funeral cadences of their identifications acquire the cumulative impact of row upon row of gravestones: 'Constable McGoldrick, a fifty-nine-year-old married man, was from Co. Cavan. He had thirty-eight years' police service, having been a farmer before joining the RIC ...' Here is a considerable antidote to the blurring effect of uniforms and titles, which lend themselves to stereotypes, statistical aggregation and erasure.

Names also force us to see the complications lying just beneath the smoothed-out surface of received history. How many times has it been written that the Anglo-Irish War began on 21 January 1919 with the Soloheadbeg ambush led by the instant revolutionary celebrities Seán Treacy and Dan Breen? Yet how different this event suddenly feels when we see the names of the constables they killed: James McDonnell and Patrick O'Connell, from Belmullet, Co. Mayo and Coachford, Co. Cork. The Anglo-Irish War began when Breen and Treacy shot McDonnell and O'Connell on a quarry road in Tipperary.

As the circumstances of each demise are related, they further map a geography of war which, while bequeathing many well-known battle sites, otherwise tended to follow the everyday, domestic details of the lives that were taken. Again and again we see the familiar turned fatal, with men shot down in or near homes, pubs, clubs, shops and churches.

Each death also carries an imaginative charge resident in the details of the life that preceded it. What was it like for veteran constables in their forties or fifties to find their long-time neighbours turn away from them or against them? To see their colleagues bleed to death on the roads they had harmlessly patrolled for so long? What was it like for the families so many left behind, who so often occupied their last thoughts: 'Mary I am done! What will you and the babies do?' 'Oh my poor mother, I would not mind only for her.' What of the young 'Tans', the victorious and often decorated survivors of the Great War? Now they found themselves fighting a vicious, doomed campaign within their own country, yet in a foreign land where they could trust no one and were despised. Sharing a lonely, fierce comradeship they felt these deaths with the sting of betrayal, and with a rage that was driven against other men, other families, other victims.

Richard Abbott has written a careful, composed book based on some outstanding research. It is a work of reference to which many will turn, not just for its definitive casualty lists but also for a mass of other information on everything from medals to pensions. More than a compendium, however, it is also a chronicle which does justice to its subjects and holds the reader, who will be repaid with new insight into the lives behind these deaths.

Peter Hart
2000

1

INTRODUCTION

In July 1920 Colonel Ashley asked the chief secretary in the House of Commons if it had been decided to erect a Roll of Honour at the headquarters of the Royal Irish Constabulary (RIC) and the Dublin Metropolitan Police (DMP) respectively in memory of those members who, while serving, met their deaths through violence.

Sir Hamar Greenwood said that no decision had yet been reached with regard to the proposal but he assured the colonel that it would receive the most sympathetic consideration. He felt there should be some public mark of appreciation of the gallant service of those officers who gave their lives for the state.

In June 1921 this question was again raised in the House of Commons when Major Kelly requested that the prime minister ask parliament to authorise the erection of a national memorial to soldiers and police killed in Ireland. Austen Chamberlain, then leader of the Tory Party, replied that he much appreciated the spirit which prompted the question and stated that the suggestion would be considered at the proper time.

Unfortunately, this Roll of Honour and the national memorial were never erected as the tragic occurrences that unfolded during this very turbulent period of Ireland's history overtook events. The only public mark of appreciation of these men, and all those who served in the RIC, are two small memorial plaques which were erected after the force had been disbanded. One, in Westminster cathedral, shows the RIC crest and the dates 1836–1922; the other, in the crypt of St Paul's cathedral, London, likewise shows the RIC crest and the dates 1836–1922, beneath which is the following inscription:

> In memory of the Royal Irish Constabulary and of the officers and men who fell in the discharge of duty during the existence of the Force and in the Great War 1914–1918.

It would appear that no specific memorial has ever been erected in remembrance of the police officers who lost their lives between 1919 and 1922. So in order that some lasting record be made of their names, I have compiled a list of those who, it can be verified, lost their lives as a direct result of political violence. This list is as comprehensive as possible and includes members of the RIC, DMP, Auxiliary Division of the RIC and the Ulster Special Constabulary. It includes only serving officers of these forces who can be identified and does not include those members who were either accidentally shot by their comrades or themselves – sadly accidents of this kind were numerous. It also omits the sixteen men who were kidnapped and believed to have been killed at various times but whose bodies have never been recovered.

In May 1922 the total number of police officers recorded as serving in the RIC on 11 July 1921 (the date on which the Truce between the government and Sinn Féin came into force) was 12,902 regulars and 3,052 temporary officers. The following statistics illustrate the possible numbers of casualties estimated by other sources. These reports stated that from 1 January 1919 to 11 July 1921 5 per cent of RIC members were killed and 8.3 per cent wounded. Working on these figures, this would mean that approximately 700 officers were killed, with well over 1,000 being wounded.

I hope that the following short histories of each of the leading protagonist organisations (RIC, DMP, IRB and IRA) in the unfolding conflict will enhance the readers' knowledge and understanding of them and of their origins and structures. The new police divisions which strove to maintain law and order in Ireland as the violence escalated, including the Auxiliary Division of the RIC, the Ulster

Special Constabulary and a strengthened RIC (mostly by British ex-servicemen who became known in Ireland as the 'Black and Tans', a name that was often also applied to the members of the Auxiliary Division), will be examined in more detail in the appropriate chronological place.

THE ROYAL IRISH CONSTABULARY

Ireland had the unique distinction of having been in the vanguard of policing, with a force formed in Dublin in 1786 and a similar one set up in Belfast the following year. There was also a Baronial Police Force throughout Ireland from 1787.

Robert Peel, chief secretary in Ireland, was behind the introduction of the Peace Preservation Act of 1814 which established a uniformed body of men available to be sent to any part of Ireland requiring their presence to restore law and order. This force was named the Irish Peace Preservation Force. Peel's police experiment was later consolidated by the Constabulary of Ireland Act (1822), which established an organised police force with uniform, training and pay for all members.

This force was called the Constabulary Police and when fully operational it had 313 chief constables and 5,008 constables responsible for policing throughout Ireland. It was under the supervision of four inspectors general, one for each province, and appeared to be four separate bodies of police, with little or no central control. Even so, it is recognised as the first organised national police force in the British Empire.

In 1836 an Act amending the previous Act of 1822 was passed, which improved the rank structure and consolidated the force under the leadership of one inspector general, Colonel Shaw Kennedy, as the Constabulary of Ireland. This force had a uniform system of management with centralisation of control, standardisation of the rules governing the force and a code of regulations for its officers and men, which made it more efficient.

On 6 September 1867, after the failed Fenian Rising earlier that year, nine officers and men of the Constabulary of Ireland, who were to be presented with awards for conspicuous gallantry in the recent discharge of their duty, paraded at the force's depot in Phoenix Park, Dublin.[1] The Marquis of Abercorn, the lord lieutenant, and the Marchioness attended this parade to present the awards. During the presentations, the lord lieutenant said, 'I am now authorised to inform you that, as proof of Her Majesty's satisfaction of the gallant conduct of the Irish Constabulary and of her confidence in their loyalty and devotion, she has been graciously pleased to command that the force shall be henceforth called The Royal Irish Constabulary and that they shall be entitled to have the harp and crown as badges of the force.'

So the RIC emerged to become the first 'royal' police force and soon became the model for other colonial forces. Officers upon appointment to other forces had to undergo a period of training at the RIC depot. Some of these officers were appointed to the colonial police forces, as well as forces in England and Scotland.

When the Anglo-Irish conflict erupted into violence in 1919, the RIC had approximately 11,000 officers and men, along with a headquarters and depot staff. Each county was under the control of a county inspector whose area of responsibility was subdivided into districts under the command of a district inspector. The sub-district was further divided into areas covered by individual RIC barracks. Monthly inspections were made at each barracks by the local district inspector and quarterly by the county inspector, with each district headquarters being inspected biannually by the inspector general.

The Police's Lack of Preparation for Conflict

The early policing system which developed in Ireland was different to other systems in Britain, as it was armed, had a military appearance and was trained and organised on quasi-military lines with no local control. Control was directed from Dublin Castle by an inspector general, who answered directly to the chief secretary, a political appointee, who was a member of the British cabinet at Westminster.

Initially, the people did not find it easy to accept this system of control of policing, though it followed the original concept of policing in Ireland in seeking to reduce the dependence on troops to govern the island. The fact that the police retained their weapons provided nationalist critics with ammunition to attack their credibility throughout the nineteenth century.

However, the wide range of duties assigned to the RIC provided an important counterbalance to the paramilitary image, with the police effectively becoming the public face of government in Ireland. Their routine patrolling, the collection of agricultural and other statistics, and their extensive civil and local government duties ensured that the RIC became a very familiar part of Irish daily life. These generally peaceful civil duties, and the force's acceptance in rural Ireland, helped to integrate policemen into Irish society. To limit the possibility of improper local influence or control of the police, the RIC enforced a policy that members were not to be stationed in their counties of birth. Their integration was helped by the social standing many policemen had, and wished to preserve, in their communities. This attitude substantially transformed and domesticated the RIC's character.

Violence within Irish society as a whole had begun to subside in the latter part of the century for a variety of reasons, including increased emigration after the Famine and stricter clerical control. The RIC's weapons became progressively less visible and, although not formally disarmed, by the early twentieth century the RIC had lost its military edge and no longer constituted a formidable fighting body. It had become a civil police force which reflected the socio-economic structure of Irish society in its composition and in its operations, the needs of small, relatively law-abiding, rural communities.

By the end of the nineteenth century the RIC had earned the reputation of being an organised, well-trained and disciplined police force. However, despite its excellent reputation, there were serious flaws in its administration, which needed reform.[2] This reform was not forthcoming and it became even more necessary with the outbreak of the First World War, when over 800 RIC officers and men volunteered for military service, thereby further diminishing the operational efficiency of the police.

During the First World War morale in the RIC became a problem, the key issues being pay and, in particular, the government's promise of increased war bonuses. The grievance over RIC pay went back many years and was shared by the DMP and other police forces in the rest of the United Kingdom. However, as the war progressed, the issue of pay became more acute due to the rise in wartime prices, which had not been remotely covered by the government's bonuses. This grievance was further compounded by the fact that the RIC's responsibilities had increased considerably during the period. This controversy was aired in the columns of the *Constabulary Gazette* throughout 1918 and 1919.[3]

The inadequacies of reform, aggravated by the pay and bonus issues, together with the Irish administration's enforced economies after the war, began to seriously undermine the morale and operational effectiveness of the RIC. Added to the lack of intelligence, this left the police unprepared for the renewed Republican challenge after the Armistice.

In 1905 the new chief secretary, Walter Long, who was to remain in the post for only nine months, had implemented steps to ensure that the police improved their intelligence-gathering work.[4] His directions included the removal of the 1903 rule requiring the disclosure of the names of informers, and gave the police the authority to spend more in their quest for good intelligence. However, after Long's departure, his liberal successors abandoned his directives on intelligence matters.

Although the police continued to put a good deal of effort into intelligence gathering, by following known troublemakers, watching suspect premises and taking notes at public meetings, it had become a highly ritualised undertaking. This resulted in the recording of essentially trivial information, which produced plenty of background material but nothing definite on what extreme nationalists were planning. There is no doubt that by following old routines the police lost touch with potentially seditious organisations and had no really worthwhile informants on, or penetration of, such organisations when they were needed. Furthermore there were no formal intelligence links between the RIC and the DMP, which meant that available resources were not being utilised to their full potential.[5]

After 1916 the RIC bore the brunt of escalating Republican intimidation and violence. Control of the police was particularly important to all political and religious groupings because of its highly visible manifestation of state power and its conspicuous role in the accumulation of political intelligence. As the police occupied the centre of the political stage, their political affiliations and religious composition were important to ordinary people. Controlling the police or depriving them of their authority became crucial to those seeking to retain, or to gain, power, and became a matter for struggle between the interested groups.

After Sinn Féin's landslide victory in the general election of 1918, they set about supplanting British authority with their own administration, complete with a police and local justice system.[6]

Because of its potency as a symbol of imperial power, and the threat it posed to Sinn Féin's efforts to set up their own administration, attempts were made to humiliate and isolate the pre-existing police force. Efforts to have the RIC ostracised spread and diversified, culminating in the economic and social isolation of many RIC members and the active boycotting, intimidation and victimising of their relatives.[7] This organised campaign, which became increasingly effective, together with the more subtle but equally effective practice of threatening letters, had a psychological impact on the morale and recruitment of police.[8]

The Dublin Metropolitan Police

The Dublin Police Act of 1786 established the first full-time police force in the British Isles, which soon took the name Dublin Metropolitan Police. This force's area was split into six divisions covering the city: A (or Castle) Division; B (or College) Division; C (or Rotunda) Division; D (or Barrack) Division; E (or Donnybrook) Division and F (or Kingstown) Division.

G Division was added to the force later. This section contained the detectives attached to the force and was subdivided into three sections with responsibilities for political crime, ordinary crime and carriage supervision.[9] Detective headquarters was at Brunswick Station and each member had his own notebook from which he transferred, at the termination of his tour of duty, all relevant details into a central intelligence book which was maintained there.

The DMP was an unarmed force and its jurisdiction was confined to an eight-mile radius around Dublin Castle. It was commanded by a commissioner, who had seven superintendents, twenty-four inspectors, 100 sergeants and 1,000 constables under his command. There was also a surgeon attached to the force and an assistant commissioner. Later the rank of chief superintendent was added.

Recruits to the early DMP force had to be unmarried, between twenty-two and twenty-six years of age and able to read and write. They had to be at least 5' 9" in their bare feet and 'proportionally stout'. Each recruit had to satisfy the force surgeon that they were fit for appointment and were, therefore, advised to see their local doctor before travelling to see the DMP surgeon, as they did so at their own expense with the risk of rejection if found unfit.

On his arrival at the DMP depot, the recruit was required to be dressed in a respectable suit and have with him two pairs of strong, serviceable half-boots, three good shirts and four pairs of stockings. He was also required to have with him two testimonials covering the preceding five-year period. One had to be from his former employer, the other from either a clergyman or magistrate. Two testimonials from housekeepers, of which one had to recommend him to the police commissioner for service with the DMP, would be similarly acceptable.

At first, if the recruit had other public service experience he had to produce a certificate of good conduct. Later this rule was changed to prevent any recruit who had previous public service from joining. Any recruit discharged from the army as unfit for duty, or a constable of the RIC receiving a pension or other gratuity were, under no circumstances, to be admitted to the force, and members of the force were not allowed to have any other employment.

As the force was paid one week in arrears, each recruit was also required to have with him fourteen shillings to support himself until his first issue of pay, which was ten shillings, plus lodgings and fuel. The level of the recruit's intelligence determined the length of time he had to remain in the depot, but the average period was eight to ten weeks. Once allocated to a division, a recruit was required to reside wherever appointed.

In 1919, other than the height requirement having been raised to 5' 10" and the recruit needing a minimum chest size of 36" and weight not less than 11 stone, little had changed. Then, the force had twenty-four stations with a strength of 1,202 made up of one chief superintendent, six superintendents, twenty-seven inspectors, forty-one station sergeants, 145 sergeants, 928 constables, eighteen detectives and thirty-six supernumeraries.

By 1921 the number of stations had been reduced to twenty-one and the force had been increased by one superintendent, one inspector, three station sergeants, thirteen sergeants and four constables. The number of detectives was not stated. The requirements for recruits had also changed as they could now be married, aged between eighteen and thirty-three and 5' 8" in height. They were still required to have a minimum chest size of 36" but the weight condition was now not less than 10 stone.

The DMP would remain in being for a short time after partition in 1922, before it was finally absorbed into An Garda Síochána in 1925.

The Irish Republican Brotherhood

The Irish Republican Brotherhood (IRB), a secret oathbound society, was founded on St Patrick's Day 1858 by James Stephens and Thomas Clarke Luby, following the suspension of an earlier revolutionary group, the Phoenix National and Literary Society. This new society was committed in principle to using force to compel the British to grant self-government to Ireland.

In America the IRB was led by John O'Mahony, who gave the American branch of the society the name of the Fenian Brotherhood.[10] In 1873, as a result of their ill-fated attempt to invade Canada in 1866, the American wing of the society was reorganised, but by the beginning of the twentieth century the whole organisation seemed to be a spent force and had been successfully penetrated by British informers.

A second reorganisation of the society took place in 1907, when the older, less active leadership was replaced and a system to screen new members was introduced in an attempt to prevent infiltration by British agents. The society also adopted a cell or circle system, whereby the only person who knew all the individuals in any particular circle was the circle leader or head, and he was also the only member of the lower circle who knew how to make contact with the circle above. Circles were grouped to form districts under a district centre, and a number of these districts then formed a county circle under a county centre. The whole organisation was divided into eleven divisions, eight in Ireland, two in England and one in Scotland.[11] The society was governed by a supreme council, with the president of the council being the chief of the entire Brotherhood.

Many of the new recruits to this revamped IRB took their secret oath to the society in a newsagent/tobacconist shop in Dublin, which the future Easter Rising leader Thomas Clarke had opened in 1907 after his return to the city from America. (Clarke had been released from prison in 1898, having served fifteen years for his part in the dynamite campaign in Britain in the early 1880s.)

After the reorganisation of 1907, the IRB's supreme council adopted a policy of infiltrating other potentially useful organisations in order to place IRB members in positions of power and influence. The IRB successfully infiltrated organisations such as the Gaelic League and the Gaelic Athletic Association (GAA).[12] However, in the formation of the Irish Volunteers in November 1913 on the prompting of Eoin MacNeill, the IRB leadership saw an opportunity to establish an openly armed and trained force in the country, which would be ready at any favourable moment to strike against Britain. The IRB looked upon this as a heaven-sent opportunity, as its members had been drilling in secret and were waiting for an opportunity to appear under an unchallenged guise in public. IRB members were instructed to join the new Volunteer movement but to take orders from their 'superior officers'.[13]

MacNeill believed that the Volunteers should be utilised only to prevent any attempt to frustrate Home Rule's introduction at the end of the First World War. The IRB leadership, however, intended that the Volunteers should not be used as a defensive force but rather as an offensive one, and they were in contact with their American wing (which now used the Gaelic name of Clan na Gael) to ensure that this objective was achieved.

With the outbreak of the First World War, the leadership of the IRB decided that they were not going to allow their generation to miss Ireland's opportunity as their predecessors had done during the Boer War.[14] In August 1914 a small group of IRB leaders met secretly in Dublin and pledged to mount a rebellion aimed at gaining Ireland's total independence. Early in 1915 the IRB, through John Devoy, liaised with the Germans, which enabled one of the society's Irish leaders, Joseph Plunkett, to make contact, via the German foreign office, with Chancellor Theobald Von Bethmann-Hollweg.[15] Plunkett arranged that the following spring the Germans would send a shipment of weapons and ammunition, which would be used in Ireland in an insurrection timed to coincide with a German offensive on the Western Front.

In the spring of 1915 the IRB formed a military committee, which very soon after its formation became known as the military council and consisted of five leading IRB leaders. This council went to great lengths to ensure that its plans remained secret from both Dublin Castle and MacNeill. It also attempted to have the Volunteers and James Connolly's Irish Citizen Army united, but was unable to persuade MacNeill.[16] In order to prevent Connolly and his plans for the Citizen Army from derailing their own strategy, the IRB leaders confided in him, and on 16 January 1916 he was sworn into the IRB, becoming a member of its military council.

British intelligence, through their cypher centre in Room 40 at the Admiralty, London (under the leadership of the brilliant maverick Captain Reginald Hall), were aware of the IRB's plans, having intercepted and decoded German diplomatic transmissions between Washington and Berlin.[17] This intelligence ensured that the British were well briefed on the links between the Germans and the Irish-Americans, and on Republican leader Sir Roger Casement's progress in Germany as he sought aid for the planned rebellion. This information bore fruit on Good Friday, 21 April 1916, when a German shipment of munitions aboard the *Aud*, a disguised German steamer, was captured off the Kerry coast and escorted towards Queenstown before the captain, Karl Spindler, scuttled her at the approach to Cork Harbour, and in the capture of Casement after a U-boat (U-19) had landed him and two companions near Banna Strand in Co. Kerry.

On 23 April, when MacNeill's order to cancel Easter Sunday's activities appeared in the *Sunday Independent*, the IRB's military council convened a meeting in the Liberty Hall, Dublin. Despite the widespread uncertainty that prevailed, they decided to proceed with the planned rebellion the following day, no matter how unpromising the circumstances, as they feared the authorities were poised to carry out arrests. The military council also believed that Irish nationality had sunk so low that only a 'blood sacrifice' would revive it, and so, on Easter Monday, 24 April 1916, the Rising began.

After this failed insurrection, the Irish prisoners held at Frongoch, a military camp in Wales being utilised as an internment camp, debated the pros and cons of static warfare. Michael Collins, who in November 1909 had been sworn into the IRB at Barnsbury Hall by Sam Maguire, and who had become the society's treasurer for the London and south of England areas, was a believer in the hit-and-run approach to warfare during these debates.[18] He supported the thinking of one of those executed for his participation in the Easter Rising, Major John MacBride, who had fought for the Boers against the British in South Africa. He felt Irishmen should never again allow themselves to be locked up in buildings, outnumbered and facing superior firepower. Another reappraisal of IRB thinking began.[19]

On 27 October 1917 a secret convention was held by the Irish Volunteers at the GAA's Jones Road ground, Drumcondra. The IRB dominated proceedings, and had their members placed in key posts within the Volunteers. By 1919 the IRB had a strong controlling influence on the movement.[20] This secret control was further strengthened with the election of Michael Collins as the president of the IRB's supreme council, shortly after Éamon de Valera's departure for America on 1 June 1919. The hand of the IRB would be the driving force behind the forthcoming increase in political violence.[21]

The Irish Republican Army

In the 1860s a group known as the Fenian Brotherhood was active in the United States with the aim of liberating Ireland and establishing a Republic. Most of the support for the Fenian cause came from the thousands of ex-soldiers from both the Union and Confederate armies, many of whom accepted ranks and appointments with the Fenian organisation.

On 4 March 1866 the Brotherhood held a mass meeting in New York and suggested an invasion of Canada. The result was that on 31 May 1866 a group of 800 armed Fenians (who were mostly *émigré* Irishmen) marched into Canada from the USA. They carried a green flag adorned with the gold harp of Ireland and the letters IRA. Just inside the border, at a place called Ridgeway, they met a hastily assembled Canadian force, which they defeated. However, on hearing that a larger Canadian force was approaching them, they fled back across the border. This was the first time that any Irish group or society calling itself the Irish Republican Army had ever taken to the field.

On 1 November 1913 Eoin MacNeill, vice-president of the Gaelic League (an organisation which had been founded in 1893 by Douglas Hyde, a Protestant, in order to preserve and revive Gaelic culture, language and traditions) wrote in the league's paper – *An Claidheamh Soluis* (The Sword of Light) – an article entitled 'The North Began' proposing that a body of southern volunteers be formed on the same lines as the recently formed Ulster Volunteer Force (UVF).

MacNeill then organised a private meeting, the first of five, in a room at Wynn's Hotel, Lower Abbey Street, Dublin, on 11 November 1913, with a handful of like-minded men for the purpose of starting a body of volunteers. Another of these meetings was held on 14 November 1913 and from that gathering was born the Provisional Committee of the Volunteers. About half of those present at the private meetings were members of the IRB, but this was unknown to MacNeill and most of the others.[22]

A public meeting to form the Irish Volunteers was held on 25 November 1913 in the Rotunda Hall, Dublin and on 1 December 1913 the first assemblies of Irish Volunteers took place in halls which had been secured for them in Dublin. A number of men who had served in the British Army acted as drill instructors, and from the start the Gaelic title *Óglaigh na hÉireann* was used as an equivalent of 'The Irish Volunteers'.[23]

The head of the IRB in Dublin was a Belfast Quaker called Bulmer Hobson, who encouraged MacNeill in his new venture. Unlike the UVF, which had been formed by the unionists in the north-east of the island to frustrate the Liberal government's plan to introduce Home Rule to all of Ireland, the Irish Volunteers saw themselves as a counterbalance to ensure that this British Act of Parliament was carried out without hindrance from the unionists. The vast bulk who joined this new movement did not foresee themselves being actively engaged in any fighting, but the IRB members had other plans and intentions, as the 1916 Rising was to prove.

The Irish Volunteers aroused national enthusiasm and general support, which caused the rapid growth of the organisation into a widespread national movement. This convinced the IRB leadership that if they wanted independence they would be better off fighting for it rather than waiting for the constitutionalists at Westminster to decide on how much or how little (or when) Home Rule would be granted.

John Redmond, the leader of the Irish Parliamentary Party, at first viewed this new movement, over which he and his party had no control, with a resentful and unfriendly eye. He feared it would jeopardise the prospect of Home Rule, for which he and his party had worked so long and hard, being granted. Having tried everything to discourage the growth of the Volunteers, Redmond, in May 1914, through secret negotiations with their leader MacNeill, tried to gain control of the organisation.[24] When this failed he sent a letter to the press on 9 June in which he insisted that he be given control of the Volunteers and that unless their leaders agreed to add twenty-five persons nominated by himself to their committee (which he believed contained twenty-five members) he would call upon his supporters in the Volunteers to break away and form their own organisation. Faced with the prospect of a split in the Volunteers, the majority of the members of the committee decided to surrender to Redmond's demand and he then took control.

In August 1914 the First World War broke out and Redmond agreed to postpone the implementation of the Home Rule Bill until after the war, encouraging members of the Volunteers to join the British Army, which they did in large numbers. It was a recruiting speech by Redmond in favour of the British Army at Woodenbridge on 20 September 1914 that caused the inevitable split within the Volunteers. Approximately 170,000 remained with Redmond and became known as the National Volunteers, while 10,000–12,000 remained as the Irish Volunteers under the influence and leadership of the IRB.[25]

By 1915, because of enlistment, the influence of the National

Volunteers was reduced, while the Irish Volunteers started to rebuild and reorganise. The chosen date for the Rising was the spring of 1916 but, on learning of these plans, Eoin MacNeill, who was the Irish Volunteers' chief of staff but not a member of the IRB, countermanded the mobilisation order. The other leaders knew that this revolt would likely end in disaster because of the earlier split in the movement, the recovery by the government of the arms destined for the Rising, and the uncertainty of the Volunteers as to whether or not the mobilisation was still to take place. They felt, however, that their sacrifice and example would put new heart into the Irish people and give rise to an Irish revolutionary independence movement, so they carried on with their plans for Easter week.

During the insurrection, one of the leaders of the Volunteers, Patrick H. Pearse (who styled himself commandant-general of the army of the Irish Republic) proclaimed a Republic from the steps of the General Post Office (GPO) in Sackville Street, Dublin, on Easter Monday 1916.

After the failed uprising, the Volunteers spent their time re-organising and re-equipping. Then, on 21 January 1919, when a Provisional Government sitting in the Mansion House, Dublin, formed departments (including that of defence), it was confirmed that the Irish Volunteers were now the army of the Irish Republic. The Department of Defence automatically made them the defence force of the new government, to be known henceforth as the Irish Republican Army, under the control of the minister for defence. This was announced by Éamon de Valera, the president of the Provisional Government, on 11 March 1921, when he proposed that the Provisional Government should formally acknowledge a state of war with Britain, and should, therefore, publicly take full responsibility for the military actions of the Volunteers as the army of the Republic. This proposal was unanimously adopted and so, on 30 March 1921, de Valera made the following statement to the newspapers:

> One of our first Governmental acts was to take over the control of the voluntary armed forces of the nation. From the Irish Volunteers we fashioned the Irish Republican Army to be the Military arm of the Government. This Army is, therefore, a regular state force under the civil control of elected representatives and under officers who hold their commissions under warrant from those representatives. The Government is, therefore, responsible for the actions of this Army.[26]

Although the Volunteers had stated in August 1918, in their monthly paper *An tÓglach* (The Volunteer), which had been published for the first time in that month, that they were the army of the Irish Republic, they did not confirm this until after a special Volunteers' convention held in the spring of 1919. On 10 April in that year, at the second sitting of the Dáil, the minister for defence, Cathal Brugha, was 'in close association' with the voluntary military forces, but not in control of them, and the issue of the autonomy of the Volunteers remained.[27]

On 20 August 1919 Cathal Brugha proposed a motion that every Irish Volunteer should swear an oath of allegiance to the Dáil and the Irish Republic and, once this was taken, that the Irish Volunteers would become the standing army of the Irish Republic. The Dáil approved this oath but it was not administered until the autumn of 1920.[28] Although no order was issued from their headquarters (HQ) to have the Volunteers' name changed, it did in fact change as the fighting increased and the people, newspapers and even the British Government began to refer to the Volunteers as the IRA.

From the outset, the Irish Volunteers had organised themselves on a coordinated military basis and modelled themselves on the British Army, forming companies, battalions and brigades. A company had three officers: a company commander (captain) and two half-company commanders (first and second lieutenants). Each company was subdivided into four sections with a section commander and two squad commanders. A section was itself subdivided into two squads. Each squad had seven men attached to it, including a pioneer or signaller. The squads of a company were numbered 1 to 8. As well as officers, a company also had a company adjutant, a signaller and a bugler, piper or drummer. Early in 1920 companies also appointed intelligence officers.

Companies in Dublin and other cities were distinguished by a letter, whilst those in country areas were usually named after the parish in which they were formed. No company was officially recognised as permanent until it had existed for two months and fulfilled the requirements of the Volunteers. The true strength of companies varied, with only a few in towns and cities being at the required levels; the remainder were on average approximately thirty to thirty-five in number.

The captain attached to a company was elected by ballot at a general company meeting but was not given command until his election had been ratified by HQ. HQ also had the power to relieve a captain of his command either at his own request or at the request of the company. Between five and eight companies formed a battalion which was to be self-contained with its own engineering, signals, transport, supply, intelligence and quartermaster departments. The officers attached to a battalion were: commandant, vice-commandant, adjutant, quartermaster and assistant, engineer commander and surgeon. All these officers were appointed by ballot at a meeting of all the officers of the companies comprising the battalion.

Between three and five battalions were formed into a brigade, the officers of which were elected by its battalion's staff and in some counties there was more than one brigade (Cork, for example, had three). A brigade's officers included a brigadier general, who presided at meetings with his brigade staff and took the final decision on any operation. He travelled constantly around his area, keeping in touch with battalions and companies in order to familiarise himself with the territory for which he was responsible.

The second-in-command of a brigade was a vice-brigadier general, who deputised for his commandant, inspecting battalions and companies, paying particular attention to training, special services and signals. The brigade adjutant was responsible for the correspondence and communications system between battalions and brigade, and also between HQ and brigade.

An intelligence officer attached to a brigade was required to obtain all available information on military and police in his area regarding movements, disposition, posts, weapons, vehicles and identities. He had to build up an information network on which he could rely, and each company within a brigade was responsible for appointing a number of 'call houses' and despatch riders within the company area. These 'call houses' were to be off main roads on an organised route which was known to despatch riders of other companies.

During 1920 there was no higher formation within the IRA than a brigade, but by the end of 1921 the whole country had been divisionalised. On 26 April 1921 the First Southern Division was formed, containing nine brigades, three each in Kerry and Cork, two in Waterford and one in West Limerick. Before 11 July 1921 the Second Southern Division and the Fourth Northern Division had been formed, with the rest following. In the area that was to become Northern Ireland, the IRA formed a northern military council and also a Belfast Guard which had approximately 600 men attached to it.[29]

As well as these formal units, the IRA's General Headquarters (GHQ) ordered that flying columns be formed. These first came into being at the end of May 1920, when two senior Limerick IRA men, in broad daylight, were able to move across open country for approximately thirty miles without being discovered. They achieved this by the careful use of the countryside's natural cover and the avoidance of towns, among other things. As a result, the IRA came to the conclusion that the same could be done by a larger body of armed men and the principle was first put into practice in the East Limerick area. The concept was soon adopted by other IRA brigade areas, and the flying column developed into one of the IRA's chief offensive weapons.[30]

At first these flying columns were small, self-contained bands of men who were on full-time active service and who operated whenever the opportunity presented itself. Local companies provided these columns with safe houses and guards while a column was resting in their area. The number of men attached to any column varied, but the largest one was in Co. Cork and numbered 105 men in total. Orders were issued to flying columns about their security as follows:

> When [the column is] resting scouts or sentries should be posted on vantage points commanding a view of the whole country about. At night they should be posted on all roads and should be provided with horns (or other sounders) to signal the approach of the enemy. When moving, columns should have advance and rear guards connected with the main body.
>
> Columns should never move into country until it is first scouted and the OC has satisfied himself that it is either free of the enemy or that he is aware of the exact position he occupies.[31]

In cities the IRA did not use columns but instead formed Active Service Units (ASUs), though some rural areas also formed ASUs rather than flying columns. An ASU was formed in Dublin at the end of 1920 and was organised in sections that corresponded with the Dublin battalion areas. This ASU had fifty men attached to it who were on full-time operations and were, therefore, paid £4–£5 per week. The Dublin ASU acted in much the same way for the Dublin Brigade as Collins' Squad (of which we shall hear later) did for the intelligence section of the IRA. Another ASU was formed in Cork city in September 1920 from members of Cork's two city battalions.[32]

A few days after the IRA attack on the Custom House in Dublin on 25 May 1921, the Dublin ASU and Collins' Squad were amalgamated into the 'Dublin Guard', which allowed Éamon de Valera (president of both the Dáil and Sinn Féin) and Cathal Brugha (minister for defence) more control over the Squad, which they viewed as Collins' personal autonomous unit.

On partition in 1922, the Dublin Guard became the first regular unit in the new National Army.

The Political Background

During the failed uprising of 1916 the citizens of Dublin and the population of Ireland had little sympathy for those who had participated, but this attitude was soon to change dramatically for a number of reasons.

The government handled the aftermath of the Rising badly, particularly the execution of its leaders. This caused public opinion to focus on the remaining prisoners being held in prisons in Britain, and the population of Ireland also began to examine the doctrines of Sinn Féin. On 22 December 1916 the first batch of prisoners was released from gaol and returned to Ireland. The people received them as heroes, with bonfires, bands and torchlight processions through densely packed streets.

On this new tide of popular support, Sinn Féin won a number of by-elections early in 1917. With the prisoners' return to Ireland, the ranks of the Irish Volunteers grew and they started reorganising and rearming. On 16 April 1918 the government (against all advice) passed the Conscription Act in Ireland. This was as a direct result of the need for fresh troops to replace the large number of men killed and wounded during the German offensive (the Ludendorff Offensive) in March 1918. In the end, the need for conscription receded but it had the effect of uniting all strands of opposition against the government and swelling the ranks of both Sinn Féin and the Irish Volunteers.

The government compounded this problem when, on the night of 17–18 May 1918, it had the leaders of this opposition arrested, alleging that they had been involved with the Germans in a plot against the British. These arrests threw the leadership of the nationalist movement into the hands of men less well known to the authorities and, therefore, not so easily arrested.[33] (Michael Collins was not arrested as he had been forewarned of the pending arrests by a DMP detective.)[34]

On 4 July 1918 the Volunteers, Sinn Féin, Cumann na mBan and the Gaelic League were all proscribed. This had little effect, as the people gave Sinn Féin a landslide victory in the general election held in December 1918. From the outset, all Sinn Féin candidates pledged that, if elected, they would abstain from taking their seats at Westminster. This policy was taken further when the Sinn Féin candidates set up their own national parliament (Dáil Éireann) on 21 January 1919 in the Mansion House, Dublin, establishing a Provisional Government of the Irish Republic as proclaimed at Easter 1916.

Coinciding with the first sitting of Dáil Éireann, Dan Breen, Seán Treacy and several other Tipperary Volunteers, acting without orders from either their headquarters in Dublin or from the Provisional Government, took matters into their own hands, as they had grown impatient for military action against the British. As Breen stated in his book, *My Fight for Irish Freedom*, the Volunteers were in great danger of becoming merely a political adjunct to the Sinn Féin organisation. (Breen said, 'we had nothing definite in mind, but we proposed to engage in some enterprise that would start the ball rolling in Tipperary.')[35]

The action which started the ball rolling, not only in Tipperary but in the whole country, was the killing of two constables by the

Tipperary Volunteers on 21 January 1919 at Soloheadbeg. These killings triggered the military stage of the Anglo-Irish conflict, which became known as the War of Independence and within Republican circles as the 'Tan War', by which name it is still known.

2

1919

21 January 1919,
Soloheadbeg, Co. Tipperary
James McDonnell, Con 50616
Patrick O'Connell, Con 61889

These two policemen were escorting 168lbs of gelignite, in three cases of half a hundredweight each, and thirty-eight detonators from the military barracks' magazine in Tipperary town to Soloheadbeg quarry.

The IRA needed high explosives for grenades and demolition work, so when they received information that explosives were soon to be conveyed to the quarry, which was in a small townland about two and a half miles from Tipperary and one mile from Limerick Junction, they planned to take them. (Seán Treacy, the vice-brigadier of the IRA's South Tipperary Brigade, also believed that the forcible taking of the gelignite from a police escort would have a salutary effect on the morale of the IRA.)

So, from 16 January 1919, the IRA lay in ambush, moving into their position each morning before daybreak and waiting until 2 p.m. before abandoning it, as they felt certain that the police would not come with the explosives after that time of day. On leaving the ambush location they made their way to the nearby home of Dan Breen, where they would stay before moving back into their ambush position the next morning.

After three days, the number of IRA men involved in this ambush was reduced to nine. They were Séamus Robinson (OC

South Tipperary Brigade), Seán Treacy (vice-brigadier), Dan Breen (brigade quartermaster), John Joseph Hogan (who was known as Seán), Tadhg Crowe, Patrick McCormack, Patrick O'Dwyer, Michael Ryan and Seán O'Meara. Each man knew the area very well, having been born and brought up in the vicinity. Treacy's old home was only a stone's throw from the quarry.

On 21 January O'Dwyer was acting as lookout when he saw the cart and police escort making its way towards the quarry. He warned the others, who had taken up their positions in a ditch which was topped by a whitethorn hedge. They had stationed themselves along the ditch from the nearest pillar of a gate into a field in the direction of the quarry. Treacy, who was armed with a 0.22 automatic rifle, took up a position behind the other gate pillar. As the cart approached it was led by Edward Godfrey, the driver. Constable James McDonnell had been driving the cart but he got down from it 150 yards from the quarry and the two constables now walked a short distance behind it with a county council employee, Patrick Flynn. Flynn, who was to take delivery of the explosives, walked between the policemen, who had their rifles slung over their shoulders.

As the cart came abreast of the gate, Treacy issued a challenge. Flynn crouched behind the cart and Godfrey looked round in bewilderment as the two constables fumbled with their rifles. Treacy shot both officers with his rifle, his shots being followed by a burst of revolver shots from the ditch. Both constables fell dead on the roadway. Treacy and Breen leaped over the gate into the roadway and as he did so Breen's mask slipped. (On 29 January the government issued a wanted poster with a reward of £1,000 for his arrest.) Robinson and O'Dwyer, revolvers in hand, came onto the road ahead of the cart, securing it and covering Godfrey. The others secured the rifles and equipment from the constables' bodies.

The cart, with Hogan at the reins and Treacy and Breen on either side, was driven away. The others escaped in different directions, with

Crowe and O'Dwyer (already a wanted man on the run) dumping the rifles in a safe hiding place some distance away. The IRA men forgot about the detonators, which remained in Patrick Flynn's pockets.[1] All sources studied, including Republican ones, agree that Constable McDonnell was a typical, harmless village constable, whose great joke was to ask children to spell 'rhododendron' and then teach them the correct spelling.[2]

The coroner declared that the constables were killed on the spot. He described the tragedy as one of the saddest cases that had happened in Co. Tipperary, or any part of Ireland, for many years. He said he knew the deceased constables well and added that Constable McDonnell had been in Tipperary for thirty years, and a more quiet and inoffensive man he had never met, while Constable O'Connell was also a decent, quiet man who, during the recent influenza epidemic, had acted as a nurse to his comrades. It was terribly sad to see these men shot down while doing public duty and not doing anything that would injure anybody.

Constable McDonnell, a fifty-seven-year-old married man with five children, was from Belmullet, Co. Mayo. He had thirty-six years' police service, having been a farmer before joining the RIC. A relief fund was later opened for his family. Constable O'Connell, a thirty-six-year-old single man, was from Clonmoyle, Coachford, Co. Cork. He had twelve years' service, having also been a farmer before joining.

The explosives passed through a number of hands in a short time. Once removed from the scene in the cart, they were taken on the Dundrum to Tipperary road to Lisheen Grove, where they were dumped in a ditch at the roadside and covered with leaves. A few sticks were taken for misdirection and thrown onto the roadway when the three IRA men had covered a good distance from the hiding place and before they abandoned the horse and cart at Ryan's Cross. Later, school children found 1lb of the missing explosives in a field near Allen Creamery, midway between Tipperary and

Dundrum. Later, more were found thirty yards from where the horse and cart were discovered.

The following Friday the explosives were moved by a man called Tom Carew (later to become the intelligence officer for the South Tipperary Brigade). He and his brother, who travelled in a cart in front of him, made their way towards the explosives. On reaching them Carew waited for the all-clear signal from his brother, who had travelled further along the road, before placing the three boxes into his cart. Having collected the explosives, Carew was stopped a short distance away by an RIC patrol for not having lights on his cart. On being questioned as to his movements by the sergeant in charge of the patrol, Carew produced a receipt for the sale of timber from Tipperary Barracks and stated that he was taking the timber home. (This was not the case as the timber had been bought at an earlier sale in the barracks by his father.)

A constable then confirmed Carew's alibi by pointing out that the load of timber had a label from Tipperary Barracks attached. Carew was allowed to proceed and took the explosives to a neighbour's farm. The next day he placed the three boxes in a dugout on his own family farm, where they remained until 9–10 November 1919. At that point they were again moved, with a box going to each of the following units: headquarters South Tipperary Brigade, Tipperary town and Rosegreen.[3]

The first time the explosives were used was on 18 January 1920 during the attack on Drumbane village hall, which was being used as a police barracks. Before this, security forces almost discovered the explosives on three occasions as follows:

1. When a military lorry broke down on the roadway beside their hiding place at Lisheen Grove.

2. When the Carew brothers were stopped, as described above.

3. When Carew's farm was searched by the security forces and they began to dig right above the dugout containing the explosives.

During their searches for the missing explosives, soldiers found a box in a dyke near a rath at Donour Creenane, which was about two miles from the scene of the ambush. This box contained charcoal and some gelignite that was not from the same consignment as those from Soloheadbeg.

On 24 January 1919 Constable McDonnell was buried in St Michael's Cemetery, Tipperary. On the same day Constable O'Connell was buried in Coachford, Co. Cork. (Treacy was to follow them to his own grave on 14 October 1920.)

On 31 January 1919 the Irish Volunteers' paper, *An tÓglach*, announced that the Volunteers were entitled morally and legally to kill British police and soldiers.

6 April 1919, Limerick city
Martin O'Brien, Con 62375

Constable Martin O'Brien was shot dead whilst guarding a prisoner at Limerick Workhouse. The prisoner, Robert Byrne (adjutant of Limerick city's Second Battalion of the IRA), had been arrested for the unlawful possession of a revolver and ammunition, and on 13 January 1919 was sentenced to twelve months' imprisonment with hard labour.[4]

Once sentenced, Byrne commenced a struggle to secure political status for the prisoners in Limerick gaol. During the course of this campaign he instigated a riot, which failed. He then went on hunger strike. No attempt was made to forcibly feed him due to the adverse publicity for the government following the death of Thomas Ashe on 25 September 1917 at Mountjoy gaol in Dublin. After three weeks Byrne was in a weakened condition and had to be moved to Limerick

Union Hospital, where he was placed in Ward One, a general ward. The rescue of Byrne on Sunday 6 April 1919, by a group under the leadership of Michael 'Batty' Stack, a section leader of the IRA's E Company, Second Battalion, would appear to have taken place as follows.

On that day Byrne was in his bed in the ward, which was in an alcove and out of view of other patients. Constables O'Brien and Spillane sat at either side of it, while Sergeant Goulden and Constables Tierney and Fitzpatrick, along with Warder Mahoney, were on duty in the ward, being at vantage points to scrutinise visitors.

Approximately twenty IRA men entered the general ward as visitors, drifting into it singly and in pairs towards the end of visiting hours at 3 p.m. A further fifteen IRA men were in the hospital's corridors and grounds. Once the rescue began, they were to cut the hospital's telephone wires. A blast on a whistle was given as the signal for the IRA to mount their rescue.

Bewildered by the alien sound, the policemen attempted to draw their revolvers. Byrne, who knew of the rescue plan, tried to get out of bed. Startled visitors sprang to their feet and, panic-stricken, stampeded for the ward doors. Constable O'Brien hurled himself bodily on top of the prisoner.

Stack approached the alcove and shot Constable Spillane in the back, shattering his spine with a 0.38 bullet. He then shot Constable O'Brien, who fell to the floor dead. The other RIC men were all wounded during this rescue.

Byrne was moved from the hospital by the IRA but that was when their plan began to go wrong. Originally they were to going have a car at the hospital to remove Byrne from the scene, but this was required at short notice to move Dan Breen and Seán Hogan, two of the IRA men involved in the Soloheadbeg killings on 21 January, so alternative transport had to be obtained. As cars and drivers were few in those days, the alternative transport used was a horse-drawn mourning coach which had been lent to the IRA by a local undertaker. This coach, along with a nurse, clothes and a disguise for Byrne, waited at the rear entrance to the hospital, but the IRA party removed him from the hospital by the front entrance.

Once into the roadway the rescue party noticed that Byrne had been shot and could not be moved far on foot. A horse and trap driven by a John Ryan came on the scene. Byrne was placed in the trap and taken to Ryan's home, which was near Meelick, Co. Clare, about three miles from the hospital. At 8.30 p.m. that Sunday evening Byrne died and the next morning the police found his body in Ryan's cottage.

Constable O'Brien, a thirty-five-year-old married man with one child, was from Co. Tipperary. He had twelve years' service, having been a farmer previously. He was stationed at Caherconlish and had only been on temporary duty in Limerick at the time of his death. He was buried on 9 April 1919 in Birr, King's County (now Offaly).

13 MAY 1919,
KNOCKLONG RAILWAY STATION, CO. LIMERICK
Peter Wallace, Sgt 56438
Michael Enright, Con 62005

Two police officers were killed as they escorted a prisoner by train from Thurles, Co. Tipperary, to Cork city.

The Arrest
Seán Hogan, Séamus Robinson, Dan Breen and Seán Treacy, four of the IRA men involved in the Soloheadbeg killings in January, had attended a dance at Ballagh on 11 May 1919. It had been intended that after the dance all four men would return to the O'Keeffes' house at Glenough, but Hogan and Brigid O'Keeffe went instead to the Meagher house at Annfield, near Thurles. (The Meaghers were cousins to the O'Keeffes.)

Next morning a police party was sent to search this house, the home of a known active IRA family, unaware that a wanted man was inside. Hogan, who had been warned of the RIC's approach, left the house via the rear door, making his way towards the roadway. The RIC party, which comprised Sergeant Wallace, Constables Ring and Reilly and three others, saw this and waited for Hogan to come out onto the road, where they stopped and searched him, finding a revolver.

They then searched the house but found nothing. As the RIC party were leaving with the prisoner, Brigid O'Keeffe said, 'Goodbye Seán.' Believing her to be a daughter of the householder, the police left, not realising that a short distance away in the O'Keeffes' house three more wanted men were hiding. The police took their unidentified prisoner back to Roskeen Barracks, where his identity was established later that morning, and then Hogan was moved to Thurles Barracks.

On hearing that Hogan had been arrested and taken to Thurles, Treacy at once knew that the police would move their prisoner by train to Cork city, as this was the usual destination for prisoners arrested under the Defence of the Realm Act (DORA) in Munster, and he and the others began to plan a rescue.[5]

The Plan

Having satisfied themselves that any attempt to attack the barracks at Thurles was impossible, the three IRA men made their way to Maloneys of Lackelly, near Emly. They planned to attack the police escort party at Emly Railway Station, but at the very last minute dropped this plan in favour of Knocklong, which was in quiet countryside and deserted on one side, with the two nearest police barracks being at least three miles away.

Treacy sent May Maloney to Thurles to tell the IRA of Hogan's movements by coded telegrams. Hogan was given the code name 'greyhound' and these messages were to be sent to Thomas Shanahan, the manager of Knocklong Coal Store. This man was supposed to have been told to expect these coded messages but he was not. When Shanahan, a coursing enthusiast who had sent a greyhound to stud in Co. Dublin on the previous day, received the first coded telegram which stated, 'Greyhound in Thurles still', he thought it was about his own dog and did nothing.

Treacy also sent for help from the Galbally unit and five IRA men arrived at Maloneys. They were Éamon and John Joe O'Brien, Jim Scanlon, Edward Foley and Seán Lynch.

The plan was then explained by Treacy: four of the Galbally IRA men were to board the train in which Hogan travelled without arousing suspicion at Emly. A Thurles IRA man, McCarthy, was to board the train at Thurles and once in Emly Station he was to wave a white handkerchief from the window to inform the IRA party at Emly which train to board. As it happened, this signal was not seen, but the IRA men in Emly boarded the right train by luck.

Treacy, Robinson, Breen and Éamon O'Brien were to go to Knocklong Station and, once there, Robinson and Breen were to guard the entrance while Treacy and O'Brien were to board the train and, along with the others already on board, attack the police escort and rescue Hogan.[6]

The Incident

On his arrival at Knocklong, Treacy had expected a messenger would meet him with the coded message; when no one arrived, he sent Éamon O'Brien in search of Shanahan. O'Brien returned to Treacy with the first message, which stated that Hogan was not coming. Treacy decided to wait for the train anyway, in case the Galbally men were on it.

As Treacy and O'Brien waited, the Dublin-bound train arrived into the station. (As a rule the Cork and Dublin trains arrived simultaneously into Knocklong Railway Station.) At once the two IRA men saw that one compartment of the Dublin train contained soldiers, who remained on board. After the Dublin train left and just as the Cork train arrived, Shanahan arrived and handed O'Brien a second message, which he placed into his pocket without reading. (This message stated 'Sending Wednesday evening by 6.30 p.m.') Then, as Treacy and O'Brien turned to leave the station, John Joe O'Brien raced up to them from the Cork train telling them that Hogan was on it.

Treacy and Éamon O'Brien boarded the train with their revolvers drawn. They made their way to the carriage which contained the police and their prisoner. Hogan, handcuffed, sat with his back to the engine between Sergeant Wallace and Constable Enright. Opposite them sat Constables Reilly and Ring, each armed with a rifle.

The sliding open of the compartment door took the RIC party by surprise and all four officers half-rose. Treacy and O'Brien opened fire and Constable Enright fell back dead. Sergeant Wallace was able to knock Treacy's gun from him and started to wrestle fiercely with him. Hogan hurled himself at Constable Ring, hitting him full in the face with his manacled hands, while Constable Reilly wrestled with O'Brien. The other IRA men rushed in and wrenched Constable Reilly's rifle from him, clubbing him with it, until he collapsed unconscious on the floor. One of the IRA party, Lynch, moved Hogan from the carriage, and Constable Ring, who was in a half dazed state, was thrown out of the carriage window.

Sergeant Wallace's great physical strength defied the combined onslaught of Treacy and O'Brien and he was able to get his revolver out and in the cramped and constricted carriage crowded with struggling men, he shot Treacy in the throat. The revolver was wrenched from the sergeant's hand and he was shot twice by Treacy, collapsing to the floor.

Constable Reilly, who had recovered his senses towards the end of the struggle, noticed Constable Ring's rifle under one of the seats. He secured it and, unnoticed, crawled out onto the platform. He then opened fire on the IRA party through the carriage window, wounding Éamon O'Brien as he held Sergeant Wallace from behind; Scanlon was also wounded.

This rifle fire brought Breen and Robinson hurrying down the platform, which was thronged with excited passengers. An exchange of shots then took place between Breen and the constable, with Breen being shot through the lung and right arm. Robinson, in the meantime, had stopped with the engine driver to prevent him moving the train. Constable Reilly, having engaged Breen, fell back, still firing at the other IRA men as they tried to leave the train. The incident had lasted from 8.13 p.m. to 8.27 p.m.[7]

The Aftermath

The IRA party hurried from the scene, Hogan being taken into a neighbouring butcher's shop where his handcuffs were removed with a butcher's cleaver and heavy weight. Breen was helped from the railway station onto the roadway by a soldier in khaki uniform, who had cheered for the Irish Republic while the fight raged.

All the IRA men then made their way to Michael Shanahan's, near Knocklong, where Doctor Hennessy of Ballylanders (later a member of the Dáil) attended to Breen and Treacy. Breen's condition was so serious the doctor was certain that he would not survive his wounds.

Soon after their arrival at Shanahan's, Breen and Treacy were moved by pony and trap to Cush, where they stayed one day. The following night two cars arrived at Cush, and Breen and Hogan were placed in the second car, which was kept in darkness, while the first car, with its lights full on, went in front to act as a decoy. The vehicles sped through the town of Kilmallock and eventually reached their destination between Newcastle West and Drumcollogher in West Limerick.

Éamon O'Brien and Scanlon were moved also by car to Co. Cork, the vehicle being fired at by a military guard at Moore's Camp when it failed to stop. Both these men later went to America and did not return to Ireland for many years. Treacy remained in the general East Clare area.[8]

Sergeant Wallace died from his wounds on 14 May 1919 in Kilmallock. He was a forty-eight-year-old married man from Co. Roscommon. He had been a postman before joining the RIC and would have completed twenty-five years' police service on 16 May. He was buried on 22 May in the graveyard near Curraghroe, Co. Roscommon. Constable Enright was a thirty-five-year-old bachelor from Ballyneety, Co. Limerick. He had twelve years' service, having previously been a clerk.

Six men were charged with these killings, three of them being found guilty at their trial in Armagh on 9 March 1920. Of these three men, Edmund Foley and Paddy Maher were hanged in Dublin on 7 June 1921. The third, Michael Murphy, was released shortly after the Truce on 11 July 1921.

23 JUNE 1919,
THURLES, CO. TIPPERARY
Michael Hunt, DI 55727

This RIC officer was shot dead in the square at the top of Main Street, Thurles, after he had performed his duty at the Thurles Races. A police report gave the following account:

> I regret to have to report that at 5.30 p.m. this date, DI Michael Hunt of Thurles was shot when returning in uniform from Thurles Races.
>
> When entering the square from New Street the DI was fired at three times in quick succession. Sergeant Joseph Grove 59311 and Constable Patrick Murphy 52292, who were about 15 to 20 yards in front of the late DI, turned around at once and saw him lying on

the ground face downwards. They rushed to him at once, raised him up and carried him to the footpath. There was a rush in all directions from the scene by the very large crowd then returning from the races and there is no doubt the murderer got away in the crowd.

The sergeant, then having failed to trace the murderer, blew his whistle and Constables William Walsh 55430 and F. R. Doyle 66082, Sergeant John McFarland 55453, Constable Richard Doyle 58557, Sergeant Joseph Meardy 58726 and the other police who were on duty near the scene rushed to the place.

Sergeant Grove then sent word to the RIC Barrack and the Military Barrack, and also sent for a clergyman. Doctor Thomas Barry, who lives at the place, was in immediate attendance but could do nothing for the late DI as he died in less than five minutes. The late DI's lips and mouth moved as if to speak but he was unable to do so. With the consent of Mrs Scully's son the body was removed to her home and Doctor Barry more fully examined it.

He found that one bullet had entered the spine about six inches below the collar of the overcoat, another bullet had entered higher up under the left shoulder blade, one of those bullets showed itself below the right nipple just under the skin.

On receiving the report I went with a party of police to the scene and having seen that nothing further could be done for the late DI, we looked up suspects and searched every suspicious person. We also searched every person in the public houses, closed them out and moved off the crowds, but failed to get any trace of the assassin. I shall continue to make enquiries. It is likely that the murder was directed by persons who were anxious to remove the late DI, who had prosecuted several Sinn Féiners, and was an important witness in pending cases of a similar nature. Probably the murderer came from a distance and took opportunity of the Race Day to commit the murder.

S. Patterson

HC 56146 for DI killed.[9]

On further researching this incident, one publication stated that this killing was carried out by an IRA man, Jim Stapleton. It would appear that he was accompanied by some others but he was the only one to fire.[10]

DI Hunt, a forty-five-year-old married man, was from Co. Sligo. He had twenty-six years' police service, having been a farmer before joining the RIC. He was buried on 26 June 1919 in Monasteraden Catholic Cemetery.

RIC BENEVOLENT FUND

On 29 July 1919 a meeting was held at the library in the RIC depot Phoenix Park, Dublin, to consider the establishment of an RIC Benevolent Fund. Brigadier General Sir Joseph A. Byrne, KBE, CB, Inspector General of the RIC, presided. This meeting proposed the inauguration of a benevolent fund to make provision for hardship cases, which at the time were dealt with through special appeals to the generosity of individual members of the force.

Prior to this meeting the public had subscribed liberally to a fund inaugurated by the Earl of Granard, Lieutenant Colonel Sir Hutcheson Poe.[11] Lieutenant Colonel Poe had conceived the idea to start a fund on 19 May 1919, after the Knocklong incident, and on 3 June 1919 he held a public meeting in the Royal Irish Automobile Club in Dawson Street, Dublin, in order to form the RIC indemnity fund.[12]

Members of the RIC felt that it was only right that the force should also make an organised effort to meet this pressing need. The inaugural meeting of the Benevolent Fund, held in the RIC depot, unanimously agreed that money should not be paid out if men had been killed or injured in the execution of their duty, as the recent Criminal Injuries Act would compensate for this, but moneys should be used for the dependants of men who died or were required to leave the RIC because of sickness.

The meeting also agreed that the fund should be administered by a sub-committee of one county inspector, one district inspector, one head constable, two sergeants and four constables, all of whom had to be subscribers to the fund. It was further agreed that benefits from the fund would be payable from 1 April 1919. The sum of £4,113 5s 10d was then raised by public subscription in response to an appeal issued by the committee of the RIC Benevolent Fund in recognition of the splendid services which the RIC had rendered the country during a period of great difficulty and disorder. That period sadly was only a forerunner of the political violence that was to come.[13]

This was not the first time the RIC had proposed such a scheme, as District Inspector John Charles Milling, 56627, had in 1914 suggested that a large insurance scheme be started and that this scheme be used as a benevolent fund. On 2 January 1915 Mr Milling became a resident magistrate, proving unpopular in Westport, Co. Mayo, because of his willingness to send Irish Volunteers to prison for unlawful assembly and drilling. On 31 March 1919 he was shot through the window of his drawing room and was hit in the abdomen. He died the next morning from his wounds. At the time of the attack Mr Milling had been putting his clock on to the new summer time before going to bed, when four revolver shots were fired at him.

30 July 1919,
Millmount Avenue, Drumcondra, Dublin city
Patrick Smyth, D/Sgt DMP

This officer was the first member of the DMP to be killed. He had just got off a tram car at Drumcondra Bridge when he was attacked by five gunmen, who fired numerous shots. The sergeant was able, although severely wounded, to make it to his own front door at 51 Millmount Avenue, where he collapsed.

Background

On 7 April 1919 Michael Collins was smuggled into the DMP detectives' headquarters at Brunswick Street by a friendly member.[14] (Detectives in the DMP were attached to G Division and as such were known as G-men long before the name became famous from American gangster films. They were what would now be called Special Branch officers and as such were the lynchpin in the government's intelligence system.) Collins spent the night going through G Division records, which gave him the *modus operandi* of the intelligence system and also showed him how to combat it.

On 9 April Collins took the first step in using the intelligence gathered at Brunswick Street and had a number of G-men assaulted and warned against their involvement in intelligence work.[15] Sergeant Smyth was threatened in an attempt to make him drop charges against a Sinn Féin member, but he refused.

Collins realised that more would have to be done to paralyse G Division, so he formed an elite 'hit unit' to eliminate its members.[16] This unit was known as the Squad and its specially selected operatives were under the direct orders of Collins. (Although officially founded on 19 September 1919 at 46 Parnell Square, the Squad had killed twice before.) Collins impressed on the Squad that no organisation in Irish history had ever had a unit to deal with spies but that had now changed. In January 1920 Collins expanded the Squad to twelve in number and they soon became popularly known as the 'Twelve Apostles'.[17]

The Incident

Some of the Squad members had waited several nights for Sergeant Smyth near his home at Drumcondra before he was shot. They fired on him, wounding him several times, and were amazed to see him continue running. (Collins analysed the reasons for this and from then on the Squad members were armed not with 0.38 but 0.45

revolvers. They also began to work in pairs, walking up to their victim, with one shooting the victim in the body to knock him down while the other fired into the victim's head to kill him. Moreover, in further killings involving the Squad, eight members were used, this number including back-up and lookouts.)

On hearing the gunfire the sergeant's children rushed out into the street and saw their father about fifteen yards away in the direction of Drumcondra Bridge. He was leaning against the wall of a house with his hand on his hip. When one of his sons reached him he said, 'I am shot; get the ambulance quick.' Another son and daughter then helped their injured father to their home.

Later, in hospital, the sergeant spoke to Sergeant Lynch and, as reported in *The Irish Times* of 23 September 1919, told him: 'I was coming home soon after 11 p.m. When I got off the tram at the end of my own avenue I saw four or five men against the dead wall and a bicycle resting against the curb stone. Just as I turned the corner into Millmount Avenue I was shot in the back. I turned and said to them, "You cowards", and three of them fired again with revolvers at me and one bullet entered my leg. I then ran away and they pursued me to within about fifteen yards of my own door and kept firing at me all the time. In all about ten or twelve shots were fired at me. I shouted for assistance but no one came to me except my own son. I had no revolver myself and I am glad now I had not one as I might have shot some of them when I turned round after the first shot, as I would not like to have done that.'

Sergeant Smyth died from his wounds on 8 September 1919 in the Mater Misericordiae Hospital, Dublin. He was a forty-eight-year-old native of Co. Cavan, married with seven children. He had twenty-eight years' police service and was the first police officer killed in a grim process, masterminded by Collins, which targeted DMP detectives who were becoming well-informed about the IRA and their activities.

4 August 1919,
near Ennistymon, Co. Clare
John Riordan, Sgt 57242
Michael James Murphy, Con 69587

These two RIC officers were cycling back to a protection hut at Illaunbaun, Ballyvoreen, near Ennistymon, when they were ambushed at Eighth-One Crossroads, under Mount Callon, by three armed men who sprang from behind a bush. (A protection hut was a steel building used as a temporary police barracks and this one had been erected for the purpose of protecting the members of a family named Marrinan, who had been witnesses for the crown in the Kildea murder case some years before.) As a result of the ambush Constable Murphy was killed outright, while Sergeant Riordan was mortally wounded.

While lying on the ground the sergeant scribbled an entry on the flyleaf of his prayer book, which he had been given by his sister, a nun: 'Shot by three assassins wounded them.' On another page he had written: 'A repeater did us.' He was removed to the Union Hospital, Ennistymon but died on 5 August. A forty-five-year-old widower with no family, from Macroom, Co. Cork, he had twenty-three years' service, having been a labourer before joining the RIC. He was buried at Kilnamartyra on 8 August 1919.

Constable Murphy, a twenty-year-old bachelor, was from Co. Westmeath. He had eight months' police service on the day prior to his death, having been a farmer before joining the RIC. He was buried at Augharaso Cemetery, Co. Leitrim, on 8 August 1919.

2 September 1919,
between Lorrha and Carrigahorig, Co. Tipperary
Philip Brady, Sgt 54833

An RIC cycle patrol of three men was ambushed near a disused quarry, midway between Lorrha and Carrigahorig. Sergeant Brady, a married man who had only arrived at Lorrha on 30 August 1919 from Enniskillen, was killed outright, while Constable Foley received serious head injuries. He was taken to the Workhouse Hospital at Borrisokane. Republican sources stated that six to eight IRA men from the local Lorrha unit were involved in this attack and that three police rifles were captured.

The Incident

On 2 September 1919 James Carroll, along with his uncle, John Gilligan, an ex-British soldier, met Michael Hogan and John Madden. All four men went to Ballyquirk, where they hid behind a wall. At this point Carroll produced a parcel, which when opened was found to contain four guns. This was the first Gilligan knew of the coming attack and stated that he wanted nothing to do with it. He was told, 'Sit down if you don't want to see what happens.'

The police patrol left the barracks at 10.30 a.m. and went to Ballyquirk crossroads. At 11.30 a.m., as it was returning, the patrol reached the gate to a farm owned by people called French, when a noise was heard from the wall at the right, which was four to six feet high. The head and shoulders of a man were then seen coming up from behind the wall.

As the gunfire started, the sergeant called out, 'My God I am shot.' A constable, on seeing the man appear above the wall, ran towards it and fired his rifle, forcing the attackers to flee. After the ambush was over Carroll told his uncle, 'There are no informers in these days.' John Gilligan then made his way to Birr and re-enlisted; Carroll also enlisted in the army a short time later.

On 22 April 1920 John Madden who, it was stated, was the man seen appearing above the wall, was tried for the death of Sergeant Brady at Green Street Courthouse, Dublin. The court was guarded by military – some stood at the rear of the courtroom itself, while in front of the judge three soldiers with fixed bayonets stood guard. The gallery facing the judge was occupied by RIC men armed with carbines.

Sergeant Brady, a forty-six-year-old married man with six children aged between two and eleven, was from Co. Cavan. He had twenty-eight years' police service, having been a farmer before joining the RIC. He was buried at Redhills, Co. Cavan on 6 September 1919.

12 September 1919,
Townsend Street, Dublin city
Daniel Hoey, D/Con DMP

On 12 September 1919 Detective Constable Hoey was shot dead in Townsend Street by members of the Squad as he was heading for the Central Police Station in Brunswick Street. (Within a few days of his death he was to have taken up duty with the Special Branch at Scotland Yard.) Earlier that day security forces searched Sinn Féin headquarters at No. 6 Harcourt Street, Dublin, and the government announced that Dáil Éireann was banned. Some sources alleged that Hoey took part in this search, and Michael Collins reacted by having him shot, both as a result of this alleged involvement and also as a direct reaction against the government's banning of the Dáil.

(Republican sources studied also state that Hoey, a deeply religious man, had picked out one of the leaders of the 1916 Rising for the firing squad. These sources allege that this man was Seán Mac Diarmada who, though well-known in Dublin, had not been identified at Richmond Barracks after the Rising and had been chosen as one of those to be interned until he was identified by Hoey. Official papers from the time appear to show that the leaders of the Irish Volunteers had been under surveillance for some time before the Easter Rising. In the case of Mac Diarmada this surveillance had lasted for more than three years, with Hoey keeping detailed notes of the pubs he visited and his other movements, along with details of people he associated with.)

Hoey, a thirty-two-year-old man, had been born near Edenderry, King's County (now Offaly). He had joined the DMP in September 1910. On 16 September 1919 he was buried at Rhode, King's County.

19 OCTOBER 1919,
HIGH STREET, DUBLIN CITY
Michael Downing, Con DMP (A49)

The constable, who was stationed at Chancery Lane, was on beat patrol in High Street, Dublin, when he was shot and wounded. He was taken to the Mercer's Hospital but died from his wounds. A twenty-three-year-old man with three years' police service, he was from Castletownbere, Co. Cork. He was buried at Adrigole, Bantry, Co. Cork on 22 October 1919.

Constable Neary of the DMP later received a special service cross from the British Red Cross for giving one pint of blood in an attempt to save Constable Downing.[18]

31 OCTOBER 1919,
BALLIVOR RIC BARRACKS, CO. MEATH
William Agar, Con 63198

The constable, who was on duty as the barracks orderly, was shot when he answered a knock at the barracks' door in the village of Ballivor, nine miles from the town of Trim. Shots rang out and the constable staggered into the barracks' day room and fell dead. Men wearing masks then pulled shut the door into the room. Other police in the room fired through the door four times at the masked men, but they escaped, taking some arms from the barracks.

The constable had only been in the barracks for ten days, having transferred from Navan. A thirty-seven-year-old man, he was from Tullow, Co. Carlow, and had been married on 22 May 1919. His wife was expecting their first child. He had eleven years' service, having previously been a labourer. He was buried at Rathrilly, Co. Carlow on 4 November 1919. He was the first police officer to die as the direct result of an attack on a barracks, but he was not the last. Constable Agar's brother was stationed in Belfast at the Springfield Road Barracks.

29 November 1919, College Street, Dublin city
John Barton, D/Sgt DMP

This officer was shot and wounded in College Street as he was going towards the central police station. He was taken to the Mercer's Hospital but died a short time later. A short time before his death the detective sergeant had, through his informants, discovered an IRA arms dump in Dublin. Also, according to information contained in official papers, it would appear that he had given evidence against Joseph Plunkett, one of the leaders of the Easter Rising, whom he had been watching for some time before the rebellion. He was, therefore, a marked man whom the IRA wanted to kill.

Background
At the end of the summer of 1919 Treacy, Breen, Hogan and Robinson, who by this time were known as the 'Big Four' within Republican circles, had made their way to Dublin. They arrived just after the Squad's official formation and they soon formed a close alliance with its members. On Collins' instructions they acted as auxiliaries to the Squad and as such played a part in most of its activities. As the Squad attacked Barton, Treacy was not only present but seems to have fired the two shots which fatally wounded the detective sergeant.

Barton was thirty-six, single and had joined the DMP in 1903. He was from Ballymacelligott, Co. Kerry and was buried in Keel, Co. Kerry, on 3 December 1919.

14 December 1919, Kilbrittain, Co. Cork
Edward Bolger, Con 54668

The constable, who was unarmed, was shot dead as he was going from his home to the barracks in Kilbrittain, a village seven miles from Bandon, Co. Cork. He was attacked by two men, who continued to shoot him several times after he had fallen.

At this time, small parties of RIC or groups of military led by a policeman who knew the people and the countryside intimately were continually searching for IRA arms and literature. These patrols also tried to arrest known IRA men whenever possible and this activity by the security forces was having an effect on the IRA, disrupting the whole organisation. Constable Bolger was involved in these search-and-arrest operations and, according to Republican sources, was successful in his duties. He had arrested seven IRA men in October and had been the principal witness against them at their trial in November, during which a serious riot developed at the courthouse. On 12 December these men were released and two days later Constable Bolger was killed.

Bolger, a forty-seven-year-old married man with four children, was from Co. Kilkenny. He had twenty-eight years' service, having had no other employment before joining the force.

Conclusions for 1919

My research into the incidents in 1919 has, to date, shown that a total of fifteen police officers were killed as a result of political violence.

Another officer died in August from a bullet wound, but it has never been established how he received this wound. One was accidentally shot in December by a colleague, while another constable was reported as having been shot in Killarney in December during a fight between soldiers and civilians. However, later reports stated that he too had been accidentally shot by a comrade.

During the first six months of 1919 the campaign of attacks against the RIC was sporadic and, to a certain extent, spontaneous, with the number of police casualties being small. However, as the year progressed, with improved organisation, the IRA was able to spread its attacks throughout the whole country. It embarked upon a deliberate and systematic guerrilla campaign to neutralise the police. These physical attacks, and the ongoing local ostracism, petty persecution and intimidation of RIC members, their families and relations (coupled with a wage increase in 1918 that only gave a police veteran with fifteen to twenty years' service forty-three shillings per week and a recruit in the depot thirty-one shillings) ensured that morale within the force remained low. Times of national distress had always been associated with increases in resignations from the police, but the onset of political unrest in 1919 produced a marked increase in such numbers.

The problems of morale and force numbers were further compounded by the then inspector general of the RIC, Joseph Byrne (1916–20), who exercised the authority given to him by the Constabulary and Police (Ireland) Act 1883 and initiated a policy which compulsorily retired men, in order to rid the RIC of officers whom he, for one reason or another, felt no longer met the required standard.[19] It was somewhat ironic that this power was invoked on 18 January 1919, just three days before the first major incident of the year which resulted in the deaths of policemen. This mandatory retirement policy removed loyal, seasoned men from the ranks as any semblance of 'normal' policing was fast disappearing.

These problems with police numbers and the low morale of the force were making it painfully obvious that the RIC could not cope and was beginning to show signs of collapse, and were exacerbated by the force's archaic administrative procedures.[20] The lack of police intelligence had not been addressed in 1919 and the RIC still did not have a detective unit to deal with separatist organisations, while its Crime Special Branch remained no more than a records section.

Although the DMP did have such a unit in the form of its G Division, it had fared little better, as it was heavily undermanned and poorly led. It had come under heavy IRA attack, with five of its total membership of ten being attacked, resulting in the death of two officers and the serious wounding of a third. These attacks ensured that the DMP's efficiency in its intelligence work virtually ceased, a problem compounded as the embattlement of the RIC had resulted in that force's reduced contact with the general public. Consequently, its ability to gain an understanding of political developments throughout the country was similarly reduced.

This lack of intelligence forced the military, in the spring of 1919, to develop its own network, but like the police they too were unable to obtain much useful information on the development and control of the IRA.[21]

Despite the growing crisis in 1919, the British cabinet remained remarkably uninterested in the 'Irish problem', being devoid of ideas and indecisive in getting to grips with it. Although the authority of the government was diminishing daily, the administration in Dublin Castle continued to be riven by internal disputes, had no coherent policy and was seldom able to produce a consensus on what action to take. This situation ensured that, even when agreement was reached, there was little confidence within the administration that effective measures would follow from any decisions. No planned or sustained campaign was launched, which resulted in disorganised responses to successive IRA actions in 1919.

An example of the administration's ineptitude was their designation of Tipperary South as a special military area under the DORA after the Soloheadbeg killings. The punishing of everyone simply made life less pleasant for the entire population and was ineffective in apprehending the perpetrators. This made the people progressively more hostile to the government and also increased support for the IRA.[22]

However, not all Dublin Castle initiatives failed. A licensing system for fairs, markets and meetings introduced throughout Ireland proved a very effective way of controlling agitation, pushing the IRA's own 'police' underground, and by November 1919 'open lawlessness' had practically been suspended.[23]

Despite this the RIC was forced to rely increasingly on military assistance. Urgent funding required for the police in Ireland was refused by the Treasury. This problem increased and military officers warned that the garrison in Ireland would not be in a position to continue carrying out policing duties as their strength was being reduced. It can be seen then that, as 1920 approached, urgent measures were required to address the deteriorating policing situation in the face of increased political chaos in Ireland.

3

1920

20 January 1920, Thurles, Co. Tipperary
Luke Finnegan, Con 65234

The constable had just finished duty at 10.15 p.m. and was making his way home to his residence in the Mall, Thurles. A few yards from his home he was fired at three times by four men in fawn overcoats who had been standing twelve to fifteen yards from the constable's front door. The lamp near the officer's home had been turned off and the area was in complete darkness.

The constable was wounded in the abdomen but was able to stagger to the front door of his home, where his wife let him in. He gasped to her on the doorstep, 'Oh Mary I have been shot,' and once into the house he said, 'Mary I am done! What will you and the babies do?'

After the attack the men involved escaped up the mall.

Constable Finnegan was removed to Steeven's Hospital, Dublin, but died from his wounds at 11.30 p.m. on 22 January. In an attempt to save Finnegan's life, blood was transfused from Constable Patrick McGirr. This was a new concept in medicine at the time, whereas today blood transfusions are commonplace.[1]

The Aftermath
On seeing their wounded colleague, the local police smashed the windows in the houses of twelve prominent Sinn Féiners. Eleven panes of glass in the local Sinn Féin hall were also broken and a number of volleys were fired down the street as a reprisal, but no one was

injured. These incidents were later described as the 'Sacking of Thurles'. It was the first time that members of the RIC had reacted after the shooting of one of their colleagues.[2] Despite the IRA's campaign against them, which was backed by an intense social boycott, until then they had not retaliated in any undisciplined form, with their morale holding remarkably well. During attacks on patrols and barracks, the police had almost always refused to surrender and fought bitterly, often driving off superior numbers. However, the attack on Constable Finnegan was to establish a pattern of unofficial reprisals by police officers after attacks on their colleagues.

British Prime Minister David Lloyd George wrote as follows to the *Daily Chronicle* about the incident:

> Nobody can fail to deplore such occurrences but equally obviously no one can wonder at them. Indeed it is obvious that if these murderous clubs pursue their course much longer, we may see counter clubs springing up and the lives of prominent Sinn Féiners becoming as unsafe as prominent officials.

The prime minister then warned, if indirectly, through this article of the possibility of counter-insurgency measures being adopted, and before the end of the year his government had introduced a policy of 'official reprisals'.

Constable Finnegan's remains were taken to Ballinlough, Co. Roscommon, where they were met by a funeral party including Mr Patrick Kelly, an ex-RIC sergeant, who was his father-in-law. On 29 January 1920 he was interred at the Catholic churchyard at Williamstown, Co. Galway. An RIC party from Dunmore took part in the funeral.

Finnegan, a twenty-nine-year-old married man with two children, was from Tuam, Co. Galway. He had nine years' service, having been a farmer before joining the RIC.

21 January 1920, Harcourt Street, Dublin city
William Charles Forbes Redmond,
Second Assistant Commissioner, DMP 57951

Redmond was shot dead as he made his way from his office in Dublin Castle to the Standard Hotel in Harcourt Street. He had been due to vacate his rooms in the hotel for the safety of accommodation in the Castle. At 6.10 p.m. he was shot twice by IRA man Paddy Daly (a member of the Squad) and fell mortally wounded in Harcourt Street. He had been hit in the left jaw and the back, severing his spinal cord. Dr Robinson, who resided at 13 Harcourt Street, was on the scene at once but Redmond was dead within a minute. After the attack five men were seen running from the scene.

On 25 January 1920 the government issued a reward notice of £10,000 for evidence to convict the offenders in the killings of Redmond or the other police officers (both RIC and DMP) killed. They also offered £1,000 reward for secret information about Collins and £10,000 for his body, dead or alive.

Background
As a result of previous killings and other pressures on G Division personnel, the intelligence department of the DMP had begun to falter and the government realised that urgent measures were required in order to prevent its total collapse. They approached this problem on two fronts:

1. They placed Redmond, an experienced detective, in charge of G Division in order to reorganise the demoralised detective division.
2. A British Secret Service Agent was placed close to Collins himself.

In November 1919 Redmond made a serious mistake that would

cost both himself and that agent their lives. Underestimating Collins' inroads into the ranks of the G-men, he ordered that they all parade in Brunswick Street one night, where he addressed them. During this pep talk he is alleged to have remarked, 'It was extraordinary that you who know Dublin so well could not catch Michael Collins, whereas a man who had only just arrived from England had managed to meet him more than once.'[3] This information, coupled with the fact that Redmond had brought with him a squad of RIC detectives from Belfast who did not appear at any Dublin police station but lived about the city as civilians and worked closely with him, was passed to Collins.

From Republican sources studied it would appear that Collins had penetrated right into the heart of the British Secret Service and was able to confirm that they had an agent close to him. He also knew that Sir Basil Thompson, the head of the service, described this agent as one of the best and cleverest England ever had. (He was later identified as a DI's son from Newcastle West, Co. Limerick. His real name was Byrnes but he called himself Jameson, a salesman of musical instruments with an interest in bird watching.)[4]

Byrnes began infiltrating Irish circles in London, posing as one of the fiery communist speakers whose podium adjoined the Irish Self-Determination League's platform at Speakers Corner in Hyde Park. Through a London IRB man called Art O'Brien, Byrnes was able to make contact with Collins, stating he had two objectives:

1. Provide the IRA with arms.
2. Foment mutiny in the British Army and Navy, both in England and Ireland.

As evidence of his good faith, Byrnes visited Dublin and handed over a suitcase of handguns to the IRA. He then had the building into which he had seen this suitcase taken searched by the security forces, but the weapons had been moved before the search. This search was one of the main reasons that the IRA suspected him of being a British agent.

Collins realised that Redmond and the British Secret Service agent were forces to be reckoned with and he would have to deal with them, but first he had to identify them. He sent one of the Squad, Frank Thornton, to Belfast to link up with an RIC sergeant named Matt MacCarthy at Musgrave Street Barracks. The sergeant, a Kerryman, installed Thornton in the barracks for the night, claiming he was his cousin. It was the evening of the Police Boxing Championship and every policeman who could was attending, including the DI. During the night Thornton entered the DI's office, removed Redmond's photograph from his file and the following day handed it to Collins.

Collins then had Redmond watched by the Squad, but did not order any action against Byrnes, whom he had come to like, in the hope that he would go back to England and never return after Redmond had been killed. However, Byrnes did return to Ireland, so two of the Squad, Paddy Daly and Joe Dowling, called on him at the Granville Hotel, Dublin, telling him that Collins wished to see him. They took him by tram to the back entrance of the Albert College in Ballymun, where they informed him they knew he was a British Secret Service agent. Both IRA men stated that, once confronted, Byrnes stood to attention and clicked his heels while they cocked the hammers of their 0.45 revolvers, but they gave differing accounts of what he said. Daly, who killed Byrnes by shooting him in the head, alleged he said, 'That's right. God bless the King. I would love to die for him.'

A contemporary report records that at 5.15 p.m. on 2 April 1920 seven shots, three in rapid succession, followed after a short pause by four more, were heard in Hampstead Lane. This lane led from Ballymun Road, Glasnevin, to the Model Farm, Glasnevin, and was a quarter of a mile from the tram terminus. After these shots were heard the body of a well-dressed man was found lying on the roadway with several bullet wounds to the head and body. His clothes had been singed by the flames from the firearms used to kill him.

Byrnes' body was removed to the Mater Hospital, where it remained for several days before being identified as being that of a Mr Jameson. This closed the first chapter in the battle between the Squad and the British Secret Service, but others were to follow.

During the First World War Redmond had been a major in the Sixth Battalion of the Royal Irish Rifles. He rejoined the RIC in the early part of 1918. He was from Co. Armagh, forty-seven and married with two daughters aged thirteen and sixteen. He had twenty-three years' service, having previously been a clerk, and was buried on 23 January 1920 in Mount Jerome Cemetery, Dublin.

24 January 1920,
Baltinglass RIC Barracks, Co. Wicklow
James Joseph Malynn, Con 67903

On 24 January 1920 the IRA attacked yet another barracks. Constable Malynn answered a knock at the door from a newspaper messenger but when he opened it a volley of shots was fired at him, hitting him twice. He was seriously wounded in the spine during the attack and died on 1 December 1920 in the Mercer's Hospital. Malynn was thirty, married and from Co. Cork. He had seven years' service, having previously been a constable in Hull. He was buried at Burngreave Cemetery, Sheffield.

Before the attack two motor cars had entered the village and within two minutes of the attack they had left again, at speed.

Background
Early in 1920 the IRA began to carry out concerted attacks against

RIC barracks and refined its operational techniques in these attacks. From merely attempting to burn them down by the use of inflammable liquids, in hit-and-run attacks, it progressed to deploying significantly larger attacking forces, using prearranged drills. These drills soon included the virtual holding of a town or village by a section of the attacking force, whilst a small, more experienced core, using a variety of improvised explosive devices, tried to penetrate the barrack defences. Whilst this stage of the attack was underway, the police occupants were kept under sustained gunfire.

These two physical attacking elements were normally drawn from IRA flying columns, whilst local company resources were utilised in wider rings of outer protection, which could extend for several miles from the centre of the attack. These outer protective rings were also responsible for the disruption of road and communications links with the barracks under attack, in an effort to prevent or hinder any reinforcements coming to its aid. The use of these tactics resulted in the smaller barracks in outlying districts being evacuated.

In March and April attacks on RIC barracks increased dramatically, with approximately 150 being burned on the night of 5–6 April 1920 alone. This campaign accelerated, with official figures recording that between 1 January 1919 and 30 June 1920 the number of barracks attacked was as follows:[5]

Vacated barracks	Destroyed 351	Damaged 105
Occupied barracks	Destroyed 15	Damaged 25

The reason behind this increase in attacks was mainly twofold:

1. To prevent their being reoccupied by the new recruits to the RIC from England. (These new members of the RIC began to arrive in Ireland from 25 March 1920 and were mostly ex-service personnel who were to become known as the Black and Tans.)

2. To seize the garrisons' weaponry which was required to arm further IRA units. This was most likely when they succeeded in capturing a small outlying barracks.

RIC Barracks

The word 'barracks' means a permanent building for lodging soldiers or a building that gives that appearance. Each RIC sub-district was divided into areas covered by a police barracks, which varied in size from extensive buildings, the property of the Board of Works in cities and towns, to six- to eight-roomed houses in country areas.

The number of police officers attached to any particular barracks also varied, with almost 100 men being stationed in some barracks in Belfast as a result of the civil disorder and rioting which had been prevalent in the city during the late nineteenth and early twentieth centuries, whilst in the country districts barracks were normally manned by a sergeant and four constables. Each barracks was located in as central a position as possible within its area of responsibility, taking its name from the town or village in which it was situated. However, in many instances the RIC barracks was a lone house at a crossroads, in which case it took its name from that locality, or the townland in which it stood.

Most RIC barracks were rented from private individuals, usually on a twenty-one-year lease, but with a clause enabling the inspector general to give up the premises as a barracks after seven years of the lease period. Prior to being utilised as an RIC barracks, a building had to meet required standards, the main ones being as follows: it had to have a staunch slated roof with its chimneys drawing well; it had to be free from damp and have sufficient rooms for the strength of the party, along with rooms for the family of one married man. All windows had to have wooden shutters. There had to be a sufficient supply of good water on or near the premises and, where possible, a garden and walled-in yard.

All men were required to live in the barracks, except married men, who were allowed to live with their families within a proper distance from their barracks. All the parties attached to a barracks were subject to barracks regulations, seventy-three in all, which covered all aspects of life within it. The RIC was always a barracked force, which was good for discipline and also provided a reservoir of personnel for security purposes or for dealing with emergencies and calls for assistance.

As well as barracks, the RIC also supplied manpower in protection posts or temporary police huts to provide security for victims of cattle rustling and other serious offences. These huts were utility buildings normally erected in the area in which police wished to provide a localised body of officers to prevent or contain trouble. Protection posts could either be a hut or a small dwelling in the area which offered a more permanent police presence. Temporary police huts were not uncommon from the 1880s into the early twentieth century and were mainly to be found in Cork, Kerry, Clare, Galway and Mayo.

In 1919, when trouble once again flared in Ireland, the RIC had a total of 1,299 barracks, of which fifty-one were hut stations, and twenty-four protection posts, these being situated mainly in the midland and south-western counties. By the beginning of 1921 these numbers had been reduced to 865 barracks, with eleven hut stations and five temporary barracks, and six protection huts, two of which were located in Galway East Riding, one in Galway West Riding and the remaining three in King's County.

Of the 452 barracks and protection huts that disappeared over this period a large number included smaller, isolated barracks which were hard to defend. The barracks that closed had been attacked and destroyed by the IRA, who then embarked upon an organised campaign of attacks upon those barracks which were mostly rented houses and not originally built to withstand attacks by large numbers of armed men. It soon became necessary to have the remaining barracks put into a suitable state of defence. In order to provide protection the RIC began to use barbed wire, steel shutters, sandbags and other military devices. During 1920 a number of orders were issued in relation to the defence of police barracks. One of these was about the expense involved in the carriage of items to defend barracks:

> Office of Public Works,
> Dublin.
>
> All expenses incurred in connection with the carriage of steel plates and fittings from Railway Stations to Royal Irish Constabulary Barracks are to be paid direct by the Constabulary Officer who arranges for the carriage. The bill to be sent by him to the District Inspector in charge of the Barracks. When collected together the District Inspector will please furnish all such claims as a disbursement account direct to the Account, Office of Public Works, Dublin.
>
> M. J. Burke, 1 Apr 1920[6]

As the force had little or no experience in the art of defending their barracks or in the proper utilisation of these new materials, they employed ex-army officers to undertake this task. These officers were called 'defence of barracks sergeants' and, as far as can be ascertained, the first of thirty-three men recruited for this purpose was George Charles Peel Davis, 71440, who joined the RIC on 18 May 1920 from America. These men organised the defences of the barracks and were to take command in the event of an attack, but were not to interfere with ordinary police duties. They were paid £7 a week and had to sleep in the barracks, being responsible for their own messing.

Men transferred from the smaller barracks were garrisoned in overcrowded barracks behind their new defences.

Attacks on Police

During the early part of 1920 the IRA began to attack police officers when they were at their most vulnerable, either going to or coming from their lodgings, or at their homes when on leave. This kind of attack was highlighted to the force by the following circular:

> D 196
> 1920
> RIC Office, Dublin Castle,
> 4 February 1920

> Attacks on Police:
> Having regard to recent attacks on the police, it is essential men off duty should take greater precautions for their safety. In disturbed localities they should not go out singly; they should carry revolvers and should return to Barracks before dusk. When returning from Barracks to their lodgings at night they should be accompanied by armed men, the escort keeping a little apart. In places which are not disturbed, it is desirable that men should go out alone as seldom as possible and never after dusk where there is any possibility of danger.
> T. J. Smith Actg Depy Inspector General[7]

The campaign of violence against off-duty police officers intensified, with a number of men belonging to both the RIC and DMP being killed whilst home on leave during the month of June 1920. Because of these attacks, a large portion of the RIC was forced to cease visiting their homes when off duty. This placed extra pressure on the force, which the government helped remove by offering travelling expenses to officers who could not take leave in Ireland in the terms of the following circular:

324
1920 F
Royal Irish Constabulary Office, Dublin Castle,
18 June 1920

Finance Circular

Travelling Expenses Incurred in Proceeding on Leave to Great Britain

I have much pleasure in notifying to the Force, with the sanction of Government, that Head and other Constables entitled to leave will, if desirous, be granted return cost of transport from an Irish port of embarkation to London, or to a place of less distance in Great Britain, provided the County Inspector concerned certifies that it is unsafe for the applicant to take leave in Ireland. Claims for such expenses may be approved by the County Inspectors, the general rules with regard to travelling charges for the Force being observed – Finance Code, Sections 296 to 298 and 300.

   T. J. Smith Inspector General
   3044 F
   3,508[8]

The contents of this circular were later reiterated on 2 September 1920 with particular emphasis on the county inspector being required to certify that it was unsafe for an officer to take leave at his home in Ireland. The travelling expenses incurred were to be limited to the emergency and covered the cost of one return journey for each individual per year.

However, despite these precautions police officers continued to be killed when they were at their most vulnerable, a number of them losing their lives as they attended their places of worship.

12 February 1920,
Allihies RIC Barracks, Co. Cork
Michael Neenan, Con 62412

The attacks against RIC barracks continued, with an outlying occupied barracks at Allihies, Co. Cork, being targeted. Between 3 and 4 a.m. the IRA mounted their attack, placing a bomb at the gable end of the building which, when detonated, blew it in. This explosion wounded two constables, one of whom, Michael Neenan, died later that afternoon from his wounds. Neenan, a thirty-two-year-old single man, was from Co. Clare. He would have had thirteen years' service on 4 March 1920, having previously been a farmer.

As the year progressed, there appeared to be a change in IRA tactics, whether by design or not, which involved the selecting and attacking of more vulnerable targets.

The Constabulary Medal

In 1842 the Irish Constabulary and not the crown instituted this medal as a reward for its members, whose conduct was 'exemplary and who showed a high degree of intelligence, tact or courage'. The medal was first awarded in 1848 after the Irish Constabulary had been brought face to face with rebellion for the first time. Approximately 335 such medals were granted, most of them during the years 1916, 1920 and 1921, with the last one presented in 1922.[9]

The medal had a dark-green ribbon and the earlier version had a fixed bar suspender with a female figure on the obverse side, whilst on the reverse was engraved the name and rank of the recipient, the date of the award and (sometimes) the place of the award. Later the obverse design changed to a harp and wreath, with the suspender of the medal being altered to a swivelling wire suspender. It is believed that only seven men received a second award of this type and they were either given a second medal or a bar for their original medal. This medal was only awarded after exceptional acts of bravery and normally during times of political unrest and violence.

During the period 1919–1922 a large number of these medals was awarded, many posthumously. The following list contains police officers who received this medal during the period 1919–1922 and also lost their lives.

The first award made posthumously was to Michael Neenan, Constable 62412, on 3 March 1920, as a result of the incident described above.

No.	Name	Rank	Died	Medal
60741	Boylan, John	Con	23.04.1921	11.09.1921
62175	Burke, Peter	H/Con	20.09.1920	no date found
58743	Carroll, Patrick J.	Sgt	18.04.1920	28.05.1920
59764	Clarke, Christopher	Sgt	13.03.1922	no date found
60459	Curtin, Jeremiah	Sgt	13.01.1920	15.09.1921
71631	Dray, Ernest	Con	31.12.1920	22.04.1921
62633	Dunne, Edward	Con	10.05.1920	16.03.1920
65154	Fallon, Martin	Con	03.05.1921	15.09.1919
56899	Flynn, John	Sgt	10.05.1920	16.03.1920
55730	Gilmartin, John	Sgt	15.03.1922	19.10.1921
70996	Gorbey, Robert	Con	06.11.1920	13.07.1920
69264	Heffron, Thomas	Con	26.01.1921	11.09.1920
55093	Kane, Thomas	Sgt	28.05.1920	04.06.1920
57392	Kingston, James	Sgt	06.05.1921	16.08.1920
65056	McFadden, John	Sgt	24.04.1921	12.01.1921
68892	McNamara, John	Con	24.08.1920	06.05.1920
70142	Malone, Michael F.	Con	01.01.1921	21.04.1921
54291	Morton, Joseph	Con	28.05.1920	04.06.1920
70256	Mullan, John	Con	27.08.1920	18.11.1920
61673	Mulloy, Michael	Sgt	20.01.1921	No date found
62412	Neenan, Michael	Con	12.02.1920	03.03.1920
59193	O'Sullivan, Tobias	DI	20.01.1921	04.06.1920
77306	Perkins, Walter P.	Con	30.05.1921	22.04.1921
69729	Quinn, Michael	Con	26.01.1921	06.05.1920
62069	Shannon, Peter	Con	17.12.1920	22.04.1921

70853	Shelsher, Joseph	Con	01.07.1921	15.10.1921
70974	Will, Alexander	Con	11.07.1920	22.12.1920

20 February 1920,
Suffolk/Grafton Street, Dublin city
John Walsh, Con DMP (63B)

Constable Walsh was on duty and had just reached the corner of Suffolk Street and Grafton Street, Dublin, when he was shot dead. Sergeant Dunleavy, who was accompanying the constable, was also wounded in the attack. Walsh was thirty-seven and unmarried. He was buried at the Catholic burial ground at Galbally, Co. Wexford, on 23 February 1920.

4 March 1920, Bouladuff, Co. Tipperary
John Martin Heanue, Con 69188

The constable was shot and critically wounded in the village of Bouladuff (Ragg) near Thurles, Co. Tipperary, as he called at a grocer's shop. He was moved to Tipperary Military Hospital but died from his wounds on 5 March 1920. On 8 March his body was taken to Clifden, Co. Galway and he was buried on 12 March.

Heanue, a twenty-four-year old single man, was from Co. Galway. He had two years' service, having been a pawnbroker's assistant before joining the RIC.

8 March 1920,
Hugginstown Barracks, Co. Kilkenny
Thomas Ryan, Con 60822

The barracks at Hugginstown, a village fifteen miles from Kilkenny town, was attacked by the IRA using bombs. Constable Ryan was wounded, having an arm blown off, and died at 6.30 p.m. on 10 March 1920. The scene of this attack is within a stone's throw of the famous Carrickshock Boreen, where nearly eighty-nine years earlier seventeen policemen were killed in a cul-de-sac during the Tithe War. It was stated later that Constable Ryan had been killed because his own grenade detonated prematurely during the attack, but this could not be confirmed. A thirty-five-year old married man from Co. Limerick with four children, he had seventeen years' police service, having previously been a farmer.

10 March 1920, Rathkeale, Co. Limerick
George Neazer, Sgt 59800

The sergeant and Constable Garret Doyle were in plain clothes escorting Michael O'Brien, the land steward for a Miss Ella Browne of Rattoo House near Ballyduff, Co. Kerry, to the March Fair in Rathkeale, Co. Limerick.[10] All three men were in the dining-room of Ward's Hotel when the commandant of Rathkeale Company of the IRA, which was attached to the Fourth Battalion, West Limerick Brigade, along with Paddy O'Shaughnessy, Seán Reidy, Jimmy and Paddy Roche (all Rathkeale IRA men) and Seán Hogan ('Big Four'), entered the room. It is alleged by some sources that the sergeant attempted to draw his gun and was shot dead, while Constable Doyle was wounded. Other sources state that the sergeant was one of the most active policemen in the Tralee area from 1912 to 1920 and that it is likely he was killed because of the zeal he showed in the performance of his duties.

After the attack the weapons were removed from the policemen by their attackers, who then left the scene.

Neazer, a forty-three-year-old married man with two children, was from Ballycahane, Pallaskenry, Co. Limerick. He had nineteen years' police service, having been a farmer before joining the RIC.

11 March 1920, Glanmire, Co. Cork
Timothy Scully, Con 49471

The constable was part of an RIC patrol returning to its barracks at Glanmire, a village four miles east of Cork city, when it was ambushed. Constable Scully was shot dead during the attack. From Adrigole, Skibbereen, Co. Cork, he was sixty-four and married with a family. He had thirty-eight years' police service, having been a farmer before joining the RIC, and was buried in Skibbereen on 14 March 1920.

17 March 1920, Toomevara, Co. Tipperary
James Rocke, Con 67945
Charles Healy, Con 69198

The two constables were shot as they left the church in the small village of Toomevara, four miles from Nenagh, Co. Tipperary, after evening devotions on St Patrick's Day. They were the first officers to be shot as they left their place of worship.

The two constables were attacked within 120 yards of their barracks by a number of men hiding behind a hedge between the graveyard and the church. As Healy lay wounded on the ground he was shot three more times by his attackers before they made their escape. Police rushed to the scene from the barracks. When they arrived, Healy stated, 'Oh Sergeant, I am shot. May God forgive them anyhow because I do. Oh my poor mother, I would not mind only for her.' As both men were being carried back to the barracks, Healy kept repeating, 'May God forgive them.'

On the way back to the barracks Rocke stated, 'I forgive the man that shot me and anything that I have I leave to my mother.' He died at 11.15 p.m. He had six brothers, one of whom had served in the American Army during the First World War. Constable Healy was removed to Limerick Hospital, where he succumbed to his wounds later that night.

During this incident a civilian was wounded in the ankle by a bullet fired by the attackers, which ricocheted off a wall.

Constable Healy, twenty-five, was from Glengarriff, Co. Cork and had four years' police service, having previously been a farmer. Rocke was from Killimor, Co. Galway and would have been twenty-seven in three days' time. A farmer before joining the RIC, he was single with five years' service. On 19 March 1920 his remains were taken to Killimor.

19 March 1920, Pope's Quay, Cork
Joseph Murtagh, Con 57783

Constable Murtagh was shot dead at 11 p.m. as he walked along the quay, returning from the funeral of Constable Healy.[11] He was a widower with two grown-up children and lived in Sunday's Well police station. By all accounts he was an inoffensive officer who was held in high esteem by his colleagues. He was forty-six and from Westmeath. A farmer before joining the RIC, he had twenty-three years' police service.

At approximately 1 a.m. the next morning armed men with blackened faces forced their way into Tomás MacCurtain's home in Cork city and shot him dead. MacCurtain was the lord mayor of the city and also the commandant of Cork No. 1 Brigade of the IRA. His death upset Michael Collins, who decided not to take action until after the inquest. The retaliatory action he did take was to have far-reaching consequences for the town of Lisburn, Co. Antrim.

The inquest jury's verdict stated: 'we return a verdict of wilful murder against David Lloyd George, Prime Minister of England; Lord French, Lord Lieutenant of Ireland; Ian MacPherson, late Chief Secretary of Ireland; Acting Inspector General Smith of the

Royal Irish Constabulary, Divisional Inspector Clayton of the Royal Irish Constabulary, District Inspector Swanzy and some unknown members of the Royal Irish Constabulary.'

THE BLACK AND TANS

Who or what were the Black and Tans? The simple answer to this question is that they were recruits to the regular RIC who had to wear a hybrid dress of police and military uniform. This situation arose because so many men joined the RIC that it was impossible to secure sufficient quantities of dark-green police uniforms. The RIC was, therefore, compelled to look for some other source of uniform to supply the temporary deficiency. So the shortages of RIC uniform were made good as far as possible with military service dress, which created a strange mixture of khaki and dark-green uniforms.

It is believed that members of the RIC in this unfamiliar uniform first began to operate from a police station near Upper Church, Co. Tipperary, an area which was home to a famous pack of hounds known locally as the Black and Tans. The local inhabitants promptly applied the familiar title of these hounds to the newly arrived police recruits and by the late summer of 1920 the term was in popular use throughout Ireland.

Another result, and perhaps more serious than their look, was the impression given that these men were not members of the RIC in the sense of being regular constables as heretofore. The uniform appeared to indicate they were a quasi-military force under the control of the military authorities. This impression died hard, long after all the deficiencies of uniform had been made good by the end of 1920, with all the men being equipped in standard police uniform.

This influx of recruits happened for two main reasons. The first was that because of the Sinn Féin and IRA campaign to ostracise police officers from the rest of Irish society, the number of men resigning or retiring from the RIC had increased. There are different sets of figures for the number of men leaving the RIC as offset by new recruits. The following tables, however, show the true number of men who left the RIC from 1919 to 1922 and those who were appointed per month from January 1919 until its final disbandment in August 1922.

	Resigned	Pensioned	Died (Natural causes/ accidents)	Gratuity	Absent Deserter	Discharged	Dismissed	Medically Unfit	Totals
1919	99	234	66	25	0	63	8	0	495
1920	1,647	1,126	63	41	16	167	138	31	3,229
1921	1,638	425	99	20	57	266	591	112	3,208
1922	7	126	13	5	1	7	29	2	190

Recruitment

	1919	1920	1921	1922
January	9	184	1,451	–
February	23	287	817	–
March	20	481	675	–
April	29	370	600	–
May	39	175	473	1
June	39	244	768	5
July	37	425	313	–
August	32	702	10	24
September	26	757	7	–
October	36	1,631	213	–
November	55	1,214	477	–
December	60	1,399	30	–
Totals	**405**	**7,869**	**5,834**	**30**

(These details of men who resigned, died or left the RIC for any other reason and all those who joined the force have been obtained from the *Royal Irish Constabulary General Personnel Register* (PRO HO 184/1–48).)

After the Truce on 11 July 1921, a number of men received RIC numbers, which might indicate that recruiting was continuing for the RIC. However, on closer examination it was found that the numbers issued from August to December 1921 were only given to temporary constables or cadets. It was further found that the men joining these ranks had been appointed to the RIC before the Truce, but only received their force number in the latter part of 1921. The thirty numbers issued in 1922 were given to ex-members of the DMP, the first being issued on 7 May to David Neligan, a member of the DMP's G Division, who was also an intelligence officer for Michael Collins. (He wrote a book about his exploits, *The Spy in the Castle*.) It is, therefore, possible that the remaining numbers issued to ex-members of the DMP went also to men who had been attached to its G Division.

The first Black and Tan to be recruited for the RIC in England in 1920 was one William Robert Bird, who had been a gas-fitter and a member of the Royal Navy. He was recruited by Major Fleming in London and was issued the force number of 70014.

The second reason for the increase in the number of recruits was the fact that as the political violence increased the government was forced to proclaim the worst affected areas as being in a state of disturbance and requiring an additional establishment of police. The areas proclaimed were as follows: Cork city and West and East Ridings, Co. Kerry, Co. Limerick and city, Co. Roscommon and Tipperary North and South Ridings (10 April 1919). The following areas were also proclaimed: Dublin, Co. Louth, Co. Longford, Co. Sligo, Co. Waterford, Co. Westmeath and Co. Wicklow (25 February 1920). Co. Clare and Co. Galway had been proclaimed on 27 August 1907. This meant that by February 1920 all of Ireland, except the northern-most counties, had been proclaimed and required extra officers for policing, necessitating an increase in RIC strength.

An appeal for new recruits to the regular RIC was originally made to men who had been demobilised from the army. Their wages of ten shillings a day and all found (a princely sum in 1920) meant that there was no shortage of applicants. Men applying for appointment had to supply the name of their regiment, proof of their army discharge and character. No man was eligible with less than a 'good' character. Although the majority of these new recruits were ex-servicemen who had been recruited in specially opened recruitment offices, a large number, possibly as many as one-third, were recruited in Ireland. These new recruits were never maintained as an autonomous force, although a large number of them joined the RIC Transport Division as drivers. The remainder were allocated to individual stations to either maintain or increase the barracks' strengths.

Due to the high rate of recruits joining the RIC, Gormanston was converted into a depot for them in late September 1920. The first of the new recruits appeared in Ireland on 25 March 1920 with their unfamiliar uniforms. Five days later they were greeted with a proclamation which was posted throughout the south of Ireland:

i) Whereas the spies and traitors known as the Royal Irish Constabulary are holding this country for the enemy, and whereas said spies and bloodhounds are conspiring with the enemy to bomb and bayonet and otherwise outrage a peaceful, law abiding and liberty loving people.

ii) Wherefore we do hereby proclaim and suppress said spies and traitors, and do hereby solemnly warn prospective recruits that they join the RIC at their own peril. All nations are agreed as to the fate of traitors. It has the sanction of God and man.

By order of the GOC
Irish Republican Army[12]

What came to be known as the 'Tan War' had been declared.

9 April 1920, Lackamore Wood, Co. Tipperary

William Finn, Con 69209
Daniel McCarthy, Con 67704

An RIC cycle patrol of three men was ambushed at Lackamore Wood on a bleak and desolate bog road midway between Rearcross and Newport, Co. Tipperary, in the heart of the Silvermine Mountains. The patrol was on its way to Newport Petty Sessions to appear in cases of unlighted vehicles. Two constables were killed outright, with Constable Byrne being seriously wounded. He rolled over into a ditch and then scrambled over a wall, from behind which he was able to return fire against the attackers.

The patrol was ambushed by twenty masked men who had taken cover behind some trees at Sycamore Wood. They allowed the police to pass before opening fire from both the entrance into the wood and a nearby fence.

Constable Finn, a twenty-three-year-old single man, was from Castlerea, Co. Roscommon. He had two years' police service, having been a farmer before joining the RIC.

Constable McCarthy was twenty-five and from Waterville, Co. Kerry. He had six years' service, and like his colleague was a farmer before joining the RIC.

Background

The local DI's report of this incident dated 9 April 1920 stated the following: 'We found the late Constable Finn lying on his back on the centre of the road quite dead, both eyes blown away and the lower part of his forehead, brain matter scattered on the road and a large pool of blood. About five yards in advance, on the left-hand side of the road, we found the late Constable McCarthy in a sitting posture against the wall of the road and a bullet wound in his neck.'

14 April 1920, Lower Camden Street/Pleasants Street, Dublin city
Henry Kells, D/Con DMP (93B)

Detective Constable Kells had been on plain-clothes duty. As he neared the corner of Lower Camden Street and Pleasants Street, Dublin, he was shot dead by Paddy Daly, the commander of the Squad, after another member of the Squad told him where he could find the constable. Daly fired at the policeman three times, with one bullet passing through his windpipe.

Background
Whilst approximately 100 IRA prisoners were in the exercise yard of a gaol in Dublin, an army officer called out twenty names he had on a list. The men named were then marched back towards their cells. As rumours within the gaol a few days prior to this incident had stated that the prisoners were to be broken into small groups and deported, the prisoners expected to be taken to their cells to collect their belongings. However, at the last moment they were marched into a long open area, stopping opposite some steps. A group of men stood on these steps with their backs towards the prisoners. This group of men quickly turned to face them and then turned back again from the prisoners. However, one of this group, Detective Constable Kells, made his way towards the prisoners, who by this time realised it was an identification parade and turned their backs.

Kells was recognised by one of the prisoners, Peadar Clancy, who called out his name. A few days later a note was smuggled into the prison for Clancy. This note read 'I am going to Kells tomorrow. Signed MC.'[13] The next day Kells was shot and killed. He was forty-two, married, but with no family and had been twenty-two years in the service. He was buried at Mount Jerome Cemetery, Dublin on 17 April 1920.

14 April 1920, Balbriggan, Co. Dublin
Patrick Finnerty, Sgt 56458

The sergeant was shot and wounded at Balbriggan. He died from his wounds at 8.30 a.m. on 16 April 1920 in the Mater Misericordiae Hospital, Dublin.

Background
An RIC patrol of one head constable, one sergeant and three constables had followed a crowd of approximately 150 Sinn Féin supporters to a bonfire at Clonard Hill, which was three-quarters of a mile outside Balbriggan. The police had cautioned a man that the procession was illegal but did not take any other action.

On their return, the police again followed the crowd, with twenty to twenty-five people in a smaller group following behind the police. On reaching Clonard Street a flash was seen behind the sergeant, about three or four feet from him. He called out, 'I am shot.' The police did not anticipate trouble and, in the confusion, the smaller crowd behind them got into the larger one in front, with a person in the larger crowd calling out, 'That's the stuff to give them.' The wounded sergeant was taken to a nearby house and a doctor was summoned. At 1.15 a.m. he was removed to hospital with bullet wounds in the back and abdomen.

The sergeant's remains were taken by train to Athenry for interment at the burial ground at Clonkeen. RIC men from various country barracks accompanied the remains to Broadstone Railway Station, with a few RIC men from Balbriggan travelling to the funeral. Messages of sympathy were telegraphed to the relations of the late sergeant. One, from the inspector general, stated, 'The Inspector General directs relatives to be informed that the Inspector General is deeply grieved to learn of the death of Sergeant Finnerty, who has been brutally murdered in the honourable discharge of his duty.'

Another message was from the lord lieutenant, which stated, 'Convey to relations of the late Sergeant Finnerty His Excellency's deep sympathy on his cruel murder while gallantly performing his duty.'

Finnerty, a fifty-one-year old single man, was from Clonkeen. He had twenty-five years' service, having been a labourer before joining the RIC.

17 April 1920, near Waterville, Co. Kerry
Martin Clifford, Con

The constable, who was stationed at Cahir, was ambushed and wounded at Bradley's Cross, Dromod, about four miles from Waterville, Co. Kerry. He was home on leave and was cycling from Waterville to his home two miles away at Derinaden. He died a short time later from his wounds. (No further details could be found in relation to this incident and it is possible that the constable was a retired member of the RIC.)

18 April 1920, Kilmihil, Co. Clare
Patrick J. Carroll, Sgt 58743

Three police officers had just left the church in Kilmihil when they were fired on. Sergeant Carroll was killed outright, while Constable Collins was seriously wounded. The IRA man responsible for this attack is believed to have been John Breen, who was shot dead by another police constable, while two or three other IRA men were injured. The ambush took place sixty yards from the church.

Sergeant Carroll had been escorting his two comrades who had been to Mass. As they left the chapel, the IRA men, one of whom was Breen, followed them. Constable Martyn saw Breen behind the sergeant with a Webley service revolver in his hand; Breen was also wearing a gun belt and holster. But before the constable could take any action this man shot the sergeant and was in turn shot by the constable.

The sergeant had only transferred to Co. Clare from Co. Down a short time before his death. He was a forty-three-year-old single man from Dublin. He had twenty-one years' police service, having been a railway clerk prior to joining the RIC. The sergeant's father lived at Scurlogstown, Trim, Co. Meath.

20 April 1920,
Mountjoy Street, Dublin city
Laurence Dalton, D/Con DMP

At 12.45 p.m. the detective constable was on his way to work at the Broadstone terminus of the Midland Great Western Railway when he was shot and wounded. The detective constable was going to the terminus in order to meet the 1.10 p.m. train when he and Constable Spencer were attacked. Dalton ran off towards St Mary's Place with two men running after him. He was heard to call out, 'Let me alone', and then three more shots rang out. He was found shot twice in both legs and once in the right thigh and pelvis. He was taken to the Mater Misericordiae Hospital but died from his wounds two hours later. The policeman with him was unhurt.

Dalton was a twenty-six-year-old single man and was buried on 23 April 1920 at Newcastle West, Co. Limerick. A member of the DMP's B Division for six years, he had only been attached to the detective division for a short time.

The Background
It was standard practice for G Division members of the DMP to keep watch on railway terminuses to look for wanted or suspected members of the IRA. It would appear from research that Dalton was a man with a mild disposition, being involved in only one incident

against a Sinn Féin member. During a search to arrest J. J. Walsh, a well-known Sinn Féin member, the detective constable was sent to cover the rear of the premises. When Walsh ran out the back door and into the policeman he tried to persuade the officer to allow him to escape but he refused.[14]

23 April 1920, Deelis, Co. Kerry
Patrick Foley, Con 70111

The constable was found with his hands tied behind him. A bandage covered his eyes and he had twenty-six wounds, believed to have been inflicted by a shotgun at close range. The body was recovered in an auxiliary creamery yard of J. M. Slattery and Sons at Deelis.

Foley, who was attached to the RIC barracks at Kilkern, Ballinasloe, Co. Galway, had been on fourteen days' leave at Annascaul. On 21 April he went, with another ex-soldier, to Moriarty's Hotel, where they had met a man from Inch. As this man was under the influence of drink, the constable and his friend were helping him across the railway tracks when they were ordered by a number of men to put up their hands. These men then took Foley away and his body was found a few days later, on 23 April. A 1914 Mons Ribbon was found on the body. He had enlisted in the army twice (the first time whilst still at school), joining the Royal Munster Fusiliers and later the First Battalion of the Irish Guards. He spent four years as a prisoner of war in Germany, being repatriated after the Armistice.

Constable Foley was twenty-five and single, and had only three months' service.

23 April 1920, near Clonakilty, Co. Cork
Michael McCarthy, Con DMP

Constable McCarthy was home on leave and was working in a field on his brother's farm at Lackenalooha, three miles from Clonakilty, when he was shot and wounded six times. He died from his wounds on 24 April 1920 at Cork Military Hospital. He was twenty-six, single and had five years' service.

25 April 1920, Ballinspittal, Co. Cork
Cornelius Crean, Sgt 55059
Patrick McGoldrick, Con 48684

A three-man RIC patrol from the barracks at Innishannon, near Bandon, Co. Cork, was on the road from Upton about 5 p.m. and had just reached Ballinspittal, six miles from Bandon. It was ambushed by IRA members from the Cork No. 3 (West) Brigade under the leadership of Jim O'Mahoney, the local battalion adjutant. The sergeant and Constable McGoldrick were killed outright; the other constable managed to escape. He returned fire on the patrol's attackers but was unable to prevent the removal of the weapons from the dead officers.

Background
Sergeant Crean had a good local knowledge of both the people and the area. Because of this knowledge and understanding of the local people, the IRA viewed him as very dangerous to them and had placed him on the 'Black List'. He was forty-eight, married, and came from Annascaul, Co. Kerry. He had twenty-eight years' police service, having been a farmer before joining the RIC. He had been a member of a famous tug-of-war team. His brother had accompanied Sir Ernest Shackleton on his voyage to the South Pole in 1909.[15]

Constable McGoldrick, a fifty-nine-year-old married man, was from Co. Cavan. He had thirty-eight years' police service, having been a farmer before joining the RIC, and had resided with his family at Innishannon before his death.

29 April 1920,
Rush RIC Barracks, Co. Dublin
John Edward Brady, Sgt 55744

During an attack on the RIC barracks at Rush, Co. Dublin, Sergeant Brady, a fifty-year-old married man from Bray, Co. Wicklow, was shot and wounded. He was removed to Steeven's Hospital, Dublin, where he died on 9 May 1920. He was buried in Mount Jerome Cemetery, Dublin, on 12 May 1920. His coffin, draped with a Union Jack, was carried from the hospital to a waiting hearse by his comrades. The RIC band played funeral marches as it made its way to the cemetery. After the funeral was over a firing party from the RIC depot fired a volley over the grave.

Brady had twenty-seven years' police service, having been a footman before joining the force.

3 May 1920,
Gale Bridge, Co. Kerry
Francis McKenna, Sgt 58789

The sergeant and Constables Colgan and Rabbett were cycling back from Listowel Quarter Sessions to Ballylongford, Co. Kerry. Approximately two miles from Listowel, the RIC officers reached two field gates facing each other near the O'Connor farm at Gale Bridge. Here IRA men from the Ballydonoghue Company lay in ambush. Those involved were Michael Aherne, John and Patrick Walsh, T. P. O'Shea, Thomas Connor – who acted as a scout – Patrick Corridan and John Galvin. The sergeant was shot dead, and during the fight Constable Colgan shot O'Shea. Believing he had seriously wounded his attacker, the constable moved from his cover, but was in turn shot by O'Shea, who had not been badly injured.[16] The ambush ended in a bloody hand-to-hand struggle, with both constables being seriously wounded. The sergeant died from eighty pellet wounds in the face.

(It is interesting to note that Sergeant McKenna had arrested Sir Roger Casement, which may or may not have played a part in his death. Casement was tried on 26 June 1916 on a charge of high treason and was sentenced to death on 29 June. He was hanged at Pentonville prison on 3 August.)

Sergeant McKenna, a thirty-nine-year-old married man with three children, was from the city of Waterford. He had twenty-one years' service, having had no other employment before joining the RIC. He had been a detective in Tralee, Co. Kerry for some years.

10 May 1920, Goold's Cross, Co. Tipperary
Patrick McDonnell, Sgt 55303

The sergeant was shot dead at 1 p.m. while making his way, along with Constable Hayes, from the railway station at Goold's Cross to the RIC hut at Clonoulty. The sergeant had been involved in the stubborn defence of this RIC hut, which he commanded, on 31 March 1920 when it had been attacked by members of the IRA's Second Battalion, South Tipperary Brigade. He was a member of the Cavan force and had only been on temporary duty in Tipperary, which was originally to have been completed on 5 May. It was extended for a further period owing to Sergeant Hamilton having sustained injuries.

Sergeant McDonnell's wife resided at Cootehill, Co. Cavan, whilst his parents lived at Straduff, six miles from Omagh, Co. Tyrone. From Co. Tyrone, he was forty-nine, with twenty-eight years' service, having been a farmer before joining the RIC. He was buried in the Catholic cemetery at Dromore, Co. Tyrone.

10 May 1920,
near Timoleague, Co. Cork
John Flynn, Sgt 56899
William Brick, Con 64151
Edward Dunne, Con 62633

A police patrol on its way to Dungourney left its barracks at Butlerstown and was ambushed from both sides of the road by approximately forty men one mile from the village of Timoleague, Co. Cork, at Ahawadda. The sergeant and two constables were killed outright, with Constable Grimsdale, an ex-soldier, being wounded. He was removed to Cork Military Hospital.

This attack was carried out by IRA men under the leadership of Charlie Hurley, who was, at that time, vice-OC of the Bandon Battalion. He later became brigade commander of the Cork No. 3 (West) Brigade. On 19 March 1921, at Ballymurphy, Upton, Co. Cork, Hurley was shot and killed by soldiers (see p. 268).

During the ambush Constable Dunne ran for cover but fell. He got up and began to run again, but only covered twenty yards before being shot by a man in a crouching position near a mill dam.

After the ambush Sergeant Flynn's body could not be found at first. On his arrival at the scene, DI Connor found only Flynn's boot and a blood track. The DI followed the blood trail for some distance, finding the body lying on its back in a stream, being completely covered by water. There were signs of a struggle on the stream's bank and some discharged cartridges were found there, along with an empty pint whiskey bottle. The sergeant's revolver had been taken.

Flynn, a fifty-one-year-old married man, was from Kildysart, Co. Clare. He had twenty-five years' police service, having been a farmer before joining the RIC. Constable Brick, a thirty-two-year-old single man, was from Tralee, Co. Kerry. He had eleven years' police service, having been a postman prior to joining the RIC. Constable Dunne was from Maryborough, Queen's County. A forty-year-old married man, he would have had thirteen years' police service on 21 May 1920. He was a farmer before joining the RIC. Flynn, who was in charge of the barracks at Butlerstown, and Dunne were two of the officers who successfully defended Timoleague Barracks when it was attacked in February.

Members of the inquest jury later received letters threatening that if they did not publicly withdraw their verdict of murder they would suffer serious consequences.

11 May 1920, Cork city
Denis Garvey, Sgt 56861
Daniel Harrington, Con 59401

The sergeant and two constables had just left their station at Lower Glanmire Road, Cork, and boarded a tram car. As they sat in the tram a number of men – who had been seated in it when it stopped – drew revolvers and approached them. They opened fire on the sergeant and Constable Harrington. The other policeman, Constable Doyle, was seriously wounded and taken to Cork Military Hospital.

The sergeant had figured prominently at the inquest of the lord mayor of Cork, Tomás MacCurtain. A forty-seven-year-old married man from Co. Kerry, he had twenty-five years' police service, having been a labourer before joining the RIC.

Harrington, a forty-four-year-old single man, was from Co. Cork. He had twenty years' police service, having been a farmer prior to joining the RIC. His funeral took place in Bantry, Co. Cork.

15 May 1920, Derry city
Denis Moroney, D/Sgt 59644

The detective sergeant was the chief of the Crimes Detective

Department in the city and was the first member of the RIC to be killed in Ulster since the beginning of 1919. Along with a small party of detectives, he had accompanied uniformed police in a bayonet charge to disperse rioters. As the police moved along the quay near the Great Northern Station, a person in the crowd shot and wounded the detective. He was taken to the Metropole Hotel, where he died from his wounds.

Background
At 10.30 a.m. a riot developed between two crowds, one in Fountain Street, the other in Bridge Street, Londonderry. The police charged down Bridge Street and the crowd scattered in all directions at the end of the street. A portion of the crowd made its way into Rookery Lane and across Foyle Street, through Fish Lane and onto the quay. The police followed this crowd, who fired revolvers at them as they ran away. Once on the quay the crowd concealed themselves behind wagons and continued to fire at the police. Shortly after reaching the quay Moroney said to Detective Constable Patrick Kelly, 'My God, Kelly, I am shot.' Kelly, along with Detective Constable Darragh, then helped the sergeant from the scene. As they did so he said, 'Help me, boys! I am falling.'

Moroney lived at 16 Grove Place and at 11.20 a.m. on 18 May his remains were carried the entire distance from his home to the Great Northern Railway Station by his former comrades, with all the available police in the city attending the funeral. His body was taken to Ballinrobe, Co. Mayo, and was later interred at Roundfort, Hollymount, Co. Mayo. The body was exhumed by relations and brought to his native Co. Clare for reinterment. Moroney, from Tulla, Co. Clare, had nineteen years' police service, having been a farmer before joining the RIC.

19 May 1920,
Mallow Street, Limerick city
Kyran Dunphy, Sgt 65998
Patrick Hearty, Sgt 54232

At 5 p.m. the two sergeants were shot at by three IRA men armed with revolvers in Mallow Street, Limerick. Sergeant Dunphy was killed outright, having been shot in the head, with Sergeant Hearty being mortally wounded.

Dunphy and Hearty, who were both attached to Ballinacurra RIC Barracks, which was one mile outside the city boundary, had gone to the residence of Dr John Roberts in Mallow Street, as Hearty was on the sick list. When the two officers left they were fired at twelve to fifteen times by three IRA members from B Company of the local Limerick City Battalion. After the attack the IRA men made off towards the People's Park.

The IRA men, along with others under the leadership of Michael Hartney, B Company's IRA captain, had been preparing an ambush in the area of the People's Park when the two police officers were first noticed. Their appearance forced the IRA to abandon their planned ambush and resulted in a different attack.[17]

Sergeant Hearty had been wounded in the leg but knelt down and returned fire, before being wounded again. He was later taken to the Military Hospital. Sergeant Dunphy lay dead on the other side of the street. After this attack police and military began a follow-up search and as the evening wore on a number of properties were set on fire and gunfire could be heard in several areas.

The next day Hearty was moved to a Dublin hospital but died from his wounds on 22 June. On 24 June, at the sergeant's inquest in the hospital, Constable Eugene Igoe, when asked to sign his deposition, stated he wished to say something before doing so, after which he said, 'I wish to state here that if the Sinn Féin organisation think they will terrorise the police force in carrying out their duties they are making a very big mistake. On the contrary, they are making them more determined every day to carry out their duties.'

A man was arrested for killing the two officers on 12 August 1920.

Sergeant Dunphy was thirty, single, and from Queen's County. He had eight years' police service, having previously been a farmer. On 25 May 1916 he had joined the Leinster Regiment and had volunteered to remain as part of the army of occupation. He rejoined the RIC on 18 October 1919.

Sergeant Hearty, a fifty-three-year-old single man, was from Cregganbane, Crossmaglen, Co. Armagh. He had thirty years' service, having been a farmer before joining the RIC.

28 May 1920,
Kilmallock RIC Barracks, Co. Limerick
Thomas Kane, Sgt 55093
Joseph Morton, Con 54291

These officers died as a result of the attack on Kilmallock Barracks by the IRA in the very early hours of 28 May 1920.

Background
In April 1920 a very large number of outlying (and mostly evacuated) RIC barracks were attacked by the IRA and destroyed by fire. One of those attacked, on 28 April, was Ballylanders, Co. Limerick. It had been occupied during the attack, which was carried out by the East Limerick Brigade of the IRA under the command of its vice-OC, Thomas Malone, who used the name of Seán Forde. (Thomas Malone was attached to the GHQ staff of the IRA and had a roving commission to stiffen up IRA activities throughout Ireland. Another man who had such a commission was Ernie O'Malley.)

As a direct result of this attack RIC weapons were captured and this gave Malone the idea to attack Kilmallock Barracks. This was to be the first of a more deadly and destructive type of operation against RIC barracks which required the assistance of IRA men from Co. Clare, South Tipperary and East Cork.

The Barracks
Kilmallock Barracks was a soundly constructed building which had steel-shuttered windows. It was fronted by a lawn and set back from the street, the front face of the barracks being in line with the rear of Carroll's shop next door. There was a slight gap between the two buildings but the roof of Carroll's was higher than that of the barracks. Other buildings overlooked it, and business premises dominated the rear.[18]

The Plan
The different IRA units in the attack party were to make their way to an assembly point in a field close to the town. This was to avoid the detection of the main party, which numbered approximately sixty, and also to ensure the exact timing of their arrival at the different attack points. These men were then to be taken by local IRA members to the different locations from which the assault on the barracks was to be launched.

The buildings used were Willie Carroll's house, which was situated about six paces from the gable end of the barracks, towered over it and was to be the main attack point, under the command of Thomas Malone; the houses directly facing the barracks and Clery's Hotel, under the command of Tim Crowley; Herlihy's shop, under the command of J. MacCarthy, who was accompanied by Michael Brennan, the East Clare IRA commander, in whose uniform the IRA man Byrne had been buried after the incident on 6 April 1919 in Limerick city; and the Provincial Bank, under D. O'Hannigan, the IRA man who first had the idea of forming flying columns.

As the attack was taking place, the local IRA unit was to cut telegraph wires into the town and block roads leading into the area to prevent reinforcements gaining access to the barracks. The unit using the hotel was to be admitted by an IRA man who had taken a room earlier that day, posing as a commercial traveller. The windows of the houses facing the barracks used to mount the attack were to be barricaded by pre-filled sandbags. Heavy iron weights were to be pushed out of Carroll's skylight window onto the barracks' roof to smash a hole in it. Once breached, oil and petrol were to be poured into the barracks and set alight. The signal to initiate the attack was to be a torch flash from Carroll's rooftop.[19]

The Attack

Before the attack began, the occupants of the buildings to be used were ordered by armed men to leave, and were conveyed to Lyon's Hotel, where they remained under guard until the attack had finished. Local units blocked all the approach roads to the town at various places for several miles and the telephone in the railway signal box at Emly was removed. The main Dublin to Cork railway line was cut, with part of it being removed. (It was reported that the night mail train on arrival at Limerick Junction had fragments of clothing attached to the engine and a kidney was found in the fire box.)

On the given signal at approximately 1 a.m., the attack opened on the barracks from three sides and was met by stubborn resistance from the ten RIC officers inside, the sound of rifle fire and bombs being heard for many miles around in the stillness of the night.

The weights dropped from Carroll's began to break the slates of the barracks, which enabled the IRA to pour oil and petrol into the western wing of the building. However, a number of attempts to ignite this fuel failed and the roof space of the barracks was set on fire only after a Mills bomb had been dropped into it. Once the building caught fire, the police inside were called on to surrender, but they refused. The fire in the western wing of the barracks, from where Sergeant Kane and Constable Morton were returning gunfire, was quickly extended by the IRA, who threw more fuel into the building and within a comparatively short time the whole wing was ablaze.

At 5 a.m. the top of the barracks was a howling conflagration and the roof fell in, reportedly killing the two police officers. Their charred bodies were found that afternoon in the debris of the barracks. (There are differing reports stating that before the collapse of the roof both RIC officers had died from wounds.) The remainder of the police party withdrew to the ground floor, the only portion of the barracks still intact, and continued their resistance. They were repeatedly called on to surrender but refused each time.

By 7 a.m. the barracks was nearly in ruins, with the roof and most of the upper floor having collapsed to ground level, and could not be defended any longer, so the remaining garrison dashed to a small detached building in the yard. (Newspaper reports stated that during the withdrawal from the barracks the police had fixed bayonets and charged.) During this withdrawal Constable Arthur Hooey, 66674, was shot and seriously wounded. He was not expected to live, but he survived to retire from the Royal Ulster Constabulary (RUC) in 1947 with thirty-five years' service.

Of the remaining police officers only two escaped unscathed. Sergeant Tobias O'Sullivan had been struck with a bullet on the left breast but a pocket book he carried diverted the shot and saved his life. (He was later killed in Listowel, Co. Kerry, on 20 January 1921.)

An IRA man, Liam Scully, from Glencar, Co. Kerry, was also wounded, as the police made their way to the outbuilding. He was attended by two women, one of them a nurse, who had come with the IRA. Scully was then moved from the area by motor vehicle but died from his wounds.

At 7.15 a.m. the remaining IRA men in the town withdrew. Later in the day a large number of military reinforcements, along with an armoured car, arrived, while an aeroplane circled above the town. A private residence that, until a few weeks before, had been a local solicitor's office, was taken over and converted into a temporary RIC barracks.

Sergeant Kane had only been transferred two days earlier to Kilmallock from the depot in Dublin. On 1 June 1920 his funeral took place from Aughrim Street, Dublin, to Glasnevin Cemetery.

Constable Morton's Funeral, 30 May 1920

This impressive ceremony took place to the local Catholic churchyard in Kilmallock. It was led by three members of the clergy followed by a guard of honour and a hearse drawn by two horses. The coffin was draped in a Union Jack, which had several wreaths placed upon it. The hearse was followed by a number of mourning carriages and three RIC firing parties totalling 100 men, who carried their arms reversed and were under the command of DIs Marrinan, Egan and Regan. The band of the Royal Welch Fusiliers played the funeral march.

Very few townspeople attended the funeral, but as the coffin passed, small groups lifted their hats. At the corner of Main Street and Water Street the horses drawing the hearse refused to go on and the coffin had to be carried the last few hundred yards by an RIC guard. At the end of the funeral three volleys were fired and the Last Post sounded, after which all the RIC members formed up and marched back into town, halting in front of the ruined barracks. Here they were briefly addressed by Major General Tudor, police adviser to the viceroy, who awarded each of the survivors a Constabulary Medal and promotion. Sergeant O'Sullivan, the inspiration behind the defence of Kilmallock Barracks, also received a special gratuity of £50, while each constable received £25. Major General Tudor then made his way to the local hospital, where he bestowed the same rewards on the wounded officers.

Points of Interest
- Constable Morton was the son of a policeman who had been shot dead during fierce rioting in Belfast in 1872. The late constable's mother left her home in Thurles to attend her husband's funeral and gave birth to a son while waiting in the train at Kingsbridge Terminus, Dublin. That son, Joseph, died at Kilmallock.[20]
- The word 'Kilmallock' was used as the password by the RIC garrison in Schull Barracks, Co. Cork, but on 4 October 1920 an IRA party, aware of this information, raided the barracks and were able, through the use of the password, to take it.[21]
- Kilmallock Barracks had been attacked during the Fenian Rising of 1867, and three of the attackers were killed. (One of the dead was a stranger in the area and a monument was erected to the 'unknown Fenian'. History almost repeated itself as the IRA man Scully was also a stranger in the area and his identity was not known for a short period.) Another IRA man who took part in the attack on Kilmallock Barracks was Jeremiah O'Mahony, who accidentally shot himself in December 1920 whilst cleaning a rifle in his home at Paddock, Enniskeane, Co. Cork.
- As a result of the action taken during the attack on Kilmallock Barracks in 1867, Sub-Inspector Millings was granted a Constabulary Medal. When he and other police officers who had also been awarded Constabulary Medals for their actions during the Fenian Rising were receiving them in a ceremony at Phoenix Park in Dublin on 6 September 1867, it was announced that from then on the police force in Ireland was to be known as the Royal Irish Constabulary. The wording that announced this award to Sub-Inspector Millings in the *Police Gazette* was as follows: 'Millings Oliver First Sub Inspector Medal and Special Grant from Government. In command on the morning of 6 March when the Barrack of Kilmallock was attacked by a large party of armed insurgents'.

After the 1920 attack at Kilmallock this circular was issued to the RIC:

> No. D 326
> 1920
> Royal Irish Constabulary Office Dublin Castle
> 23 June 1920

Defence of Kilmallock Barracks on 28 May 1920

I have pleasure in transmitting for the information of the Force the following copy of a minute of the Chief Secretary's regarding the conduct of the Royal Irish Constabulary during the recent attack on Kilmallock Barrack. I feel sure the remarks of the Chief Secretary will be highly appreciated by all ranks.

T. J. Smith Inspector General

copy:
This was a really splendid defence against overwhelming odds and brutal conditions. The heroism and sacrifice of the defenders command the respect and admiration of the civilised world. It forms another great chapter in the splendid records of the Royal Irish Constabulary. Let me know if everything possible has been done for the dependants of the gallant dead.

H G 6/6/20[22]

Sergeant Kane, a forty-nine-year-old married man with eight children, was from Co. Meath. He had twenty-eight years' police service, having had no other employment before joining the RIC.

Constable Morton, a forty-eight-year-old married man with a family, was from Dublin. He had twenty-three years' police service, having had no other employment before joining the RIC.

Favourable Awards

Almost from the beginning, the Irish Constabulary had a system whereby police officers who performed outstanding acts of bravery or good police duty could be given an award. The RIC continued this system and graded the favourable awards scheme into three classes. Normally the saving of a life or other acts involving outstanding bravery merited a first-class favourable record, whilst the performance of good police duty in cases of murder and other serious crimes merited a second-class award. A third-class award was made for other police duties but mainly for action in cases of cruelty to animals and such like offences.

As well as favourable records, police officers could also receive monetary rewards for the performance of acts of bravery or good police duties. These monetary rewards were called grants and they were normally given in conjunction with some other kind of award but, on occasion, by themselves.

The money used for these grants, awarded by the police reward fund, was raised from fines imposed on police officers for minor breaches of force discipline. However, as the number of grants awarded increased during the years 1920 to 1922, the funds used for them were supplemented by money set aside by the government for this purpose. These new monies were announced to the RIC in the following circular:

> F 306
> 1920
> RIC Office Dublin Castle
> 31 May 1920

Constabulary Force Fund (Reward Branch)
The Government having decided to augment the funds of the Ward Branch of the Constabulary Force Fund, it is intended in future to

grant substantial pecuniary rewards to members of the force who perform exceptionally good duty in the detection of crime or in the defence of their Barracks, etc.

T. J. Smith Inspector General[23]

During the period covered, a number of police officers who were killed received favourable awards, with some of them also receiving grant awards. The following is a list of the officers who received such awards during this period:

No.	Name	Rank	Died	Favourable Record
59293	Benson, Francis	H/Con	14.05.1921	18.09.1919 & 01.03.1920
58519	Bloxham, Henry J.	Sgt	21.01.1921	22.07.1920 & £5
78576	Blythe, Sydney	Con	02.06.1921	09.09.1921
70823	Boyd, Robert A. E.	Con	17.01.1921	16.08.1920 & £10
55744	Brady, John	Sgt	09.05.1920	18.06.1920
54833	Brady, Philip	Sgt	02.09.1919	19.02.1919
69992	Bridges, Thomas	Con	14.05.1921	20.07.1920
61507	Brogan, Michael	Con	25.09.1920	18.06.1920
70259	Brown, Walter T.	Con	05.05.1921	02.09.1921
66998	Burke, Michael	Sgt	05.06.1921	22.02.1920 & £10 11.04.1922
58743	Carroll, Patrick*	Sgt	18.04.1920	28.05.1920
59764	Clarke, Christopher	Sgt	13.03.1922	20.02.1921, 02.09.1921
59658	Creegan, Francis	Sgt	02.06.1921	20.07.1921 (2) & 09.08.1921
60459	Curtin, Jeremiah*	Sgt	13.01.1921	02.06.1920, 15.09.1920 & £10
74477	Devine, Thomas	Con	15.07.1921	09.07.1921
57303	Doherty, Francis	Sgt	07.10.1920	19.07.1920
62633	Dunne, Edward*	Con	10.05.1920	16.03.1920
65998	Dunphy, Kyran	Sgt	19.05.1920	12.05.1920
71187	Enright, Thomas	Con	14.12.1921	06.06.1921 & 20.08.1921 (2)
65154	Fallon, Martin*	Con	03.05.1920	15.09.1919
58968	Foody, Patrick	Con	03.02.1921	19.07.1920 £3 & 17.09.1920 £5

70351	Gallagher, Francis	Con	12.10.1920	21.09.1920 & £2
70996	Gorbey, Robert	Con	06.11.1920	13.07.1920
59218	Hallissy, Michael	Sgt	30.03.1921	12.11.1919 & 20.02.1920
64249	Hanlon, John	D/Con	21.08.1920	10.02.1920
69198	Healy, Charles	Con	17.03.1920	21.06.1919
68430	Heaslip, William	Con	19.05.1922	26.10.1921 & £2
69264	Heffron, Thomas*	Con	26.01.1921	01.09.1920 & 22.07.1920
55504	Higgins, John	Sgt	01.04.1921	25.03.1920
64330	Hughes, Joseph	Sgt	21.02.1921	09.09.1919
55727	Hunt, Michael	DI	23.06.1919	09.09.19219 & £5 (good police duty at Sinn Féin meeting)
53643	Keany, Michael	DI	11.02.1922	02.02.1921 & £10 (actions during an ambush)
63544	Kelly, Michael	Con	22.09.1920	12.05.1919
65275	Kenny, Michael	Con	06.04.1921	28.03.1920
74724	Kenyon, Edmund	Con	17.05.1921	18.03.1921 & 20.07.1921
57392	Kingston, James*	Sgt	06.05.1921	16.08.1920 & £20
58083	Lucas, Samuel	Sgt	04.11.1920	14.03.1920
76409	MacDonald, John Cyril	Con	22.04.1921	16.03.1921
64858	McDonagh, Peter J.	Sgt	21.05.1921	02.06.1919
55303	McDonnell, Patrick	Sgt	10.05.1920	05.05.1920
65056	McFadden, John*	Sgt	24.04.1921	19.07.1920
68892	McNamara, John*	Con	24.08.1920	06.05.1920
54713	Maguire, James	Sgt	06.03.1921	01.07.1920 & £3
66577	Maguire, Joseph	Con	23.05.1921	27.07.1920
68276	Mahony, John	Con	19.09.1920	14.04.1920
55061	Maunsell, Daniel	Sgt	21.08.1920	03.02.1920 & £10
54291	Morton, Joseph*	Con	28.05.1920	04.06.1920
61051	Mulherin, William	D/Sgt	25.07.1920	25.02.1919 & 13.05.1920
65685	Mullany, Patrick	Con	02.02.1921	28.02.1920, 28.05.1920 & 10.09.1920
70256	Mullan, John*	Con	27.08.1920	18.11.1920
61673	Mulloy, Michael	Sgt	20.01.1921	09.09.1919
55316	Mulrooney, Edward	H/Con	04.04.1921	04.06.1920 £3 & 12.01.1921 £10

59800	Neazer, George	Sgt	10.03.1920	18.02.1920
67167	O'Regan, Christopher	Con	03.05.1921	04.02.1920
59193	O'Sullivan, Tobias*	DI	20.01.1921	04.06.1920 & £50
73253	Perrier, Frederick	Con	23.02.1921	18.03.1921
69729	Quinn, Michael*	Con	26.01.1921	06.05.1920, 14.08.1920 & £5
57242	Riordan, John	Sgt	05.08.1919	12.05.1919
68650	Satchwell, Thomas	Con	22.02.1921	05.03.1921
56877	Storey, William	H/Con	08.05.1921	13.03.1920
74612	Taylor, Frederick	Con	13.12.1920	18.03.1920
70974	Will, Alexander*	Con	11.07.1920	20.08.1920 & £10
50239	Wilson, William H.	DI	16.08.1920	16.08.1920 & £5 (for silver mines murder case on 18.09.1919)
70264	Woods, James T.	Con	15.11.1920	14.08.1920 & £2

The above list includes awards made only during the period covered and is not, therefore, a complete list of awards made to men who were subsequently killed.

Those names with an asterisk after them indicate the award of a Constabulary Medal as well as their favourable record and it is clear that the favourable record was awarded as a direct result of the political violence that prevailed at the time. The major proportion of the others (and especially those that were accompanied by a large grant award and those awarded in the later years) can be assumed to have been awarded as a direct result of the ongoing violence. This was because the normal functions of policing in Ireland had begun to be submerged under the tide of politically organised incidents.

6 JUNE 1920, CULLYHANNA, CO. ARMAGH
Timothy Holland, Sgt 60721

A police patrol from Crossmaglen Barracks was attacked in the village of Cullyhanna, 300 yards from the disused police barracks.

The sergeant and a constable were seriously wounded, the sergeant dying in Louth Infirmary, Dundalk, on 9 June 1920. He was an ex-inspector of weights and measures and was on the list for promotion.

At 8.15 p.m. the sergeant and two constables were on duty in the village as people began to leave an *aeraíocht* (open-air entertainment). The sergeant was standing midway between a public house and the school when seven or eight men walked into the middle of the road to the right and in front of him. They opened fire on the sergeant, wounding him in the arm and stomach. He returned fire and then ran to McGrainey's public house where Constable Raisdale, who had also been wounded, had taken cover. He asked the constable to reload his revolver as he was unable to do it.

When he arrived at the hospital he told his wife, 'I forgive the man who shot me and I want you to do the same.' The sergeant died at 7.15 p.m. on 9 June. He had two brothers, one of whom was also a member of the RIC.

At 7 p.m. on 10 June his body was borne by police from the Infirmary to Friary church, Dundalk. On 11 June, after a service in the church, the 'Dead March' was played on the organ as the coffin, draped in a Union Jack with a belt and tunic on top of it, was placed on a gun carriage drawn by six black chargers. Six sergeants from the Royal Field Artillery acted as drivers, while a firing party of twelve members from the same regiment, with arms reversed, headed the cortège as the sergeant's remains were taken to the 10.22 a.m. train for Belfast.

On its arrival at the Great Northern Railway terminus in Great Victoria Street, the cortège was met by large crowds, who watched the coffin being borne from the train to the hearse. The sergeant was then buried with full military honours in Milltown Cemetery, Belfast.

Sergeant Holland, a forty-one-year-old married man with five children, was from Dunmanway, Co. Cork. He had eighteen years' police service, having been a farmer before joining the RIC.

11 June 1920,
Railway Hotel, Limerick city
John J. Carroll, Con 62341

Constable Carroll had recently been transferred to Limerick for detective duties from Ballyporeen, Co. Tipperary. He and another constable were at the bar of the Railway Hotel when they were attacked by an armed man from the bar door. Constable Carroll was shot and killed. Constable Cruise pursued the man, firing at him, but he managed to get away along the side of the railway.

Constable Carroll was thirty-eight and single. A native of Co. Mayo, he had thirteen years' police service, having previously been a labourer.

12 June 1920,
near Glengarriff, Co. Cork
Thomas King, Con 69878

The constable had been on eight hours' leave in Bantry and at 7 p.m. was cycling, in civilian clothes and unarmed, back along the Bantry to Glengarriff road to his barracks at Glengarriff. At Snave Bridge he was attacked by masked men armed with revolvers. Although wounded, the constable was able to make his way to a nearby house, where he hid in a cupboard. His attackers followed and, on finding him, dragged the wounded man into a yard where they shot him again, throwing his body onto a manure pit. It was later found that the constable had ten wounds.

The IRA men involved in this incident were under the command of, and led by, Ted O'Sullivan, OC of the Bantry Battalion. Constable King, a twenty-six-year-old single man, was from Roundstone, Co. Galway. He had eight months' police service on 1 June 1920, having been a stoker in the Royal Navy before joining the RIC.

15 June 1920,
Gorey, Co. Wexford
Percival Lea-Wilson, DI 65448

At 9.45 a.m. the district inspector was shot and killed as he was going to his home in the village of Gorey, Co. Wexford, having bought a newspaper. A car with four men and a driver was seen in the vicinity of the attack and afterwards went in the direction of Ballycanew. The car used in this incident had been taken at gunpoint from a man in Enniscorthy. Newspaper reports of the incident stated that the DI's body was riddled with bullets.

Lea-Wilson had joined the army from the RIC in 1915, as a musketry instructor. He had been a captain in the Fifth Battalion of the Royal Irish Regiment. During the Easter Rising of 1916, he had charge of about 250 prisoners who had surrendered and been taken under strong military guard to the gardens in front of the Rotunda Hospital, Dublin. Some of these men were concerned by the treatment he was alleged to have meted out to prisoners, and in particular two of their leaders, Tom Clarke and Ned Daly. Two of the prisoners present at the Rotunda at this time were Michael Collins and Liam Tobin (who was later to become one of Collins' chief intelligence officers) and they vowed that they would have revenge for this alleged ill treatment.[24]

Lea-Wilson rejoined the RIC in late 1917. A thirty-three-year-old married man with no family, he was from Kent. He had nine years' police service, having had no other employment before joining the RIC. He was the great-grandson of Samuel Wilson, lord mayor of London. His funeral took place on 19 June 1920 to Putneyvale Cemetery, Beckenham, Kent.

15 June 1920, Belmullet, Co. Mayo
Pierce Doogue, Con 60412

The constable, who was stationed at Ballycroy, had been on one day's leave and was attending a fair at Belmullet. During the fair, police were about to arrest a man for some ordinary disturbance when a full-scale riot broke out. The constable is said to have gone to the aid of his colleagues at 9 p.m. but was killed by a blow to the head from a stone whilst in Main Street. Two other constables were slightly injured during this fierce street riot. After this incident the RIC garrison was strengthened, with the police and military commandeering the workhouse as a barracks. On 16 June 1920 a man was arrested for this attack.

Constable Doogue, forty-two and single, was from Queen's County. He had eighteen years' service and had been a farmer before joining the force. His body was removed on 20 June 1920 for interment in Queen's County.

21 June 1920, Clonee Wood, Co. Cork
James Brett, Con 54026

An RIC cycle patrol was ambushed at Clonee Wood, Clonee, near Bantry. Constable Brett was shot dead, and another constable and Sergeant Driscoll were seriously wounded. The attack was carried out by six Bantry IRA men under the leadership of Maurice Donegan.

No inquest could be held for the dead constable as only three of the twelve jurors who were summoned attended; later, use of a hearse for the funeral was refused.

Constable Brett, a fifty-year-old married man with four children, was from Waterford. He had thirty years' police service, having been a farmer before joining the RIC.

25 June 1920, Co. Tipperary
Michael Horan, Con 61494

Constable Horan had been on temporary duty in Co. Tipperary when he was shot dead. He had been attached to Mountfield RIC Barracks in Tyrone but was transferred to Beragh when Mountfield was closed.

Soon after he arrived in Co. Tipperary on 8 April 1920, the IRA placed his name on the 'Black List'. I have been unable to find out any further details in relation to the incident in which he lost his life. He was thirty-eight, single and from Co. Roscommon. He had been a farmer before his fourteen years in the RIC.

2 July 1920, Ballinure, Co. Tipperary
Robert Tobin, Sgt 57569

A four-man RIC patrol was making its way back from Cashel to its barracks at Ballinure when it was ambushed midway between Dualla village and the barracks. The sergeant was killed and Constable Brady was wounded. (Tobin volunteered for service early in the war, joined the Irish Guards and was wounded in action abroad.) Michael Burke, who lived about three miles from the scene, was arrested on 9 August 1920 to await trial by court martial for this incident. It was alleged that at the time of his arrest he had in his possession an automatic revolver which had been removed from Constable Maloney, another member of the ambushed patrol.

Sergeant Tobin, a forty-five-year-old married man with six young children, was from Co. Wexford. He had twenty-seven years' police service having had no other employment before joining the RIC.

11 July 1920,
Rathmore RIC Barracks, Co. Kerry
Alexander Will, Con 70974

In the early hours of 11 July 1920, IRA members of the Fifth Battalion, Kerry No. 2 Brigade attacked the RIC barracks at Rathmore. It is alleged that during this attack the IRA used an obsolete cannon from Ross Castle which had been placed on a railway truck to move it to its firing position.[25] The railway bridge was fortified with sandbags from behind which the IRA men were able to fire on the barracks. The attack opened with the IRA firing rifles and shotguns, and throwing bombs, which were, in turn, answered by rifle fire from the RIC garrison. The attack continued throughout the night and as dawn neared, a bomb was hurled into one of the upper windows of the barracks. The explosion that followed killed one of the defenders, Constable Will.

Will, twenty-four and single, was from Forfar in Scotland. He would have had four months' service on 30 July, having been a farm worker and a soldier before joining the RIC. On 14 July, after a service in Abbey Presbyterian church at 47 Rutland Square Dublin, his body was removed to Aberdeen for interment.

RIC Recruitment

Constable Will was the first fatality among the police officers who had been recruited in Britain as part of the government's efforts to increase the RIC's strength. He had been recommended for police service by DI (formally Major) Fleming, the RIC's recruitment officer in London. His death was technically the first casualty of a policeman termed a 'Black and Tan'. However, it should be remembered that not all recruits from England or Scotland would merit this title as recruitment for the RIC had taken place in these areas before the upsurge in political violence in 1919.

Between the land war of 1881–82 and 1916 the RIC had not been seriously challenged by any major unrest or controversy, with the result that it stabilised as an occupation, with the force settling down to low-key routine policing. Improved pay and conditions in the latter part of the nineteenth century helped to reduce resignations from the force, with longer-serving officers being less likely to resign, their pensions doubtlessly being a great inducement for them to stay.

The whole system of police pensions had been fundamentally reorganised by the Constabulary and Police (Ireland) Act (1883), which allowed officers to retire after the completion of twenty-five years' service, regardless of age, as opposed to the original system whereby an officer could retire only on reaching sixty years of age. Then he was awarded a proportion of his pay, according to his length of service, as a pension. By 1908 RIC members who had completed thirty years' service and attained the age of fifty were encouraged to retire.

As policing established itself in Ireland, it generated local traditions of family enlistment, with a high incidence of multiple family membership, both within and across generations in the RIC. By the end of the nineteenth century, RIC regulations reflected that these emerging 'police families' formed a very important source of reliable recruits already familiar with the police culture, its demands and prospects. Sons of RIC officers were allowed to join the police a year younger and an inch shorter than other recruits.

The religious composition of the RIC was very close to the recorded Catholic proportion of the population during 1861–1911, but with the onset of political violence the socio-economic background of recruits changed significantly. This was due to the fall in native Irish recruits and a very large increase in the number of officers resigning. These were replaced by an influx of demobilised ex-military personnel, the majority of whom were Protestants from large urban industrial areas in Britain. These new recruits did not have an understanding or appreciation of Irish rural life, which did nothing to endear them to the Irish population, regardless of their religious or political views.

These facts, combined with the multitude of other policing problems, almost inevitably ensured that conflict with the police would increase.

12 July 1920,
Rearcross RIC Barracks, Co. Tipperary
John Stokes, Sgt 71609

Approximately fifty IRA men from three IRA brigades – East Limerick Brigade and North and South Tipperary brigades – attacked the RIC barracks at Rearcross, Co. Tipperary. The assault lasted for eight hours, during which time the barracks was set alight by the attackers.[26]

Two IRA men, Ernie O'Malley and Jim Gorman, an Irish-Australian who had deserted from the Australian Army when on home leave and who was now an officer of the Hollyford Company, were on the roof of the barracks trying to smash a hole in it so that the building could be set on fire.[27] Sergeant Stokes must have become aware of this, as he opened the front door of the barracks and aimed his rifle at these two men. However, he was shot and killed by an IRA man, Paddy Dwyer, who was in charge of the attacking party at the front of the station. A constable, on seeing the sergeant fall, ran out and dragged him back inside. His body was moved further inside the barracks by his comrades each time they were forced to fall back, so that it would not be consumed by the advancing flames.

Sergeant Stokes was a defence of barracks sergeant and the first officer employed as such to be killed by the IRA. He had undertaken the defence of the barracks, which stood back a little from the main road and was built under a gradually sloping hill, with great care. The precautions he had taken included a garden wall at the rear being cut away close to the ground and the top slanted in order to remove cover to anyone attacking the barracks from that direction. The backyard was covered in netting wire, with the windows of the barracks having steel plate attached to them. Openings had been made in these steel plates allowing sufficient space for the defenders to return fire, and these were protected by netting wire to prevent bombs from entering the barracks. The whole area around the barracks had also been defended with wire.

Sergeant Stokes' funeral took place on 16 July to Cloghogue chapel in Newry. He was a twenty-one-year-old single man from Co. Down. He had one month's police service, having joined the RIC as a defence of barracks sergeant. Prior to this he was an army officer.

The Attack

The attack on Rearcross RIC Barracks was to have taken place the previous evening but was cancelled by the local IRA brigade staff as the plans had not been discussed with them.[28] In order to overcome this problem O'Malley, as an IRA GHQ staff officer, assumed charge and ordered the attack be postponed.

On the night of the attack the wind was blowing strongly and it was raining heavily, which helped mask any noise made by the IRA as they made their way towards the barracks carrying bombs, paraffin, spray pumps, etc. The IRA men on their way from the mobilisation point to the police barracks had a long length of rope, along which men were spaced, so that they would not get lost in the darkness. The plan was to enter Flannery's Store, which was to the left of the barracks, and via the store gain access to the barracks' roof.

Once the IRA had access to the roof they intended to strip it away with mud bombs. These were half-sticks of gelignite with a detonator and fuse attached, wrapped in a sticky clay. The clay fastened the bomb to the roof and when it exploded slates were blown from a large portion of roof. Through these holes the IRA planned to spray paraffin from a pump they had brought with them. Once the barracks was on fire, cart bombs were then to be thrown through the holes in its roof. (Cart bombs were metal cart boxes packed with explosives and scrap iron, which weighed between 20 and 25lbs.) A number of these bombs, which had been left over after the attack on Doon RIC Barracks in March, were brought by the local IRA company to Rearcross.

While the barracks' roof was under attack, other IRA units were to cover the front and rear of the building with gunfire, whilst all roads into the village were to be blocked by other IRA companies to prevent reinforcements reaching the barracks.

At 1 a.m. the attack began, but during it the spray pump gave up, forcing the IRA to fill bottles with paraffin and throw them at the barracks to fuel the flames. As Seán Treacy, O'Malley and Dan Breen were doing this a policeman threw a grenade at them from behind a wall at the rear of Flannery's. The grenade exploded as they ran into the store. The three were wounded by hand-grenade splinters; O'Malley, being the more seriously wounded, had to receive help to make his way from the scene. Gorman was wounded by police gunfire through the roof and also had to be helped from the scene.

O'Malley, an IRA GHQ staff captain, was a very important member of the IRA, and Collins had supreme trust in him. He was later placed in charge of the Second Southern Division of the IRA which covered five counties with overall command of twelve IRA brigades.

At 9 a.m. the attack finished as the police had moved back into part of the barracks that had not been destroyed. They continued their stubborn defence, forcing the IRA to withdraw.[29]

13 July 1920, near Dingle, Co. Kerry
Michael Lenihan, Con 63592
George Roche, Con 62449

A police mobile patrol was ambushed between Cloghane and Dingle, Co. Kerry. Two constables were killed outright, while the driver and DI Fallon of Dingle were seriously wounded. The vehicle had been returning to Dingle after the DI had inspected the barracks at Cloghane.

Constable Lenihan was thirty-four and single, and came from Co. Cork. He had twelve years' police service, having been a clerk before joining the RIC. His funeral took place from St Mary's church, Limerick, to Mount St Lawrence Cemetery on 16 July 1920. RIC officers had to carry the coffin in relays from the chapel to the cemetery as a hearse could not be obtained.[30]

This attack is believed to have been carried out by the IRA's flying column attached to the West Kerry No. 1 Brigade and some of those involved were Tadhg Brosnan, Dan Jeffers (a Tralee IRA officer), and J. Dowling (who had been OC of 'A' Boherbee Company, Tralee Battalion, Kerry No. 1 Brigade).

Constable Roche, a thirty-two-year-old single man, was from Co. Clare. He had thirteen years' service, having been a farmer before joining the RIC.

14 JULY 1920, NEAR FOYNES, CO. LIMERICK
Patrick Fahy, Con 69396

At 8 p.m. a six-man RIC cycle patrol consisting of a sergeant and five constables was ambushed near Foynes, on the main Limerick to Glin road in the district of Adare, by IRA men from the West Kerry Brigade under the leadership of the brigade's commander, Séan Finn.

The constable was shot and died from his wounds at 4 a.m. on 15 July 1920. The other members of the patrol returned fire and were able to make their way into a position overlooking their attackers. A gun battle then developed which forced the IRA party to withdraw. The rest of the RIC patrol escaped uninjured.

Constable Fahy, twenty-five and single, was from Co. Galway. He had two years' police service, having previously been a farmer. It was reported that the constable had intended to resign from the RIC.

14 July 1920,
Lanesborough, Co. Longford
Martin Clarke, Con 64977

A party of police were making their way to the assizes at Roscommon when they were ambushed at Wakefield near Lanesborough. One constable was killed; another, Constable Macken, although seriously wounded, was able to return to Lanesborough.

Constable Clarke was attached to Mount Talbot Barracks. He was thirty-one and from Co. Cork. He had ten years' service, having had no other employment before joining the RIC. It was reported that his coffin was taken to Co. Galway.

17 July 1920,
near Newcastle West, Co. Limerick
James F. Masterson, Con 62862

Constable Masterson was attached to Newcastle West and was making his way home on leave by motor car when he was ambushed just outside the town. From Co. Leitrim, he was a thirty-five-year-old married man with two children. He had twelve years' police service, having been a farmer before joining the RIC.

17 July 1920, County Club, Cork city
Gerald Brice Ferguson Smyth, Lt Col DSO,
Divisional Police Commissioner for Munster

At 10.30 p.m. Smyth was in the smoking-room of the County Club along with RIC County Inspector Craig, when a party of IRA, possibly thirteen, entered the building. Some remained on guard at the entrance with a waiter, Ned Fitzgerald, who was involved in the attack. Six made their way upstairs to the smoking-room: Séan (Jack) Culhane, John J. O'Connell, Seán O'Donoghue, Daniel Donovan, Cornelius O'Sullivan and Daniel Healy, all IRA men from various battalions of Cork's No. 1 Brigade. It is alleged that one of these IRA men walked up to Smyth and said, 'Your orders were to shoot on sight. You are in sight now so prepare', after which Smyth was shot a number of times.[31] Craig was wounded in the leg. After the attack all those involved made their way out of the club and mingled with the crowds coming out of the cinemas.

Lieutenant Colonel Smyth was born on 7 September 1885 at Dalhousie in the Punjab, India. He joined the Royal Engineers in 1905 and was promoted to captain in 1914, going to France with the expeditionary force. In October 1914, as a result of a serious wound, he lost his left arm. During the war he was wounded six times, was awarded a DSO and on 2 December 1916 was appointed to command a battalion of the King's Own Scottish Borderers, being mentioned in despatches four times.

During the war Smyth had been a subordinate officer in the Ninth Division under General Tudor, who was later to become police adviser to the viceroy and commander of both the RIC and DMP. Tudor recommended Smyth for the post of divisional police commissioner for Munster, which he took up on 3 June 1920.

After his death, three days of rioting ensued in Belfast and a number of people lost their lives. There was also rioting in Banbridge and Dromore, Co. Down, with one person being killed in Dromore.

On 21 July 1920 Smyth was buried with full military honours in the family burial ground at the public cemetery on the Newry road, Banbridge, Co. Down. It would appear that he was not issued with an RIC number.

Background

On 19 June 1920 Smyth made a speech to RIC personnel at Listowel Barracks, Co. Kerry. During this speech he spelled out RIC policy. As a result of this, Constable Jeremiah Mee placed his revolver on a table and refused to do his duty as he considered the speech to be inflammatory and alleged that it was also an incitement to murder. When other senior police officers present ordered that Mee be removed, the other constables refused. This incident became known as the Listowel Mutiny. On 10 July 1920 a newspaper published an extract from the *Irish Bulletin*, an underground newspaper of Sinn Féin's publicity department, outlining these events. (The *Bulletin* was edited by Robert Brennan, Frank Gallagher and Erskine Childers.) Smyth subsequently published his account in *The Times*.[32]

Because of the alleged content of this speech, Seán O'Hegarty, acting commander of Cork No. 1 Brigade, planned to have Smyth killed, but first he needed information about his movements. The County Club in Cork was frequented by high-ranking military officers and persons loyal to the government. The staff were also viewed as being loyal and so the IRA found it very difficult to obtain information about the club and those who visited it. However, this situation was to change when Seán Culhane, the intelligence officer of B Company of the IRA's First Cork Battalion, made contact with the waiter Fitzgerald, who supplied the necessary information. On the night of the attack Fitzgerald was held at the door by the IRA, whom he was expecting. As a result of his information the IRA men were able to mount their attack, with one of them using words that were alleged to have been used by Smyth himself during his speech at Listowel, just before the IRA opened fire.

In the month before his death Divisional Commander Smyth issued a number of orders to all police officers in his area of responsibility in an attempt to enhance police efforts against the IRA. As can be seen from some of these orders, which are reproduced below, Smyth was a radical and astute thinker whose operational procedures and proposed changes to police strategy would have had a pronounced effect on the IRA. The IRA leadership probably realised the impact these new measures would have against their organisation and its ability to carry on the campaign, so they ordered that he be killed.

Some of these orders, issued on 10, 11 and 17 June 1920, were as follows and show how seriously he took his appointment:

Order No. 1; 10.06.1920

1. Every effort will be made to bring the garrisons of all stations up to 15 men.
2. The police will occupy the same building as the military wherever there is a military post, except as Co. and District Headquarters. At Headquarters' stations they will also occupy the same building unless there are excellent reasons to the contrary. These reasons will be forwarded to this office by return of post.
3. The number of police at combined military and police stations will be reduced to a minimum. At outstations three will be sufficient. The men left at these stations will be the men with the best local knowledge and will act as guides to the military. At least one must be a sergeant or Head Constable. The other police will be used to strengthen weak stations.
4. When the police vacate a barracks to occupy the same house as the military, the Sinn Féiners may burn the old Barracks. I do not much mind if they do, but as a preventative the following procedure will be adopted. (a) Before vacating the Barracks select the house of a leading Sinn Féiner and send me the particulars of it. I will then send you an order to requisition it and you will be ready to act. (b) Warn the occupier that if the Barracks are burnt his house will be seized in lieu in 24 hours. (c) If the Barracks are burned, give the occupier 24 hours to clear out and then evict him. Leave the house empty in case we need it. (d) Consider this

house as the Barracks, select another, send me particulars and warn the occupier as before.
5. Report when paragraphs 2, 3 and 4 of order have been fully complied with.

(Signed) G. F. Smyth Lieut. Colonel D.C.

Order No. 2
By Lieut. Colonel G. F. Smyth, D.C.
(a copy of this order is to be posted in every Barrack.)
1. In every station where the Police or combined Police and Military number over 14, strong patrols will be sent out at night on at least five nights a week and preferably every night. Patrols to be at least eight strong.
2. Stereotyped patrols are useless. We are up against a cunning enemy and will only defeat him if every man uses his brains.
3. The following are some obvious hints. (a) Never go out before dark. (b) Never go out through the front door if you can get over the back wall or through a side window. (c) Never go out twice at the same time or follow the same route twice. (d) Never go along the road if you can avoid it. Go across country. (e) Wear shoes if you have them. (f) Make sure that you are not followed. Let one man drop in a ditch whilst the rest of the patrol moves on a couple of hundred yards. He will soon see if anyone is following.
4. The main object of patrolling is to stop illegal movement by night. Therefore get across country to a road, lie up behind the hedge and hold up everyone who comes along. Put out a man a hundred yards on either side of the main group. He will shout 'Halt in the King's name' to all motors. Other traffic he will let pass and the main group will halt and search them, whilst the single man will hold up anyone who tries to escape.
5. Patrols should not as a rule move outside a three mile radius from their Barracks. If the Barracks are attacked in their absence so

much the better. The patrol can then take the attackers in the rear by surprise. Remember that even seasoned regular troops will not stand if surprised by night from the rear. So as long as patrols are intelligently led and surprise the enemy they have nothing to fear and everything to gain.

6. If a patrol finds roads blocked they can soon tell if their own Barracks is threatened or not. If it is not, the leader must decide which is the most likely Barracks in the neighbourhood to be attacked and move in that direction. He may be wrong but there is a chance that he may be right and may be able to take the attackers in the rear. If he does nothing he can expect no results and I will have him reduced to the ranks for inefficiency.

(Signed) G. F. Smyth 10.6.1920 Lieut. Colonel, D.C.

Order No. 4

By Lieut. Colonel G. F. Smyth, D.C.

1. In every Barrack each man must have a definite position to occupy in case of alarm.
2. Each man's name will be written on the wall above his position, also a list of the bombs, etc., which he requires.
3. There must be a reserve in each Barracks to meet any unforeseen occurrence, even if it only consists of the Sergeant and one man. The best position for this reserve should be carefully thought out.

(Signed) G. F. Smyth 10.6.1920 Lieut. Colonel, D.C.

Notes on Defence of Barracks

1. The only forms of attacks to be expected are: (a) An explosive charge placed against or outside a wall to blow it down. (b) An attack on the roof from an adjoining house. (c) An explosive charge in a neighbouring house.
2. Petrol and oil will probably be used in both forms of attack.
3. For 'A' we want barbed wire. The easiest way to put up barbed

wire is to drive nails, spikes or staples into the wall about 6 feet up and pickets into the ground about 5 feet from the wall. Run the wire criss-cross from the pickets to the nails and pull it as tight as possible. Then throw in loose wire to fill up. Leave gaps opposite the doors and make knife-rests to close them at night. Remember that wire which cannot be fired into is not much use and that wire which cannot be either fired into or bombed is useless as the attackers can cut it up at their leisure.

4. The existing bombing holes are far too small. We want a hole big enough to allow a man to put his head and shoulders through and listen for attackers. We want a hole big enough for a man to put out his arm and shoulder and aim and throw a bomb instead of poking it out. We want to protect the man whilst he is doing this from rifle fire. Try this method. Take two stout pieces of wood about 4 feet long and 3 or 4 inches in diameter. Near one end of each cut a deep groove across the piece of wood into which the steel plate will fit tightly. Then nail the piece of wood into the bottom corners of the bombing hole so that they are horizontal and the grooves are 9 inches beyond the outside face of the wall. Take a small steel plate from one of the windows and fix it in the grooves. Drive in nails to steady it and, if necessary, fix two pieces of wood similarly in the top corners of the hole. The plate will then sit 9 inches clear of the wall and will cover a man who is firing or bombing from the hole.

5. Remember that if you have no barbed wire you must be particularly careful that no one can work against the wall without you being able to firstly hear him and secondly bomb and shoot him.

6. Remember that it must be possible from some loophole in the Barrack to fire on every possible position which an attacker may occupy.

7. To defeat 'B', which is now the Sinn Féiners' main method, adopt the following expedients. (a) The Sinn Féiner has to break a hole in

the neighbouring roof to get at ours. If we hear him and are ready we can shoot him as soon as he pokes his head out. To do this we must have a fire position all ready. So at the head of the Barrack furthest from the adjoining house cut a good big hole in the ceiling and rig up a rough ladder so that a man can get up into the ceiling joists in a minute. If the rafters are far enough apart to let his shoulders through he will then only have to knock off the slates to fire. If they are not, cut a piece out of one at once. The roof will still stand. (b) When the Sinn Féiner has got on to the next roof he then drops bombs and weights onto the roof, firstly to break in the roof and secondly to break in the ceiling. We cannot stop him breaking in the roof except by shooting him, but if we nail meshed rabbit-wire to the undersides of the roof and rafters for a distance of 6 feet from the neighbouring house it will catch the first of his bombs and give us some time. With luck the bombs will roll down the wire and burst on top of the side wall. (c) Then the Sinn Féiner pours in oil and petrol. We have found by experiment that if the top of the ceiling is covered with a layer of earth a quarter to half an inch thick the petrol burns away and sets fire to nothing. So cover your ceiling with each for a distance of six feet from the adjoining house. Do not put in a thick layer or you will break the ceiling.

8. To defeat 'C' if the Sinn Féiners blow in the party wall between the Barracks and the neighbouring house we are still alright if we have the opposite wall of the room loopholed. If they try to come through the breach we can shoot them. So get your loopholes made now.

Order No. 5
By Lieut. Colonel G. F. Smyth, D.S.O.
Divisional Commissioner R.I.C., Munster No. 2
Cork, 17th June 1920

1. I wish to make the present situation clear to all ranks.

2. A policeman is perfectly justified in shooting any man who is seen with arms and who does not immediately throw up his hands when ordered. A policeman is perfectly justified in shooting any man who he has good reason to believe is carrying arms and who does not immediately throw up his hands when ordered.
3. Every proper precaution for protection will be given to police at inquests so that no information will be given to Sinn Féin as to identity of individuals and movements of police. This was ably managed by Counsel at a recent inquest at Limerick.
4. I wish to make it perfectly clear to all ranks that I will not tolerate any 'reprisals'. They bring discredit on the police. I will deal most severely with any officer or man concerned in them.

(Signed) G. F. Smyth, Lieut. Colonel
Divisional Commissioner, R.I.C.[33]

The Aftermath

On 11 October 1920 Smyth's brother, Major George Osbert Stirling Smyth, DSO, MC, who had also been wounded in the war, was killed as he commanded a party of soldiers trying to arrest Dan Breen and Seán Treacy at Fernside in Drumcondra, Dublin, the home of Professor John Carolan, who was employed at St Patrick's Training College, Dublin. As the major was about to enter a top-floor bedroom, shots were fired from inside, killing him. A Captain White who was with him was also killed and Corporal Worth, who had been on the stairs, was seriously wounded. Although badly wounded, both Breen and Treacy escaped. Major Smyth was later buried with his brother in the graveyard in Banbridge.

Republican sources studied indicate that on hearing of his brother's death, Major Smyth, who was on military service in Egypt with the Royal Field Artillery, applied for intelligence duty in Ireland. They state that he came to Ireland along with eleven picked men to avenge his brother's death, believing that Breen had been responsible.

At that time General H. Tudor had requested that Brigadier General Sir Ormonde de l'Épée Winter, KBE, CB, CMG, DSO, be appointed chief of intelligence. The brigadier general was nominated as deputy inspector general of the RIC, an appointment which would enable him to replace General Tudor during any absences and give cover to his actual position as chief of combined intelligence services. Within a short time Winter had totally reorganised the intelligence services and once more a flow of accurate information began to be received. Because of his success the IRA nicknamed him 'The Holy Terror'. Information supplied by an informant known to Republicans as 'Bow Tie' sent Major Smyth to search for the two wanted men at Fernside, Drumcondra, Dublin, and this resulted in the incident described above.[34]

After the IRA men's escape, intense police and military activity continued throughout Dublin. Breen was taken the next day to the Mater Hospital, where he remained under the assumed name of Shine, while Treacy moved around the city from safe house to safe house. On 14 October police and military surrounded the Mater Hospital but they did not find Breen. At the same time a search was also carried out at Peadar Clancy's draper's shop in Talbot Street, Dublin, which was known as the 'Republican Outfitters' to IRA men and their supporters.[35]

An IRA meeting in the shop, which had been discussing the plight of Breen, had just broken up, with four IRA men remaining behind after it had finished. These men were Seán Treacy, Dick McKee (OC, Dublin Brigade), Leo Henderson (officer, Dublin Brigade) and Joe Vize (a member of the Squad and also director of purchases and head of arms smuggling). When they realised that the premises were about to be searched, all four men ran into the street and tried to escape.

Treacy and three others (two civilians and an army officer) were killed in the gun battle which developed, with another army officer (who was in plain clothes) dying later from his wounds. He was an intelligence officer. All the other IRA men managed to escape. Treacy, one of those involved in the ambush at Soloheadbeg, was killed while Breen was being moved from the Mater to a safe house. In October 1920 Scotland Yard offered £1,000 for information which would result in the arrest of Daniel Breen.

19 July 1920, near Tuam, Co. Galway
James Burke, Con 66147
Patrick Carey, Con 66045

A motor vehicle containing four RIC men, who were returning from the Galway assizes, was ambushed at Aughle, three miles from Dunmore, as they were making their way back to their barracks. It was stated that a tree had been felled across the road in order to stop the vehicle. Once stopped, the car was fired on by IRA men who were in cover behind a hedge. Two of the constables were killed outright, the other two were disarmed and told to return to Tuam. Prior to the ambush police had received a warning not to attend the assizes as someone was aware that the IRA meant to attack them.

Police and soldiers sent to the area to help search for the persons responsible for this attack arrived at the barracks in Tuam at 4.30 a.m. on 20 July. When they saw the bodies of the two dead constables on the floor of the mess room, pent-up feelings overcame them and they took revenge on the town, burning the town hall to the ground and causing much destruction to other property.

Constable Burke was twenty-eight and came from Birr, King's County. He had eight years' police service, having had no other employment before joining the RIC. (His father, James Burke of Newbridge Street, Birr, was an ex-member of the RIC.) On 23 July 1920 his remains were conveyed by military motor car to Birr church and the funeral was to Clonoghill Cemetery.

On the same day the body of Constable Carey, twenty-nine, single, from Skibbereen, Co. Cork, was buried at Caheragh, Skibbereen. He had nine years' police service on 17 July 1920, having been a farmer before joining the RIC. After the funeral the hearse was set upon and burnt.

21 July 1920, Ballina, Co. Mayo
Thomas Robert Armstrong, Sgt 53611

The sergeant and a constable were on duty in Knox Street, Ballina, just outside the Moy Hotel and within 100 yards of their barracks, when they were fired on. The sergeant was mortally wounded while Constable Regan was seriously hurt. As Sergeant Armstrong lay dying he said, 'I do not think any Ballina man would do this to me.'

Sergeant Armstrong, a fifty-six-year-old married man with eleven children, was from Co. Cavan. He had twenty-one years' police service, having been a farmer before joining the RIC. On 24 July 1920 he was buried with full military honours in the Protestant cemetery at Ballina.

24 July 1920, Henry Street, Limerick city
Walter Oakley, Con 71636

Three English recruits were walking in Henry Street, Limerick, when they were attacked by IRA men from E Company, Second Battalion, Mid Limerick Brigade under the leadership of William Barrett. Two of the constables were wounded and fell. The third, Albert Jones, a brother to one of the other constables, gave chase to their attackers but was hit by a revolver bullet in the chest. He was very fortunate that the round hit the clasp of his braces and glanced off, probably saving his life.

Constable Oakley died from his wounds on 29 July 1920 and on 2 August his remains were taken to West Ham in London, where his interment was to take place.

One of the IRA men involved in this attack is alleged to have hidden his revolver during the incident by dropping it into a post box. The next morning the weapon was recovered by other IRA men who confronted the postman as he opened the post box.[36]

Republican sources also stated that two ex-soldiers named Patrick Blake and James O'Neill, both from Rossbrien, were arrested for this killing. Both men were taken to Dublin for a military court martial which acquitted them. On 20 November 1920 these men, along with their relations, set out on their journey home from Dublin. At Limerick Junction the two families split to make their way home. At Oola the Blake party was stopped by a number of masked men who shot Michael Blake, a brother of Patrick, who was in the car with him and their parents. The O'Neills were also stopped by masked and armed men near Limerick Junction. James was removed from the vehicle and taken away. The next day he was found shot dead.

Constable Oakley, a twenty-year-old single man, was from Essex. He had one year's service, having been a seaman and a Royal Marine before joining the RIC.

25 July 1920,
Bandon, Co. Cork
William Mulherin, D/Sgt 61051

The detective sergeant was the chief intelligence officer for the area of West Cork, being stationed at Bandon. The information he gained was very accurate and the raids and arrests which followed from it were having an effect on the IRA. He realised that his life was in danger because of his duties and, therefore, took every precaution to ensure his safety. In early 1920 he had received several threatening letters and had survived an attempt on his life in March that year.

However, he went to his place of worship regularly and on 25 July was planning to attend 8 a.m. Mass at St Patrick's, Bandon. He had just made his way up the seventy steps that led to the church and was in the chapel porch, when he was shot and killed by two men.[37]

Detective Sergeant Mulherin, thirty-eight, was a married man from Co. Mayo. He had seventeen years' service, having previously been a farmer.

27 July 1920,
Rossa Street, Clonakilty, Co. Cork
James Murray, Con 69939

Four IRA men followed Constable Murray and, as he was about to enter a greengrocer's shop in Rossa Street, two of them shot him in the head.

The constable, a twenty-six-year-old single man, was from Queen's County. He had eight months' police service on 4 July, having been a soldier and seen war service with the Irish Guards before joining the RIC.

Auxiliary Division of the RIC

Winston Churchill is credited with the conception of the Auxiliary Division of the RIC, when, early in 1920, he suggested that a special force of 8,000 ex-soldiers be raised at once to reinforce the RIC. This was agreed in principle by the government and the Auxiliary Division was formed later in the year.[38] Churchill believed that this second force should be recruited from ex-army officers and viewed it as a means of bolstering the RIC, while at the same time avoiding the appearance of all-out military conflict in Ireland.

On 10 July 1920 the Auxiliary Division was advertised in London as a *corps d'elite* for which only men who had held commissions in the British armed services would be accepted. Newspapers at the time carried reports that the RIC was being strengthened by the recruitment of high-ranking officers ('Generals as Police Cadets') in a new scheme to combat Sinn Féin. The media also reported that General Tudor, the commander of police in Ireland, recommended this scheme in order to coordinate the activities of the military and police in stamping out the Sinn Féin campaign.

Men wishing to apply for appointment were interviewed at Scotland Yard and, if accepted, were given a first-class single ticket to Ireland. Due to the economic situation that prevailed after the First World War, coupled with the fact that the majority of the applicants were in their early to mid-twenties and had seen only military service, there was an abundance of men wishing to apply, not only in the London area but from all quarters of the globe. Within the first fortnight over 1,000 applications were received.[39]

The qualifications required were that applicants had to be ex-officers with the highest military and personal standards, physically fit and able to give names of persons who would supply references for them. Prospective recruits were informed that they would first of all be put through a short training course before being posted throughout the RIC, in order to take up their duties of instructing the rank and file in the best tactics to adopt against the surprise methods of the IRA, and to act as advisers in matters of defence of police barracks.

They were informed that their rank would be that of temporary cadet but graded as an RIC sergeant for the purpose of discipline, and that their service would be on a short service system. They were guaranteed employment by the government for at least twelve months. Further to this they were told they would receive preferential treatment for permanent RIC commissions and, whilst employed as temporary cadets, would be paid the rate of £1 per day, with certain other allowances in addition.

Because these new members were to be ranked as sergeants, it caused some apprehension in the RIC about future promotions within the force. In order to explain the situation the RIC issued a notice to all its members as follows:

> Royal Irish Constabulary Office
> Dublin Castle
> 9 August 1920
>
> Promotion
>
> It having been brought to notice that some apprehension is felt among constables that the temporary cadets now joining the RIC with the rank of Sergeant are actually filling vacancies in that rank to the detriment of the prospects of Constables who are already serving, I wish to make it clear that the temporary cadets' are a temporary service only, inaugurated to assist the Constabulary in the present pressure, that they are supernumerary to the establishment and their appointment as sergeant will in no way operate adversely in the promotion of constables to that rank, which will continue under the existing rules of the service.
>
> T. J. Smith
> Inspector General
> Issued to DCs, CIs, DIs and all existing stations.[40]

The RIC recruiting officer in London was a Major Fleming, who stated to the newspapers:

> Applications are being received from ex-officers of every class from the West End clubmen to soldiers who were commissioned from the rank and file of the Regular Army. Quite a number of the applicants are Irishmen and many are well-to-do men who are taking on the job in a spirit of duty or adventure. There is no

class bar against candidates. We are still open to take recruits and a man's social position will not affect his chances of acceptance. We are also recruiting to the rank and file and are enlisting a large number of ex-soldiers as Constables. It is quite incorrect to say that there is at present an abnormal number of resignations from the RIC. The force is doing splendidly and many of the ex-officers who have joined have done so purely out of admiration for the fine work which the men are doing in Ireland under most trying circumstances.

On 27 July 1920 the first Auxiliary recruit, Harold C. Pearsons, 72096, arrived in Ireland. The first recruits arrived at the North Wall Dock, Dublin, and were then transferred to Hare Park Camp at the Curragh Military Training Camp, where they underwent a shortened police course. During this course they received firing and bombing practice for which they provided their own instructors.

The temporary cadets were formed into the Auxiliary Division and maintained as an autonomous force under the command of Brigadier General Frank Percy Crozier, CB, CMG, DSO (72229), who joined on 4 August 1920.

At first the uniform of the Auxiliaries was British Army officers' khaki service dress with RIC badges and a Glengarry cap. They changed their uniform to a distinctive blue one but retained the Glengarry cap and the crowned harp as a badge. They soon became known as the Auxies, but many of the Auxiliaries preferred to be known as 'Tudor's Toughs'.[41]

On joining the Auxiliaries each man was allocated an Auxiliary force number and also an RIC number. However, the RIC number did not, as one would have expected, show the member's seniority from his date of appointment, as the date on which he received an RIC number varied from the day after he joined the Auxiliary Division to a number of weeks after the event, which meant that a man who joined in August or September could have a lower RIC number than a man who joined in July, and so on.

The Auxiliaries' value as a specially trained police mobile force was soon recognised, and they were formed into companies and deployed into areas where the IRA was most active, moving from place to place as the need arose.

Companies were commanded by a divisional staff, with each company being 100 men in strength. The officer in charge of a company was normally a lieutenant colonel holding the RIC rank of DI1 and his second-in-command holding the RIC rank of DI2. Each company had four sections and each section had an officer ranked as a DI3 in charge, whilst his second-in-command was ranked as a head constable. The men chosen to fill these command posts within a company were not picked because of any experience of the work but mostly by virtue of having held senior rank during military service.[42]

As well as their distinctive blue uniform, the Auxiliaries wore breeches and puttees. Their accoutrements included a black bandolier worn across the chest, a black leather belt with bayonet and scabbard attached to it, and an open black holster for their 0.45 revolver, which was normally strapped to their hip; in some cases members wore two weapons. They were also armed with 0.303 rifles.

By the end of August the first four companies had been established in Counties Kilkenny, Cork, Galway and Dublin. By the end of October nine companies had been formed, the new companies being stationed in Counties Limerick, Mayo, Clare, Meath and Kerry.[43] In April 1921 Q Company (mostly ex-naval members) was formed. This company was used as a special search squad for weapons in Dublin Harbour. In order to maintain their effective mobility each company had two Ford cars and six Crossley tenders, most of which were ex-Royal Air Force (RAF) and capable of carrying twelve men.

Not all Auxiliaries had been ex-officers; a few were ex-policemen and at least two had been privates in the army, but it was the most decorated force in the world, with two of its members having the VC, and DSOs being quite common within its ranks. A very large percentage of its members also held the MC, *Croix de Guerre* and other coveted war medals. These awards showed the Auxiliaries' undoubted courage and gallantry when under fire and they seemed to many IRA men to be super-fighters and nearly invincible. In order to dispel this belief the IRA leadership offered a £50 reward for each member killed.

The total number who served in the Auxiliary Division was just over 2,000, with no more than 1,500 serving at any one time. In April 1921 there were fifteen companies located in the following areas – three in Co. Cork, three in Dublin city and one each in Counties Clare, Kerry, Galway, Meath, Kilkenny, Longford, Sligo, Roscommon and Tipperary. When the division began to be run down, and was then finally disbanded, a large number (some believe in the region of 750) were offered jobs in the Palestine Police Force. On 16 March 1922 it was reported that an advance party of ex-RIC officers and men who were to join the Palestine gendarmerie had arrived at Devonport, where 700 were to be assembled, pending their embarkation for Palestine. This, it was thought, would take place about 5 April.[44]

Later it was reported that some ex-members of the RIC Auxiliaries joined the force in Morocco (Riffs) in their rebellion against the Spanish Government in Morocco.[45]

7 AUGUST 1920, NEAR KILDORRERY, CO. CORK
Ernest S. Watkins, Con 71756

A six-man RIC foot patrol was ambushed near Kildorrery, Co. Cork. All six men were wounded with one, Constable Watkins, dying from his wounds at Fermoy Military Hospital. He had recently been recruited in England and on 11 August his body was returned to England for interment. He was twenty-nine, married and from Monmouth. He would have had been two months in the service on 29 August, having been an engineer and a soldier before joining the RIC.

The patrol was attacked by eleven men from a flying column attached to the Castletownroche Battalion, Cork No. 2 Brigade, under the command of Tom Barry, and fourteen IRA men from the East Limerick Brigade flying column, led by the column's OC Donnchadh O'Hannigan. After the attack the IRA removed the weapons and ammunition from the wounded RIC men.[46]

15 August 1920,
Edward Street, Limerick City
Cyril Henry Nathan, Con 71627

On 15 August Constable Nathan was returning from church when he was shot and wounded in Edward Street, Limerick. Serious riots took place that day, with widespread destruction of property. Nathan and another constable were set upon and beaten, with their weapons being taken before Nathan was shot and wounded. He was taken to the Military Hospital but died a short time later. No inquest could be held for the constable as only ten of the fifteen jurors attended.

Nathan was from London, nineteen and single. He had two months' service on 11 August, having been a clerk and a soldier before joining the RIC.

16 August 1920,
Templemore, Co. Tipperary
William Harding Wilson, DI 50239

The DI, who was in plain clothes, was shot dead at 6.45 p.m. as he was about to enter Percy's grocery shop in George Street, Templemore.

He was wounded in the head by a shot fired from an adjoining archway. Police and military from the nearby police barracks rushed to the scene, but shortly after the shooting a motor car containing unknown men was seen leaving the town at speed.

DI Wilson was a man of giant stature who was well known in North and Mid Tipperary. He had served in Templemore for eight to nine years, but two months before his death he had a narrow escape as two bullets grazed his head when he was on duty in the village of Templetuohy. After this attack he took great precautions at his home on the outskirts of the town.

The DI had risen from the ranks and for some time had been employed as a special shorthand writer at Dublin Castle, being the official notetaker in the Maguire (Trillick) murder trial of 1898. After the death of DI Hunt he had taken temporary charge of Thurles. On 19 August he was buried in the local Protestant cemetery in Templemore. Republican sources studied state that the IRA man who shot DI Wilson was Jim Stapleton, the same man who, it was alleged, shot DI Hunt in Thurles on 23 June 1919.

DI Wilson, a fifty-six-year-old married man with three sons and a daughter, was from Ballycumber, King's County. He had thirty-seven years' police service, having had no other employment before joining the RIC.

21 August 1920,
Macroom, Co. Cork
Daniel Maunsell, Sgt 55061

Sergeant Maunsell, a forty-nine-year-old married man from Tralee, Co. Kerry, was returning at 9.20 p.m. from his home in Inchigeela (where he had, until a short time before his death, been in charge of the local RIC barracks) to Macroom, when he was ambushed and killed. A police patrol returning from the scene of his killing were themselves ambushed, with several of them being hit, Sergeant Runane being the most seriously wounded.

Maunsell had twenty-nine years' police service, having been a farmer before joining the RIC.

21 AUGUST 1920, KILRUSH, CO. CLARE
John Hanlon, D/Con 64249

Detective Constable Hanlon, thirty-three and married, with two children, was a member of the Kilrush detective department. He was shot dead at 4 p.m. in a pub in Moore Street, Kilrush. His body was removed on 24 August to his native Co. Kerry for interment. He had twelve years' police service, having been a farmer before joining the RIC.

21 AUGUST 1920, GREENHILLS, CO. KILDARE
Patrick Reilly, Sgt 56526
Patrick Haverty, Con 60160

A police patrol which left Killen Barracks was ambushed at Greenhills, about three-quarters of a mile from Killen, four miles from Naas, Co. Kildare. Reilly, who was mortally wounded, was taken to Steeven's Hospital, Dublin, where he died on 31 August. Constable Haverty was shot through the chest and died immediately from his wound.

Sergeant Reilly, a forty-seven-year-old married man from King's County, had twenty-six years' police service, having been a farmer before joining the RIC.

Haverty was forty, single and from Eyrecourt, Ballinasloe, Co. Galway. He had nineteen years' police service, having been a herdsman previously.

21 August 1920, Oranmore, Co. Galway
Martin Foley, Con 64007

A police cycle patrol was ambushed on the morning of 21 August 1920 at Oranmore, near a railway bridge which was known locally as the Red Bridge. Constables Foley and Brown, along with Sergeant Mulhearn, were hit, Foley being wounded four times and dying later as a result of shock and haemorrhage.

Constable Foley, a thirty-three-year-old single man, was from Castlerea, Co. Roscommon. He had twelve years' police service, having been a labourer before joining the RIC.

21 August 1920, Dundalk, Co. Louth
Smyth Thomas Brennan, Con 59297

An ambush was carried out by the IRA in Jocelyn Street, Dundalk, as a police patrol made its way along the street. The dead constable, who came from Tubbercurry, Co. Sligo, was forty-two and a married man, whose wife resided in Omeath. Two other constables were critically wounded. On 25 November 1920 Constable Witherden, who was wounded during this incident, was accidentally shot in the head with a revolver whilst he was in a Dundalk pub. He and a friend were examining the firearm, which was described as a toy, when it went off. This accident left him in a critical condition.

Brennan had twenty years' police service, having been a farmer before joining the RIC. On 24 August 1920 his body was removed to Tubbercurry for burial.

22 August 1920, Athlone, Co. Westmeath
Thomas M. Craddock, Sgt 56968

The sergeant had just left the comrades of the Great War Club in

King Street at 12.30 a.m. when he was shot and killed. A son of a former head constable, he was employed at Crime Special HQ Athlone in Fry Place RIC Barracks, having formerly been stationed at Lisburn Road, Belfast.

The sergeant, who looked after his widowed mother and sister, had served in the Boer War, receiving the South African War Medal. His body was taken to St Peter's parish church. He was buried on 25 August after a military funeral in Ballinasloe. A forty-three-year-old single man from Co. Monaghan, he had fifteen years' police service, having been a soldier before joining the RIC.

22 August 1920, Lisburn, Co. Antrim
Oswald Ross Swanzy, DI 61367

The DI was shot and killed as he left Christ Church cathedral, Market Square, Lisburn. He lived at 31 Railway Street, only a short distance from the scene of his death, and was buried on 25 August at Mount Jerome Cemetery, Dublin.

Background
Michael Collins, believing that DI Swanzy led the party of unidentified men who killed Tomás MacCurtain (lord mayor of Cork and commandant of Cork No. 1 Brigade of the IRA) on 20 March 1920, began to search for the DI after his transfer from Cork. Collins had Swanzy traced to Lisburn with the help of RIC Sergeant Matt McCarthy, who had helped him in the past. As a result of the information received from this RIC man, Collins sent Seán Culhane, the intelligence officer of B Company, First Cork Battalion (a man who knew the DI by sight), to Belfast to link up with the Belfast IRA.

On the Sunday of the attack, Culhane and a number of Belfast IRA men, one of whom was Roger McCorley, left Belfast in a taxi and made their way to Lisburn. After the DI left the cathedral,

Culhane and McCorley walked up to him, shot him at close range and then headed back to the waiting taxi.

DI Swanzy was killed at 1.06 p.m. at the entrance to the Northern Bank. He died at the scene. At the time of the attack he was walking with two men into Railway Street. After the attack the IRA men ran in pairs on either side of the street, with a fifth man in the centre of the roadway and a little behind the others. They continued to fire as they ran away along Castle Street to the waiting taxi, which was sitting at the Technical Institute. Before McCorley reached the taxi it had started to move off and he was forced to throw himself into the vehicle. As he did so he landed in a heap on the back floor of the car, which caused him to accidentally fire a round from his revolver inside the taxi.

As the taxi was leaving the town a person was able to take its number and its driver was arrested at 4 p.m. When arrested he stated that he worked for the Belfast Motor Cab and Engineering Co. at Upper Library Street, Belfast, and had been sent at 11.45 a.m. to the Great Northern Railway Station in Great Victoria Street to collect a fare, who wanted to take a run along the Co. Down coast.[47] The taxi driver was later tried for the DI's killing but was found not guilty. In total, six other men would be arrested.

As a result of the DI's death, rioting broke out both in Lisburn and Belfast, with twenty-two people being killed in one week in Belfast and most of the Catholic community's premises in Lisburn being burnt. Mill workers in Lisburn were called upon to sign the following declaration: 'I _____ hereby declare that I am not a Sinn Féiner nor have any sympathy with Sinn Féin and do declare that I am loyal to King and Country'.[48]

As the situation deteriorated, with Lisburn and Belfast being engulfed in sectarian rioting, the authorities had to swear in a number of special constables on 24 August to try to regain control. On 26 August the following advertisement appeared for the enrolment of special constables in the *Belfast Telegraph*:

Belfast 26 August 1920

Special Constables
Special Constables will be enrolled for the preservation of the peace and the protection of property in the city of Belfast. Such Special Constables will have all the powers of Special Constables under 2 and 3 William IV Chap. 108 and will be entitled to compensation if injured. Details as to enrolment will appear later.
(Signed) E. G. T. Bainbridge
Major-General
Commanding First Division

This was possibly the first time since the start of the campaign in 1919 that special constables had to be used, but on 1 November 1920 the government was to introduce them on a formal, organised basis in Northern Ireland.

Although DI Swanzy was from Co. Monaghan, his family had a long connection with Lisburn, with a direct ancestor, Henry, from Blaris, Lisburn, being baptised on 7 October 1666 in the same cathedral close to which the DI was to be killed almost 264 years later. On 5 February 1689 Henry joined a local regiment that had been raised by Colonel Arthur Upton and after the Battle of the Boyne settled at Arelreagh, Co. Monaghan.[49]

In February 1921 a memorial was erected in the north wall of Lisburn cathedral by the DI's mother and his sister, Irene. It was a mural brass tablet mounted in Irish oak with the following inscription: 'In proud and loving memory of Oswald Ross Swanzy, D.I. Royal Irish Constabulary, who gave his life in Lisburn on Sunday 22nd August, 1920, and of all his gallant comrades who, like him, have been killed in the unfaltering discharge of their duty and in the service of their country. Be thou faithful unto death and I will give you a crown of life'.[50]

DI Swanzy, a thirty-nine-year-old single man, had fifteen years' police service, having had no employment before joining the RIC.

24 August 1920, Glengarriff, Co. Cork
John McNamara, Con 68892

At 8 p.m. an RIC patrol was ambushed at Glengarriff, Co. Cork. Constable McNamara was shot dead and Constable Patrick Cleary, who was badly wounded, was taken to Cork Military Hospital in a critical condition. The dead constable had been wounded earlier in the year during the attack on Durrus Barracks. On 27 August 1920 it was reported that the constable's body had been removed to Co. Clare for interment.

McNamara, twenty-four and single, was from Crusheen, Co. Clare. He had three years' police service, having been a farmer before joining the RIC.

Discipline

The RIC had a code of regulations covering all aspects of discipline within the force and all members were required to strictly adhere to this code. Any breach of these regulations normally resulted in the offending officer being fined. The money raised from these fines was placed into the force's grants fund, which was used to reward police officers who had performed outstanding acts of bravery or good police duties. Even minor disciplinary offences could result in a fine being levied against an officer.

During the period covered, a number of police officers who were killed had already been fined for breaches of discipline, although what these offences were cannot be established. The following is a list of these officers:

No.	Name	Died	Fined
70259	Brown, Walter T., Con	05.05.1921	10s, 15.09.1920
74985	Depree, Frederick H., Con	07.05.1921	£2, 13.01.1921
75392	Ednie, Charles F., Con	02.02.1922	5 days' pay, 18.11.1921; 10s, 22.11.1921; £1, 30.11.1921
59169	Gorman, Michael, Con	02.12.1921	£2, 20.09.1921
82097	Gourlay, William, Con	03.02.1922	£1, 10.12.1921
75772	Grant, John, Con	17.03.1921	7/6, 19.03.1921
73968	Kershaw, Frank, Con	03.02.1922	£1, 12.12.1920; 10s, 20.04.1921; £2, 29.04.1921; 30s, 24.08.1921; £1, 22.12.1921
70142	Malone, Michael F., Con	01.01.1921	10s, 24.08.1920
72217	Moore, Stanley L., Con	31.03.1921	2 days' pay, 14.02.1921
76409	MacDonald, John Cyril, Con	22.04.1921	1 day's pay, 06.09.1921
77543	Sterland, Frederick, Con	08.05.1921	1 day's pay, 28.04.1921

25 August 1920, Bantry, Co. Cork
Matthew Haugh, Con 68052

At 1.45 p.m. a party of police from Bantry was ambushed at the church wall in Chapel Street, Bantry. The attackers had taken up a position in a small groove in the wall within the church grounds that overlooked the street. As a result of this ambush Constable Haugh, twenty-five and single, from Co. Clare, was shot dead. On 28 August Haugh, who had been a farmer before his five years' service, was buried in his native county. An inquest could not be held as only two of the jurors appeared.

26 August 1920,
Drumquin RIC Barracks, Co. Tyrone
James Munnelly, Con 66662

At 10 a.m. on Fair Day, the IRA attacked the RIC barracks at Drumquin, Co. Tyrone. During the attack Constable Munnelly and Sergeant Bradley were wounded. Both were taken to the Tyrone County Infirmary at Omagh, but the constable died from his wounds at 6 p.m., having been shot through the head. The inquest later recorded that 'dumdum' bullets were used to kill him.

The Attack

IRA men from Co. Tyrone dressed as cattle dealers arrived in the village in two motor cars. They cut the telegraph wires and captured two RIC men who were on duty at the fair. At 10 a.m. they attacked the local RIC barracks. This was a determined and partially successful attempt to take the building.

On answering a knock at the door Constable Munnelly was shot and the IRA party rushed into the barracks. Sergeant Bradley was upstairs and, on hearing the activity downstairs, came down to see what was happening. As he did so he was shot and wounded, falling down the stairs and fracturing his left collarbone. However, the sergeant was able to struggle back up the stairs and armed himself with a hand grenade. (The RIC had been furnished with this type of weapon on 22 September 1919 in order to provide the men with all possible modern means of defending themselves and their barracks. These were small grenades, which were entrusted only to men who had received special instruction in the method of using them.) The sergeant then dropped the grenade down the stairs into the party of raiders. This forced the IRA to leave the barracks, the whole attack being over in four minutes.

As they left the RIC barracks, a witness outside stated that he saw one dead IRA man being placed into one of the cars, whilst a seriously wounded man was put into the second car. The vehicles then left the area. It was later reported that the dead IRA man was buried shortly after the incident at Castlefin. During the attack the IRA was able to take three RIC rifles from the barracks.

Constable Munnelly, a thirty-year-old single man from Ballycastle, Co. Mayo, had eight years' police service, having been a farmer before joining the RIC.

26 August 1920,
Knockcroghery, Co. Roscommon
William J. Potter, Con 61150

At 9 p.m. Constable Potter, a thirty-five-year-old single man from Roscommon, was cycling from Roscommon to Kiltoom, where he had been transferred temporarily from the Castlebar District. He was shot at the railway crossing at Knockcroghery. His remains were removed to Athlone.

He had first joined the RIC on 16 December 1902, but had been discharged as medically unfit by the surgeon the next day. He rejoined the RIC on 2 March 1903 and had no previous employment.

27 August 1920,
Graigue, Co. Longford
John Mullan, Con 70256

At 9.30 a.m. police were escorting a mail car from Drumlish to Ballinamuck when they were attacked at Graigue, Co. Longford. Constable Mullan, a single man who would have been twenty-six on 5 September, was killed and Constable Brogan was seriously wounded. Constables Reidy and King were slightly wounded.

Mullan was from Co. Tyrone and had six months' police service, having been a shipyard stager before joining the RIC.

1 September 1920,
Rathmacross, Co. Roscommon
Martin McCarthy, Con 66580
Edward Murphy, Con 69231

Five RIC men were making their way on bicycles from Ballaghaderreen to Frenchpark Petty Sessions when they were ambushed at Rathmacross. Constable Murphy was killed outright and Constable McCarthy, seriously wounded, died the next day.

Murphy was a single man who had just turned twenty-four on 24 August. He was from Co. Mayo and had two years' service, having been a farmer before joining the RIC.

Constable McCarthy was twenty-eight, single and from Co. Clare. He had eight years' police service, having been a farmer before joining the RIC.

3 September 1920,
Kilmacthomas, Co. Waterford
Martin Morgan, Sgt 58174

Sergeant Morgan, a forty-four-year-old married man with no children from Co. Galway, was shot and wounded when he was ambushed near Kilmacthomas, Co. Waterford. He was stationed at Leamybrien and was cycling along with a constable from the bank at Portland back to their barracks when they were attacked. The wounded sergeant was removed to Waterford City Infirmary but died on 27 September 1920.

Morgan had twenty-two years' police service, having been a farmer before joining the RIC. On 28 April 1916 he had joined the South Irish Horse, rejoining the RIC on 14 July 1918.

8 September 1920,
Tullow, Co. Carlow
Timothy Delaney, Con 65728
John Gaughan, Con 64181

A patrol of four RIC men was ambushed near Tullow at 10.30 p.m. Two constables were killed outright, their bodies being discovered at the scene an hour after the attack. Another constable in the patrol was seriously wounded.

Constable Delaney, thirty, was married and from Queen's County. He would have had three months' police service on 14 September 1920. He was a signalman with the GS&W Railway before joining the RIC.

Constable Gaughan was thirty-four and single. A native of Co. Mayo, he had twelve years' police service, having been a Gaelic teacher prior to joining the RIC.

8 September 1920,
Galway Railway Station
Edward Krumm, Con 72372

At 12 midnight Krumm was shot dead at Galway Railway Station and it is thought he killed one of his attackers. He was employed as a driver and was stationed at Eglinton Street Barracks. His body was removed to Wimbledon for interment.

Constable Krumm had been stationed in Galway for only ten days, having been attached to Dunmore as an RIC transport driver. At 11.45 p.m. the constable, who was in plain clothes, and a hotel guest, a Mr C. Yorke, both of whom were sober, left Baker's Hotel, Eyre Street, to go to the railway station and collect newspapers. Having collected the papers they were leaving the station when a man tried to take the constable's revolver. Constable Krumm told the man, 'If you touch me you are a dead man.' Gunfire then broke out, with Mr Yorke returning to the hotel at 12.20 a.m. in a very upset state. He informed the hotel staff, 'He's gone, he's dead. Constable Krumm is dead. He's been killed at the station.' Constable Krumm's body was removed to the hospital but his revolver was missing.

A military inquiry instead of an inquest was held under the Restoration of Order Act. This was the first time that such a military inquiry had been held and was a direct result of inquest jurors not attending after they had been summoned.

Krumm, a twenty-five-year-old single man, was a native of Middlesex. He would have had one month's police service on 10 September 1920, having been an electrical engineer and a soldier before joining the RIC.

15 September 1920,
Dundalk, Co. Louth
Terence Patrick Wheatly, Con

The constable, an ex-soldier from Dublin who was employed as a motor driver, was attached to Dundalk RIC Barracks. At 1 a.m. he was shot and wounded in the stomach whilst in Market Square, Dundalk.

Background
Constable Wheatly was stationed at Ann Street Barracks. At 3.15 a.m. on 15 September, Head Constable Gallagher spoke to him in the barracks' day room, when Wheatly stated that he had been shot and that two men had taken his revolver and fled.

The head constable noticed that Wheatly had drink taken, but when he checked him he found that he was wounded. He then had him removed to hospital. On further checks the following items were found in Wheatly's pockets: twelve silk handkerchiefs and a document as follows:

Poblacht na hÉireann – To Driver Wheatly RIC:
Take warning, relinquish your present occupation and leave Ireland within one month from this date or the sentence of death already passed on you will be carried out. Signed by the Commandant Louth Area IRA. Dated 02.09.1920.

At a later inquest Head Constable Gallagher stated that he believed the notice found in the dead constable's pocket had been written by himself. He also said that the silk handkerchiefs had been removed from J. D. Melville draper's shop in Clanbrassil Street, Dundalk, when the constable had smashed a plate-glass window.

Later a witness stated that he had noticed squabbling between three or four men and two women, and then heard four shots over a period of approximately five minutes. The head constable stated that Wheatly should not have been out of the barracks that night and that he did not know why or by whom the constable had been shot.

Wheatly died from his wounds on 18 September 1920 in Louth Hospital and was buried in Dundalk. He was twenty-five years old and it would appear that he had not been issued with an RIC number.

19 September 1920, Mountmahon, Co. Limerick
James Donohoe, Con 66183
John Mahony, Con 68276

At 11 p.m. a joint RIC/military patrol was returning by lorry from Abbeyfeale to Limerick when it was ambushed at Mountmahon. Three constables were wounded. On 20 September Constable Donohoe died from his wounds at the Military Hospital, Limerick. He was twenty-nine and single, from Co. Monaghan. He had eight years' police service, having previously been a farmer.

Constable Mahony also died from his wounds. His father was a boat builder from Castletownshend, Skibbereen, Co. Cork, and his remains were removed there for interment. Constable Mahony had five years' police service, having been a postman before joining the RIC. He was a twenty-six-year-old single man.

This ambush was carried out by the West Limerick flying column which numbered approximately thirty members. The column was made up of two members from each company of Limerick's Second Battalion IRA. They were armed with rifles, revolvers and shotguns and after the attack they moved to Athea, six miles away.

20 September 1920, Balbriggan, Co. Dublin
Peter Burke, H/Con 62175

The head constable and his brother, Michael, a sergeant in the RIC, were making their way from Dublin to Gormanston depot, three miles from Balbriggan. Both men were in plain clothes and had stopped at Mrs Smith's public house for refreshments when they were shot. Peter was killed outright by 'dumdum' bullets and Michael was wounded.

Head Constable Burke had won special promotion to his rank eighteen months previously after a very courageous defence of Moyona police hut in Co. Clare. He was also awarded a Constabulary Medal for his actions on that occasion. He had been an instructor at Phoenix Park RIC depot, Dublin, involved with the Auxiliary Division, and was an exceedingly popular officer. It was believed that he would probably have been promoted to DI in the course of a few days. His remains were taken to his home in Glenamaddy, Co. Galway, where he had been a farmer before joining the force. He was thirty-six and single, with thirteen years' service.

After this incident Auxiliaries who had recently transferred from Phoenix Park depot arrived at the scene in lorries from their depot at

Gormanston and, on seeing the head constable, who had been one of their instructors, got completely out of hand and carried out reprisals in Balbriggan which resulted in property being destroyed and the deaths of two local men. This incident became known as the 'Sack of Balbriggan'.

Republican sources studied state this affair unfolded as follows: the Burke brothers and some Auxiliary cadets had arrived at 9 p.m. at the public house and as it was after hours were refused service by the landlady. An argument allegedly ensued with the local RIC being called, but on finding out who the travellers were, the RIC left. Two Sinn Féin police members apparently then called at the public house and asked the travellers to leave and when the head constable drew his gun the Sinn Féin police fired in 'self defence'.[51]

21 September 1920, Ferbane, King's County
Denis P. McGuire, Sgt 57625

The sergeant was attached to the RIC barracks at Shannonbridge and had gone along with the army to carry out searches at Ferbane. While he sat on the windowsill of a house that was being searched, a shot rang out and the sergeant was wounded in the head. He was taken to King's County Infirmary at Tullamore, but died from his wounds on 22 September. His right eye had been completely blown away, leaving him with a gaping wound on his scalp which exposed his brain.

Locals at the scene of this incident stated that the shot that killed the sergeant came from the house being searched at the time by soldiers.

Sergeant McGuire, a forty-five-year-old married man with six children, was from Killyon, Co. Offaly and lived in Kilkenny. He had twenty-four years' police service, having had no other employment before joining the RIC.

22 September 1920, Rineen, Co. Clare

Michael J. Hynes, Sgt 66009
Reginald Hardman, Con 71746
Michael Harte, Con 66362
John Hodnett, Con 66278
Michael Kelly, Con 63544
John McGuire, Con 69743

An RIC patrol in a motor vehicle attached to the barracks at Ennistymon was ambushed as it was passing Rineen schoolhouse, midway between Miltown Malbay and Lahinch, Co. Clare. Four of the policemen were killed outright, another's body was found the next day, while the sergeant died from his wounds on 24 September. An official report into this incident on 20 October confirmed that 'dumdum' bullets had been used by the IRA and that already wounded RIC officers had been killed by their attackers, one of them being assaulted some distance from the ambush scene.

Background

At 11 a.m. on the morning of the ambush a military non-commissioned officer stationed in Ennistymon received information that there was to be an attack mounted on the RIC on the Miltown Malbay to Lahinch road.[52] Troops were sent along the road to examine likely ambush positions, but when they reached the junction where the Miltown Malbay and Liscannor roads separate at Lahinch, they heard shooting ahead. These soldiers rushed to the scene and brought a Lewis gun into action. Another small party of troops came up in support of the others in the lorry, which forced the IRA ambush party to scatter and run. After the soldiers had driven off the IRA, they found the bodies of the RIC men on the roadway about twenty-five yards from the railway line.

On examination of the scene the soldiers found that the ambush point had been between the railway line and the roadway and that hay had been strewn down for the attackers to rest on. From the evidence it was clearly seen to be a well-planned attack, with the IRA party of some fifty men having been in position from before dawn. Two houses near the scene had also been used during the attack on the military lorry, and soldiers later burned them as a reprisal. The ambush on the RIC patrol appeared to have unfolded as follows:

1. As the car which contained the RIC travelled slowly up a hill to a bend in the road, it was attacked by approximately fifty IRA men armed with rifles and shotguns.
2. The policemen were wounded by 'dumdum' bullets and then were also fired on at close range by shotguns.
3. Constable Harte, although wounded, managed to crawl some 400 yards away from the ambush but was hunted down and killed. His body was not discovered until the next day.

During the time that the IRA remained in their ambush location at least two trains passed within 6–10 feet of them, but the passengers, guards and the drivers of the trains did not report this ambush to the authorities, even though every detail must have been visible from the line.

The IRA's Ennistymon Battalion of the Mid Clare Brigade, under the command of an ex-Irish Guardsman Ignatius O'Neill, had been watching the RIC at Ennistymon. They became aware that the police went twice a week from Ennistymon to Miltown Malbay, so an attack was planned. At 2 a.m. on 22 September men from Inagh, Ennistymon and Lahinch IRA companies made their way to Moy church, moving again at 4 a.m. into the ambush location, where they were joined by other IRA men from another three companies. All the roads in the area were then scouted by IRA men, with signallers being placed on nearby hills.

The weapons used by the IRA at the ambush point included six army rifles captured in July from a patrol at Ennistymon and others captured from the RIC. One IRA man, Peter Vaughan, who was an ex-American soldier, also had two hand grenades. The ambush party was under the command of Seamus Hennessy, the IRA's Moy Company captain, whilst a party of IRA riflemen, who had been placed opposite the ambush location, were under the command of O'Neill. On the arrival of the army at the scene, the IRA riflemen engaged them in order to allow the other IRA men time to escape. During this gun battle O'Neill was wounded.[53]

The bodies of the six RIC officers passed through Ennis on their way to their native places, with the remains of Sergeant Hynes being taken to St Mary's church, Athlone. He died from his wounds on 24 September. On 26 September he was buried with full military honours at Drum, Athlone.

Sergeant Hynes, a twenty-nine-year-old single man, was from Co. Roscommon. He had nine years' service, having been a farmer before joining the RIC. The sergeant had been promoted on 1 February 1920.

Constable Hardman, from London, was a Black and Tan who had served in the Royal Artillery. His funeral took place to East Finchley Cemetery, London on 4 October. He was twenty-one and single and would have had three months' police service on 29 September 1920, having been a driver before joining the RIC.

Constable Harte, a twenty-eight-year-old single man, was from Co. Sligo. He had eight years' police service, having been a farmer prior to joining the RIC.

Constable Hodnett, thirty-one and single, was from Co. Cork. He had eight years' police service, having previously been a farmer.

Constable Kelly, a thirty-two-year-old single man, was from Co. Roscommon. He had twelve years' police service, having been a farmer before joining the RIC.

Constable McGuire, a twenty-year-old single man, was from Co.

Mayo. He had one year's police service, having been a farmer prior to joining the RIC.

25 SEPTEMBER 1920, BROADFORD, CO. CLARE
Michael Brogan, Con 61507

A five-man RIC patrol was ambushed at 9 p.m. in the village of Broadford, Co. Clare. Constable Brogan was killed, with Constable Brennan being seriously wounded.

Constable Brogan was a single man who had just turned forty-one on 15 September. He was from Co. Galway and had fourteen years' service, having previously been a herdsman.

25 SEPTEMBER 1920, FALLS ROAD, BELFAST CITY
Thomas Leonard, Con 62331

The constable was stationed at Springfield Road RIC Barracks and was on beat patrol along with Constable Carroll at Broadway on the Falls Road. Shortly before midnight they were ambushed and wounded by two armed men. Following the attack, other police on duty in the area saw two men running from the direction of Broadway. They were able to catch one of them, but the other escaped. On searching the man they had caught, the police found that he had a revolver on him with four rounds for it in his pocket. It was also discovered that this man had been in the Royal Marines for four years. He was not believed to have been involved in the attack as his weapon had not been fired. In October two Falls Road men were arrested for the constable's killing.

Constable Leonard died from his wounds in the Royal Victoria Hospital. On 28 September his funeral left from the hospital for his father's home at Knockcroghery, Co. Roscommon. Three of his brothers – Sergeant Leonard from Cavan, Constable Patrick Leonard from Mountpottinger and Constable Edward Leonard from Smithfield – acted as pallbearers. A thirty-five-year-old married man with three children, Leonard was from Knockcroghery. He had three years' police service and was a farmer before joining the RIC.

29 September 1920, Killoskehan, Co. Tipperary
Terence Flood, Con 64194
Edward A. Noonan, Con 70978

At 1.30 p.m. a four-man police patrol was ambushed at Killoskehan, five miles from Templemore, as it was returning from Borrisoleigh to its barracks at Goldings Cross. Constable Noonan, a Black and Tan, was killed outright. He was twenty-six, married with three children and from Co. Galway. He would have had six months' police service the next day, having been an electrician and a soldier before joining the RIC. During the First World War he had been severely wounded on active service.

Constable Flood, thirty-five and single, was from Drumsna, Co. Leitrim. He was initially reported missing, but was found a short time later at Gortalough, approximately four miles from Templemore. His body, riddled with bullet wounds, lay beside a hedge. He had twelve years' police service, having been a labourer before joining the RIC.

Constable Ferris was wounded during the ambush while another constable escaped uninjured.

29 September 1920, O'Brien's Bridge, Co. Clare
John Downey, Con 63680
John Thomas Keeffe, Con 67115

The policemen were in John Ryan's Pub, a licensed house at O'Brien's Bridge, Co. Clare, which was beside the barracks, when they were shot. Constable Downey, who was planning to resign from the RIC, was killed outright, while Constable Keeffe died from his wounds shortly afterwards. Both were buried at St Joseph's Cemetery, Cork on 4 October.

Constable Downey was thirty-five and married. From Co. Cork, he had first joined the RIC on 24 March 1908 but had resigned on 17 May 1913. On 22 September 1914 he rejoined. Prior to joining the RIC he had been a farmer.

Constable Keeffe, a thirty-year-old single man, was from Co. Clare. He had seven years' police service, having been a tea agent before joining the RIC.

30 September 1920, Chaffpool, Co. Sligo
James Joseph Brady, DI 70381

At 5.30 p.m. an RIC patrol in a motor lorry was ambushed between Bunninadden and Tubbercurry, Co. Sligo, at Chaffpool. The DI, an ex-Irish Guards officer, was wounded three times, the injuries caused by 'dumdum' bullets. He was the son of Captain Louis Brady, the Harbour Master in Dublin, and a nephew of P. J. Brady, MP for St Stephen's Green, Dublin. DI Brady was due to return to his permanent station at Ballymoney, Co. Antrim, the next day.

Head Constable O'Hara was seriously wounded during this attack, while Constable Brown received minor head wounds from shotgun pellets.

Approximately fifty IRA men were involved in this ambush and, afterwards, were seen withdrawing in a southerly direction, which indicated there was a strong probability that those involved were from the South Sligo Brigade.

There was evidence that another party of IRA men had lain in ambush on the only other road the RIC lorry might have taken back to the barracks. A military officer who visited the scene of the ambush stated that a person with a good deal of military knowledge had selected the spot and had something to do with the preparation of the ambush location.

A police report of this incident records the facts as follows:

I beg to state that on 30 September District Inspector Brady, Head Constable O'Hara and seven men from Tubbercurry went to Sligo on duty via motor lorry by direct road. They left Sligo for their station about 4 p.m., taking a different route via Ballymote.

When they arrived at Leitrim, which is about two miles from Tubbercurry on the road between Bunninadden and Tubbercurry, they were fired on with rifles from an elaborately prepared ambush behind loopholed walls situated on elevated ground on each side of the road. The spot was a regular death trap and afforded no chance of success to the police, even if they had been in a position to dismount and attack.

District Inspector Brady received three dreadful wounds in the region of the kidneys, apparently caused by expanding bullets.

The calf of Head Constable O'Hara's right leg was practically blown away and the big toe of his left foot shattered. Constable Brown received a slight superficial wound on the cheek. The lorry drove on under heavy fire to which the police replied as well as they could. They could not see their cowardly assailants, who were safely entrenched in strong numbers behind their loopholed walls.

On their arrival at Tubbercurry they found the telegraph wires to Sligo had been cut and so a party of police from Tubbercurry had to come into Sligo by motor lorry to inform the County Inspector, arriving there at 9.15 p.m.[54]

After the incident had been reported, DI Russell took a party of sixteen RIC from Sligo, along with DI Dease (who was returning to Tubbercurry from sick leave) and ten soldiers under the command of an army officer, to Tubbercurry, arriving after 11 p.m. When the two DIs entered the barracks they found that DI Brady had died at approximately 8.30 p.m. His naked body was lying on the kitchen floor having just been washed after death. Head Constable O'Hara was lying in a room off the kitchen suffering intense pain. On seeing this, the RIC and military left the station and carried out reprisals against property in Tubbercurry, which their officers were unable to prevent.

On 4 October DI Brady was buried at Glasnevin Cemetery, Dublin after a service at Aughrim Street church. He was a single man who would have been twenty-two years of age on 9 October 1920. He was from Dublin and had seven months' service, having been an army officer before joining the RIC.

3 OCTOBER 1920, PATRICK STREET, CORK CITY
Clarence Victor Chave, Con 72072

Constable Chave was a single man who had just turned twenty-four on 24 September. He was from Sheerness and had three months' police service, having been a tailor and a soldier before joining the RIC. He was attached to Empress Place Barracks and was shot and wounded in Patrick Street, Cork. He was taken to the Military Hospital in Victoria Barracks but died from his wounds two hours later.

Two other constables were wounded during this attack, which happened at 12.35 a.m., and was directed against four constables. They were opposite Blackthorn House when at least six shots were fired at them from two windows in the building. Constable Chave received a large wound in his left shoulder and fell to the ground.

6 October 1920,
Bishop Street, Londonderry City
John Flaherty, Con 57717

At 10 p.m. Constable Flaherty, a forty-six-year-old married man with a young family, was on beat patrol with Constable Dykes. They were in Bishop Street, Londonderry, on the Long Tower side of the road and had just reached Bishop's Gate when they were fired on. Constable Flaherty was wounded in the left breast and staggered to the gate, where he fell, vomiting blood. He was taken to the City Infirmary but died from his wounds on 16 October. He was stationed at Bishop Street and lived at Stanley's Walk with his wife and children. From Co. Galway, he had twenty-four years' police service, having been a farmer before joining the RIC. He was later buried at his native place.

7 October 1920,
Feakle, Co. Clare
Francis Doherty, Sgt 57303
William Stanley, Con 58371

A party of six RIC had left their barracks in Feakle, Co. Clare, to make their way to the local post office when they were ambushed. Constable Stanley was killed outright. Sergeant Doherty, a forty-six-year-old single man from Mohill, Co. Leitrim, was wounded and died one hour later. He had twenty-four years' police service, having been a farmer before joining the RIC.

Constable Stanley, forty-six, married with four children, was from Co. Cork. He had twenty-two years' police service, having been a farmer prior to joining the RIC.

OSTRACISM OF THE RIC

As political violence in Ireland worsened, Sinn Féin and the IRA began to enforce a campaign to ostracise all members of the RIC and their families from the rest of Irish society.[55] The IRA's GHQ issued a number of orders about actions to be taken against the RIC and people who supported them. Two of these orders were as follows:

> A General Order of Óglaigh na hÉireann (The Irish Volunteers) numbered 1920 (New Series) No. 6 and issued from General Headquarters on the 4th June 1920, is headed *Boycott of RIC*:
>
> Volunteers shall have no intercourse with the RIC and shall stimulate and support in every way the boycott of this force, order by the Dáil. Those persons who associate with the RIC shall be subjected to the same boycott and the fact of their association with and toleration of this infamous force shall be kept public in every possible way. Definite lists of such persons in the area of his command shall be prepared and retained by each Company, Battalion and brigade Commander.
>
> By Order Adjutant General
> Irish Republican Army
>
> To Commandant   Brigade Headquarters
> _____ Battalion
>
> A Chara
>
> You will furnish answers to the accompanying queries.
>
> _____ Brigade Adjutant
>
> Subject 'Police Boycott'
>
> Query
> 1. How has boycott been declared in your area?
> 2. What are the visible results of boycott order?
> 3. Do general population speak to members of the RIC?

4. Has a list been compiled of persons who are 'friendly' with the police?
5. Are police forced to commandeer supplies?
6. Have merchants been ordered to refuse supplies?
7. What steps have been taken to deal with persons who disobey the order?
8. Have you any suggestions to offer as a means of intensifying the boycott in your area?[56]

Depending on which part of the country the police officer was stationed in, and the amount of unrest existing in it, this order drastically affected the campaign of ostracism against the RIC.

The IRA went to great measures to enforce this policy, killing people who objected to it and cutting the hair of women who associated with members of the RIC.[57] One such attack occurred in May 1921, when a woman who had recently placed a wreath on a constable's grave was held up by two masked and armed men in the Dunfanaghy district of Co. Donegal and had her hair cut off. The men accused her of being friendly to police and warned her that their action was only a caution and that they would shoot her if she did not take their warning. Police officers' relatives did not escape this campaign and many were killed or injured, although the exact number is unknown.

The first effect this campaign had was on inquest courts, as jurors refused to attend them for fear they would be assaulted or killed by the IRA. Later members of the public were afraid to show sympathy to the cortèges of police officers as they passed, making the RIC social outcasts even in death.

The tactics of boycott had first been used by Sinn Féin against those people who had voted against Éamon de Valera in the East Clare elections of 1917. On seeing their effect, de Valera requested that the tactics of boycott be applied universally to the police so that they be treated as pariahs and outcasts.

Apart from the violent aspect of this campaign, there were also financial problems. In order to help with the financial hardship encountered by police officers and their families, the RIC announced the introduction of a bonus for the force in the following circular:

F 414
1920
Royal Irish Constabulary Office
Dublin Castle
7 October 1920

Bonus for Royal Irish Constabulary

The Treasury has sanctioned the payment to married men of a non-pensionable addition to their pay in respect of the increased cost of living at the following rates:

As from the 1st July 1920 to 30th September 1920:

Constables 8/– weekly

Sergeants 9/– weekly

Head constables 10/– weekly

As from the 1st October 1920 to 31st March 1921:

Constables 12/– weekly

Sergeants 13/6– weekly

Head constables 15/– weekly

This bonus is only payable to permanent members of the Force. It is payable to unmarried men at half the above rates. Widowers with dependent children may draw the bonus at the same rates as married men. Payment of arrears should be made at once. A further communication will be sent later authorising payment of a bonus to certain higher ranks.

T. J. Smith

Inspector General
Issued to DCs, CIs, DIs and all existing stations
17727F
573[58]

As this boycott against the RIC hardened, being enforced by intimidation and violence both against persons and property, clothes and food became even more difficult for policemen and their families to buy, and in certain areas the government had to supply the boycotted men directly. Later the RIC not only helped with financial problems faced by members of the force, but also offered accommodation to members' families who were forced to leave their homes.

In September the government took over a camp at Newtownards to house the wives and families of married RIC members who were obliged to live in their barracks. Notice of the accommodation at Newtownards was conveyed by a circular to county inspectors as follows:

D 437
1920

Accommodation for married families at Newtownards Camp
CI
Quarters can now be provided for several married families at Newtownards Camp. If the families of any member of the Force in your county are desirous of occupying these quarters, full particulars of their cases should be submitted at once.

(Sgd) T. J. Smith IG[59]

This campaign not only ostracised serving members of the RIC and their families, but it also drastically affected recruiting in Ireland for the RIC, which necessitated the recruitment of thousands of men from Britain.

12 October 1920,
Ballinderry, Co. Roscommon

Peter J. McArdle, Sgt 57940
Martin G. O'Connor, Sgt 51713
John Crawford, Con 67464
Francis Gallagher, Con 70351
Michael Kenny, Con 63217

A police motor patrol travelling from Roscommon to Ballaghaderreen was ambushed at Fourmile House, Ballinderry. The dead and wounded were taken to Strokestown.

Constables Kenny and Crawford were killed outright, while Constables Gallagher and O'Rahilly were wounded. Sergeant O'Connor was also wounded and died from his injuries. On 15 October he was buried at Achill. Police had to commandeer a hearse for his funeral. Constable Crawford was interred in the New Cemetery at Roscommon. Constable Gallagher died from his wounds at Strokestown. Large cards were attached to the coffins of these four dead RIC men which read 'Behold the work of Sinn Féin. Is this Irish? Murdered by Irish Savages and Sinn Féin. Shame on you.'

Sergeant Peter J. McArdle, a forty-two-year-old married man from Co. Cork, died from his wounds on 30 January 1921. He had twenty-four years' service, having been a shop assistant before joining the RIC. Sergeant O'Connor, fifty-three and married, was from Co. Sligo and had thirty-four years' police service, having had no other employment prior to joining the RIC.

Constable Crawford, a twenty-nine-year-old single man, was from Miltown Malbay, Co. Clare. He had seven years' police service, having previously been a farmer. Constable Gallagher was thirty and from Co. Donegal. He would have had eight months' service on 16 October 1920, having been a riveter and a soldier before joining the RIC. Constable Kenny, a married man from Clare, was thirty-eight.

He would have had three years' service on 16 October 1920, having previously been an asylum attendant.

17 October 1920,
Capel Street/Ormond Quay, Dublin city
Daniel Roche, Sgt 59912

Sergeant Roche, a forty-five-year-old married man, was from Co. Cork. He had nineteen years' police service, having been a coachman before joining the RIC. He was one of two sergeants who had been brought to Dublin on special duty to identify the body of Seán Treacy, who had been killed in the search of the Republican Outfitters in Talbot Street on 14 October. At that time Treacy's corpse was being referred to as 'the man in the fawn coat'. The two sergeants, both of whom were stationed in Co. Tipperary, knew the identity of IRA men from that area and were also to have assisted in the search of hospitals in the Dublin area for Dan Breen.

On the day Sergeant Roche was shot he was chatting with David Neligan, a DMP detective attached to G Division who was one of three detectives in Dublin Castle working for Michael Collins as intelligence officers. Neligan had arranged for the Squad to kill the sergeant, and three men – Joe Dolan, Tom Keogh and Jim Slattery – were involved.[60] Dolan shot the sergeant six times and the other two fired a few more times before all three escaped.

18 October 1920,
Ruan RIC Barracks, Co. Clare
John Longhead, Con 65478

The RIC barracks at Ruan, six miles from Ennis, Co. Clare, was attacked and captured by the IRA. Constable Longhead was killed, while two others, Roddy and Farrelly, were wounded. Two constables from Ruan who were on patrol were also reported missing: Constable Wilmott reappeared at Boston RIC Barracks; Constable Carroll sent a telegraph from Kinvarra to say he was fine. As the police believed he was probably a traitor and had been involved in the IRA's attack on the barracks, he was dismissed from the RIC on the date of the incident, 18 October.

Constable Longhead, a thirty-six-year-old single man, was from Co. Sligo. He had ten years' police service, having been a farmer before joining the RIC.

21 OCTOBER 1920,
GLANDORE, CO. CORK
Bertie Rippingale, Con 71838
Albert Rundle, Con 71830

Three policemen were returning to their barracks in Leap, Co. Cork, when they were ambushed at Glandore, seven miles from Skibbereen. All three were wounded. Constable Rippingale died on 22 October in Cork Military Hospital and Constable Rundle died in the same hospital on 4 November.

Rippingale, twenty-five and single, was from Essex. He had three months' police service, having been a labourer and a soldier before joining the RIC. Rundle, a twenty-six-year-old married man, was from London. He had three months' police service, having previously been a rubber worker and a soldier.

23 OCTOBER 1920,
PARKWOOD, KING'S COUNTY
Harry Biggs, Con 73983

Three lorries of police were making their way from Gormanston to Ballinasloe when they were ambushed at Parkwood, Clara,

King's County, which is approximately two miles from Moate and Kilbeggan. Constable Biggs was the driver of the first lorry.

Biggs, twenty-three and single, was from London. He had two weeks' police service, having been a motor driver and a soldier before joining.

25 October 1920,
Tempo RIC Barracks, Co. Fermanagh
Samuel Wilfred Lucas, Sgt 58083

At 7.15 a.m. on 25 October 1920, a raid was carried out against Tempo RIC Barracks by the local IRA company which resulted in the deaths of Sergeant Lucas and a civilian, Philip Breen.

This IRA attack had been planned by ex-Constable Bernard Conway of the RIC, who had resigned from the force in August 1920. He became an IRA officer in the Colloney Company. Conway had persuaded his friend and ex-comrade Constable Hugh O'Donnell, who was stationed at Tempo, to help facilitate the capture of the barracks.

When the plan had first been devised, Conway went to see the local Fermanagh Brigade commander, Frank Carney, to obtain assistance in the raid in return for half of any weapons captured. At first Carney rejected the plan, but when other sympathetic members of the barracks party agreed to help in the raid, approval was given for it to be undertaken. On 25 October an RIC patrol left the barracks and on its return was captured by the Tempo IRA and held until the raid on the barracks was over.

Three IRA men entered the barracks (which contained only Constable Bannon and Sergeant Lucas) via the back door, which had been deliberately left unlocked. The sergeant, on hearing a noise, went to investigate and met the three raiders inside the barracks. A struggle developed between the unarmed sergeant and the IRA men, during which the sergeant attempted to make his way back to the day room to arm himself, but he was seriously wounded as he did so by one of his attackers. The constable, who had come to the aid of the sergeant, was tackled and overpowered by the raiders, who then held him at gunpoint while the barracks was searched for weapons.

During this incident the IRA raiders had fired shots which alerted a number of unionists from the area who were in the village parochial hall. These people armed themselves and opened fire on some IRA men who were positioned at the rear of the barracks. As a result of this gunfire, along with the fact that flares and the church bell had begun to be rung as a warning to other unionists in the area, the IRA attackers withdrew, being able to remove only a few rifles from the barracks.

After the attack had ended, Sergeant Lucas made his way out of the barracks to the pavement outside, where he was found by the Reverend Scanlon. The sergeant told the minister, 'Do not try and lift me, I'm shot in the back.' The wounded sergeant was removed to the Royal Victoria Hospital, Belfast, but died on 4 November. He was interred in Cloveneden burial ground in Loughgall, Co. Armagh. As the sergeant's remains approached the grave, they passed between an avenue of police with their heads bowed and arms reversed, and after the funeral was over the grave was filled in by RIC men.

Philip Breen, who was well known in the area as a prominent Republican, had not taken part in the raid as he knew he would be high on the list of suspects for such an action. After the incident had ended he appeared at his doorway in order to create an alibi, but an unknown person shot and killed him.

Background
Bernard Conway of Cliffoney, Co. Sligo, joined the RIC in February 1913 and was party to the IRA raid on Cookstown RIC Barracks on 17 June 1920.

This attack was almost a carbon copy of the later attack on Tempo

Barracks. Conway and three other constables from the west of Ireland, all with Sinn Féin sympathies, were stationed in Cookstown. One of them, Denis A. Leonard, who had been reduced from the rank of sergeant because of his sympathies, contacted a prominent Sinn Féin man in Cookstown at the end of March 1920 to discuss their proposal for the IRA to take over Cookstown Barracks.

A few weeks later Conway and Leonard, with two IRA officers from Dungannon, attended a meeting in Keady, Co. Armagh, at which it was decided to carry out a raid on the Cookstown Barracks on 4 June. However, this attack did not take place as the IRA men from Keady and Dungannon who were to participate feared that they might walk into a carefully prepared trap – their scouts had reported unfavourably on the proposed attack, believing the barracks had been taken over by the military.

The four constables again made contact with the IRA and succeeded in getting the raid rescheduled for 17 June. Two of the constables, one being Conway, were then sent on temporary duty to other barracks in the area. The IRA was informed of this but intimated that it would continue with the plan. So on the agreed date IRA men from Dungannon and Keady entered the barracks via an unlocked back door. However, when two of their number tried to enter a locked bedroom belonging to Head Constable Henry O'Neill, shots were exchanged which awakened the remaining sleeping policemen and a great deal of shooting followed in which one of the IRA men was seriously wounded.

RIC men on their way from Dungannon to Cookstown to assist their comrades stopped a car outside Newmills and found it contained a wounded IRA man, Patrick Loughran from Quinn's Lane, Dungannon. He was taken to Dungannon Hospital where it was found that he had already received medical attention. However, it was felt that he had to be operated on at once, so he was conveyed to the Mater Hospital, Belfast, where he died.

As a result of the IRA raid on Cookstown RIC Barracks, Constable Leonard was dismissed and Constables Conway, Hargaden and O'Boyle resigned within three months.[61]

After the attack on Tempo Barracks the IRA threatened to kill local police and the DI for the area if any action were taken, including arrests, for the attack. At the inquest the local DI stated, 'This thing won't intimidate the RIC.' He continued vehemently, passionately striking the table: 'Never, never by the IRA that was born in cowardice and lives on murder. They will never intimidate us by shooting a couple of hundred policemen.'[62]

In March 1921 two men from the Tempo area were tried by general court martial in Victoria Barracks, Belfast, for their part in this incident. They were both alleged not to have been involved in the actual raid on the barracks but were part of the general scheme, acting as Republican Police. One was alleged to have been one of the twenty men who held up the RIC patrol as it returned to the barracks; the other was allegedly involved in the holding of other RIC men in O'Rourke's public house during the attack. This man was stopped by police the next day between Fivemiletown and Tempo and found to have a medal inscribed 'RIC Tournament 1913', which belonged to Constable Breen, a well-known athlete stationed at Tempo.[63]

Sergeant Lucas, a forty-seven-year-old married man, was from Co. Tyrone. He had twenty-four years' police service, having been a bread server before joining the RIC.

25 October 1920, Moneygold, Co. Sligo

Patrick Perry, Sgt 56270
Patrick Keown, Con 69697
Patrick Laffey, Con 60083
Patrick Lynch, Con 63750

A police patrol, consisting of a sergeant and eight constables who were stationed at Cliffoney Barracks, was ambushed between Grange and Ahanlish at Moneygold, eight miles from Sligo. Three of the patrol were killed outright, namely Sergeant Perry, Constable Laffey and Constable Keown. Perry, a fifty-one-year-old married man with ten children, was from Ballivor, Co. Meath. He had twenty-six years' police service, having had no other employment before joining the RIC. Laffey was forty-one and married with five children and came from Co. Galway. He had nineteen years' police service, having previously been a farmer. Constable Keown was twenty-five and single. From Co. Fermanagh, he had four months' service, having been a farmer before joining the RIC. He had first joined the RIC on 3 May 1919 but had been discharged as unfit by the force surgeon. He rejoined on 3 June 1920.

Constable Lynch was removed to the County Infirmary where he died from his wounds on 27 October. A thirty-three-year old married man from Co. Cavan with two children, he had twelve years' police service, having been a farmer prior to joining the RIC.

Two other constables, Clarke and O'Rourke, wounded during this incident, were removed to a Dublin hospital. A lorry conveying the bodies of the dead to Boyle had an inscription displayed in large letters which read: 'A Sinn Féin victory, three widows and seventeen orphans'.

The ambush was carried out by an IRA unit under the command of William Pilkington, the Sligo Brigade commandant, who eventually became OC of the IRA's Third Western Division. In 1924 Pilkington joined a Redemptorist Order, and was ordained a priest in 1931.

30 October 1920, Castledaly, Co. Galway
Timothy Horan, Con 60534

An RIC cycle patrol, consisting of one sergeant and four constables who were stationed at Kilchreest, was ambushed at Castledaly, midway between Kilchreest and Peterwell, as it was returning from Peterwell. Constable Horan was killed outright, with Constable Keane being seriously wounded during the attack.

Horan, a forty-year-old married man with a young family, was from Co. Kerry. He had eighteen years' service, having been a farmer before joining the RIC.

31 October 1920, Tullamore, King's County
Henry Cronin, Sgt 56371

The sergeant was shot and wounded three times near his home in Henry Street, Tullamore, as he was leaving to go to the RIC barracks. He died on 1 November 1920 at 7.45 p.m. in the County Infirmary. After the shooting, the sergeant's wife ran out into the street and met her husband, who fell into her arms saying, 'I'm shot, I'm shot.' It was later found that he had been shot at very close range as his clothing showed signs of having been singed.

He was forty-seven with a young family and from Co. Cork. He had twenty-six years' police service, having been a labourer. His eight-year-old son, Patrick, was later head of the Columban Fathers in the Philippines and became an archbishop. Forty years after the death of his father, he returned to Tullamore to the cheers of the townspeople.

31 October 1920, Granard, Co. Longford
Capt Philip St John Kelleher, DI 71645

The DI, who held the rank of captain in the Fourth Leinster Regiment and had won an MC and other honours for gallantry, had not been in the RIC very long. He was in Kiernan's Hotel in Granard when he was shot and killed at 9 p.m. on 31 October.

Kelleher, twenty-three and single, was from Macroom, Co. Cork. He had four months' police service, having been promoted DI3 on 7 August.

31 October 1920, Hillville, Co. Kerry
Albert Caseley, Con 71924
John Herbert Evans, Con 71269

At 10 p.m. the two constables, who had only been in the RIC a short time and were stationed in Killorglin, Co. Kerry, were shot dead at Hillville, half a mile from the town, as they returned from leave.

Constable Evans, twenty-two and single, was from Belfast. He had six months' service in the RIC. Prior to this he worked for five years as a GPO telegraphist in Belfast and then joined the RAF and served in the First World War. His father was W. G. Evans, an ex-RIC sergeant who had seen war service with the Royal Irish Regiment. Constable Evans was buried at Dundonald Cemetery on 4 November.

Constable Caseley, a twenty-four-year-old single man, was from Kent. He had four months' police service, having been a soldier before joining the RIC. He was buried with full military honours at Lambeth Cemetery, Tooting. His home had been at Heredene Street, Somers Road, Brixton Hill, London.

31 October 1920, Ballyduff, Co. Kerry
Robert Gorbey, Con 70996
William Madden, Con 65081
George Morgan, Con 70802

A large party of IRA men picked from the Ballyconry, Ballydonoghue, Ballyduff, Leam and Lixnaw companies of the IRA took up positions in the village of Ballyduff, Co. Kerry, on 31 October and attacked the local RIC barracks and a police patrol which was in the village. During the attack on the patrol Constable Morgan was killed and Constable Madden and Constable Gorbey were wounded. Both wounded constables were removed to Cork Military Hospital where they died from their injuries.

Constable Gorbey died on 6 November. He was twenty-three and single, and from Newcastle West, Co. Limerick. He had six months' police service, having been a manservant and a soldier before joining the RIC.

Madden, a thirty-year-old single man, was from Co. Tipperary. He had eleven years' police service, having had no other employment prior to joining the RIC. The date of his death could not be established.

Morgan, twenty-three and single, was from Co. Mayo. He had seven months' police service, having been a grocer's assistant before joining the RIC.

1 November 1920, near Ballinalee, Co. Longford
Peter Cooney, Con 60641

The constable was on leave from his barracks at Granard and had stayed at Ballinalee. Whilst he was making his way back to Granard he was attacked. His body was found on 2 November riddled with bullets. He was forty-three, married and from Co. Sligo. He had eighteen years' police service, having been a farmer before joining the RIC.

The Ulster Special Constabulary

On 1 November recruiting began in Belfast for the Special Constabulary, with the scheme being introduced to the rest of the province by pairs of counties, the last pair being Antrim and Londonderry, where recruiting began on 27 November 1920.

Official documents and correspondence of the time referred to these new police officers as 'The Special Constabulary', but unofficially they became known as the 'Royal Irish Special Constabulary'. As the prefix Royal was unauthorised it was not retained and the Special Constabulary became the Ulster Special Constabulary, with the introduction on 24 May 1922 of the Constabulary Bill (Northern Ireland).

In November 1920 men between the ages of twenty-one and forty-five who wished to assist the authorities in the maintenance of order and the prevention of crime, and who wanted to join the Special Constabulary, were asked either to call in person or send a letter to the police station most convenient to their residence. These applications were then considered by a selection committee, one being formed for each county. These committees consisted of justices of the peace, who could co-opt other inhabitants from the county in order to gain the most accurate knowledge of each candidate. The names agreed by these committees for appointment into the Special Constabulary were then given to their respective local RIC DIs for final vetting.

No new legislation was required for the formation of the Special Constabulary as the necessary authority for their establishment under the Government of Ireland Act 1920 was contained in the Special Constabulary (Ireland) Acts of 1832 and 1914 and subsequent enactments and orders in council. Therefore, in theory, special constables could have been recruited throughout Ireland, but in practice recruitment was only attempted in the six counties of north-eastern Ireland. From 1 November 1920 four grades of special constables were recruited as follows:

1. A Specials. These were men who were recruited for full-time duty. The upper age limit of forty-five years was strictly adhered to, with applicants also being required to pass a medical examination.

They were paid ten shillings per day and other sundry allowances, being employed on six-month periods. A Specials were required to serve only in the six counties, but were required to take the same oath of allegiance as regular members of the RIC and were also bound by the RIC's code of discipline. These new A Specials were deployed in two ways, with half of the recruits being used as reinforcements to the RIC and attached to RIC barracks, whilst the remainder were formed into platoons. By the end of 1920, 1,500 Specials had been sworn in, with the first two platoons being formed on 6 December 1920, one being utilised in Belfast and the other being deployed in the border area of Co. Down. Each platoon had two officers, a head constable, four sergeants and sixty special constables, formed into four sections, each under the leadership of a sergeant. A platoon had a Ford car, two armoured cars and four Crossley tenders so that it could retain its mobility. By early 1921 a number of A Special platoons had been formed and were trained at Newtownards.

2. B Specials. These men were used only occasionally, on duty one evening a week, exclusive of training drills. They were used on day duties only in emergencies. These men were not paid but received £5 each six months for wear and tear on their footwear, etc. They also received 2s 6d for each drill they performed in excess of the one training drill required each week. In the beginning the only uniform these men were issued with were police caps and armlets. However, by February 1922 they had been fully armed with rifles and bayonets and had also been issued with uniforms. Their uniforms at the start were only available in three sizes, being 1914–18 army tunics, trousers and puttees dyed dark green. They were also issued with webbing equipment, and recruits in country districts were allowed to keep their arms at home for protection. The B Specials had their own officers but remained under police authority, coming under the command of Lieutenant Colonel Sir

Charles George Wickham, DSO, the divisional commissioner for the RIC in Northern Ireland, who was based in Belfast. Each county had a commandant in charge of its B Specials, who co-operated closely with the county inspector of the RIC. The county force of B Specials was divided into districts, which in turn were divided into sub-districts, each being under the control of a district and sub-district officer.

By the middle of November 1920, 750 men had joined the B Specials in Belfast, nearly half of them ex-soldiers. On 4 February 1921 the first patrol of B Specials began to patrol in Belfast. Prior to taking up duty as a B Special, a man had to be formally appointed by two justices of the peace, being required to take the following oath of allegiance – 'I do swear that I will well and truly serve our Sovereign Lord the King in the Office of Special Constable without favour or affection, malice or ill-will and that I will to the best of my power cause the peace to be kept and preserved and prevent all offences against the persons and properties of His Majesty's subjects; and that while I continue to hold the said Office I will to the best of my skill and knowledge discharge all the duties thereof faithfully according to law. So help me God.'

3. C Specials. These were older men who were to be used as a reserve in an emergency. They received no pay or allowances and only performed occasional drills.

4. CI Specials. In the middle of 1920 tension began to increase in Northern Ireland, with a number of minor attacks being carried out by the IRA. The IRA was weak in the six counties because of a large unionist population, which was fanatically loyal to the crown and held a violent hatred of Sinn Féin. This meant that the IRA was unable to carry out the same number of attacks as in the south and west of Ireland. However, as the number of incidents increased, it had the effect of heightening tensions in the six coun-

ties, which caused spasmodic outbursts of sectarian rioting, mostly in Belfast. The RIC had adopted a policy of abandonment of its smaller barracks, which caused the unionist population to come to the conclusion that if nothing was done disorder would become worse, so they decided to take measures to protect themselves and their property. Vigilante groups and defence committees of various kinds began to be formed and using their own arms they mounted guards. On 8–9 June such a group was able to prevent property in Lisbellaw, Co. Fermanagh, from being burnt by the IRA, forcing the attackers to flee. On 24 June 1920 a decision to revive the pre-war UVF was made. Lieutenant Colonel Wickham outlined in a circular on 9 November 1921 that the better members of the UVF should be taken under police control as special constables. He believed it was easier to try to incorporate these men into a police scheme to prevent any unauthorised actions or reprisals. This secret circular became known as the 'Wickham' circular and was later used by Michael Collins when negotiating with the government in an attempt to embarrass them.

In April 1922 a new class of C Special Constabulary for UVF members was formed, called the CI Special Constabulary. It was formed into regular military units of battalion strength on a territorial basis, being available for duty during a grave emergency anywhere in Northern Ireland. 6,000 in number, they were unpaid unless called up for service. Two-thirds were to be recruited in Belfast, with the remainder from Lisburn and Londonderry. With the introduction of the Constabulary Bill (Northern Ireland) on 24 May 1922, the CI Specials were separated from the rest of the Special Constabularies, becoming a kind of Northern Ireland Territorial Army. They did no police work except static guard and were formed into three brigades called groups, two of which were active in Belfast. Each group had four battalions or districts, which in turn had four companies.

On 17 November 1920 an advisory board concerning the discipline and general welfare of the Special Constabulary was formed. This board consisted of three magistrates, a county inspector of the RIC and a county commandant of the Special Constabulary.

Two of the main rules which governed the 'B' Specials were:

a) When on patrol they had to be accompanied by a member of the RIC.
b) They were not allowed to carry out searches.

Background to the Special Constabulary:

The prevailing circumstances which led to the government establishing this new body of police in Northern Ireland can be summarised as follows. The original reason was the shortage of troops and regular police, coupled with the demand by the population of north-eastern Ireland for protection. As the escalation in the troubles increased, the need for more police officers to deal with the campaign was obvious. However, because of the IRA's boycott of RIC men and their families, enforced by intimidation or violence, recruiting for the RIC was almost at a standstill, with the force's overall strength falling dramatically due to the number of men who resigned rather than have themselves or their families ostracised from the rest of Irish society.

The army, which until then had been deployed mainly in guarding government buildings, providing escorts for stores and prisoners, and helping to hold outlying police stations, began to be used more to counter the wave of violence. Another eight battalions were sent to Ireland in May 1920, with an increase in the use of motor vehicles to make them more mobile. However, the army's officers were mainly young men who were inexperienced in mobile operations, having been involved in a prolonged war that was extensively fought from trenches. In order to counter this it was proposed to raise a Special Emergency Gendarmerie. This never reached fruition but on 1

January 1920 recruiting began in England for the RIC, the result of which was the recruitment of those men who became known as the Black and Tans, and also, later, of the Auxiliary Division. These new English recruits brought the RIC back up to strength by September, with Major General H. H. Tudor being appointed police adviser to the viceroy, in command of both the RIC and DMP.

As the situation worsened in the six counties in 1920, Captain Sir Basil Brooke, who had been most active as an organiser of several thousand men into defence groups in Co. Fermanagh (which were collectively known as Fermanagh Vigilance), travelled to Dublin to request that Dublin Castle organise an official Special Constabulary in the six counties as he was concerned that the trouble would spread there. His request was turned down; however, he was informed that his unofficial force could wear armbands and carry whistles but were not to be armed.

In June 1920 a telegram was sent to the king by the Ulster ex-servicemen's association in Belfast pledging the support of 3,000 trained ex-servicemen to restore law and order. On 23 June a conference was held in London at which David Lloyd George presided. Most of his cabinet was present, along with ministers and officers of the Irish administration, including Generals Macready, Tudor and Sir James Craig. Winston Churchill, who was then secretary of state for war, asked what would happen if the unionists in the six counties were given arms and charged with keeping law and order, in order that seven battalions and several thousand police could be sent to the south and west of Ireland.

Mr Wylie, the assistant attorney general, stated that this would be disastrous and would lead to civil war. Sir John Anderson said that such an action would set the south ablaze and might well lead to the massacre of Protestants in the south and west of Ireland. Major General Tudor was against using an irregular force for the purpose of maintaining law and order and was determined that the pre-war

UVF should not be used. Sir James Craig stated that the proposal was quite practicable if it was official and legal, with the men being properly sworn in with an oath of allegiance and the force having its own officers. He said that if such a force were maintained with military-type discipline it would prevent mob law and actions or reprisals.

At another conference held on 2 September Craig proposed that 2,000 full-time special constables be formed to assist the RIC. He said they should be armed and organised on military lines and that part-time special constables, for use when required under RIC officers' command, should also be formed. He pointed out that the situation in the six counties had deteriorated, and that the law-abiding people were rapidly losing faith in the government's ability to protect them and were threatening recourse to arms, which Craig feared would lead to civil war. It was also proposed that should a general rising by Sinn Féin take place in the six counties, and if it was beyond the capability of the government to deal with it, as a last resort the UVF should be rearmed and mobilised.

As killings continued in the south and west of Ireland, unionists in the north-east became more incensed and tensions increased. On 3 September the Ulster Unionist Council called upon the government for immediate action for the protection of lives and property. A deputation of unionists, including members of the Ulster Unionist Labour Association, met members of the cabinet in London on 7 September to underline their concerns. As a result of this pressure a ministers' meeting was held on 8 September. General Macready disapproved of arming an irregular force, saying it would sow the seeds of civil war, and proposed that eight battalions be specially raised in Britain for use in Ireland. It was agreed that Hamar Greenwood, the chief secretary for Ireland, would take the necessary steps to organise a Special Constabulary.

On 22 October Dublin Castle announced its intention to raise a Special Constabulary for the six counties. On 1 November the government acceded to Sir James Craig's request for a force of both full-time and part-time special constables, and recruiting began.

2 November 1920,
Auburn Glasson, Co. Westmeath
Sydney G. Larking, Con 71468

A motor lorry driven by the constable was ambushed as it made its way between Carrick-on-Shannon and Athlone, at Auburn Glasson, which is about six miles outside Athlone. Larking was to have given evidence at a court martial. Sergeant Meaney and Constable Costello were badly wounded during this attack.

Constable Larking, a twenty-two-year-old-single man, was from London. He had four months' police service, having been a footman and a soldier before joining the RIC.

2 November 1920,
Cloughjordan, Co. Tipperary
William M. Maxwell, Con 71234

Constable Maxwell, twenty-four and single, with five months' service, was shot dead in a public house in Cloughjordan. He was an ex-soldier, having served for three years with the Irish Guards during the First World War and had earlier been a postman. He was buried in Ballynahinch, Co. Down, his home town.

3 November 1920, Ballymote, Co. Sligo
Patrick Fallon, Sgt 55021

Sergeant Fallon was forty-nine, married and from Co. Galway. He had twenty-one years' service, having previously been a farmer. He was on duty at Ballymote Fair when he was shot dead. He was buried on 6 November in the local cemetery at Ballymote.

In July 1921 a man from Ballynaglogh, Co. Sligo, was tried by court martial in Victoria Barracks, Belfast. It was stated at the court martial that Fallon had been an orderly sergeant, whose job it was to parade men going out on duty. It was also stated that it was his custom to take his meals in his lodgings at Mill Street, 130–140 yards from the barracks. At 2 p.m. he was making his way back to the barracks when he was shot, which caused him to stagger and fall. Police rushed to the scene and carried him back into the barracks, but he died within seven minutes.

At the time of the attack there were sixty to seventy people in the vicinity, who ran off after the shooting. Two of them were the men who carried out the attack, one of whom police in the barracks recognised. On 8 November 1920 this man was arrested by police at Boyle. At first he said that he had been in Ballymote to sell cattle at the fair, but he made the following statement at the court martial: 'I was with _____ in Ballymote on the Third and did fire a shot at Sergeant Fallon. _____ and I then ran down Jail Street and we parted and I have not seen him since. I cannot say who ordered us to do this as my brother and sister would be shot.'[64]

9 November 1920,
Ballybrack Railway Station, Co. Kerry
Archibald Turner, Con 71552
James Thomas Woods, Con 70264

The two constables were returning from leave by train to Farranfore when they were observed boarding at Tralee platform by members of the IRA. This information was sent to Ballymacelligott. Local IRA men then went to Ballybrack Railway Station to wait for the train. Once the train pulled into the station, IRA members began scanning the carriages for the two constables. They found them seated facing each other and opened fire on them.⁶⁵

Constable Turner, a twenty-eight-year-old single man from Kent who had served with a Welsh regiment, died a short time after the attack. He had five months' police service on 4 November 1920, having been a labourer before enlisting.

Constable Woods, twenty-nine and single, from Lancashire, died from his wounds on 15 November. During the First World War he had been a member of the Grenadier Guards and had nine months' police service. On 18 November his remains were removed to Glasgow.

It was thought the IRA gunman involved in this incident was a Dublin man called Foy.

13 November 1920, Inches Cross, Co. Tipperary

Charles Buntrock, Con 74436
Jeremiah Leary, Con 65367
Patrick Mackessy, Con 62820
John Miller, Con 71096

An RIC patrol of eight men was making its way by lorry from Galbally to Bansha when it was ambushed at Inches Cross in the Glen of Aherlow. The driver was shot in the head and killed, which caused the lorry to crash into a ditch. The other police alighted from the lorry and began to return fire. One of these officers, Constable Mackessy, who was a clerk in the DI's office, took cover under the lorry but during the fighting the petrol tank ignited. His badly charred body was found later.

Constables Leary's last words to his comrades were, 'Carry on!' A thirty-year-old single man, he was from Cork and had ten years' police service, having been a labourer prior to joining the RIC.

Mackessy, thirty-five and married with three children, was from

Co. Kerry. He had nine years' police service the day before the attack, having been a farmer before joining the RIC. His remains were removed by train on 16 November to his native place.

Constables Buntrock and Miller, both seriously wounded, were removed to the Military Hospital in Tipperary. Buntrock, a twenty-seven-year-old married man, was from Essex. He would have had one month's service on 15 November, having been a boilermaker and a soldier prior to joining the RIC, but he died on 13 November from his wounds. His brother was also in the lorry when it was attacked, but was not injured.

Constable Miller, a twenty-two-year-old single man from Co. Wicklow, died on 14 November. He had six months' police service, having been a teacher before joining the RIC.

This attack was carried out by No. 1 flying column attached to the IRA's Third Tipperary Brigade under the command of Dinny Lacey. The IRA had lined a ditch on one side of the roadway near a bend. Two other IRA men were in a tree on the opposite side, about fifty yards away from the ambush point. It was alleged that they acted as lookouts.[66] After the attack, a house near the scene was burned as the occupants refused to give shelter to the wounded police. The IRA took the police weapons but did not get any ammunition as it had all been expended by the police during the attack.

17 November 1920, White Street, Cork city
James Donoghue, Sgt 58216

The sergeant, who was stationed at Tuckey Street Barracks, was shot three times, twice in the back and once in the head, as he walked down White Street. He had just left his home in Tower Street and was making his way to his barracks. He was to have been promoted to head constable in one week's time.

Donoghue, a forty-six-year-old married man with four children, was from Cahirciveen, Co. Kerry. He had twenty-two years' service, having been a farmer previously.

Background
Three IRA men had been standing in a small gateway into Desmond's Yard in White Street. They initially planned to attack another person, but as their target had not arrived by 5.30 p.m., they were thinking of leaving the area, when Sergeant Donoghue arrived. Acting on their own initiative and to the later fury of their superiors, they shot and killed the sergeant, who was well-liked in the area and was unarmed when attacked. A week after his death the Cork IRA officially apologised in writing to his family. Charlie O'Brien, his brother William (Willie Joe), an officer in the IRA's G Company, First Battalion, and their future brother-in-law, Justin O'Connor, were the three men involved in the attack.

Later that evening three houses in Cork city were attacked by armed men believed to have been wearing police uniforms. As a result of these attacks three men were killed and three others wounded. One of the wounded, Charlie O'Brien, lost an eye and much of his jaw as a result of his wounds.[67]

21 NOVEMBER 1920, NEWRY, CO. DOWN
John Kearney, H/Con 52729

At 8.15 p.m. Head Constable Kearney, a fifty-one-year-old married man from Westmeath with two children, had left the Dominican church and was near Needham Street when he was shot and seriously wounded. He was taken to a nursing home in the town, but died from his wounds at 2 p.m. on 22 November. He had been attached to the RIC barracks in Canal Street. He had thirty-three years' police service, having had no other employment before joining the RIC.

21 November 1920, Leap, Co. Cork
Harry Clement Jays, Con 70194

Five constables had just left Sheehan's Hotel in Leap when they were attacked. Constable Jays, a twenty-two-year-old single man from Hampshire, was killed and Constable Mills (also English) was seriously wounded. Jays had nine months' service, having been a footman/waiter and a soldier before joining the RIC. On 26 November his body was removed to England for burial.

21 November 1920, Cappoquin, Co. Waterford
Isaac James Rea, Con 70130

The constable, who was twenty and single, was shot and wounded from a passing car as he walked in the village of Cappoquin. He was taken to the Military Hospital in Cork, but died on 27 December. He was buried on 31 December at his home in Durrus, Bantry, Co. Cork. His mother had died a few days before his own death. Constable Rea had ten months' police service, having been a farmer prior to joining the RIC.

21 November 1920, 28 Earlsfort Terrace, Dublin City
John Fitzgerald, Sgt 71614

Sergeant Fitzgerald was in bed in his lodgings at 28 Earlsfort Terrace, Dublin, when the front doorbell rang at 9 a.m. The door was opened by the maid, who was asked by a man, a member of the Squad, to show him Colonel Fitzpatrick's room. The girl stated there was no Fitzpatrick in the house, but said there was a Capt. Fitzgerald staying. At this the man called in other armed men, whom he placed in the hallway outside the sergeant's room, which he then entered.

Police later found the body of Sergeant Fitzgerald in bed. He had been shot four times at point-blank range – twice in the forehead, once in the heart and once in the wrist, which suggests he had tried to protect himself. He had, until just before his death, been employed as a defence of barracks officer in Co. Clare. Whilst on that duty he was kidnapped by the IRA, who tried to kill him with his own revolver, which misfired. He was then dragged into a field and placed against a wall to be shot. During this struggle his arm was dislocated and when the IRA shot at him he dropped to the ground pretending he was dead, later seizing an opportunity to leap over the wall and escape.[68]

He was attending a hospital in Dublin for treatment for his injured arm and had only been released a few days before being killed. He was buried at Glasnevin Cemetery, Dublin, on 24 November with full military honours, which included an RIC and Auxiliary guard of honour. He was twenty-two, single and had five months' police service, having been an army officer prior to joining the RIC.

21 November 1920, Northumberland Street, Dublin city
Frank Garniss, Cadet 79177
Cecil A. Morris, Cadet 79106

An IRA party entered a house at 22 Lower Mount Street, Dublin, in which two agents of the British intelligence service were lodging. One of these men was killed, while the other, whose door had been locked, escaped uninjured when seventeen shots were fired through it. During the attack, the maid made her way to a top-storey window, where she called out for help to a party of Auxiliaries from Beggars Bush Barracks, who were making their way to the railway station to catch an early train southwards for duty. The Auxiliaries alighted from their vehicle and entered the house, with two being despatched back to their barracks for reinforcements.[69]

The IRA men involved in the attack ran from the rear of the house and one of them, Frank Teeling, was shot, wounded and captured. All the other IRA men escaped.

The two cadets sent for help never made it to their barracks; they were stopped on the Canal Bridge at Mount Street and overpowered, being dragged struggling into a hallway of a house in Northumberland Street, where they were questioned. When one stated that they were from Beggars Bush Barracks they were taken into the garden of the house and killed.[70]

Their fate was unknown until other Auxiliaries reached Lower Mount Street and it was discovered that these reinforcements had arrived at the scene because of the sound of gunfire and not as a result of any message sent. A search was then undertaken for the two missing men, whose bodies were later found in a nearby garden.

Cadet Garniss had joined the RIC on 18 October 1920, having completed fifteen years in the army. He was thirty-four and single. On 25 November his body was taken by ship to England to be buried in his native Yorkshire. He had been a second lieutenant in the Leicester Regiment and his Auxiliary number was 755.

Cadet Morris, who lived at Mitcham, had served as a second lieutenant in France with the Middlesex Regiment and the Machine Gun Corps. He was a twenty-four-year-old single man from London. His Auxiliary number was 756.

These were the first members of the Auxiliary Division of the RIC to be killed and their deaths caused great resentment.

Background
Michael Collins realised that the security forces were closing in on him when three of his top intelligence agents, Thornton, Tobin and

Cullen, were arrested, though later released. Through his network of informers and sympathisers, Collins became aware that the government had a new network of agents living and working in Dublin. He ordered that detailed reports on these people be made and that Thornton collate all the information. Collins decided to attack all the addresses these men lodged at simultaneously, picking Sunday 21 November 1920 as the date for the attacks. He favoured this date for two reasons: (a) he wanted to carry out the attacks as soon as possible and (b) on that Sunday a big match was to take place at Croke Park, Dublin, between Dublin and Tipperary, which meant that Dublin would be unusually crowded.

On the evening of 20 November, Collins met David Neligan, one of his main intelligence agents in the DMP, and later Dick McKee and Peadar Clancy, the commander and vice-commander of the Dublin Brigade, to put the finishing touches to his plan. Unknown to Collins, these two men were arrested early on the Sunday morning at Lower Gloucester Street, Dublin and taken to Dublin Castle. On the evening of 21 November it was reported that these men, along with a man named Conor Clune, had been shot dead in controversial circumstances.

At 9 a.m. on Sunday morning members of the Squad, augmented by Dublin Brigade ASU members, called at a number of addresses throughout the city, which resulted in the deaths of eighteen men, some being members of the intelligence network, others being military officers or civilians, and one a member of the RIC. One young man who took part in these attacks was Seán Lemass, who later in life was Taoiseach (prime minister) of the Irish Republic.[71]

After these attacks security forces went to Croke Park to search it. They said they were looking for some of those involved in the attacks. There are conflicting reports as to how the shooting began, but when it had ceased fourteen people were dead. 21 November 1920 became known throughout the world as 'Bloody Sunday'.

The Funerals

The remains of seven of the army officers and the two cadets killed on 21 November, along with two Auxiliary cadets accidentally killed earlier that week, were removed from the King George V Hospital, Dublin, to the North Quays, where a naval vessel waited to take them back to England.

At 10 a.m., before the funeral procession passed along the route, it was checked by police officers from the RIC, Auxiliary Division and DMP, and at 11 a.m. trams on the route were suspended, while six aircraft circled overhead as the procession got underway. One thousand troops along with detachments from the RIC, Auxiliary and DMP forces were posted along the route. The procession was led by a double-turreted armoured car, with another bringing up the rear.

The coffins were draped with Union Jacks and placed on six horse-drawn field-gun carriages and three RIC lorries. They were accompanied by a firing party with arms reversed, along with infantry, cavalry and police detachments. The bands of the Wiltshire Regiment, Lancashire Fusiliers and the RIC played the 'Dead March'. Military headquarters staff, along with senior members of the RIC and DMP led by army chaplains, were also in the procession.

24 November 1920, Infirmary Road, Phoenix Park, Dublin city
Thomas Dillon, Con 68998

The constable had been in charge of a picket of eight soldiers in Infirmary Road, Phoenix Park, Dublin, when he was shot and killed.

Constable Dillon, a twenty-five-year-old single man, was from Co. Roscommon. He had three years' police service, having previously been a farmer.

27 November 1920, near Castlemartyr, Co. Cork
Timothy J. Quinn, Con 62234

Constable Quinn, thirty-four and married and from Co. Tipperary, and Sergeant Curley were visiting the constable's wife at Killeagh. The two officers were making their way back from Killeagh to their barracks at Castlemartyr when they were attacked and wounded. Quinn died from his wounds on 28 November in Cork. He had fourteen years' police service on 15 November 1920, having had no other employment before joining the RIC.

27 November 1920, Cappoquin, Co. Waterford
Maurice Quirk, Con 63192

Constable Quirk, a thirty-four-year-old married man from Kerry with three children, was shot and badly wounded leaving his lodgings at Cappoquin. He died from his wounds on 29 November and he was buried in Cappoquin on 1 December. He had thirteen years' police service, having been a farmer before joining the RIC.

28 November 1920, Kilmichael, Co. Cork
Francis William Crake, DI 72473
William Barnes, Cadet 72849
Cecil James W. Bayley, Cadet 72843
Leonard Bradshaw, Cadet 72847
James C. Gleave, Cadet 72825
Philip Noel Graham, Cadet 72813
Cecil J. Guthrie, Cadet 72863
Stanley Hugh-Jones, Cadet 72307
Frederick Hugo, Cadet 79333

Albert G. Jones, Cadet 72818
Ernest William H. Lucas, Cadet 72845
William Pallester, Cadet 79151
Horace Pearson, Cadet 71615
Arthur F. Poole, Const. 73356
Frank Taylor, Cadet 72824
Christopher Wainwright, Cadet 72850
Benjamin D. Webster, Cadet 79332

On Sunday 28 November 1920, No. 2 Section, C Company of the Auxiliary Division left their barracks at Macroom Castle, into which they had moved in August, to carry out a routine patrol. This patrol of eighteen men was under the leadership of DI Crake and was travelling in two Crossley tenders, intending to take their usual route of Macroom to Dunmanway, then on to Bandon and across country back to Macroom.

The reason the patrol set off on a route they regularly used was outlined by a member of the Auxiliaries stationed at Macroom: 'Winter was now coming on and our patrols were no longer looked forward to, indeed they were becoming most unpleasant. We had only open cars and as it rained nearly all the time, as it knows how to in south-west Ireland, we finished each patrol soaked to the skin despite our mackintoshes. This discomfort I think may have been responsible for our disinclination to deviate from known roads. We would take patrols which we knew would only last so long, then we would be back to the dubious comfort of the castle. However it came about, it is certain that each section officer got into the habit of doing the same patrol each time he was on duty, on any particular day we knew where his patrol was going. All this was not lost on the other side. There was always careless talk in the town and it was easy for them to find out which section would be patrolling on any day some days ahead, and make any plans they thought fit'.[72]

This, then, was the reason that, on that wet and wintry day, these two tenders were travelling along a minor roadway through bleak and barren countryside of bogland, which was interspersed with heather and rocks, near Kilmichael, when they were ambushed. After the attack had finished sixteen policemen lay dead. One constable, H. F. Forde, was badly wounded and taken to Cork Military Hospital, and remained paralysed with brain damage for the rest of his life. Although Republican sources state there were no survivors, a photograph of this man appeared in the 17 January 1921 issue of *The Freeman's Journal*. Another man, C. J. Guthrie, vanished, and his body was not located, although the commander of the IRA unit involved in the ambush stated that he was wounded and crawled off the roadway into a boghole where he sank to his death. This was not, in fact, the case. Cadet Guthrie had been the driver of the second Crossley tender in the patrol and was the only member to escape from the scene of the ambush. He made good his escape under gunfire and was able to get to within two miles of Macroom before being spotted and recaptured by two local IRA men, who pretended to be armed. Two days later Guthrie was shot by the IRA and buried secretly south of Macroom in Annahala bog. His body was discovered and exhumed in 1926, being reburied in the Church of Ireland graveyard at Inchigeela.[73]

The Ambush
Although the exact details of this ambush are not accurately known, it is believed to have happened as follows. It was carried out by the Cork No. 3 (West) Brigade flying column under the command of Tom Barry, who was an ex-British soldier and the son of a policeman. Barry stated that on the Monday before the ambush the column began to train for it and that he and Michael McCarthy, the vice-commandant of the Dunmanway Battalion, inspected the ambush position during the week.

At 2 a.m. on 28 November 1920, the column was at O'Sullivans of Ahilina, where Father O'Connell, PP of Ballineen, heard the men's confessions before he gave them absolution. The IRA unit then made its way to the ambush site, arriving at 8.15 a.m. The site, chosen for the ambush by Barry, was not on the Macroom side of Kilmichael as he believed that police and military reinforcements could quickly react to a location on that side.

Once at the location for the ambush, Barry divided the column into four sub-units and explained his attack plan, telling his men that this was a fight to the end and that the outcome was not only vital to West Cork but to the whole nation.

He then had the sub-units take up their positions as follows:

1. The command post was situated behind a small narrow stone wall, which faced the direction the police patrol was expected to arrive from.
2. No. 1 Section of the IRA flying column was placed behind a large heather-covered rock approximately forty yards from the command post, and once the ambush had been initiated they were to move to the crest of the ten-foot-high rock, which gave them a vantage point with a good field of fire that dominated the entire ambush location.
3. No. 2 Section was placed about 150 yards from No. 1 in a rock outcrop with some of this party situated in such a way that they could fire on the second Crossley tender if it had not rounded the bend when the ambush commenced.
4. No. 3 Section was divided in two, some of them being positioned in a chain of rocks to prevent the ambushed Auxiliaries getting into positions on the roadway, from which it would be extremely difficult to dislodge them, whilst the remainder were placed further up the road towards Macroom in case more than two lorries drove into the ambush.

The IRA also had two scouts on the Macroom side of the ambush and one towards Dunmanway to prevent surprise from that direction.

No. 3 Section was under the command of Stephen O'Neill and they were told to take the utmost care as their crossfire could hit the IRA sections on the other side of the road.

The IRA had taken up their positions by 9 a.m. and begun their wait. During the day another IRA man, John Lordan, who was vice-commandant of the Bandon Battalion, joined the ambush and the people in the house near the site sent food and tea to the IRA men in the area. At 4.05 p.m. the scouts on the Macroom side reported the arrival of the two expected vehicles; at the same time, a horse-drawn cart with five fully armed IRA men rounded the bend into the ambush site, not knowing that the police patrol was only a short distance behind them. These particular IRA men were on their way to join the flying column during their ambush and were told to gallop their horse up the farm laneway and out of sight.[74]

As the lorries entered the ambush area, Barry, in full officer's uniform, stood on the roadway near the command post. He believed, rightly, that this would slow the vehicles as the Auxiliaries probably had never seen this kind of uniform or would mistake it for a military one. The first lorry slowed and was about to stop when a bomb thrown by Barry landed in the front of the vehicle, killing the driver and front-seat passenger. At this the rest of the IRA men opened fire. The nine officers in this lorry were killed, with the last of the fighting taking place on the roadway in hand-to-hand conflict. (The Mills bomb used in this attack had been captured by the IRA on 22 October 1920 at Toureen when a military patrol was ambushed and Captain Dixon was killed. His sidearm was taken and given to Tom Barry, who had been present during the attack.) The IRA men in the command post then made a crouched run up the side of the roadway and began to attack the police in the second lorry (who were fighting from the vehicle and the roadway) from the rear.

When the ambush was over the IRA had two dead, Michael McCarthy and Jim O'Sullivan of Knockawaddra, Rossmore. Sixteen-year-old Pat Deasy, the Bandon Battalion's signalling lieutenant, later died of wounds sustained in the fight. Another IRA man, Jack Hennessy from Ballineen, had a slight head wound. After the incident Barry harshly reprimanded the column and made them drill and march on the roadway among the corpses and burning lorries for five minutes, as they were in a state of shock and needed to be 'jerked back to their former efficiency'. He then had the weapons and documents removed from the dead Auxiliaries. Within thirty minutes the column was on the move south and by 11 p.m. it crossed the Bandon River at Granure, which was eleven miles from Kilmichael and where they stayed in an empty labourer's cottage. The local Ballinacarriga Company of the IRA was waiting for them and they produced food and also protection as the column rested.[75]

After this incident a number of conflicting points arose, the main ones being as follows:

1. The reason the patrol was on such a minor road was that it was stopped by a civilian or person in military uniform who said he had been sent by the officer of an army patrol which had broken down and was in need of help a little further up the side road.
2. When the lorries containing the Auxiliaries drove into the ambush location, there was one or possibly two lorries with a number of men in khaki uniforms clustered round them and the police stopped to render assistance.[76]
3. During the fighting the Auxiliaries in the second lorry had made a bogus surrender call to the IRA No. 2 Section and when some of these IRA men exposed themselves they were killed.
4. It was claimed that the bodies of the policemen were badly mutilated with axes. (The IRA stated that they did not have axes with them, but it is fair to assume that they were carried in the

Crossley tenders to be used in the removal of trees, etc., felled to block roadways.) In retrospect it would appear that some bodies had been mutilated, not with axes or shotguns, but by bayonets and revolvers used at point-blank range.
5. The IRA stated there were no survivors.
6. It was stated that several of the police officers were killed after they had surrendered.

The first army officer on the scene stated that it was the worst sight he had ever seen and he had witnessed thousands of men lying dead during the First World War. A doctor at the inquest affirmed that there was no doubt that some of the injuries inflicted on the cadets had been carried out after their deaths.[77]

It became known as the 'Kilmichael Ambush' and it was to be the largest single loss of police lives during the period 1919–1922. It had a heartening effect on the IRA, who had viewed the Auxiliary Division of the RIC as super-fighters.

After this attack, two notices were printed in the daily press:

1. New Police Order in Macroom

1 December 1920

Whereas foul murders of servants of the Crown have been carried out by disaffected persons, and whereas such persons immediately before the murders appeared to be peaceful and loyal people but have produced pistols from their pockets, therefore it is ordered that all male inhabitants of Macroom and all males passing through Macroom shall not appear in public with their hands in their pockets.

Any male infringing this order is liable to be shot on sight.
By Order Auxiliary Division RIC Macroom Castle

2. Notice

2 December 1920

The General Officer Commanding 17th Infantry Brigade, Cork, requests that all business premises and shops be closed between the hours of 11 a.m. and 2 p.m. on Thursday 2 December 1920 as a mark of respect for the Officers, Cadets and Constables of the Auxiliary Division RIC killed in ambush near Kilmichael, 28 November 1920, and whose funeral procession will be passing through the city on 2 December 1920.

F. R. Eastwood Major Brigade Major 17th INF Bde.[78]

On 2 December 1920 the bodies of the men killed were taken by destroyer to Fishguard to be buried. The men were:

Barnes, William, DFC, Cadet, twenty-six years, single, joined RIC 18 August 1920 (Aux. No. 269). Ex-lieutenant, RAF. Buried in Bexhill churchyard, Sutton. From 47 Glebe Road, Sutton, Surrey. A native of Surrey.

Bayley, Cecil James W., Cadet, twenty-two years, single, joined RIC 18 August 1920 (Aux. No. 328). Ex-lieutenant, RAF. From 24 Reynard Road, Chorlton-Cum-Hardy, Manchester. A native of Lancashire.

Bradshaw, Leonard, Cadet, twenty-two years, single, joined RIC 18 August 1920 (Aux. No. 297). Ex-lieutenant, Royal Field Artillery. From 24 Larkhill Terrace, Blackburn. A native of Lancashire.

Crake, Francis William, DI, MC, twenty-seven years, single, joined RIC 14 August 1920 (Aux. No. 205). Ex-captain, Hampshire Regiment. Buried Elswick, Newcastle-on-Tyne. From 22 Westgate Road, Newcastle-on-Tyne. A native of Northumberland.

Gleave, James C., Cadet, mentioned in despatches, twenty-one years, single, joined RIC 18 August 1920 (Aux. No. 266). Ex-lieutenant, RAF. From near Canterbury, Kent. A native of Worcester.

Graham, Philip Noel, Cadet, thirty-one years, single, joined RIC 18 August 1920 (Aux. No. 274). Ex-captain, Northumberland Fusiliers. Buried Abingdon. From 14 Wootton Road, Abingdon, Berkshire. (He would have been thirty-two on 6 December 1920.) A native of Berkshire. On 3 October he had been promoted to section leader.

Guthrie, Cecil J., Cadet, twenty-eight years, married, joined RIC 19 August 1920 (Aux. No. 294). Ex-lieutenant, RAF. (His wife was residing at Macroom.) Buried Inchigeela. A native of Fyfe.

Hugh-Jones, Stanley, Cadet, twenty-seven years and single (Aux No. 413). Ex-lieutenant, Northumberland Fusiliers. Buried Holcombe, near Bury. A native of Hampshire.

Hugo, Frederick, Cadet, OBE, MC, Mons Star, forty years, single, joined RIC 16 November 1920 (Aux. No. 820). Ex-major, Royal Engineers/Indian Army. Buried Southgate. From Gove House, Southgate. (His fortieth birthday had been on 23 October 1920.) A native of London.

Jones, Albert G., Cadet, thirty-three years, single, joined RIC 18 August 1920 (Aux. No. 268). Ex-second lieutenant, Shropshire Regiment. From 56 Swindon Road, Wroughton, Wiltshire. A native of Northamptonshire.

Lucas, Ernest William H., Cadet, thirty-one years, single, joined RIC 18 August 1920 (Aux. No. 292). Ex-second lieutenant, Royal Sussex Regiment. From 42 Fox Street, Shaldon, Tidworth. A native of Sussex.

Pallester, William, Cadet, twenty-five years, single, joined RIC 22 October 1920 (Aux. No. 822). Ex-captain, West Yorkshire Regiment. Buried Burngreave Cemetery, Sheffield. From 71 Primrose Avenue, Sheffield. A native of Yorkshire.

Pearson, Horace, Cadet, twenty-one years, single, joined RIC 31 May 1920 as a defence of barracks sergeant (Aux. No. 835). Ex-lieutenant, Yorkshire Regiment. A native of Co. Armagh.

Poole, Arthur F., Const., twenty-one years, single, joined RIC 24 September 1920. Ex-Motor Fitter/RAF. He and four brothers came through the First World War unscathed. Funeral on 6 December to Kensal Rise Cemetery, London. Lived Muriel Street, King's Cross, London. (He would have been twenty-two on 23 December 1920.) A native of London.

Taylor, Frank, Cadet, twenty-two years, single, joined RIC 18 August 1920 (Aux. No. 331). Ex-lieutenant, RAF. From 21 Seaview Road, Gillingham, Kent. A native of Kent.

Wainwright, Christopher, Cadet, mentioned in despatches, thirty-six years, single, joined RIC 18 August 1920 (Aux. No. 330). Ex-captain, Royal Dublin Fusiliers and Royal Irish Rifles. He had ten years' army service. From 13 Brunswick Road, Gravesend, Kent. A native of Lancashire.

Webster, Benjamin D., Cadet, thirty years, single, joined RIC 16 November 1920 (Aux. No. 832). Ex-lieutenant, Black Watch. From 300 Langside Road, Crosshill, Glasgow. (He would have been thirty-one on 5 December 1920.) A native of Lanark.

Within a month of the Kilmichael Ambush, C Company was moved to Dublin, where it ceased to act as an independent unit. On 14 December 1920 it was reported in the *Belfast Telegraph* that four men, two of them from Macroom, Co. Cork, were arrested in a farmhouse at Cappagh, Inistioge district, Co. Kilkenny. It was also said that during the search of this farmhouse a large quantity of bombs, guns and ammunition was found and that the two men had in their possession cigarette cases, pipes, watches and personal jewellery identified as belonging to some of the cadets killed at Kilmichael.

On 4 February 1922 the body of a man who had shot himself in the head was found on Clapham Common, London. It was later found to be that of a forty-six-year-old ex-army colonel, Barton Smith, who had been in command of the Auxiliaries at Macroom at the time of the ambush. He had resigned from the RIC on 25 February 1921.⁷⁹

3 December 1920, Youghal, Co. Cork
Maurice Prendiville, Con 57219

While on patrol from Youghal, the constable was crossing the Blackwater Bridge near the town when he was wounded. He was taken to hospital in Cork but died from his wounds on 3 December 1920.

Constable Prendiville, a forty-five-year-old married man with five children, was from Kerry. He had twenty-five years' police service, having been a farmer before joining the RIC.

5 December 1920, Sallymount Avenue, Leeson Park, Dublin city
Hedley A. Balls, Cadet 72875

This officer was shot during a house search in Sallymount Avenue, Leeson Park, Dublin. Cadet Balls, a twenty-nine-year-old single man from Suffolk, would have had three months' police service on 18 December. His Auxiliary number was 281 and he had been a lieutenant in the Machine Gun Corps before joining the RIC.

11 December 1920, Dillons Cross, Cork city
Spencer R. Chapman, Cadet 77834

At 8 p.m. a lorry carrying Auxiliary police was going from the military barracks to Cork city. It had travelled about 200 yards and had just reached Dillons Cross when it was ambushed by IRA men armed with revolvers and bombs. A bomb was dropped over a wall into the lorry wounding eleven men. Cadet Chapman, a twenty-seven-year-old single man, died from his wounds. He lived at 490 London Road, Westcliffe-on-Sea, his Auxiliary number was 495 and he had been a member of the Fourth Battalion, London Regiment during the First World War. He would have had three months' police service the next day and before joining the army he had been a stock jobber.

One of the wounded cadets was from Londonderry and in 1915, at the age of seventeen, he had joined the Black Watch. He was later commissioned into the Tenth Reserve Battalion of the Royal Irish Fusiliers, serving on the Front with the Ulster Division.

13 December 1920,
Ballinalee RIC Barracks, Co. Longford
Frederick Taylor, Con 74612

The attack on the RIC barracks in Ballinalee resulted in the death of Constable Taylor and the serious wounding of Constable E. Shateford, with another two constables being slightly wounded.

When the RIC garrison was called on to surrender, a piano could be heard playing in the barracks, as the police sang 'God Save the King', after which the police returned the attackers' fire.

Constable Taylor was a single man who would have been nineteen on 19 December 1920. He was from Surrey and would have had two months' police service on his birthday, having been a handyman before joining the RIC.

16 December 1920,
Kilcommon, Co. Tipperary
Patrick J. Halford, Con 70628
Ernest F. Harden, Con 73877
Albert H. Palmer, Con 72263
Arthur Smith, Con 73844

An eight-man RIC foot patrol of one sergeant and seven constables from Kilcommon Barracks was ambushed as it was going to the post office in Kilcommon, twelve miles from Thurles, Co. Tipperary. Four constables were killed outright and another was seriously wounded.

Constable Halford, a twenty-seven-year-old single man, was from Co. Meath. He had nine months' police service, having been a clerk and a soldier prior to joining the RIC.

Constable Harden, twenty-one and single, was from Essex. He had two months' police service, having been a labourer.

Constable Palmer was twenty-four and married. From Farnham, Surrey, he had four months' police service, having been a labourer and a soldier before joining the RIC.

Constable Smith, a twenty-two-year-old married man, was from Bermondsey, London. He had two months' police service on 5 December, having been a soldier before joining the RIC. The constable had requested to resign from the RIC on 3 November, but had withdrawn his request on 30 November.

17 December 1920, Henry Street, Dublin city
Philip John O'Sullivan, DI 72019

DI O'Sullivan, twenty-three and single, from Skibbereen, Co. Cork was shot and killed as he walked along Henry Street, Dublin, with his fiancée, whom he had just met a few minutes before, at 6.15 p.m., at Nelson's Pillar. As they passed a jeweller's doorway in which two men stood, a shot rang out and the DI fell. As the wounded man lay on the ground a man came over and pointed a revolver at him. His fiancée tried to wrestle it from him but he fired into the DI's body before running off. The wounded man was taken to Jervis Street Hospital but died soon after admission, at 6.30 p.m.

O'Sullivan was attached to the inspector general's office in Dublin

Castle and was a qualified solicitor. He had served as a lieutenant in the Royal Naval Volunteer Reserve at Toronto, training on HMS *Hermione*, and won an MC, a distinction rarely conferred on members of the Royal Navy. He served in the Mediterranean and the Adriatic, and was awarded an Italian bravery award and complimented by the admiral of the Italian fleet. His father was a solicitor in Kinsale, Co. Cork. O'Sullivan would have had five months' police service on 21 December, having been promoted to DI3 on 1 October. He was buried at Glasnevin Cemetery, Dublin on 20 December.

17 December 1920, Swanlinbar, Co. Cavan
Peter Shannon, Con 62069

A three-man RIC patrol was ambushed a quarter of a mile from Swanlinbar on the main Enniskillen road as it approached the village from the Enniskillen direction. A sergeant and a constable were seriously wounded, with the constable dying from his wounds twenty minutes later.

Shortly after this attack, Constable Byrne was shot and wounded in the arm by IRA men as he stood at his front door in Mill Street, Swanlinbar. He had come out of his home when the gunfire had commenced, in order to see what was happening.

Shannon, a thirty-six-year-old married man, was from Elphin, Co. Roscommon. He had fourteen years' police service, having been a farmer before joining the RIC. On 28 December his body was removed to Elphin for interment.

20 December 1920, near Glenbower, Co. Tipperary
Thomas Walsh, Sgt 58465

Police and army patrols were ambushed at least three times between

Callan, Co. Kilkenny, and Glenbower, Co. Tipperary. These attacks resulted in a number of running battles with IRA men in the area, and in the death of Sergeant Walsh. Sergeant Thomas Shannon was wounded, eight soldiers were killed and several others wounded. Both sergeants were stationed at Kilkenny and both had recently been promoted. The IRA losses included several men killed, with thirty others being captured, some of whom had been wounded.

Sergeant Walsh, a forty-year-old single man, was from Co. Cork. He had twenty-two years' police service, having had no other employment before joining the RIC.

22 December 1920, Newtownbarry, Co. Wexford
William Jones, Con 62330

Constable Jones was stationed in Newtownbarry, Co. Wexford. At 8 p.m. on 22 December he was in a local public house, Kelly's, when he was shot dead. Jones, along with another constable, had entered the bar a short time previously and the two were standing in an inner room when three men entered. Constable Jones was suspicious of these men; when he went to speak to them they shot him. (The previous day Jones, along with the military, had arrested a local IRA man who had been on the run.)

The constable, a thirty-seven-year-old married man with three children, was from Limerick. He had thirteen years' police service, having been a miller before joining the RIC.

27 December 1920, near Bruff, Co. Limerick
Alfred C. Hodgsden, Con 75225
John Reid, Con

On the night of 27 December members of the IRA's Third Battalion,

East Limerick Brigade held a dance to raise funds to purchase arms for the battalion's flying column. This function was held at Caherguillamore House, a vacant mansion belonging to Viscount O'Grady, which sat amidst deep woodlands with a half-mile avenue to the roadway. The house was near the village of Bruff and thirteen miles from Limerick city. The caretaker of the mansion was Tom O'Donoghue, whose son, Paddy, was a member of the Bruff Battalion of the IRA, and it was through him that the house was obtained for use by the IRA, with 200–300 people in attendance at the dance.

The IRA had posted sentries around the house and some of them became uneasy as they believed they could see movement in the area of the mansion. When Martin Conway, the local company IRA captain and vice-commandant of the Third Battalion, was checking on the sentries, he sent word to the dance that all men on the run were to clear out at once as a precaution. As Conway was talking to the O'Dwyer brothers, both of whom were on the run, in the avenue to the mansion, a large force of military and police, who had moved on foot for several miles, began their final approach to the building.

This well-mounted operation, led by Colonel Wilkinson, had a great element of surprise as it was not until they were almost at the mansion that the IRA sentries realised what was happening and opened fire. During the attack Constable Hodgsden was killed, and Constable Reid was wounded, dying the next day.

Five IRA men, including Conway, were also killed and 128 males, many of them IRA members, were taken prisoner. Female searchers were brought to the mansion and they searched all the women. The prisoners were taken to Limerick gaol for court martial by a tribunal presided over by Major General Eastwood. Many received lengthy sentences, with fifty-eight receiving ten years' penal servitude, of which five years were afterwards remitted. Those prisoners who received long sentences were moved to prisons at Portsmouth and Dartmoor; others who received shorter sentences were sent to Spike

Island in Cork Harbour. The prisoners held in England remained in prison until the general amnesty following the signing of the Treaty in December 1921.[80]

Constable Hodgsden was thirty-two, a single man from London who lived with his parents at Parish Lane, Penge. He would have had two months' police service on 5 January 1921, having served in the Royal Navy for fifteen years, seeing considerable service as a torpedo boat gunner during the First World War. On 31 December his funeral to Crystal Palace District Cemetery was attended by Metropolitan Police stationed at Penge.

Although Constable Reid was reported as having died from his wounds, no details could be found.

29 December 1920, Midleton, Co. Cork
Ernest Dray, Con 71631
Martin Mullen, Con
Arthur Thorp, Con 76333

At 9.45 p.m. an RIC foot patrol of ten men was on duty in the dimly lit Main Street of Midleton, Co. Cork, when the members of the IRA's Fourth Battalion, Cork No. 1 Brigade ambushed them. Constable Thorp and five others were wounded. Sergeant Moloney was seriously wounded and Constable Dray died from his wounds on 31 December.

According to newspaper reports, reinforcements on their way to the scene were ambushed about one mile from the village at Ballyrichard, where a tree had been placed across the road, with Constable Mullen being killed and a sergeant and five constables receiving wounds. An IRA man named Jim McCarthy was slightly wounded in the hand during these attacks.[81]

About one month before these attacks the military had been

withdrawn from Midleton as it seemed so peaceful, with the RIC taking over the task of patrolling. As a result of this incident, seven houses were destroyed on 1 January 1921 by the military in an 'official reprisal'.

Constable Dray, a twenty-one-year-old single man, was from Kent. He had six months' police service, having been a soldier before joining the RIC.

Although Constable Mullen was reported as having been killed during this incident, no details of his death could be found.

Constable Thorp, twenty-three and single, was from Middlesex. He had twenty-three days' police service, having been a fitter's mate and a soldier prior to joining the RIC. He died from his wounds on 30 December.

Conclusion for 1920

A total of 179 police officers had lost their lives during the year. At the end of March the IRA, through their paper *An tÓglach*, had announced that the period in the trenches was over and that a continuous policy of guerrilla war was now to begin.[82] Many of the police officers killed during the year were attacked when they were at their most vulnerable, either when alone or coming from their place of worship. Other police officers lost their lives when patrols were ambushed by far superior numbers from well-prepared and concealed locations, as the IRA began to move towards more ambitious operational methods. The number of police casualties caused by the accidental discharge of firearms either by the victim himself or by a colleague, along with tragic fatal mistakes between patrols, also began to rise quite rapidly as the year progressed. Despite these facts, however, the single worst month for police casualties was still to come.

The year 1920 saw the intensification of the struggle, with attacks by sniping, ambush, assassination and arson increasing. The intensity of these attacks had a profound effect on the morale of the police, which by May 1920 had reached a low point. Increased recruitment of British ex-servicemen and officers ensured that there was an injection of manpower into the police ranks and this increase in numbers had, after September 1920, notably improved morale, but the stresses of the conflict continued to take a heavy toll through resignations of men who had less than ten years' service.[83]

In December 1919 a committee had been established to formulate a consistent plan of action for policing to ensure that the demoralising and rendering useless of the police did not continue in 1920.[84] This committee recommended better transport for both the RIC and the DMP, more joint police–army patrols, the use of loyal citizens as special constables and the use of secret agents to penetrate the IRA. The improvements of the RIC's transport along with an upgrading of its armaments, together with the boost in police numbers, helped increase the force's efficiency. This was further enhanced by the end of 1920, when some exploitable intelligence began to filter through.[85]

However, the efforts to obtain worthwhile intelligence had received a number of setbacks, both physical and administrative, during the year. The main physical issues were the killings of Redmond on 21 January, shortly after he had undertaken the task of improving the efficiency of the DMP's G Division, which had been absolutely demoralised, and of a British Secret Service agent on 2 April. The effects of these two incidents were compounded by the shooting of Alan Bell, an ex-DI of the RIC and a member of the 1919 committee formed to perfect policing, by the Squad. In March 1920 he had begun an inquiry into Sinn Féin and Dáil Éireann funds, and was nominally attached to Sir Basil Thompson's Directorate of Intelligence at Scotland Yard.

Later in the year the military's attempts to obtain workable intelligence were upset, for a period, by the Bloody Sunday killings in November. However, the major intelligence difficulty at one point was the administration of all Secret Service work, with the exception of conventional police work, being for a time the responsibility of Thompson's Directorate, a situation which frequently produced chaos.

Despite these setbacks, the police under the leadership of Sir Ormonde Winter had, by the end of the year, begun to establish an intelligence system. Although the administration from Dublin Castle, at the beginning of the year, had been allowed to drift, David Lloyd George began to take more of an interest in the Irish problem and implemented a number of new initiatives. Firstly, in April, the GOC and the under-secretary for Ireland were replaced by General Sir Nevil Macready (who had been a commissioner in the London police and had improved both the discipline and morale of the force) and Sir Hamar Greenwood (a cabinet newcomer of one year's experience as a junior minister) respectively. Secondly, in May, a committee was sent to investigate the workings of the administration and found it to be in absolute chaos, having collapsed under the weight of its own inefficiency and political divisions. A drastic reorganisation then took place, marking the end of Dublin Castle government as such, with key decisions now taken by ministers in London.

The general overhaul of the Castle between 1920 and 1922 produced a radical reorganisation of the Civil Service, which ensured that the Irish state in 1922 did not inherit an outmoded ramshackle and demoralised administration but rather a thoroughly overhauled one, which was to profoundly influence the development of the new state.[86]

As these developments on the policing, intelligence and administration fronts took effect, the British cabinet decided to meet the IRA's emphasis on the use of force, and its intensification of violence in the latter part of 1920, with its own fierce campaign to defeat the IRA by military means.

4

1921

Reprisals

1 January 1921 saw the first 'official reprisal', when the army began formally to destroy houses in the wake of IRA activities, carried out under government orders in retaliation for an IRA ambush. The ambush, which had resulted in the deaths of three police officers, occurred on 29 December 1920 in Midleton, Co. Cork. Seven houses in the Midleton area were demolished by the military under the order of Brigadier General Higginson, after the occupants had been served formal notice and allowed to remove their personal belongings. The formal notice stated that the reprisals were being carried out because the inhabitants of the area had 'failed to give information to the Military or Police authorities'.

The government viewed reprisals as a punitive measure and as a deterrent, when property in the vicinity knowingly occupied by members of the Sinn Féin movement would be destroyed. On 4 January 1921 the *Daily Express* reported this first official reprisal and stated, 'This is of course martial law. It is legal and disciplined. It is, we must believe, necessary. But it is horrible.'

The policy of reprisals stimulated an outburst of protest in the press and on public platforms, which was fuelled by Sinn Féin propaganda and backed up by the IRA, whose GHQ issued orders for the destruction of unionist property in Ireland. On 14–16 May 1921 the IRA also attacked homes in England of men who were serving in Ireland as police officers. These attacks included shootings and burnings in the London, St Albans and Liverpool areas. This, and public opinion, caused the government to review its policy of reprisals and eventually dispense with it.

On 20 January 1920, after the shooting of Constable Finnegan, police had reacted to the death of this popular officer by smashing windows in property owned or occupied by members of Sinn Féin. The RIC officers involved in this unofficial reprisal were men who had joined the police to make it their life's career and were, therefore, mindful of the consequences that any disciplinary action against them would have on their future police careers. However, as the year progressed and incidences of political violence, both in number and severity, dramatically increased, the RIC was supplemented by new recruits. These new recruits were mainly ex-military and the majority came from England and Scotland, being employed under a temporary, short-service system. The ultimate threat of dismissal, the policeman's most serious punishment, held no terror for these new recruits, who had joined up in an emergency and were not embarking on a career with pension rights. They were used to the graded punishments of military discipline and the penalties enforced by the RIC were less severe and, therefore, bearable.

As the number of police casualties began to rise, feelings within the RIC and the Auxiliaries hardened, with more vengeance attacks being carried out. These started to come to a head in the latter part of 1920, when the IRA began to kill survivors of ambushes, and also with the use of expanding (or 'dumdum') bullets against the police and military, even though the Hague Convention forbade the use of this ammunition. Although most policemen had seen dead men before, especially if they had previous military service, they reported that dead RIC at ambush locations were left as 'gruesome and bloody sights'. In order to reduce attacks, proclamations were sometimes posted by the police in an area warning the locals of what would happen if any police officer was killed by the IRA, but other proclamations were placed anonymously, on occasion, by the IRA itself.

Other secret organisations were also issuing threats during this period, one being made on 11 October 1920 when the All-Ireland Anti-Sinn Féin Society Supreme Council of the Cork Circle reluctantly decided that 'if in the future any member of His Majesty's forces be murdered two members of the Sinn Féin Party in the county of Cork will be killed'.

In order to maintain discipline within the police forces, Sir Hamar Greenwood, chief secretary, addressed the RIC on 30 September 1920 at their depot in Phoenix Park, Dublin. The major part of this speech was disseminated to the force in a circular dated 28 September 1920:

Royal Irish Constabulary Office
Dublin Castle
28th September 1920

Alleged Acts of Reprisal by Police and Soldiers

Many reports have appeared in the press of alleged acts of reprisal by police and soldiers. These accounts are generally thoroughly misleading and often misrepresent acts of justifiable self-defence as reprisals; but there are cases in which unjustifiable action has undoubtedly been taken. These cases are being carefully investigated. Meanwhile it is necessary to repeat and emphasise that reprisals will ruin the discipline of the Force and cannot be countenanced by those in authority. The great provocation under which men suffer who see their comrades and friends foully murdered is fully recognised, but the police are urged to maintain, in spite of this provocation, that self-control that has characterised the Force in the past. By so doing they will earn the respect and admiration of the majority of their fellow countrymen. The police exist to restore and maintain order in the country. Destruction of buildings and institutions cannot but impoverish the country and increase want and disorder. It must, however, be made clear to all ranks that the effective use of weapons when threatened or attacked is only legitimate self-defence and that it is their duty to hunt down murderers by every means in their power. The power of the Government to bring to justice those who commit crimes is increasing every day. The police will be fully supported and protected in the discharge of their duties by every means available.

C. A. Walsh

Deputy Inspector General

issued to DCs, CIs, & DIs and all stations.[1]

On the same day as the chief secretary was addressing the RIC at Phoenix Park, District Inspector Brady was killed at Chaffpool, Co. Sligo.[2] After the death of the DI, Dublin Castle took the unprecedented step of issuing a communiqué admitting that policemen had reacted angrily, stating, 'reprisals continued till early in the morning, despite the efforts of the officers. The men were eventually got into the police lorries and while final instructions were being given by the officer, the lorries moved off and a creamery in the neighbourhood was burned.'

This incident, and two others in 1920, when police took reprisal actions – after the killing of Head Constable Burke at Balbriggan, Co. Dublin on 20 September, and on 22 September at Rineen, Co. Clare, when six policemen were killed – caused Arthur Henderson, deputy leader of the Labour Party, to move the following resolution in the House of Commons on 20 October:

> That this house regrets the present state of lawlessness in Ireland and the lack of discipline in the armed forces of the Crown, resulting in the death or injury of innocent citizens and the destruction of property; and is of [the] opinion that an independent investigation should at once be instituted into the causes, nature and extent of reprisals on the part of those whose duty is the maintenance of law and order.[3]

During the debate that followed, Sir Hamar Greenwood replied for the government in a discursive and emotional speech, part of which was as follows:

> Sir H. Greenwood: Take Balbriggan. This case has been stated, I think, by the right hon. Gentleman, the Member for Paisley (Mr. Asquith), to be comparable with a Belgian town in the War. I believe the right hon. Gentleman said he has seen some of these places. So have I. Has he seen Balbriggan?
>
> Mr Asquith: No.
>
> Sir H. Greenwood: I have. I claim to be an authority on Balbriggan. I will give the case as it is and I will admit at the start it is a case of which I, more than anyone else, have every right to regret, because it did mean a certain break in the splendid discipline of the Irish police. But when the right hon. Gentlemen or anybody else compares Balbriggan with a village [at the] Front, to the Belgian Front or any other place in the War, the statement has no relation to facts, either in the cause which led to the destruction or in the amount of destruction which resulted. Head Constable Burke, who had recently been decorated for his gallant defence of a barracks, became a marked man for the assassins in Ireland. Everyone in Ireland who gets the Royal Irish Constabulary Medal for courage, or who does anything out of the ordinary in his loyal devotion to duty, is a marked man by the terrorists in Ireland. Head Constable Burke was in Balbriggan with his brother Sergeant Burke of the Royal Irish Constabulary. It is true they had gone into a public-house. But the suggestion that the murder of Head Constable Burke and the dangerous wounding of his brother the sergeant was due to the effort of the Irish Volunteers in Balbriggan to bring about peace, as my right hon. friend the Member for Widnes suggested, is really so remote from the fact that it is in the dark. This Head Constable, unarmed, and his brother, unarmed,

were surrounded by what I call assassins – I know no other name for them – and the Head Constable was shot dead. The brother was shot and dangerously wounded. Then the assassins fled. Head Constable Burke was not only a man of great courage but a very popular man with the police. In two depots, miles away from Balbriggan, when they heard of this murder they came in lorries to Balbriggan. When they saw the bodies of Burke and of his brother they – I admit it – they saw red! I admit it with regret. I always view these actions with the profoundest regret. In Balbriggan that night 19 houses of Sinn Féiners were destroyed or damaged, four public houses were destroyed, and one hosiery factory, which employed 200 hands, was also destroyed. I admit at once that it is difficult to defend the destruction of that factory.

Lieut Commander Kenworthy: Two men were also killed.

Mr Asquith: Murdered!

Sir H. Greenwood: If the right hon. Gentlemen the Member of Paisley gets any satisfaction out of it, I will say 'murdered'. I myself have had the fullest inquiry made into the case. I will tell the House what I found. I found that from 100 to 150 men went to Balbriggan determined to avenge the death of a popular comrade shot at and murdered in cold blood. I find it is impossible out of that 150 to find the men who did the deed, who did the burning. I have had the most searching inquiry made. I have laid down a code of still more severe discipline for the Royal Irish Constabulary and I shall be glad to know that it will meet with approval. I myself had a parade of a large number of the Royal Irish Constabulary. I addressed them. I saw that what I said was published in nearly every paper in Ireland. I do not want to weary the House with a repetition of my speech, but I put the matter in as strong words as I could command that their business, and mine, was to prevent crime and to detect criminals, and when there was great provocation they must not give way. But I cannot in my heart of hearts – and, Mr Speaker, I say this – it may be right or it may be wrong – I cannot condemn in the same way those policemen who lost their heads as I condemn the assassins who provoked this outrage. My quarrel with the right hon Gentleman the Member for Paisley and his friends is that they put all the emphasis on reprisals in Ireland. I put it on the provocation.

Mr Mills: Look at Ulster!

Sir H. Greenwood: The best and the surest way to stop reprisals is to stop the murder of policemen, soldiers and loyal citizens.[4]

After the debate the government won the vote 346 to 79. The next day the *Morning Post* reported: 'Whatever we may think of these reprisals in theory, in practice they are found to be the most effective way of causing these murders to cease', and it caused Lord Hugh Cecil to observe, 'It seems to be agreed that there are no such things as reprisals, but they are having a good effect.'

The media had long since suspected that there was an official policy of reprisals, with *The Times* stating after the Balbriggan incident, 'There seems to have been behind it a directing influence.' *The Times* also stated, 'Methods inexcusable even under the loose code of revolutionaries are certainly not methods which the government of Great Britain can tolerate on the part of its servants' and on 1 October 1920 it stated, 'The name of England is being sullied throughout the Empire and throughout the world by this savagery for which the Government can no longer escape, however much they may seek to disclaim, responsibility.'

In a statement to the press on 28 September 1920 Sir Hamar Greenwood said, 'There is no truth in the allegation that the government connives at or supports reprisals. The government condemns reprisals and has issued orders condemning them and has taken steps to prevent them.'

Sir Hamar was no doubt sincere in his detestation of these reprisals and quite correct when he stated, 'the number of reprisals is few and the damage done is exaggerated', as Sinn Féin propaganda was brilliantly organised, with English and foreign journalists being taken regularly for a tour of what was known in Dublin Castle as 'The Republican Scenic Railway'.[5]

Despite the chief secretary's assurances, the reprisal campaign gathered momentum throughout October 1920 and the remainder of the year. Prior to the end of the year the RIC issued two further circulars to police officers about reprisals and discipline as follows:

> D 446
> 1920
> RI Constabulary Office
> Dublin Castle
> 12 November 1920

Discipline

The following memorandum is transmitted for the information and guidance of officers and men of the Royal Irish Constabulary.

C. A. Walsh

Deputy Inspector General

The Royal Irish Constabulary has shown unparalleled fortitude in standing up to a diabolical murder campaign. Discipline has been maintained at a very high level. To ensure uniformity of action and of discipline the following directions are issued for guidance. The RIC will have the fullest support in the most drastic action against that band of assassins, the so-called IRA. These murderers must be pursued relentlessly and their organisation ruthlessly suppressed. The initiative must be seized, the ambushers must be ambushed. The leaders and members of the criminal gang are mostly known to us. They must be given no rest. They must be hunted down. But, for the effectual performance of these duties, the highest discipline is essential. There must be no wild firing from lorries. It is useless and dangerous to innocent people. Firearms should never be fired except with the intention of hitting the object aimed at. Firing in the air or over the heads of crowds is strictly forbidden. It is dangerous to innocent people in the far distance. Property must be respected or women and children and innocent people will suffer; there must be no arson or looting. The Officers, Head Constables and Sergeants must see to this. I look to them to enforce discipline. The police exist to restore and maintain order in Ireland. They must show forbearance and preserve their discipline, whatever the provocation. Women must invariably be respected. Because the cowardly blackguards of the IRA cut women's hair, it is no reason why the RIC should retaliate by similar action. Such conduct cannot and will not be tolerated. The police grow strong every day. Decent men who have been deluded or forced into joining the IRA are resigning. By continuing their firm and resolute pressure against this criminal organisation, the police will lift the terror from the people of Ireland.

 H. H. Tudor Major General
 Police Adviser

9.11.20

issued to DCs, CIs and DIs and all existing stations

D 466
1920
Royal Irish Constabulary Office
Dublin Castle
6 December 1920

Burning of Houses, etc.

The following copy of a memorandum issued by the Police Adviser is sent for the information and guidance of officers and men of the RI Constabulary.

C. A. Walsh

Deputy Inspector General

Copy

Office of the Police Adviser
Dublin Castle

There have been recently a large number of reports of arson. Whilst by no means clear that this is done by the Forces of the Crown, I wish again to impress on all members of the Police Force the absolute necessity of stopping burnings whatever the provocation. The only justifiable burnings are the destruction of buildings which have been used to shelter ambushers or from which fire is opened on Forces of the Crown. Burnings of houses or buildings not directly connected with assassination or attempted assassination, is indefensible. I appeal to the police of all ranks to suppress all destruction of property in Ireland even of notorious Sinn Féiners. The Force will now fully recognise that the Government is giving them strong support and I feel sure that they do not wish to embarrass the Government in their very difficult task of exterminating the murder organisation. I can assure them that incendiarism tends to alienate the sympathy of many right-thinking and law-abiding citizens of the Empire and does harm to the cause of right for which we are fighting.

H. H. Tudor Major General

Police Adviser

(issued to DCs, CIs, DIs and all existing stations)[6]

Although Prime Minister Lloyd George had not publicly stated that his government had an official policy for reprisals, he hinted strongly that this was the case during a number of his speeches. On 9 October 1920, at Caernarvon, where he spoke of the necessity of breaking up the 'murder gangs', he said that: 'The police naturally feel that the time has come to defend themselves and that is what is called reprisals in Ireland. Sinn Féin could not have it both ways. If they were at war they must expect the consequences. You cannot have a one-sided war.' During the same speech he stated, 'There is no doubt that at last their [police] patience has given way and there has been some severe hitting back. Let us be fair to these gallant men who are doing their duty in Ireland. It is no use talking about this being war and these being reprisals when these things are being done [by the IRA] with impunity in Ireland.'[7]

Another speech which hinted at reprisals was made on 9 November 1920 at the Guildhall Banquet when he stated, 'We have murder by the throat, we had to reorganise the police. When the Government was ready we struck the terrorists and now the terrorists are complaining of terror.'

On 11 December 1920 members of the RIC Auxiliary Division carried out their largest reprisal when they burned part of Cork city as a direct response to an ambush on one of their patrols earlier in the day in the city at Dillons Cross. During that attack thirteen Auxiliaries were wounded, one fatally. After this act some members of the Auxiliaries began to wear pieces of half-burnt cork in their headdress or on their revolver lanyards. This one act of reprisal cost the government two million pounds in damages and caused it great political difficulties and embarrassment. The incident also probably forced the government to make official reprisals public, so that they could be performed in a disciplined manner, but these official reprisals had the effect of rallying Irish opinion, and almost the whole London press, against the government and its policy.

With this political background, the related violence in Ireland continued into 1921.

1 January 1921, Ballybay, Co. Monaghan
Michael Francis Malone, Con 70142

At 9 p.m. four policemen from Ballybay were patrolling Main Street when they were attacked by armed men from gateways on either side of the street. The patrol returned fire and was reinforced by a further three officers from the local barracks.

The fight between the police and their attackers was a prolonged one, with the police running short of ammunition. Meanwhile, the three policemen still in the barracks sent up Very lights to indicate the need for assistance. These signals were seen at Dundalk, twenty-four miles away, and a joint RIC/military force in two Crossley tenders was despatched.

As the reinforcements passed through Castleblayney they were stopped and informed that an ambushing party of 200 IRA men was entrenched on the main road three miles from Ballybay. Because of this information, the reinforcements left their vehicles at Castleblayney and proceeded on foot the eight miles to Ballybay. On their arrival, they found the body of Constable Malone lying in Main Street. He had been shot in the right side of his face at close range, probably with buckshot, and killed. He was almost unrecognisable. Close by, the body of a dead civilian called Somerville was found. He was from Ballybay.

Three Auxiliary policemen – Constables Brown, Cromwell and Van Best – were wounded, one of them sustaining a bad eye injury. These injured officers were moved to Louth County Infirmary at Dundalk.

After this incident six men were arrested and taken to Monaghan. One of them was found to have a severe head wound when he was arrested. In July 1921 ten Monaghan men were charged at a general court martial at Victoria Barracks, Belfast with the death of the constable.

Constable Malone, a thirty-year-old bachelor and First World War veteran, was from Co. Westmeath. He would have had one year's police service on 20 January 1921, having been a clerk and a soldier before joining the RIC.

1 January 1921, Parnell Bridge, Cork city
Thomas R. Johnston, Con 74669
Francis Shortall, Con 64741

On 1 January 1921, at 7 p.m., a party of ten RIC men made their way out of Union Quay headquarters, the main RIC barracks in Cork city. As they crossed Parnell Bridge a bomb was thrown at them. The RIC men then came under revolver fire from their ambushers. On their arrival, police reinforcements found that six had been wounded. They were removed to Union Quay Barracks and then to Cork Military Hospital. Five civilians were also injured by bullets and bomb splinters. The IRA had made their attack from the ruins of a public house.

Constable Francis Shortall succumbed to his wounds on 7 January. He was thirty-eight and recently married. From Co. Tipperary, he had eleven years' police service, having been a soldier before joining the RIC. On 5 August 1914 he had rejoined the Irish Guards, being commissioned later in the First World War in the rank of captain. He acted as an interpreter as he had knowledge of Irish, French and German, before being taken prisoner. On 21 February 1919 he rejoined the RIC.

On 21 January Constable Johnston, a nineteen-year-old single man from Co. Cavan, also died from his wounds. He would have had three months' police service on 20 January 1921, having been a labourer before joining the RIC.

7 January 1921, near Ballinalee, Co. Longford
Thomas James McGrath, MM, DI 65788

The district inspector was accompanying a small patrol searching for Seán MacEoin, a blacksmith from Ballinalee and the Longford IRA Brigade commander. It would appear that the DI knocked at the door of a cottage at about 4.30 p.m. at Kilshrewley in the Lislea district, which is one mile from the village of Ballinalee and about five miles from Granard. MacEoin opened the door and at once fired on the RIC officer, shooting him through the head. A bomb was then thrown at the remaining members of the RIC patrol, wounding two constables, before MacEoin escaped.

DI McGrath was thirty and single. From Co. Limerick, he had joined the RIC in 1911 as a constable, and the Royal Irish Regiment on 7 June 1916. He was commissioned into the Third West Yorkshire Regiment as a captain and rejoined the RIC on 18 October 1919. He was promoted to DI on 24 November 1920.

Seán MacEoin was captured in March on a train at Mullingar. In July 1921 Mrs McGrath and her three sons sent a letter to Lord FitzAlan, lord lieutenant of Ireland, urging mercy for John Joseph MacEoin. In the letter Mrs McGrath stated, 'I, the mother of the late DI, appeal to you in an especial manner to give effect to our wishes and in doing so desire it to be understood that the sorrow and loss sustained by us will be all the greater should it entail the loss of a single additional life.' A similar letter was sent by the McGraths to the chief secretary.

13 January 1921, Cratloe, Co. Clare
Stephen Carty, Sgt 58105
Jeremiah Curtin, Sgt 60459

An RIC patrol was making its way from Ennis to Limerick by lorry when it was ambushed at noon as it had almost reached the railway station at Cratloe, about six miles from Limerick. The lorry, which contained two sergeants and six constables, was ambushed by forty to fifty men from two unused houses, one standing at either side of the roadway. Sergeant Carty, who was severely wounded, fell from the lorry onto the road and died from his wounds a short time later. He had been in charge of the patrol. Sergeant Curtin and two constables were wounded. The remaining uninjured men picked up the body of the sergeant, and the whole party drove to Limerick, but Sergeant Curtin died as he was carried into the Military Hospital.

Sergeant Curtin was in charge of Inch police hut when it was attacked a year previously, while Sergeant Carty had been in charge of Ruan Barracks when it had recently been attacked.

Carty, a forty-five-year-old single man, was from Co. Roscommon. He had twenty-two years' service, having been a farmer prior to joining the RIC. Curtin, from Co. Cork, was forty-three and married. He had nineteen years' police service, having previously been a farmer.

13 January 1921, near Crossmaglen, Co. Armagh
Robert William Compston, S/Con

A party of five policemen was escorting a postman carrying old age pensioners' money on his rounds from Crossmaglen to Cullyhanna. The postman was cycling about fifteen yards in front of the patrol. At a sharp bend in the roadway beyond Ballyfarnham Lodge, they were ambushed by approximately fifty men with rifles, revolvers and shotguns from a vacant house and from behind the hedge that lined the roadway.

The postman was shot in the back and fell to the ground, while the police and their attackers became locked in a fierce battle that lasted for a considerable time, with Constable Boylan being hit in the chest. When the firing ceased, the police searched for the postman but could not find him so they returned to Crossmaglen with their wounded comrade.

A force of police in a Crossley tender was sent from Crossmaglen to find the postman. When they were about 200 yards from the ambush location, the police moved forward on foot, firing on both sides of the road as they went. When Special Constable Compston was about three yards inside the gate leading to the house, which sat twenty yards back from the road, a rifle shot rang out, wounding him in the groin. The police rushed the house but their attackers had gone. Compston died from his wounds as he was taken to Louth Infirmary and was the first member of the newly formed Ulster Special Constabulary to lose his life. From Whitecross, Co. Armagh, he was an unmarried twenty-four-year-old stationed at Crossmaglen. The postman also died from his wounds. He was a twenty-three-year-old ex-soldier from Crossmaglen.

The IRA man who led this attack was Frank Aiken, a twenty-two-year-old Camlough man, who later became the IRA's 4th Northern Division commandant, and later still the IRA's chief of staff.

When the house was searched, a revolver and a haversack which contained 100 cartridges full of buckshot were found, along with two parcels of food. Also on the floor of the house was some hay, on which the men in the house had apparently been sleeping. Outside the house a single-barrelled shotgun was found.

According to Toby Harnden, in *'Bandit country'*, the house later became known as the 'Ambush House', and it was not the first time that it had seen violence, having been burned by Lord Blaney's men in June 1797, as it then belonged to a rebel leader of the United Irishmen by the name of Donaldson.

14 JANUARY 1921, ARMAGH CITY
John J. Kemp, Sgt 58633

At 9.30 p.m. Sergeant Kemp was walking along Market Street and was opposite the Technical School when he was wounded by a bomb.

A civilian who was in the street at the time also received wounds in this attack. Two masked men were seen immediately after the attack running up Market Street before disappearing.

Sergeant Kemp was taken to the infirmary but died from his wounds on 23 January. Forty-two and married, he was from Co. Cavan. He had twenty-two years' service on 3 January 1921, having been a farmer before joining the RIC. On 26 January he was buried in the New Cemetery, Cavan. He had served in Armagh for twenty years. After this attack the local UVF patrolled the streets of the city, stopping and searching every person coming from Thomas Street and other areas of the city.

17 January 1921, Cappawhite, Co. Tipperary
Robert A. E. Boyd, Con 70823

At 9.30 p.m. Constable Boyd entered the licensed premises of Mrs Margaret Moran and was sitting at the kitchen fire drinking a glass of stout with his back partly turned to the door, talking to two of Mrs Moran's nieces. Four revolver shots rang out and he was shot dead in the chair. It was believed that two or three men were involved in this attack, but none of them was seen. After the shots were fired, retreating footsteps were heard. One of Mrs Moran's nieces was wounded in the leg.

Constable Boyd was a single man who had just turned twenty-four on 27 December 1920. He was from Banbridge, Co. Down, and would have had ten months' police service on 22 January. He had served with the Royal Irish Fusiliers during the First World War. In May he had been one of the defenders at the siege of Cappawhite RIC Barracks. The dead constable's father and two brothers were also members of the RIC.

On 19 January the constable's remains left Dublin on the 6 p.m.

train for Scarva, where a guard of honour of local RIC officers transferred the coffin to the Banbridge train. At 9.15 p.m. family members and a detachment of the local RIC force met the train, with the police carrying the coffin in relays from the railway station to the constable's father's home.

20 JANUARY 1921, LISTOWEL, CO. KERRY
Tobias O'Sullivan, DI 59193

District Inspector O'Sullivan, who was one of the defenders at Kilmallock Barracks on 28 May 1920, was shot dead at 1.20 p.m., twenty yards from the police barracks at Listowel, Co. Kerry. At the time of his death the DI was walking from the barracks with his seven-year-old son towards his home, which was a short distance along the street. Half a dozen shots rang out and he fell dead, shot through the head and body.

In a private letter a ten-year-old girl, who only recounted the incident to her son in 1950, stated that she was looking out of the window when she saw an officer and his son crossing the street. She saw them stop in the middle of the street, as the officer saw guns aimed at him, and he told his son to run on into the house. She watched him gunned down. (The policeman's son was a playmate of hers, although she was some three years older. The incident left a powerful mark on the witness, so much so that she effectively suppressed much of her Irishness in later life, as she concentrated on a new life in England.)

On 24 January 1921, after Mass in James's Street church, O'Sullivan was buried at Glasnevin Cemetery, Dublin, with full military honours. His cortège was led by a contingent of Auxiliary police with their arms reversed. They were followed by the bands of the Lancashire Fusiliers, DMP and RIC, with the coffin following behind. A number of RIC officers walked on either side of the coffin and acted as pall-bearers, while behind the remains a large number of senior officials followed, including the lord lieutenant, inspector general of the RIC, commissioner of the DMP and other divisional and headquarters staff of the RIC. A contingent of RIC with their arms reversed and a group from the DMP came next. They were followed by the bereaved relatives, including DI O'Sullivan's widow, son and two daughters, and a large number of friends and colleagues. The rear of the procession was brought up by the carriages of bereaved relatives and friends. At the conclusion of the service the Last Post was sounded.

Background
It is thought that early in December 1920 a top-level IRA meeting was held in Dublin at which IRA headquarters staff directed that Kerry's Sixth Battalion would shoot DI O'Sullivan, for reasons which they listed as follows:

i) The DI could identify prisoners held on Spike Island, Cork, as being persons who had participated in the attack on Kilmallock Barracks.
ii) It was believed that the DI was responsible for the death of the IRA man Liam Scully, who was a popular IRA member in the North Kerry area, during the attack on the barracks at Kilmallock.
iii) However, the main reason for this decision was probably DI O'Sullivan's dedication to duty and the courage and leadership he showed at Kilmallock, coupled with his enthusiastic and energetic approach to duty since his appointment as DI in North Kerry.[8]

Later, as a result of information, eight men were arrested, four being found guilty of murder. Two of these men were sentenced to death, but all four were released after the Truce.

The information which led to their arrests came from two people, one being Miss Burke of Charles Street, Listowel, who later had to leave the country, and a fishery inspector, James Kane. Mr Kane was an ex-RIC sergeant whom the IRA ordered to be killed in May. They alleged they had found his sworn statement about the DI's death on RIC Divisional Commander Major P. A. Holmes on 28 January 1921 when they seriously wounded him at Toureengarriv.

On 11 June 1921 IRA men from the Sixth Kerry Battalion's flying column found James Kane at Shanacool Bridge as he performed his duty as a fishery inspector. He was kidnapped and later killed, his body being found on 15 June. James Kane's brother, John, was a chief inspector, whom Scotland Yard assigned to the 'Irish Crown Jewels case'.[9]

On 1 March 1921 an RIC pensioner, Patrick Roche, was shot at Causeway, Listowel, Co. Kerry. He was taken from his home and shot, his body being found in a field a short distance away. Pinned to his body was a card with the words: 'Convicted spy. All informers beware IRA.'

DI O'Sullivan, a forty-three-year-old married man with a family, was from Co. Galway. He had twenty-one years' police service, having been a farmer prior to joining the RIC. He had four brothers in the RIC, including one who had joined the Jamaican police.

20 January 1921, Glenwood, Co. Clare

William Clarke, DI 72020
Michael Mulloy, Sgt 61673
John Doogue, Con 64362
Michael Moran, Con 69674
Frank E. Morris, Con 74768
William J. Smith, Con 72706

An RIC patrol in a Crossley tender was ambushed by a large body of men at about 4 p.m. at Glenwood, four miles from Sixmilebridge on the Broadford road. When the police patrol reached Belvoir, heavy and rapid concentrated fire was opened on it, killing the district inspector outright. As the remainder of the patrol tried to retire to shelter, they were hit by volleys of gunfire from the woods, leading to heavy casualties.

The attack resulted in the deaths of six RIC officers, the serious wounding of Sergeant Egan and the slight wounding of Constable Selve. Two other constables escaped uninjured. The wounded sergeant and constable were later taken to Limerick military barracks for treatment. After the ambush the IRA took the police weapons, except for Sergeant Egan's rifle – although seriously wounded, he succeeded in retaining it. They also set fire to the police tender before disappearing.

The bodies of the dead police officers were taken to Sixmilebridge. DI Clarke, who was in charge of the RIC at Sixmilebridge, had served with the Second Canadian Mounted Rifles at Winnipeg before being commissioned into the Royal Irish Rifles attached to the Ulster Division. He was captured in March 1918 and remained a POW until the end of the First World War. The DI first served as an Auxiliary cadet before his commission into the RIC. On 22 January he was buried at the Presbyterian graveyard in Lurgan, Co. Armagh. His body arrived in Lurgan on the 9.14 a.m. train from Dublin and was met by huge crowds.

Sergeant Mulloy, a thirty-eight-year-old married man, was from Co. Mayo. He would have had fifteen years' police service on 1 February 1921. Constable Doogue, thirty-four and single, was from Queen's County. He had twelve years' police service. Constable Moran, twenty-three and single, was from Liscromwell, Castlebar, Co. Mayo. He had one year's police service. All three had been farmers before joining the RIC. Constable Morris, twenty-seven and also single, was from Lancashire and resided at Salisbury Road, Richmond, London. He would have had three months' police service in two days' time, having been a seaman and a soldier prior to joining the RIC. Constable Smith, the same age and status, was from London and resided at Chalkpit Cottages, Sarro, West Birchington, Kent. He would have had five months' police service on 31 January, having been a clerk and a soldier before joining the RIC.

21 JANUARY 1921,
NEAR WATERFALL, CO. CORK
Henry J. Bloxham, Sgt 58519

A head constable and a sergeant were ambushed some distance from Waterfall, about five miles from Cork. Both officers were stationed at Ballincollig and had left their barracks on bicycles to ride to Waterfall. As they approached the Waterfall Railway Station, they were ambushed from behind a fence.

Sergeant Bloxham, a forty-one-year-old married man from Co. Mayo, was shot dead, while Head Constable Larkin, although slightly wounded, was able to return fire and escape. Bloxham had twenty-two years' police service, having been a clerk before joining the RIC. He was buried on 25 January at the New Cemetery.

22 JANUARY 1921,
STRANOODEN, CO. MONAGHAN
Sidney George Clarke, Con 76744
Robert Henry Hegerty, Con 73068
Frederick Taylor, Con 75307

Between 8 and 9 p.m. three off-duty policemen who were stationed at Stranooden (which was about four miles from Monaghan) went for a walk along the main Monaghan to Rockcorry road. When they had not returned to their barracks by 10 p.m., the alarm was raised and a search party sent out. The bodies of two constables were found at 10.15 p.m. about a quarter of a mile from the barracks, riddled with bullets and, from examination of the scene, it was believed that the bodies were fired into whilst lying on the ground.

Constable Clarke was not discovered until 8 a.m. the following morning, lying unconscious in a nearby creamery building. Although wounded six times, Clarke is believed to have crawled to the building. He was taken to Monaghan Infirmary but, because of his wounds and exposure, was not expected to live. He died on 30 January.

All three constables were ex-soldiers and had only been stationed in Stranooden about a month. Constable Clarke, nineteen and single, was from London and lived at Lissan Street, Edgware Road. He had just over one month's service on 17 January and was a footman before joining the RIC. His body was later taken from the County Infirmary by train to Belfast *en route* to London. It was accorded full military honours as it was being moved.

Constable Hegerty, an eighteen-year-old single man, was from Cork city. He had four months' police service on 11 January, having been a soldier prior to joining the RIC.

Constable Taylor was a single man who would have been twenty-five in three days' time. He was from Plymouth but had joined the RIC from Malta. He had two months' police service on 9 January, having been a driller and a soldier before joining the RIC.

26 January 1921, Townhall Street, Belfast city
Thomas Heffron, Con 69264
Michael Quinn, Con 69729

Three constables of the RIC's reserve force attached to the depot in Phoenix Park, Dublin, were sent to Belfast. They stayed at the Railway View Hotel in Townhall Street, a few minutes walk from the central police station, and had retired to their beds at an early hour.

At 9.45 p.m. five men who had been sitting in the snug of the bar rose and appeared to be leaving the hotel, but then made their way upstairs to the constables' rooms, where they shot them as they lay in bed. Two of the officers were killed; Constable Gilmartin was left in a critical condition and was later taken to the Military Hospital. Gilmartin was a witness in Sergeant Fallon's killing on 3 November 1920 at Ballymote, Co. Sligo, and had been sent to Belfast to identify prisoners in Belfast gaol. The other two constables were acting as his special escort.[10]

Constable Heffron, a twenty-six-year-old single man, was from Doonfeeney, Ballycastle, Co. Mayo. He had three years' police service, having been a farmer before joining the RIC. Constable Quinn, twenty and single, was from Queen's County. He had one year's police service, having been a farmer before joining the RIC. Each man was buried at his native place.

26 January 1921, Trim, Co. Meath
Robert J. W. Barney, Con 74970

Six RIC men attached to the barracks at Trim were on patrol in Haggard Street on their way to the railway station when they were ambushed from behind a wall. Three constables were wounded, with Constable Barney dying from his wounds on 2 February.

Constable Barney was twenty-three and recently married. He was from London and would have had three months' police service three days later, having been a grocer's assistant and a soldier before joining the RIC.

28 January 1921, Toureengarriv, Co. Kerry
Philip Armstrong Holmes, Divisional Commissioner RIC 58074
Thomas Moyles, Con 71364

At 12.30 p.m. Divisional Commissioner Holmes, who had replaced the dead Divisional Commissioner Smyth, was travelling with an escort of six men in two cars when they were ambushed in Toureengarriv, Co. Kerry, about seven miles from Castleisland on the borders of Counties Cork and Kerry. The patrol had left Tralee and was going to Cork via Castleisland, Kingwilliamstown and Kanturk.

During the attack Constable Moyles was killed, and all the other members of the patrol were wounded. Moyles, a twenty-one-year-old single man, was from Co. Mayo. He had eight months' police service, having previously been a farmer.

It is believed the divisional commissioner was returning from Listowel, where he had been obtaining evidence about the death of DI O'Sullivan. This evidence, along with the weapons and one car belonging to the RIC, were taken by the IRA after the attack.

Background
On 27 January 1921 IRA men saw a two-car military patrol making its way through Toureengarriv and along the Ballydesmond road. The IRA decided to prepare an ambush at the most suitable place that could be found on the off-chance that these vehicles would return by the same route.

Some sixty men from the flying column of the Newmarket Battalion, Cork No. 2 (North) Brigade, and from the local company began to prepare the ambush some twenty-four hours before the patrol's arrival in the area. They were under the command of Seán Moylan, who became a minister in the Irish Government in the late 1940s. Moylan had a trench dug across the road at a bend in the roadway. To the south-west of this trench he had a Hotchkiss light machine gun placed on a hill that overlooked the road. Behind a fence on the north-east side of the road a number of IRA men armed with rifles and shotguns were placed to cut off any possible retreat. IRA lookouts were positioned on Mount Falvey, to the north-west of the roadway, and this gave them a view over the whole area.

The Attack

The driver of the first car, on seeing the trench dug into the roadway, skidded to a halt as the Hotchkiss machine gun opened fire. All the police dismounted from their vehicles and began to return fire from behind a fence, being trapped in the rugged glen. The IRA called on the patrol to surrender several times but the RIC men refused to do so until they had exhausted their ammunition, by which time every one of them had been wounded.[11] One of the wounded men, a Constable Callery, was only on the patrol because he had taken the place of a colleague whose wife had become ill. The wounded included Sergeant Arthur E. Charman, 70290, who had been promoted on 1 January 1921, and Constables Francis Callery, 61783, James Hoare, 62479, Francis D. Calder, 70776 and John H. Andrews, 72788.

As the patrol approached the scene of the ambush Constable Callery had changed places in the car with Constable Moyles, who was to be shot dead a short time later. After the attack some of the IRA men involved began to search the pockets of the RIC officers and were heard by one of the wounded policemen to say that it was great to feel the blood of the English on their hands. As they searched the wounded RIC officers the IRA men threw their personal items into the ditches. This stopped, however, and the items were retrieved when the IRA leader appeared on the scene and threatened to shoot the individuals concerned.[12]

The divisional commissioner and all the seriously wounded were taken by private car to Castleisland and a party of military from Tralee brought in the remaining wounded and the body of Constable Moyles. Early the next morning a special train brought two Cork city surgeons to Tralee to operate on Mr Holmes. Later that day he was removed to Cork Military Hospital, but he died that evening from his wounds. During the First World War he had been commissioned into the Royal Irish Regiment and later served with the Royal Irish Fusiliers. He was wounded twice and gassed at the Front, and had to return to Newtownards. Later in the war he served in the Ulster Division with the Royal Irish Rifles, and before the Armistice he was attached to the intelligence office for the Midland District Irish Command, the headquarters of which was at the Curragh.

Constable Moyles' body was removed from Ballina Roman Catholic cathedral after Requiem Mass on 2 February 1921 for interment in Moygownagh Cemetery. His remains were escorted by an honour guard of RIC under the command of Captain White DI.

Holmes, a forty-four-year-old single man, was from Cork city. He would have had twenty-three years' police service on 2 February 1921.

1 February 1921,
Drimoleague, Co. Cork
Patrick James O'Connor, Con 69676

Around 9 p.m. four policemen were ambushed in the village of Drimoleague, nine miles from Skibbereen. The ambushers who, it was thought, numbered twenty, fired from behind a three-foot wall as the police were walking towards their barracks, which was less than fifty yards away. Constable O'Connor was shot dead as he was making his way to the barracks for assistance, while Constable Griffin was seriously wounded. The other two constables escaped by running back into Main Street. The ambush location had been used before, in October 1920 when Sergeant Dee was seriously wounded.

Constable O'Connor had served with distinction in the First World War and had been decorated. He was twenty-two, single, from Co. Mayo and had one year's police service, having been in the Royal Navy before joining the RIC. Just before the attack the constables heard the command, 'Fire, let them have it boys!' given in a loud voice from about fifteen yards away. Immediately after this command, rapid fire was opened on them.

This attack was carried out by IRA men under the command of Daniel O'Driscoll, the local IRA company captain. He hoped the ambush would draw reinforcements from the Auxiliary company at Dunmanway into a second ambush half a mile from the village of Gloundaw.

2 February 1921,
Balbriggan, Co. Dublin
Samuel Green, Con 75477

Constable Green, a twenty-two-year-old single man, was from Middlesex. He had two months' police service, having been a soldier before joining the RIC. A member of the Veterans' Corps attached to Gormanston Camp, he was shot at 9.30 p.m. by three armed men in a public house in Balbriggan. He died from his wounds the next day in Steeven's Hospital, Dublin.

2 February 1921,
Trinity Street, Dublin city
Patrick Mullany, Con 65685

Constable Mullany, a thirty-four-year-old single man from Co. Cavan, had ten years' service on 3 January 1921, having been a dairyman before joining the RIC. He had recently been attached as a driver to the transport depot of the RIC at Phoenix Park, Dublin.

On 2 February he and another constable, both in plain clothes, had been on a visit to a friend's house. They were returning by bicycle and at 9.40 p.m. were in Trinity Street near the Moira Hotel when they were called upon to stop by four men, who then fired at them. Constable Mullany was shot in the back and members of the DMP on duty nearby had him taken to the Mercer's Hospital, but he was dead on arrival.

2 February 1921,
Maryborough, Queen's County
William Vanston, Con

Constable Vanston, who was from Belfast, was on a short visit to his wife's home and was leaving the house at the Turnpike on the Dublin road when he was shot and killed. His family had long connections with the RIC, although he had only two weeks' service. He was twenty-six, married with two children and had served with the Royal Engineers during the First World War. Before his death he had worked in Glasgow.

At 6.30 a.m. when he was leaving the house, a young man on a bicycle rode up to him and hastily dismounted. This man fired twice at the constable before riding off. The wounded constable cried out for help and his wife rushed out to his aid.

The dead constable's father was an ex-head constable, whilst his uncle was a DI in Dublin. His cousin, William Hargrove, was a constable at Brown Square, Belfast.

Constable Vanston would appear not to have been issued with an RIC number.

2 February 1921,
Ballinalee, Co. Longford
Francis Worthington Craven, DSO, DSC, DSM, DI 80043
George Bush, Cadet 79943
Harold Clayton, DCM, Cadet 80248
John A. Houghton, Cadet 80249

At 2 p.m. two lorries with seventeen Auxiliaries were travelling from Granard to Longford when they were ambushed by the IRA's Longford Brigade under the command of Seán MacEoin at Clonfin, about midway between Granard and Ballinalee. Houghton was killed outright when his vehicle was blown up, DI Craven died at the scene and Cadets Bush and Clayton died from their wounds on 4 February 1921 at Steeven's Hospital, Dublin.

When crossing a small bridge at the bottom of a slight hill, the first lorry was blown up, killing Houghton and wounding all the others travelling in it. About fifty IRA men then opened fire on the second lorry from both sides of the road. A pitched battle ensued for ten to fifteen minutes until the Auxiliaries were compelled to surrender when their ammunition had been exhausted.

During the ambush DI Craven had been wounded in the leg and was bandaging it when he was struck in the neck and killed. After their surrender MacEoin, who was wearing a Sam Browne belt, stepped forward to the wounded police officers and stated, 'I am Commandant MacEoin.' He congratulated the police on their fight, gave permission for the wounded police officers to be attended to, during which time he denied that he had killed DI McGrath (see pp. 229–30), and allowed them to leave the scene for Longford Military Hospital in one of the lorries. The IRA burned the other vehicle and removed the police weapons before leaving the area, going in the direction of Ballinalee.

The next day the wounded Auxiliaries were taken by special train from Longford to Broadstone Station and then by ambulance to Steeven's Hospital. Six of the wounded were stretcher cases and were accompanied from Longford by doctors and nurses.

DI Craven, a single man, had been a lieutenant-commander in the Royal Navy and held the DSO, DSC and DSM. As the captain of a destroyer he performed outstanding duty when the *Toronto* came to grief off the north-west coast of Ireland, and hundreds of American lives were saved. He joined the RIC on 20 December 1920 and was attached to M Company with his Auxiliary number being 1305. On 31 December 1920 he was made intelligence officer. He was from Barrow-in-Furness and was buried on 5 February 1921 at Dalton-on-Furness. He would have been twenty-three years old on 29 February 1921.

Cadet Bush joined the RIC on 15 June 1920 before transferring to the Auxiliary Division on 19 November 1920. When he joined he was given the RIC number 71657; his Auxiliary number was 1073. When he joined the Auxiliary Division he was initially attached to B Company. On 29 January 1921 he was transferred to M Company. He was a single man from Hertfordshire and would have been twenty-four years old on 24 February 1921.

Cadet Clayton joined the RIC on 1 January 1921; his Auxiliary number was 1514. He was a twenty-four-year-old single man who during the First World War had served with the Royal Field Artillery, being awarded a DCM. He was from Yorkshire.

Cadet Houghton, twenty-six, also joined the RIC on 1 January 1921, being appointed to M Company. His Auxiliary number was 1375. He had been married for just two months. During the First World War he had served as a lieutenant with the Royal Sussex Regiment and he had transferred from the Staffordshire Constabulary to the Auxiliary Division of the RIC. He was from Gloucester.

The bodies of these dead officers were later taken back to England. MacEoin was captured on 2 March when he was arrested by police and military on a train at Mullingar. When he was being removed from the train handcuffed he escaped down a canal towpath near the station, but was recaptured a quarter of an hour later. In June 1921 at his court martial, three of the Auxiliary witnesses paid tribute to him for his actions at the ambush scene.[13]

3 FEBRUARY 1921, DROMKEEN, CO. LIMERICK

Samuel Adams, Con 75905
George William Bell, Con 75644
John Joseph Bourke, Con 66247
Michael Doyle, Con 71009
Patrick Foody, Con 58968

William Hayton, Con 74603
William Kingston, Con 76041
Sidney Millin, Con 73738
Bernard Mollaghan, Con 61122
Arthur Pearce, Con 72803
Henry Smith, Con 75901

A police patrol of thirteen men in two lorries was returning from Fedamore to New Pallas. At 2.30 p.m. the patrol was ambushed near Pallasgreen, about three miles from New Pallas. The ambush took place at a turn in the road where it forked for Dromkeen Railway Station and the Pallas/Old Pallas road.

The police patrol was attacked by a large party of men who were concealed near the road. They took them completely by surprise and most of the casualties were sustained in the opening volleys of fire from both sides of the road. Nine of the policemen were killed outright, with two others being severely wounded and dying later.

The IRA had placed barricades across both roads so that the police vehicles had no way of driving out of the ambush. After the attack all the weapons belonging to the police were removed by the IRA.

Background
Early in 1921 police located and captured the arms dump belonging to the Mid Limerick Brigade, which was a major setback for the IRA in the area and one which forced the East and Mid Limerick brigades to consider joint actions. The IRA was keen to strike back at the RIC.

The IRA, through John Purcell, the intelligence officer for the Mid Limerick Brigade, discovered that an RIC patrol regularly travelled to Fedamore, eleven miles from New Pallas, returning the same day normally via the same route. The IRA also became aware that this patrol usually appeared on the first Thursday of each month. On 3 February 1921 the flying columns of the East and Mid Limerick brigades, under the overall command of D. O'Hannigan, arrived at a prearranged assembly point at Cloverfield, Kilkeely, one mile from the proposed ambush site. There they remained until noon, when it was confirmed by one of the large number of IRA scouts in the area that the police patrol had made its way towards Fedamore. By 12.30 p.m. the IRA men were in their ambush positions waiting for the returning patrol.

The IRA used farm carts as barricades but did not prepare any fire positions. They were reluctant to leave any signs that they had been present in the area in case the ambush had to be postponed for any reason, as they intended to return to the same ambush location if they were unable to carry out this attack.

At 2.30 p.m. the IRA scouts reported the return of the patrol, at which stage the barricades were placed across the roads. The first RIC lorry into the ambush contained five men. The driver and DI Sampson were able to get out and later escape. One of the constables in the rear of the vehicle was seriously wounded, with the other two being slightly wounded. The two less-wounded officers began to fire from the roadway at their attackers, but were both killed under heavy volleys of gunfire.

As the second Crossley tender was forced to stop, five of its occupants were killed either in the first few volleys of gunfire or shortly afterwards as they attempted to fight back from the roadway. Another constable in this vehicle was seriously wounded and died from his wounds shortly afterwards.

The two remaining constables took shelter under the vehicle and were firing from the cover of its wheels. These two officers were called on to surrender. They refused, and their brave last-ditch stand was quickly extinguished when a Limerick city IRA man, Johnny Vaughan, who was attached to the Mid Limerick flying column, was able to get into a location from which, at close range, he could fire under the vehicle. The two constables, Smith and Pearce, died later from their wounds.[14]

Constable Adams, a twenty-one-year-old single man, was from Lanark. He had two months' police service, having been a coach painter and a soldier before joining the RIC. Constable Bell, the same age and status, was from Northumberland. He would have had three months' police service on 18 February, having been a labourer and a soldier prior to joining the RIC.

Constable Bourke was thirty and from Co. Kilkenny. He had nine years' police service, having been a gamekeeper before joining the RIC.

Constable Doyle, a thirty-one-year-old single man, was from Dublin. He would have had ten months' police service on 6 February 1921, having been a rough rider and a soldier before joining the RIC.

Constable Foody, a forty-five-year-old single man, was from Co. Sligo. He had twenty-one years' police service, having been a farmer before joining the RIC.

Constable Hayton, a twenty-one-year-old single man, was from Yorkshire. He would have had four months' police service on 19 February, having been a soldier prior to joining the RIC.

Constable Kingston was married and from London. He had turned thirty-six the day before he was killed. He had three months' police service, having been a painter and a soldier before joining the RIC.

Constable Millin, a twenty-four-year-old married man, was from London. He had four months' police service on 1 February, having been a motor mechanic and a soldier prior to joining the RIC. Constable Mollaghan was forty-four and married. From Co. Longford, he had eighteen years' service. Constable Pearce, a twenty-three-year-old single man, was from Lancashire. He would have had three months' police service on 7 February. Both men were labourers prior to joining the RIC.

Constable Smith was a single man from Selkirk who would have been twenty-four on 12 February. He would have had three months' police service on 24 February, having been a mill worker and a soldier before joining the RIC.

3 February 1921, Ballinhassig, Co. Cork
Edward Carter, Con 75523
William H. Taylor, Con 75998

At 1.15 p.m. four constables were ambushed at Tulligbeg by approximately thirty armed men. Two were shot dead and Constable Fuller was seriously wounded. He and his two dead colleagues were later removed to Cork Military Barracks.

All the constables were attached to Ballinhassig Barracks. The cycle patrol had been to a neighbouring town to buy stores when it was ambushed from a riverbank on one side of the road and from a high bank on the other. The dead and wounded police officers' revolvers were taken by their attackers.

Constable Carter, a nineteen-year-old single man, was from Lancashire. He would have had three months' police service on 16 February, having been a hotel porter before joining the RIC.

Constable Taylor, twenty-eight and single, was from Yorkshire. He had two months' police service, having been a soldier prior to joining the RIC.

6 February 1921, Warrenpoint, Co. Down
John Cummings, S/Con

A patrol of special constables was ambushed at Seaview Road, Warrenpoint, at 10.15 p.m. Their attackers had hidden behind a wall in the street and after hurling a number of bombs at the patrol, they opened fire on them. All the members of the patrol were seriously wounded. Special Constable Cummings had been wounded twice by shrapnel in the back and was taken to a nearby house where his wounds were dressed by a local doctor. His wife accompanied him to hospital but he died from his wounds on the way. He had been married on 9 July 1920 and was buried on 9 February 1921 from his father's home at 47 Oldpark Road, Belfast, to Seapatrick. As his funeral was passing Crumlin Road gaol it was jeered by IRA prisoners.

12 February 1921, Charleville, Co. Cork
Patrick Joseph Walsh, Con 68763

Constable Walsh from Churchtown was on leave in Charleville and at 9.45 p.m. had just left a public house about 100 yards from the local RIC barracks when he was shot dead. This attack was carried out by IRA men attached to Cork No. 2 Brigade, which at that time was under the command of Paddy O'Brien.

Constable Walsh was twenty-three and single. From Turloughbeg, Rosmuck, Co. Galway, he had four years' police service, having had no other employment before joining the RIC.

13 February 1921, Ballough, Co. Dublin
John P. Lynch, Con 61290

At 2.45 p.m. a patrol of thirteen RIC in a Crossley tender was proceeding from Balbriggan to Swords when it was ambushed at Ballough. Constable Lynch was seriously wounded and later died from his injuries. He was a thirty-seven-year-old married man from Co. Mayo and had seventeen years' service, having had no other employment before joining the force.

14 February 1921, Ballywilliam, Co. Tipperary
John Carroll, Con 62113

The constable, stationed at Cork city, had gone to visit his parents at Nenagh, Co. Tipperary, some days before his body was found on

14 February 1921, lying in a field blindfolded, with his hands tied behind his back. He was thirty-four and married, with fourteen years' police service, having been a farmer before joining the RIC.

He had been a member of a police convoy which was making its way from Dublin to Cork, stopping for the night at Nenagh. The dead officer left Nenagh to visit his father, who lived nearby at Ballywilliam. He arrived at his father's at 9.45 p.m. and left the next morning at 7.40 a.m., but failed to return to his comrades at Nenagh. When his body was discovered, it was found that he had been shot four times, twice in the head and twice in the body. On the night of 16 February, notices in pencil were posted along the road at Ballywilliam issuing threats against any person who attended the constable's funeral the next day. As a result no one from Ballywilliam attended the funeral, which went ahead as scheduled. On the night of 17 February, the constable's father received a threatening letter. Constable Carroll was a witness in an important murder trial that was pending and it was believed that the motive for his killing was to exclude his evidence from that trial.

At 1.30 a.m. on 6 June 1922, Constable Carroll's brother was shot dead. When the family's thatched house was set on fire, Carroll Jnr (twenty-eight years old) went out in his night attire to investigate and was shot dead. On hearing the shooting his father, Dennis, sixty-five years old, also went outside and dragged his son's body away from the burning building, leaving it in a ditch as the outhouse had also been burned down. The body remained there until after the inquest at 6.30 p.m. that evening before it was taken to Burgess churchyard for interment.

21 February 1921, Maynooth, Co. Kildare
Joseph Hughes, Sgt 64330

At 10 p.m. an RIC patrol consisting of one sergeant and five constables was attacked in Maynooth, Co. Kildare as it approached the local church. Sergeant Hughes was wounded and died the following day at Steeven's Hospital, Dublin. He was thirty-four and from Queen's County. He had twelve years' service, having been a postman before joining the RIC.

At the time what was described as a 'significant fact' was the respect paid to the funeral of the late sergeant and the universal condemnation of his killing. At Athy all the shop shutters were put up and a great number of people followed the funeral through the town, with many accompanying it the full eleven miles to the place of burial.[15]

22 FEBRUARY 1921, MOUNTCHARLES, CO. DONEGAL
Thomas Satchwell, Con 68650

A party of military and police were on their way to the fair at Mountcharles, when they were ambushed at a thickly wooded plantation a short distance outside the village commonly known as the Glen. Constable Satchwell was killed and a soldier was wounded in the same incident. Two men were later arrested.

Satchwell was twenty-five and single. From Castlerea, Co. Roscommon, he had five years' police service, having been a farmer before joining the RIC, and was stationed in Donegal town.

22 FEBRUARY 1921, DONEGAL TOWN
John William Hughes, Con 65939

The constable, who was stationed in the town, was shot dead in the main street. At first it was thought that this shooting had been an accident when a military and police patrol fired at each other by mistake. However, later reports stated that this had not been the case and that the constable had been killed by an unknown person or persons.

Following the trouble at Mountcharles, there was a short, sharp exchange of fire between police and attackers, who then withdrew. As night fell further fighting took place with the constable being shot in the head. He was thirty-three, single and from Roscommon. He had nine years' police service, having had no other employment before joining the RIC.

22 FEBRUARY 1921, BALLYLONGFORD, CO. KERRY
George Horace Howlett, Con 76830

On 22 February 1921 this police officer and a sailor named Wells were attacked as they made their way back to the barracks, which was 200 yards outside the village.

Background
The flying column attached to Kerry's No. 1 (North) Brigade split into two units so that attacks could be carried out in Ballylongford and Ballybunion simultaneously, as the IRA had information about police patrols in the two villages.

The IRA men involved in the attack at Ballylongford were led by Denis Quille, who had men placed near the barracks and on the roads leading into the village. He also had men placed at vantage points in the village, with six men taking up a position behind gate pillars by the side of the road, which the IRA knew was on the route usually taken by the police patrol as it returned to barracks.

A local IRA man from the Ballylongford Company acted as lookout and warned the ambush party of the approach of the two men. When they arrived at the ambush location they were attacked at close range with shotguns and rifles, which resulted in the death of Constable Howlett and the serious wounding of Wells, who, it was later stated, may have been a member of the Auxiliary Division.

After the attack, Very lights were fired from the barracks to summon assistance. Later reports on this incident stated that when police and military reinforcements arrived in the village, they came under intense rifle, shotgun and revolver fire from houses occupied by the IRA, some of whom it was said were disguised as police and soldiers. It was believed the IRA had used these disguises in order to aid their entry into the barracks, whose garrison was expecting reinforcements.

Three policemen in a public house at Ballybunion had a lucky escape on the same evening. As an attack was about to be carried out on these men, the alarm about the presence of IRA men in the village was sounded.[16]

Constable Howlett, a twenty-two-year-old single man, was from Yorkshire. He had two months' police service, having been a steelworker and a soldier before joining the RIC.

23 February 1921,
Parliament/Essex Street, Dublin city
Martin John Greer, Con 67768
Daniel Hoey, Con 66287
Edward McDonagh, Con 69370

Three police orderlies attached to Dublin Castle were going to a restaurant in Essex Street, Dublin, when they were attacked at the junction of Parliament and Essex streets by a Dublin IRA man named J. Conroy.[17] Constables Hoey and Greer, who were both employed on motor despatch duties, died at the scene; Constable McDonagh, an office orderly, died from his wounds the next day.

Constable Greer, a twenty-seven-year-old single man, was from Cootehall, Co. Roscommon. He had six years' police service, having had no other employment before joining the RIC.

Constable Hoey was single and from Lancashire. He would have been thirty-three on 3 March. He had one month's police service, having been a farmer before joining the RIC.

Constable McDonagh, a twenty-four-year-old single man, was from Trimbane, Tuam, Co. Galway. He would have had three years' police service on 4 March, having been a farmer before joining the RIC.

23 FEBRUARY 1921, BANDON, CO. CORK
Frederick W. Perrier, Con 73253

A number of RIC men were leaving a cinema in Bandon when they were attacked in North Main Street, sixty yards from the junction with Bridge Street. Constable Perrier was killed, while Constable Kearns was seriously wounded, with his condition regarded as hopeless. Two soldiers and two wireless naval men, who were walking in the suburbs of the town unarmed, were kidnapped, the two soldiers being killed whilst the two naval men were released.

Background
The IRA's Cork No. 3 (West) Brigade flying column, under the command of Tom Barry, entered the town intending to ambush a military patrol of the Essex Regiment when it passed over the bridge near North Main Street.

Barry had split his force into three, the main body entering the town via the Cork road at 8.20 p.m. to take over houses, a bank and the Freemason hall at the ambush location, while two units each of seven men were sent into the suburbs at 8.30 p.m., travelling via the Dunmanway road. Those IRA members were heavily armed, the majority having a rifle and a revolver. (This flying column was the one involved in the ambush at Kilmichael and the weapons were taken from the police after that attack.)

As Barry and another member of the column went forward to check the ambush site, it is alleged that they encountered the RIC men as they returned from the cinema and opened fire on them. Constable Perrier sought the safety of a nearby house but was followed into it by Barry, who shot and killed him. Perrier, a thirty-four-year-old single man, was from Hampshire. He would have had five months' police service the next day, having been a handyman and a soldier prior to joining the RIC.

At the same time the two smaller IRA units attacked the unarmed soldiers and sailors who were walking in the suburbs, later killing the two soldiers. Royal Navy personnel were posted in the Cork area from December 1920 to provide wireless communications between the different garrisons in the area.

25 February 1921, near Ballyvourney, Co. Cork

James Seafield-Grant MC, Commandant 79885
Arthur William Cane, Con 72068
Clevel L. Soady, Cadet 79905

Cork's No. 1 Brigade of the IRA under the command of Seán O'Hegarty became aware that the Auxiliary police at Macroom had a habit of making a journey beginning at 9 a.m. and travelling the nine miles to Ballyvourney. As a result of this information the IRA planned to ambush this patrol at Coolavokig, about two miles from Ballyvourney, from carefully prepared positions on high rocky ground to the north of the road. A farm cart was to be employed by the IRA as a barricade to prevent the RIC patrol from driving out of the trap.

A large number of IRA men were to be involved in this attack, with most of them being drawn from the brigade's Second, Seventh and Eighth battalions. They were well armed with rifles, shotguns and two Lewis machine guns. Over the period of a few days IRA men occupied the ambush location before dawn, withdrawing each evening. Because of this movement the police became aware of the proposed ambush and a force of seventy Auxiliaries and seven RIC constables, who acted as vehicle drivers, moved against the IRA.[18]

At the beginning of this engagement the commandant of the Auxiliaries in West Cork, Major Seafield-Grant, was mortally wounded but was able to continue to give the necessary orders to his men before dying from his wounds. Constable Cane was wounded as he waited with the vehicles and died the next day. A number of cadets were wounded during the fight that raged fiercely for over four hours, with Cadet Soady dying from his wounds on 1 March 1921 in Cork Military Hospital.

Other police moving into the area were also ambushed at Coolavokig on the main road between Macroom and Killarney, six miles from Killarney.

Major Seafield-Grant was an ex-member of the King's Own Scottish Borderers, had been awarded an MC and was twice mentioned in despatches during the First World War. On 1 March his funeral took place at Aldeburgh, Suffolk. He was a thirty-year-old single man from Aldeburgh. He had two months' police service and had only left Dublin on 11 February to take over as commandant. His Auxiliary number was 1179.

Constable Cane was thirty-seven, single and from London. He would have had seven months' police service on 27 February 1921, having been a clerk and a soldier before joining the RIC.

Cadet Soady, a thirty-eight-year-old single man, was from Hants. He had two months' police service. His Auxiliary number was 810 and he was a member of J Company. During the First World War he had been a lieutenant in the Royal Naval Reserve.

28 February 1921,
Rosscarbery, Co. Cork
Alfred V. G. Brock, Con 72038

A patrol of six RIC men on mess duty was fired on when it was 100 yards from the barracks at Rosscarbery. Constable Brock was wounded and died on 1 March. After the attack on the patrol the barracks was also fired on.

This attack was carried out by Jim Hurley, commandant of the IRA's Second Battalion, Cork No. 3 Brigade, and some of his men. Constable Brock, a thirty-one-year-old single man, was from London and had joined the RIC from India. He had seven months' police service on 23 February, having been a labourer and a soldier before joining the RIC.

3 March 1921,
Scartacrooks, Co. Waterford
Joseph Duddy, Con 75988

An RIC patrol was ambushed at Scartacrooks in the Cappoquin area of Co. Waterford and Constable Duddy was shot dead. He lived at 4 Elmgrove Street, Belfast and during the First World War had been a sergeant in the Army Service Corps and Royal Engineers.

The constable's body was taken to his father's home at 164 Dunluce Avenue, Belfast. At 2 p.m. on 6 March his coffin, covered in the Union Jack, was removed to a waiting gun carriage. A large body of RIC men with arms reversed and the force's band, who played funeral marches, accompanied the funeral to the city cemetery, along with the constable's widow, two young children and a large crowd.

Constable Duddy was thirty-three years old, from Co. Armagh and had three months' police service, having been a driver and a soldier before joining the RIC.

4 March 1921, Cashel, Co. Tipperary
James R. Beasant, Con 74691

The constable, a motor driver in the RIC, was in a public house in Cashel when two men shot him dead and seriously wounded a girl in the bar. Constable Beasant was from Wiltshire and a single man who would have been twenty-six on 19 March. He had four months' police service, having been a driver and a soldier before joining the RIC.

6 March 1921, Kilmallock, Co. Limerick
James Maguire, Sgt 54713

The sergeant was shot dead by five armed men as he was walking in the town. As a result of his death the military took reprisal action in Kilmallock. Maguire, a forty-nine-year-old married man, was from Co. Cavan. He had thirty years' police service on 2 February 1921, having been a farmer before joining the RIC.

8 March 1921, Shronebeha, Co. Cork
Nicholas Somers, Con 71336

An RIC patrol was ambushed at Fr Murphy's Bridge, Shronebeha, Banteer, Co. Cork, by IRA men from the Kanturk (Sixth) Battalion, Cork No. 2 Brigade. One constable was killed and three others wounded, all of them being disarmed by the IRA. Somers had been recommended for appointment to the RIC by DI Wilson, who was himself killed in a separate incident.

The ambush location was occupied for several days before the attack, the IRA changing their ambush party in relays. Constable Somers, a twenty-two-year-old single man, was from Co. Wexford. He would have had one year's service on 30 March, having previously been a farmer.

11 March 1921,
Victoria Square, Belfast city
Walter H. Cooper, Con 741 69
Robert Crook, Con 73850
John McIntosh, Con 76247

The three men had arrived in Belfast on 10 March 1921 on special duty from Gormanston to act as drivers and bring vehicles back to their depot. At 8.30 p.m. the next day they were walking in Victoria Square, a few paces from the corner of Church Lane, when they were attacked by four or five men. Two of the constables were killed outright, with Constable Cooper dying from his wounds in the Royal Victoria Hospital on 13 March. A civilian who was also wounded in the attack later died from his wounds. On 14 March the bodies of Constables McIntosh and Crook were taken to Scotland.

Constable Cooper, twenty-six and married, was from Surrey. He would have had five months' police service the next day, having been a driver/fitter and a soldier before joining the RIC.

Constable Crook, also twenty-six and married, was from Cornwall. He had five months' police service, having been a motor driver and a soldier prior to joining the RIC.

Constable McIntosh, twenty-six and single, was from Inverness. He had three months' police service on 8 March, having been a motor driver and a soldier before joining the RIC.

12 March 1921,
Sixmilebridge, Co. Clare
Daniel Anthony Murphy, Con 70065

The constable left Broadford Barracks on the morning of 12 March to take a despatch to Sixmilebridge, but never arrived. His body was later found with a number of bullet wounds.

Constable Murphy, twenty-two and single, was from Cork. He had one year's police service, having been a soldier before joining the RIC. He had been recommended for service in the RIC by DI Swanzy, who had been killed in 1920.

12 March 1921, Callan, Co. Kilkenny
Ernest J. Riley, Con 79407

A joint RIC/military search was being carried out at Ballybricken House, Callan, when the security forces came under fire. Three men escaped from the house but five were arrested inside. Some arms were also captured in the house and DI Hubert L. Baynham was wounded during this part of the operation.

Two miles on the Tipperary side of Callan, a separate RIC patrol came under fire, possibly in response to the earlier operation. This attack resulted in the death of Constable Riley. From Sussex, he had turned twenty-six just four days before. He was a single man who had sixteen days' police service, having been a soldier before joining the RIC.

12 March 1921, Tubrid Railway Station, Co. Kerry
Walter Falkiner, MC, Cadet 79207

A number of cadets were returning from Listowel by train when they were ambushed at Ardfert by a large body of men, who fired on them with a machine gun. When the train pulled in to the railway station at Tubrid, Tralee, Co. Kerry, it was found that the cadet had been killed.

Cadet Falkiner had joined the RIC on 1 November 1920 and was attached to H Company of the Auxiliary Division. His Auxiliary number was 925. Formerly, he had been a lieutenant in the Nineteenth Durham Light Infantry and had won an MC during the First World War. He lived at 31 Wynnstay Gardens, Kensington, London. He was a thirty-two-year-old single man from Middlesex who had three months' police service.

14 March 1921,
144 Brunswick Street, Dublin city
Bernard J. L. Beard, MC, Cadet 73551
Francis Joseph Farrell, Cadet 79075

The Saint Andrew's Club at 144 Brunswick Street (now Pearse Street), Dublin, was the IRA's headquarters and, as such, the area around the building was constantly patrolled by armed IRA men. On 14 March, at 8.10 p.m., two lorries containing sixteen Auxiliaries and an armoured car were seen making their way along the street. As they reached the corner of Erne Street, the police came under fire. They were on their way to search No. 144. At the time, some members of the IRA's B Company, Third Dublin Battalion were inside the building, whilst three sections of the same company were outside.

As a result of being attacked from four points, the Auxiliaries dismounted from their vehicles and a gun battle began which lasted for some time. In the course of the gunfire three IRA men were killed, with others being seriously wounded, and a large quantity of weapons was later found inside the building. Two armed IRA men were captured and later tried by court martial for murder, both being found guilty.

On 25 April 1921 one of these prisoners, Tom Traynor, was executed in Mountjoy gaol. The other, Jack Donnelly, faced a similar fate but was released after the signing of the Truce.[19] Donnelly had been wounded during the incident, being found near 157 Brunswick Street with a revolver. After he had recovered from his wounds in

King George V Military Hospital, he was tried by a court martial in Dublin City Hall.

During the gun battle three police officers were wounded, with two later dying from their wounds on 15 March in the King George V Hospital.

Cadet Farrell had joined the RIC on 8 October 1920. Twenty-eight, single and from Dublin, he had served with the Twenty-second Battalion of the Royal Dublin Fusiliers before receiving a commission as lieutenant in the Tank Corps, being mentioned in despatches. He had five months' police service on 8 March 1921, having been a motor fitter before enlisting. He was buried in Birmingham.

Cadet Beard had served as a sub-captain in the Sixth Cavalry Division and later as a brigadier general in the Hundred and Twelfth Infantry Brigade. He had received an MC and been mentioned in despatches three times during the First World War. During the battle, Beard, who had been a section leader in the Auxiliaries, was wounded in the head. Thirty-four and single, he was from Staffordshire and would have had six months' service in four days' time. His Auxiliary number was 579. He was buried in Nottingham.

16 March 1921, Ballymote, Co. Sligo
James O'Brien, Con 75921

An RIC patrol was fired on at Ballymote, Co. Sligo. The constable, who had been wounded during the attack, died on St Patrick's Day. He had been born in England of Irish parentage. The constable's rifle and revolver were later recovered after an ambush at Tourmakeady, Co. Mayo, in which two IRA men were killed. From Lancashire and single, he would have been twenty-seven on 23 March and would have had four months' police service on 26 March, having been a locomotive driver before joining the RIC.

16 March 1921, Clifden, Co. Galway
Charles O'M. Reynolds, Con 62614
Thomas Sweeney, Con 75734

A four-man RIC patrol was returning to barracks when it was ambushed at Clifden. Constable Reynolds, a thirty-three-year-old married man, was from Co. Roscommon. He had two years' police service, having been a labourer before joining the RIC. He was buried on 19 March.

Constable Sweeney, who was seriously wounded, had his right leg amputated and was not expected to live. He died from his wounds on 18 March. Twenty-four and single, he was from Aughrim, Co. Galway and would have had four months' police service on 19 March, having been a labourer, police officer and a soldier before joining the RIC. He was an ex-Metropolitan Policeman who had joined the Irish Guards during the First World War.

17 March 1921, Tullacremin, Co. Kerry
John Grant, Con 75772

The constable, a twenty-six-year-old single man, was from Inverness. Stationed at Abbeydorney Barracks, he was riding his bicycle when he was attacked at Tullacremin, one and a half miles from the barracks. There are two differing reports about this ambush. One stated the constable was killed outright and that his body was moved into a nearby farmhouse where a woman, on seeing it, collapsed from fright and died. The other stated that the constable, although wounded, was able to make his way to a farmhouse but was followed by his attackers into the house and shot with his own gun, which caused the death from shock of the woman.

Grant would have had four months' police service on 23 March, having been a surfaceman and a soldier before joining the RIC.

18 March 1921,
near Castletownroche, Co. Cork
William Elton, Con 76391

An RIC patrol of one sergeant and six constables was ambushed near the village of Castletownroche by 150 men. The constable died on 19 March from wounds received in this attack. A Constable Crowley was also wounded during the ambush.

Constable Elton was from Middlesex. He was a single man who would have been twenty-four on 29 March. He had three months' police service, having been a labourer and a soldier before joining the RIC.

19 March 1921, Lissagroom, Co. Cork
Arthur Frederick Kenward, Con 76391

On 19 March Constable Kenward, who was employed as a driver and stationed at Bandon, was killed, while Constable Rennie was wounded. These officers had been involved in a joint police/military operation to encircle an IRA flying column in the area of Lissagroom, Upton, Co. Cork.

Constable Kenward, a twenty-year-old single man, was from Surrey. He would have had six months' police service on 24 March, having been a motor fitter and a soldier before joining the RIC. On that day it was reported that his body had been taken back to England.

Background
On St Patrick's Day the flying column from the Cork No. 3 (West) Brigade of 104 men, led by Tom Barry, had been in an ambush location midway between Kinsale and Bandon, at Shippool, to ambush a military patrol that travelled along the main road.

Shortly after leaving on this patrol, the military became aware of the ambush and returned to Kinsale. A plan was formed to attempt an encirclement of the IRA. On realising that the military had returned, and fearing that an attempt would be made to capture the column, Barry moved his forces towards Crossbarry. There he prepared an ambush on the encircling military and police patrols. He mined the roadway with two devices and had the column split into seven sections. Six were used as an attacking force, with the remaining section at the rear of the main force to protect it.

On 19 March the military and police were moving towards this IRA column from three directions. As they went, the security forces searched houses and other buildings they came across, dividing their forces between foot and mobile units.

At Ballymurphy, a few miles from the column, soldiers searching a house found Charlie Hurley, the Cork No. 3 Brigade commander. He tried to fight his way out of the house but was killed.

As the military closed on Barry's unit, they left some vehicles with their drivers and moved forward. The IRA unit fought its way out of the encircling police and military forces and, as they were leaving the area, came upon these vehicles and their drivers. Six soldiers and one RIC constable were killed before the main party of military could come to their aid. This was the largest action during the period, with the largest flying column the IRA had at the time being involved. IRA man Peter Monahan, a deserter from the Cameron Highlanders, was killed and others wounded.

19 March 1921,
Dungarvan, Co. Waterford
Michael Joseph Hickey, Sgt 61706
Sydney R. Redman, Con 77083

A joint police/military patrol in two lorries left Dungarvan to make an arrest near Waterford. As the patrol was returning from the Pike on the Waterford road, two miles from Dungarvan it was ambushed. During the fighting a police sergeant and a military officer were kidnapped and one IRA man was killed.

A relief party of soldiers sent to the area recovered the military officer unhurt and were involved in a number of running battles with the IRA as they withdrew from the area.

At Castlequarter, in a bog about two miles from the ambush scene and one mile from Dungarvan, the body of Sergeant Hickey was found. He had been blindfolded and a card with the word 'Executed' on it was pinned to the body. Constable Redman, who had been wounded in the head during the ambush, died later from his wounds.

Sergeant Hickey, from Co. Limerick, was a single man who had just turned thirty-six the day before. He had fifteen years' police service, having been a clerk before joining the RIC.

Constable Redman, a twenty-five-year-old single man, was from Kent. He had two months' police service, having been a motor driver and a soldier before joining the RIC.

20 March 1921, Falcarragh, Co. Donegal
James McKenna, Con 66625

Constable McKenna, twenty-eight, single, from Ennybegs, Co. Longford, was shot and killed by armed and masked men firing from an empty house some fifty yards from his barracks at Falcarragh as he returned to it. He had eight years' police service, having been a farmer before joining the RIC.

20 March 1921, Mullinahone, Co. Tipperary
William Campbell, Con 62454

Constable Campbell, a thirty-seven-year-old married man, who was on sick leave, was shot dead by armed and masked men when he went into the backyard of his lodgings for coal. From Co. Leitrim, he had completed fourteen years' police service two days before his death. Before joining the RIC he had been a farmer.

22 March 1921,
Blackwood, Co. Roscommon
William Devereux, Con 49046
Michael James Dowling, Con 67499

An RIC patrol was cycling from Keadue to Ballyfarnon to investigate a raid on the post office. When it reached Blackwood the patrol was attacked, with two constables killed and Sergeant Reilly wounded.

Constable Devereux, a fifty-seven-year-old married man, was from Co. Roscommon. He would have had thirty-nine years' police service on 11 April, having had no other employment before joining the RIC.

Constable Dowling, thirty and single, was from Co. Wicklow. He had seven and a half years' police service, having been a grocer's assistant prior to joining the RIC.

22 March 1921,
near Drummin, Co. Mayo
John Coughlan, Sgt 55450

A four-man RIC cycle patrol from Cuilmore, Co. Mayo, was ambushed near Drummin, eight miles from Westport in the direction of Clifden. Sergeant Coughlan, a forty-eight-year-old single man from Co. Mayo, was killed and three constables were wounded, one of them, Constable Maguire, seriously. Coughlan had twenty-eight-and-a-half years' police service, having had no other employment before joining the RIC.

This attack was carried out by members of the West Mayo flying column under the leadership of its column commander, Michael Kilroy. The IRA had been in the area checking for possible ambush positions when the patrol suddenly came round a bend. The police dismounted and a moonlit gun battle began, which resulted in all four officers being wounded. After the attack the IRA removed the police officers' weapons and ammunition before leaving the area.

This was the first successful attack undertaken by the West Mayo column, which had been formed earlier in the spring from battalion columns attached to the IRA's Castlebar, Westport and Newport battalions.

22 March 1921, Rosslea, Co. Fermanagh
Samuel Nixon, S/Sgt

Special Sergeant Nixon's home in the townland of Tattymore was attacked by gunfire as he was about to retire for the night. Although shot and wounded, he engaged his attackers for some time, being called on repeatedly to surrender. After some time, and being on the point of collapse, he surrendered. He was dragged from the house and shot dead, despite the efforts of his wife to save his life.

On the same night the IRA mounted several attacks on unionist farms in the district of Rosslea. These began around midnight and by morning fourteen houses had been raided by IRA men working in units of eight. Most of the houses attacked belonged to members of the B Specials from the newly formed Ulster Special Constabulary.

22 March 1921, Rosslea, Co. Fermanagh
William Gordon, S/Sgt

Having attacked the home of Special Sergeant Nixon, the IRA then attacked that of Special Sergeant Gordon in the townland of Rathkeana, one-fifth of a mile from Rosslea, using bombs and gunfire. Special Sergeant Gordon returned fire from a downstairs window for some time but was killed when a bomb was thrown through the window.

It was stated that another man in the house, who was not a member of the Special Constabulary, was dragged from the dwelling and brutally assaulted, as a result of which he later died. Both Nixon and Gordon were buried after full military honours at Clough church. A strong detachment of special constables and members of the King's Royal Rifles stationed at Clones attended the funeral.

23 MARCH 1921,
SCRAMOGUE, CO. ROSCOMMON
Edward L. Leslie, Con 70378

At 7.15 a.m. a mixed party of Ninth Lancers and RIC officers, totalling nine men, was travelling in a Crossley tender. When the vehicle reached a bend in the road at Scramogue, two miles from Strokestown, it came under heavy fire. This attack was carried out by forty IRA men, whose first volleys killed one army officer and the Royal Army Service Corps driver. Four other members of the patrol were also wounded, with Constable Leslie dying from his wounds on 26 March.

Background
At 3 a.m. on the morning of 23 March, the South Roscommon flying column (which included some ex-soldiers) under the leadership of Patrick Madden, moved into an ambush location on the Strokestown to Longford road beside a crossroads at Scramogue, Co. Roscommon. The IRA company from Strokestown had also been mobilised for this attack, and was responsible for blocking roads in the area. A trench was dug behind the hedge from which the ambush was to be

launched in order to give more protection to the ambush party.

The lorry containing soldiers of the Ninth Lancers and RIC officers drove into the ambush and in a few minutes the attack was over. It resulted in the death of Captain Sir Wilfred Peek, DSO, the nephew of the Earl of Midleton.

After the attack two men in civilian clothes walked out to Madden with their hands up. They explained that they were prisoners being conveyed to Longford. As the IRA left the area they took these two men with them, but when they questioned them, they discovered that they were in fact police officers. On hearing this it was decided that both men would be killed as soon as the IRA was secure from any possible follow-up operation by the security forces. At Curraghroe the column split, with Constable Evans being taken to Clonberry bog, where he was shot and buried. Constable Buchanan was removed by members of the local Curraghroe Company, who had been involved in the ambush. They had intended to take him to an isolated bog at Derryhannen but were prevented by the activity of soldiers in the area. The IRA then decided to take their prisoner across the Shannon to the Longford side where he was to be shot. By doing this they hoped that any follow-up operations by the police and army would be on the other side of the river, allowing the IRA a better chance to escape.

As they waited on the banks of the river for a boat, the constable was informed of his fate. At this he attempted to escape but was shot and wounded, being found later under some sally branches at the water's edge. On finding him, the IRA killed him. His body was placed in a boat and taken out onto the river, where it was dumped into the water. The bodies of Constable Evans and Constable Buchanan were never found.

Constable Leslie, a twenty-one-year-old single man, was from Lanark. He had one year's police service, having been a labourer and a soldier before joining the RIC.

29 March 1921,
Ballyhaunis, Co. Mayo
William H. Stephens, Con 73707

Constable Stephens, forty-one and single, from London, was wounded in the hip and back of the right leg by revolver fire. He was taken to Galway County Hospital but died from his wounds.

At 9 p.m., whilst in Knox Street, the constable had saluted two men who had been staring at him and when he asked what they wanted they replied, 'It's all right.' The constable walked on about four yards before he was fired on. He had five months' police service, having been a clerk and a soldier before joining the RIC.

30 March 1921,
Ballyfermot, Co. Dublin
Edward Mulrooney, H/Con 55316
Michael Hallissy, Sgt 59218

An RIC cycle patrol of a head constable, a sergeant and two constables from Lucan was ambushed at Ballyfermot in Co. Dublin. The sergeant was killed outright, with Mulrooney and a constable being wounded.

On 4 April 1921 Head Constable Mulrooney, a forty-eight-year-old married man from Co. Limerick with no family, died from his wounds at Steeven's Hospital, Dublin. Most of his police service had been on the detective staff in Belfast. In nine days' time he would have had twenty-nine years' service, having been a shop assistant before joining the RIC. His father had been a police sergeant. He was buried at Holywood, Co. Down, from 24 Gainsborough Drive, Belfast, on 7 April.

Sergeant Hallissy, a forty-two-year-old married man, was from Kerry. He had just over twenty-one years' police service, having been a farmer prior to joining the RIC.

31 March 1921,
Rosscarbery RIC Barracks, Co. Cork
Ambrose Shea, Sgt 57356
Charles H. Bowles, Con 72058

The IRA attacked Rosscarbery RIC Barracks, which stood on a hill near the village, with explosives, causing the death of Sergeant Shea and Constable Bowles. Nine other constables were wounded, one of them, Constable Kinsella, seriously. (Some reports state that he died from his wounds, but I could find no evidence of this.)

Background
The flying column of the Cork No. 3 (West) Brigade led by Tom Barry entered the village at 1.10 a.m. The IRA took up a main position at the post office corner about thirty yards from the barracks. Others occupied upper windows of the building opposite the barracks and some covered the rear of the building. A small party then removed their boots and carried a bomb, which had been constructed by an ex-Royal Engineer who had fought during the First World War, to the front door of the barracks. When this device exploded most of the blast went backwards and did not cause the breach in the doorway that had been expected by the IRA.

A fiercely fought battle then began to rage between the police and their attackers, with both sides using rifles and Mills bombs. After two hours the police were forced out of the front ground-floor rooms into those at the back and eventually were forced to give these up. The police then moved to the top storey and continued their defence of the barracks. The IRA exploded two smaller bombs in the ground-floor rooms of the barracks in an attempt to bring down the floors, but this failed. They next set fire to the stairway and the ground floor was soon burning fiercely. This forced the police garrison into a single back room and not long afterwards they had no choice but to surrender. Before doing so they threw their weapons and ammunition into the flames so that they would not fall into the hands of the IRA.

The police party then lowered their more seriously wounded members through a back window before leaving the barracks by the same route. The bodies of Sergeant Shea and Constable Bowles could not be reached as they lay in the ground floor of the burning barracks where they had been killed early in the attack. The surviving RIC men took shelter in some nearby houses and the Convent of Mercy.[20]

Sergeant Shea, a forty-six-year-old married man, was from Co. Wicklow. He had twenty-six years' police service, having been a temporary sorter at the GPO before joining the RIC.

Constable Bowles, from Kent and a single man, would have been twenty-three on 18 April. He had eight months' police service, having been a switchboard operator and a soldier before joining the RIC.

31 March 1921,
Miltown Malbay, Co. Clare
Stanley L. Moore, Con 72217

At 10 p.m. the constable was shot dead by unknown men in the main street of Miltown Malbay. Constable Moore, a thirty-year-old single man, was from Glamorgan. He had seven months' police service, having been a dentist and a soldier before joining the RIC.

1 April 1921,
Lecky Road RIC Barracks, Londonderry city
Michael Kenny, Con 65275

The IRA had carried out two attacks simultaneously just before curfew in the city. These took place in two different parts of the city, one at Lecky Road RIC Barracks and the other at a military post at the electric station in Strand Road, which failed. The attack on the barracks was opened from two sides simultaneously, with bombs being hurled into the yard from Nelson Street. Constable Kenny, who was defending his barracks from a first-floor landing, received a wound to his abdomen. He was taken to the City Infirmary but died from his wounds on 6 April.

Kenny, a thirty-three-year-old married man, was from Leitrim. He would have had eleven years' service on 27 April, having been a farmer before joining the RIC.

1 April 1921,
Creggan Road, Londonderry city
John Higgins, Sgt 55504

On 1 April 1921 the IRA attacked the sergeant as he was making his way home along Creggan Road for his tea. He was shot twice at close range in the head, with his attackers escaping along William Street. He was taken to the City Infirmary but died later from his wounds.

His two attackers had been standing at Windsor Terrace and waited for the sergeant as he approached from the Rosemount direction. Just before this attack a chalk notice reading 'Wanted Sergeant Higgins the black murderer dead or alive' appeared on a wall near the scene of the ambush. During an outbreak of violence in June he had arrested a nationalist registration agent. He had only been attached to Lecky Road RIC Barracks for a brief period.

Sergeant Higgins, a forty-nine-year-old man, was from Co. Mayo. His wife had died three years before. He had two grown-up girls and had just over twenty-eight years' police service, having been a shepherd before joining the RIC.

3 April 1921,
near The Mall, Co. Carlow
James Duffy, Con 77133

The constable and a civilian, Henry James, had been drinking in a public house at Killeshin and were walking home when they were attacked by three men near The Mall, about two miles from Carlow. Henry James was wounded in the attack and the body of the constable was found the next day in a field. His remains were removed to the military barracks at Carlow.

Constable Duffy, a thirty-year-old single man, was from Co. Monaghan. He had four months' police service, having been a farmer and a soldier before joining the RIC.

6 April 1921,
Oughterard, Co. Galway
William H. Pearson, Con 72763

A cycle patrol from Maam, West Galway, consisting of a sergeant and four constables, was cycling into the Oughterard area when it came under fire. Constable Pearson was wounded and later died. A thirty-year-old single man from New Zealand, he had seven months' police service, having been a soldier before joining the RIC.

8 April 1921,
Mashanaglass, Macroom, Co. Cork
Frederick H. Lord, Con 73305

Two constables, who had been on eight hours' leave from their barracks at Carrigadrohid in the Macroom district of Co. Cork, were ambushed as they returned from Macroom at Mashanaglass. At 4 p.m. the two constables, who were travelling by horse and trap, were attacked by ten to twelve armed men. Constable Lord was shot five times and fell dead from the trap. The other constable, Lawrence, whipped the horse into a gallop and was pursued for more than half a mile by his attackers, who continued to fire at him. As he escaped, the constable returned fire whenever possible and one of his attackers was seen to fall. After the attack Lord's body was removed to Macroom Barracks.

Constable Lord was to have resigned on 11 April 1921 in order to emigrate to Canada. He was a thirty-three-year-old single man from London, who had six-and-a-half months' police service, having been an electrician and a soldier before joining the RIC.

8 April 1921, Limerick city
Hubert J. Wiggins, Con 71259

A number of attacks were carried out against RIC men in the city of Limerick during the evening of 8 April. Constable Wiggins, who was alone, was attacked by members of the IRA's A Company, First Limerick Battalion as he stood near the police barracks. A short time later ten members of the IRA attached to C Company, First Limerick Battalion, under the leadership of the battalion commandant, attacked an RIC patrol in John Street, throwing a bomb into their midst and then opening fire on them.[21]

A sergeant and a constable were wounded, the constable crawling to the safety of a nearby house. Their attackers scattered into the network of alleyways in the vicinity of Clare Street. A civilian was killed, with two others being wounded during this attack.

Constable Wiggins, a twenty-seven-year-old single man, was from Co. Donegal. He would have had one year's police service on 23 April, having been a postman before joining the RIC. His brother was stationed at the Brickfields Barracks, Belfast.

10 April 1921,
Creggan, Co. Armagh
John Fluke, S/Con

A party of five policemen, stationed at Crossmaglen Barracks, left on bicycle to go to the Protestant church in Creggan near Crossmaglen. As they approached the village they observed unusual activity in a public house and, on going to investigate, they were attacked by fifteen IRA men, who threw a bomb and directed gunfire at them. The IRA had cycled to Creggan, where they held the congregation as they arrived for the midday service at the parish church, placing them under armed guard in McConville's public house.

Special Constable Fluke was killed, while three others in the police party were wounded, with the IRA making good their escape. The dead man was from Ballydoo, Co. Armagh.

10 April 1921, Scart, Co. Cork
Joseph Boynes, Con 75994
George Woodward, Con 71533

The two constables were out walking at Scart, Kildorrery, East Cork, when both were shot and killed.

Constable Boynes, a twenty-three-year-old single man, was from Northumberland. He would have had five months' police service on 29 April, having been a labourer and a soldier before joining the RIC. Constable Woodward, of the same age and status, was from Surrey. He had ten months' police service, having been a sawyer's mate and a soldier prior to joining the RIC.

13 April 1921,
Fedamore, Co. Limerick
George Henry Rogers, Con 70266

A police patrol of five constables was ambushed at Fedamore, three-quarters of a mile from their barracks, resulting in the death of one constable and the wounding of three others. Their barracks was also attacked at the same time.

Constable Rogers, a twenty-five-year-old single man, was from London. He had fourteen months' police service, having been a soldier before joining the RIC.

15 April 1921, Tralee, Co. Kerry
John Alister Mackinnon, DCM, MM, Cadet

Major Mackinnon was the commanding officer of H Company of the Auxiliary Division of the RIC at Tralee, Co. Kerry. His Auxiliary number was 917 and he had joined the RIC on 28 October 1920. He was a man who not only directed, but led his men against the IRA and, as such, was well known and feared by those in the area who referred to him as 'the Major'.[22] On Christmas Day 1920 a search led by the major discovered two IRA men in a house at Ballymacelligott. Both these men were shot and the IRA planned Mackinnon's death.[23]

The local IRA became aware that he played golf at Tralee Golf Links and so they decided to attack him on the third green. For some days the IRA had been in the area, but it was not until 4 p.m. on 15 April that IRA scouts reported that he was on the links. Four IRA men armed with a rifle and three shotguns moved from the nearby Kenny's Fort and lined the fence near the third green. When the major arrived he was shot and wounded, dying three-quarters of an hour later. The IRA man who shot the major was an ex-British soldier, who had to borrow the rifle used in the attack.[24] The major's companion returned fire but it was not believed that any of the attackers were wounded.

The major was thirty-two; it would appear that he had not been issued with an RIC number.

15 April 1921,
Ballinamore, Co. Leitrim
Wilfred Jones, Con 75293

Constable Jones, thirty-five and single, from London, was walking with his girlfriend near his barracks at Ballinamore, Co. Leitrim, when he was shot and killed. He lived at 26 Leythe Road, Acton. His body was later removed to Carrick-on-Shannon, where he was buried. He had five months' police service, having been a stoker and a soldier before joining the RIC.

17 April 1921, Cove Street, Cork city
John Cyril MacDonald, Con 76409

Constable MacDonald, twenty-eight and single, from London, was walking with a girl in mufti when two men came up Cove Street towards Barrack Street. As they passed him one of the men jumped on his back pinning his arms behind him. The other pointed a revolver at him, which the constable tried to knock away, but he was shot in the face. As he lay on the ground he was fired at four or five more times but was not wounded again. The men then ran off down Cove Street while the girl went to the fire station to summon an ambulance. On her return she helped him into the ambulance. Five days later he died from his wounds.

MacDonald had four months' service, having been a soldier before joining the RIC. A contemporary newspaper reported that he lived at 31 Whitting Stone [*sic*] Road, Fulham, London.

19 April 1921,
Ballisodare Railway Station, Co. Sligo
James Hetherington, Con 77866
Thomas Kelly, Con 64253

The two constables were in civilian clothes, unarmed and off-duty, travelling by train from Dublin to Ballisodare, Co. Sligo. When the train reached Ballisodare the two men were dragged off by eight to ten IRA men. They were then moved down the road with their hands above their heads for approximately 100 yards before being shot and killed.

Both men were returning from despatch duties. The mayor and Sligo town council condemned their killings, and Sligo Petty Sessions Court, the Harbour Board and other local public bodies passed resolutions of sympathy. The funerals of the two men were also attended by large numbers of people from Sligo.[25]

Constable Hetherington, a thirty-one-year-old single man, was from Fivemiletown, Co. Tyrone. From No. 1 Barracks, he had six years' police service, having been a farmer before joining the RIC.

Constable Kelly, from No. 2 Barracks, was thirty-seven and married, with two children. From Co. Mayo, he had twelve years' police service, having been a farmer prior to joining the RIC.

19 April 1921, Ballyboghil, Co. Dublin
Stephen Kirwan, Sgt 58582

The sergeant was wounded during an affray in Ballyboghil, where he was stationed. He was removed to King George V Hospital but died the same day. Kirwan was a forty-four-year-old married man from Co. Wexford. He had twenty-one years' police service and had no other employment before joining the RIC.

21 April 1921, Mary Street, Dublin city
William Steadman, DMP Con

The constable was bringing despatches across the city when he was shot and wounded in Mary Street. He was taken to King George V

Hospital but died on 27 April. He was attached to B Division, having twelve years' service. The thirty-two-year-old constable's remains were later removed to Enniscorthy, Co. Wexford, for burial.

21 April 1921, Tralee, Co. Kerry
Denis O'Loughlin, Con 78430

The constable was in Knightly's public house in Castle Street, Tralee, when he was shot and killed. He had been recommended for appointment to the RIC by the local OC of the Auxiliary Division.

Constable O'Loughlin, forty-eight and single, was from Co. Kerry. He had three months' police service on the day he was killed, having been a labourer and a soldier before joining the RIC.

23 April 1921, Donegall Place, Belfast city
John Beets Bales, Cadet 82706
Ernest Baran Bolam, Cadet 81837

Two Auxiliaries were walking from the Great Northern Railway Station along Donegall Place. They had reached the corner of Fountain Lane when they were shot. Both belonged to B Company and were on escort duty from Sligo, arriving in the city on 22 April. They were to have returned on 23 April but, owing to the derailment of a train at Glaslough, their departure had been postponed.

Cadet Bales died from his wounds on 24 April in the Royal Victoria Hospital. He was twenty-three and had joined the RIC on 30 March 1921, being given the Auxiliary number 1876. From Norfolk and living at George's Park, Yarmouth, he had joined the Norfolk Yeomanry during the First World War but later transferred to the Royal Flying Corps and served in Gallipoli, Egypt and the Balkans.

Cadet Bolam, from Ealing, London, was killed outright. He had joined the RIC on 23 January 1921, being attached to O Company. On 5 March he was transferred to B Company. His Auxiliary number was 1579. During the First World War he was in the King's Liverpool Regiment and was later attached to the Chinese Labour Corps in France with the rank of captain. He was thirty-four, single and from Kent.

23 April 1921,
Kilmilkin, Co. Galway
John Boylan, Con 60741

A fourteen-man RIC cycle patrol was ambushed at 4.15 a.m. when they were searching for an IRA flying column at Kilmilkin, five miles from Maam, Co. Galway. The patrol was attacked from high ground in the vicinity of the house of Patrick O'Malley, MP. A sergeant and Constable Boylan were wounded, with the constable later dying from his wounds. He worked in the DI's office at Oughterard. On 26 April he was buried at Oughterard.

Constable Boylan, a forty-year-old married man, was from Co. Leitrim. He would have had nineteen years' police service on 16 May, having been a farmer before joining the RIC.

24 April 1921,
Kilrush, Co. Clare
John McFadden, Sgt 65056

On the night of 24 April, the RIC barracks and the Coastguard Station in Kilrush were attacked simultaneously, resulting in the death of the sergeant. Sergeant McFadden, a thirty-year-old single man, was from Co. Londonderry. He had eleven years' police service, having been a farmer before joining the RIC.

26 April 1921, Newry, Co. Down
George Graham, S/Con

At 9.30 p.m. an eight-man patrol of the Ulster Special Constabulary was ambushed by the IRA as it was making its way along Merchants Quay, Newry, at the corner of King Street.

During the attack the IRA threw two bombs at the patrol before opening fire on it. A gun battle followed, with a number of the patrol being seriously wounded. As the IRA men involved in the attack were running away from the scene they were caught by another police patrol.

Special Constable Graham died from his wounds. He was from Lisburn, Co. Antrim.

27 April 1921, near Clogheen, Co. Tipperary
Gilbert Norman Potter, DI 59414

A flying column from the IRA's South Tipperary Brigade under the command of Dinny Lacey attacked a convoy of troops which IRA brigade intelligence officers had discovered was in the habit of passing between Clogheen and Cahir at 10 a.m. on given days. After this ambush, in which a soldier was killed and two others wounded, the IRA removed their weapons and were moving along the roadway when a car driven by the DI came round a bend at Curraghclooney. The DI was captured, but as the IRA men were moving away from the area they came under attack by military reinforcements and a brisk engagement followed. The IRA men escaped, taking the DI with them.[26] Subsequently the DI was shot.

On 8 May 1921 Mrs Potter received a parcel with a Cahir postmark which contained her husband's diary, will, signet ring, gold watch and a poignant letter for her.[27] DI Potter's funeral took place on 30 August 1921 at 3.15 p.m. at Cahir. The remains of the late DI were later exhumed from an unknown grave and brought to Clonmel, where they were handed over to Mrs Potter. She had them conveyed to Cahir for reinterment.

Background

After the attack in Brunswick Street, Dublin, on 14 March 1921, six IRA men were shot and one captured. The captured IRA man was Tom Traynor, who was tried and sentenced to hang on 25 April. The IRA wanted to exchange the DI for Traynor but this swap was refused by the authorities. On hearing of Traynor's execution the IRA carried out their threat to kill the DI, as they believed any other action would be seen as a sign of weakness.

The DI's diary was completed up to the time of his death and he had written that he was locked in by an old man and woman and a young man whom he stated were known to Mrs Potter. (This pointed to the possibility that he had not been taken out of the area before being killed.) At 11 a.m. on 27 May he wrote that he had been warned he was to be killed that evening at 7 p.m. and that his guardians were not at all anxious to kill him but had received orders from their GHQ which they could not disobey. Dan Breen stated that the DI was a kind, cultured gentleman and a brave officer.[28]

After the death of the DI, ten farms in the South Tipperary area were blown up by the military as an official reprisal – one was Tincurry House near Cahir, the house where the 'Big Four' had sheltered after the ambush at Soloheadbeg on 21 January 1919.

The Sunday after Mrs Potter received her parcel, the rector of Cahir church made a touching reference to the DI after which the 'Dead March' was played on the organ.

DI Potter, a forty-three-year-old married man with four children, was from Co. Leitrim. He had twenty-one years' police service, having had no other employment before joining the RIC. His father was a canon at Christ Church, Londonderry.

28 April 1921, Parkbridge, Limerick city
Jeremiah Moroney, Sgt 57354

The sergeant was returning to Parkbridge to get his tobacco pouch, which he had left there. Two men shot and wounded him. He died from his wounds at 6 p.m. on 4 June at the Military Hospital, Limerick.

In July 1921 a military court of inquiry held in New Barracks, Limerick, heard that this attack happened as follows. At 6.30 a.m. the sergeant was returning to fetch his tobacco pouch when he met a fisherman who was returning from work. As they were standing talking, two men were seen coming from the direction of Corbally.

As they were strangers to both men, the sergeant said, 'I had better go to see who they are.' As he approached the men he said, 'You are out early this morning.' One of the men then stated that they had been out fishing while the other pulled out a gun and shot the sergeant in the abdomen. Although wounded the sergeant was able to return fire at the two men before they escaped.

Sergeant Moroney, forty-six and married, was from Co. Clare. He had twenty-six years' police service, having been a farmer before joining the RIC.

30 April 1921, near Castlemartyr, Co. Cork
William Albert Smith, Con 73965
John F. Webb, Con 75159

The two constables were going fishing on a riverbank near Castlemartyr, Co. Cork, when they were surrounded and attacked by twelve men. Constable Smith, twenty-seven and single, from Lancashire, had six months' police service, having been a turner before joining the RIC. He was killed outright. Constable Webb, a twenty-one-year-old single man, was seriously wounded. From London, he would have had completed six months' police service on 2 May, having been a carman before joining the RIC. He died on 1 May.

On 5 May full military honours were awarded the remains of two constables as they were taken to Glanmire Station in Cork en route to England. One of these constables was Webb, the other was John E. Bunce, 79386, who had been accidentally shot at Bandon Barracks.

1 May 1921, near Arva, Co. Cavan
George Cuthbertson, Con 78047
Walter Shaw, Con 78435

At 11.30 a.m. the two constables left Arva Barracks, Co. Cavan, to go for a walk. As the men had not returned by 5.30 p.m., a search party was sent to look for them. Their bodies were found on the Longford road in the townland of Fihora, each man having been shot.

It was learned that six men who had taken over a farmhouse had fired at them as they passed. Constable Cuthbertson was found to have three bullet wounds and another three caused by shotgun slugs, whilst Constable Shaw had three bullet wounds.

Constable Cuthbertson was a twenty-one-year-old single man from Sterling, who had been living at Greenan Dairy, Ayr, Scotland. He had four months' police service, having been a shepherd and a soldier before joining the RIC. Constable Shaw, twenty and single, was from Hollypark, Newtown, Yorkshire. He had exactly three months' police service, having been a post office clerk prior to joining the RIC.

3 May 1921, Tourmakeady, Co. Mayo
John Regan, Sgt 56814
Christopher Patrick O'Regan, Con 67167
Herbert Oakes, Con 78855
William Power, Con 61221

A two-car patrol left Ballinrobe travelling about 300 yards apart. When it reached Tourmakeady, the IRA allowed the first car past an ambush point and when the second car passed, both vehicles came under heavy fire from two points, one near Hewitts Hotel, the other at the gates to Drumbane House. Sergeant Regan was wounded and died two hours later. Constable O'Regan was killed outright.

Background
The South Mayo Brigade of the IRA became aware that the RIC at Ballinrobe collected supplies once a month from Birmingham & Co. for the barracks at Derrypark. A man in the shop (whose nephew, Frank Stagg, died on hunger strike in February 1976) gave the IRA information that the police were due to collect their stores and the brigade's flying column prepared to ambush the police on the main road at a sharp bend.[29]

Tom Maguire, the South Mayo Brigade commander, along with a flying column of twenty-five men who were mostly from the Ballinrobe Battalion, met men from the local companies in the village of Tourmakeady. This party, which numbered sixty, was divided into three. One group, under the command of Paddy May, took up a position at one end of the village near the entrance to Drumbane House. A second, under the leadership of Maguire, was placed in the centre of the village, while the third, led by Michael O'Brien, the South Mayo Brigade adjutant, went to the Fair Green at the northern end of the village. All the villagers were placed under guard – one of them, an RIC pensioner's wife, tried to escape to warn of the ambush, but was unable to get away.

As the first police vehicle reached May's location, an IRA rifleman, who was hidden behind a wall almost opposite the gates to Drumbane House, opened fire, killing Constable O'Regan, the driver, causing the car to crash through the gateway. The other members of the vehicle then alighted and began to return fire.

The second vehicle stopped when it came under fire from O'Brien's party. On seeing this, Maguire divided his party in two, sending half to each of the other units. With the arrival of these extra IRA men at May's location, the small police party was soon overwhelmed, with all of them being killed. The IRA then removed the dead officers' arms and ammunition before moving towards the second police vehicle, a Crossley tender, the occupants of which had carried their wounded into a small hotel which sat back a little from the roadside. From this building they had begun to return fire. This action forced the IRA to break off their attack and withdraw from the area. After the attack on the police patrol, military were sent to the scene of the ambush and, in a follow-up action, killed O'Brien and wounded Maguire.[30]

Constable O'Regan, a twenty-six year old single man, was from Co. Clare. He had eight years' police service, having been an engine cleaner before joining the RIC. Constable Oakes, twenty-four and married, was from London. He had three months' police service, having been a carman and a soldier prior to joining the RIC. Constable Power, thirty-nine and single, was from Co. Waterford. He had eighteen years' police service on 2 February 1921, having been a draper's assistant before joining the RIC. Sergeant Regan, a forty-six-year-old married man, was from Roscommon. He had twenty-six years' service, having been a farmer prior to joining the RIC.

3 May 1921, Clonakilty, Co. Cork
James Cullen, Con 79391
Martin Fallon, Con 65154

The two constables were in a shop in Barrack Street, Clonakilty, when they were fired on, after which a bomb was flung into the premises. Both were wounded, and both died on 9 May, Fallon in Cork Military Hospital.

Cullen was twenty-three, single and from Wiltshire. He would have had three months' police service on 24 May, having been a printer and a soldier before joining the RIC.

Fallon, a thirty-one-year-old single man, was from Co. Roscommon. He had eleven years' police service, having been a farmer prior to joining the RIC.

4 May 1921, near Rathmore, Co. Kerry
Thomas McCormack, Sgt 62054
Walter Thomas Brown, Con 70259
William Clapp, Con 72780
Robert Dyne, Con 75917
Alfred Hillyer, Con 73061
James Phelan, Con 63574
Samuel H. Wadkins, Con 72778
Hedley D. Woodcock, Con 72743

A large joint force of IRA men from Cork No. 2 and Kerry No. 2 brigades shot an eighty-year-old-man (Thomas Sullivan) and left his body on the Bog Road, a half-mile from Rathmore. A label was placed on the body which stated 'a spy and informer'. At 10 a.m. an RIC patrol of one sergeant and eight constables left its barracks at Rathmore to bring in the body. The patrol came under heavy fire from both sides of the road, and five members were killed outright. Constable Hickey escaped and was able to report the ambush. Constables Brown and Phelan died on 5 May from their wounds, with Sergeant McCormack succumbing on 8 May.

After this ambush an aeroplane was used to scout the district for the IRA units involved.

Sergeant McCormack, a thirty-five-year-old single man, was from Co. Roscommon. He had fourteen years' police service, having been a farmer before joining the RIC.

Constable Brown, twenty-nine and single, was from Middlesex. He had three months' police service, having been a soldier prior to joining the RIC.

Constable Clapp was twenty-two and single. From Hampshire, he would have had eight months' police service on 7 May, having been a dairyman and a soldier before joining the RIC.

Constable Dyne, a twenty-one-year-old single man, was from Sussex. He had five months' police service, having been a wireless operator and a soldier prior to joining the RIC.

Constable Hillyer was from London. Eighteen and single, he would have had eight months' police service on 10 May, having been a motor mechanic and a soldier before joining the RIC. He joined the force seven days after his eighteenth birthday.

Constable Phelan, a thirty-three-year-old single man, was from Co. Limerick. He had thirteen years' police service, having had no other employment prior to joining the RIC.

Constable Wadkins, a twenty-one-year-old single man, was from Middlesex. He would have had eight months' police service on 9 May, having been a labourer and a soldier before joining the RIC.

Constable Woodcock, a twenty-year-old single man, was from London. He had eight months' police service, having been a cook and a soldier prior to joining the RIC.

6 May 1921, Newtown, Co. Tipperary
James Kingston, Sgt 57392

An RIC patrol which had left Cappawhite Barracks was ambushed as it approached the Protestant church near Annacarthy and Sergeant Kingston was killed. One IRA man was also killed.

Sergeant Kingston, a forty-eight-year-old married man with several children, was from Clonakilty, Co. Cork. He had twenty-five years' service, having been a farmer before joining the RIC.

7 May 1921,
near Ballynacargy, Co. Westmeath
Murray, Sgt

A ten-man police patrol from Rathowen, Co. Westmeath, was ambushed at Ballynacargy by an IRA party estimated to be fifty in number. The sergeant was killed and a constable seriously wounded. No further details about this incident or the sergeant could be found.

7 May 1921, Inch, Co. Wexford
Frederick H. Depree, Con 74985

An RIC cycle patrol from Coolgreany Barracks was going to Gorey to get provisions. It had travelled one-and-a-half miles from the barracks when it was ambushed at Inch. The constable was killed and Sergeant Dolan was seriously wounded.

Constable Depree, nineteen and single, was from London. He had six months' police service, having been a clerk before joining the RIC.

7 May 1921, Lefane, Co. Mayo
Thomas Hopkins, Con 70690

Constable Hopkins, a twenty-one-year-old single man, who was stationed at Dromore, Co. Tyrone, was on leave at his father's home at Lefane. He was shot a quarter of a mile from the house.

On the evening of 7 May, he, his brother and a friend went to visit a neighbour. His brother left first to return home but was captured by IRA men, who held him prisoner. He tried to escape to warn Thomas, but failed, and as the other two men returned home from their visit, the constable was shot and killed. He had one year's police service on 5 May, having been a farmer before joining the RIC.

8 May 1921, Castleisland, Co. Kerry
William K. Storey, H/Con 56877
James Butler, Sgt 57034

Head Constable Storey, a forty-seven-year-old married man with six children, was returning, along with Sergeant Butler, from church at Castleisland. The police officers were attacked by two men, who walked up behind them before opening fire with revolvers. Storey was shot dead, being hit in the head and neck. Sergeant Butler was wounded in the spine and as he lay on the ground his wife threw herself on top of him in order to protect him from his attackers. Both men's wives were with them at the time of the attack.

Sergeant Butler died from his wounds on 19 July. He was forty-six years of age, having been a farmer from Tipperary South Riding prior to joining the RIC. He had twenty-six years' service two days before he died.

Head Constable Storey from Co. Limerick had twenty-six years' police service on 16 April, having been a clerk before joining the RIC. A detachment of military with their band, and a party of police under the command of DI Heggert, attended his funeral, as did a large number of relatives, friends and townspeople.

8 May 1921, Cook Street, Cork city
Frederick Sterland, Con 77543

While walking along Cook Street, Cork, the constable was shot and wounded. He was removed to the South Infirmary, where he died. He had earlier been lured to a hotel in Cork by men feigning friendship with him. The constable had bought them a drink, but when he left the hotel they followed and shot him.

Constable Sterland, a twenty-two-year-old married man from Birmingham, was a member of the transport section. He would have had four months' service on 11 May. He had been a draughtsman and a soldier before joining the RIC.

10 May 1921, Binnion, Co. Donegal
Alexander Thomas Clark, Con 73193

Two off-duty English constables left Clonmany Barracks, Co. Donegal, for a walk. They were shot in the townland of Binnion. The IRA men dragged the bodies away and it is believed that they threw them into the sea.

On 11 May police were informed about the body of a man on the seashore. When checked, it was found to be that of Constable Clark, who had been shot through the neck. Clark, a twenty-year-old single man, was from Hertfordshire and would have had eight months' police service on 21 May, having been a motor driver before joining the RIC.

On 17 May 1921 Mrs Murdock received a letter bearing a Londonderry postmark which stated that her husband was alive and well. Considerable doubt was placed on the authenticity of this letter at the time, which was borne out by the fact that Constable Murdock, 73788, was never seen again.

RIC Transport Division

With the fortification of RIC barracks, the IRA found it increasingly difficult to mount attacks on them, so they changed tactics and began to ambush patrols. The IRA's campaign against patrols began with the selection of suitable ambush spots from which the attackers could cover their line of retreat. Then overwhelming numbers of IRA men waited in ambush for small parties of RIC, who at first were either on foot or bicycle. The ambushes were carried out at short range, with shotguns being deployed.

As the situation worsened the police introduced armoured vehicles (mainly ex-RAF and military Lancia and Crossley tenders), each capable of carrying twelve men. The introduction of armoured police vehicles caused the IRA to mount their ambushes from a greater range with more use of rifles. They would also block or trench roads to prevent the police patrols from simply driving out of the danger area, which required more IRA men to be utilised in such attacks.

With the introduction of motor vehicles the police were faced with a major problem, namely finding men who had the necessary driving skills, which were relatively uncommon at that period. To overcome this difficulty, the police employed ex-service personnel who had acquired driving skills during the First World War and formed them into the Transport Division.

At first the police issued orders to the drivers that all three-tonne lorries and all solid-tyred vehicles were to be restricted to 12mph on open roads, 8mph in towns and villages, and 6mph in Dublin. Touring cars were restricted to 20mph, box-body vans and motorcycles were restricted to 10mph, and these limits were not to be exceeded unless by written order of an officer. Drivers were also instructed not to leave vehicles unattended outside barracks and, when parked off-duty, the petrol supply cock was to be turned off but the vehicle was to be ready for immediate duty. Only officers, head constables, sergeants and men from the Transport Division were to drive.

However, as attacks on vehicles began to increase, and the policy of closing outlying barracks unable to hold a garrison of at least twelve men began, new orders about motor transport and its tactical employment were issued.

The officers were informed that motor vehicles were substitutes for small isolated barracks that had closed and whose areas could not be patrolled by foot or cycle patrols from other barracks. They were reminded that their men were new to motor patrols and that any slackness could result in disaster. In order to prevent this, officers were instructed that personnel were to practise vehicle drills with vehicles being stopped suddenly at least once every patrol with the orders 'line the bank'. This way, the men could learn to deploy rapidly from their vehicles and to use what small cover the roadside offered.

The actions of the driver and the role of the Lewis gun team were to be determined by the officer before the commencement of his patrol and the men informed if they were all to leave via the end of the tender, if some were to jump over the sides, or if covering fire was to be kept going from the armoured lorry while the occupants of the vehicles got into position. The police officers were advised that experience showed that, once in an ambush, returning fire was of immediate importance and that every second counted to enable the patrol to return effective rifle and Lewis gun fire. They were also told that their own bombers, who had to be detailed when the vehicle began its patrol, must get into action quickly and that the men on the machine gun must be numbered off and be good shots at long range. The Lewis gun was to be placed in position and the bombs put carefully to hand and ready for use prior to the patrol setting off. As for the unprotected driver and the front-seat passenger, the officer was advised that they ought to wear a shield for protection.

Officers were instructed that, once ambushed, they were to send out their own flanking parties, which would break the main body of IRA attacking them, as they would not put up a determined resistance once this had happened. They were also informed that they had to check that the vehicle had spare tyres, jack, spare petrol, tool box, springs and tools like shovels, pickaxe, cross-cut saw and a couple of planks, so that the patrol had suitable equipment to deal with barricaded or trenched roads, but that they were not to overload a vehicle. The golden rule when in convoy, officers were told, was to ensure contact from front to rear vehicle. They were also told that the distance between each vehicle in the convoy and its speed were to be set before the patrol began, with the leading vehicle not less than 200 yards away; however, it had to see the following vehicle at least once every five minutes.

The speed of the convoy was not to exceed 20mph and officers were reminded that transport was not supplied to evade ambushes but to get to grips with them, which would not happen if the patrol was tearing up and down the country. When entering a town or village the convoy was to close up, so that it emerged unbroken; lookouts were to be posted in the vehicles; and signals between the convoy were to be maintained either by flag or (at night) by flashlight. Officers in charge of vehicle patrols were warned that they were not to wander around and that the entering of cottages, public houses and other buildings while on patrol was a grave offence.

Police officers were also informed that they were to practise daily every form of manoeuvre until it became impossible to be taken by surprise whilst on patrol; as the order stated, 'It becomes abundantly clear that once motor vehicles are handled with as much skill as, say, the old Royal Irish Constabulary did their arms drill, this new weapon of the force will be the foremost in overthrowing the tragic tyranny of terror which lies like a nightmare over Ireland.'[31]

Men from the RIC Transport Division were also attached to the Auxiliary Division of the RIC, who were being utilised as a kind of motorised reaction force and so also required drivers.

As the IRA campaign continued, they began to attack police vehicles in towns and cities by dropping grenades or bombs into them as they passed. To prevent this kind of attack Crossley tenders used in cities like Belfast, Dublin and Cork were fitted with wire netting.

11 May 1921,
Ship Street, Belfast city
Alfred Craig, Special Harbour Constable

The special harbour constable was on duty at the Ship Street entrance to York Dock West when he was shot dead. He had been sworn in as a special harbour constable in the autumn of 1920 and as such he was armed but did not wear a uniform – these constables were distinguished by a top coat, police cap and an armlet with a number on it.

Special Harbour Constable Craig was a twenty-four-year-old man who, during the First World War, served with the Seventh and Eighth Battalions, Royal Inniskilling Fusiliers. He had three brothers who also served in the army during the war. Two of them were wounded, while John was reported missing on 1 July 1916 and was not seen again. It is believed that Constable Craig was shot by the IRA, although earlier in the day he had been asked by a captain of a steamer to use his influence with some member of his crew who had shown signs of mutinous conduct.

The constable had been directing traffic and preventing unauthorised entry to the harbour when three to four men began quarrelling and scuffling with him. Having shot him, these men ran off towards Garmoyle Street.

The dead officer had been married for just three months. On 14 May he was buried from his home at 60 Kingswood Street, Mountpottinger, Belfast, to the city cemetery. A guard of honour was formed by his comrades, along with one officer from the RIC. The RIC band led the cortège, which was followed by a large crowd.

13 May 1921,
Cabinteely, Co. Dublin
Albert Edward Skeats, Con 80482

Constable Skeats, who was twenty-four, single and from London, was wounded at Cabinteely, Co. Dublin, and died on 28 May at Steeven's Hospital, Dublin. He had one month's police service on 12 May, having been a labourer and a soldier before joining the RIC.

14 May 1921, Innishannon, Co. Cork
John Kenna, Con 69312

Constable Kenna, a twenty-four-year-old single man from Co. Tipperary, was shot dead in a field about 400 yards from his barracks at Innishannon. The attack was carried out by Jim O'Mahoney, the local battalion adjutant, and three other IRA men.

He had three years' police service, having been a cycle mechanic before joining the RIC. The constable had been recommended for appointment to the RIC by DI Wilson, who was killed in a separate incident.

Background
In May 1921 a general election had been held in which Sinn Féin won an electoral success in the southern counties. The next day the IRA's First and Second Southern Divisions issued orders that synchronised attacks causing as many fatal casualties as possible were to be carried out by all IRA units against members of the security forces. These orders resulted in the death of fifty-six police officers in the month of May, which was the largest number to be killed in any month from 1919 until the Truce on 11 July 1921.

As a result of these attacks the *Daily News* declared that it had been a Black Whitsun in Ireland, while Dublin Castle announced that the casualties for the week ending 16 May 1921 had been the highest since the rebellion in 1916.

The reason these two IRA divisions had issued this order was as a reprisal for the execution of four Co. Cork IRA men on 28 April 1921. Before these executions the IRA had threatened the army commander in the area, Major General Sir E. P. Strickland, that if IRA men were executed after court martial they would take reprisal actions. These attacks placed added pressure on the government, who were about to negotiate a Truce with the IRA.

14 May 1921, Midleton, Co. Cork
Joseph E. Coleman, Sgt 61273
Thomas Cornyn, Con 64930
Harold Thompson, Con 76556

Sergeant Coleman was shot dead in a public house in Midleton. When other police arrived at the scene, two of them were sent to get a priest to minister to the sergeant. These officers were also shot and killed. A third party of police sent to fetch their bodies was also attacked, with one constable being seriously wounded. These attacks were carried out by the East Cork Brigade.

Sergeant Coleman was buried on 18 May at Glasnevin Cemetery, Dublin. The sergeant, a thirty-nine-year-old married man, was from London. He had eighteen years' police service, having been a groom before joining the RIC.

Constable Cornyn, thirty-five and single, was from Co. Cavan. He had fourteen years' police service, having been a farmer before joining the RIC. Constable Thompson, twenty-eight and also single, was from Australia. He had five months' police service on 10 May, having been a motor driver and a soldier before joining the RIC.

14 May 1921, Killarney Street, Dublin city
Robert Redmond, Con 78135

Constable Redmond was on leave from 13 to 16 May 1921. After a shot was heard at Frankfort Cottages in Killarney Street, Dublin, the wounded officer was found. He died as he was being taken to the Mater Hospital. He had been attached to the Auxiliaries HQ at Beggar's Bush Barracks, Dublin.

Constable Redmond, a forty-three-year old married man, was from Co. Wicklow. He had four months' police service on 3 May, having been a labourer and a soldier before joining the RIC. His funeral later took place to Glasnevin Cemetery, Dublin.

14 May 1921, Watercourse Road, Cork city
Peter Carolan, Con 62268
Patrick Hayes, Con 57259
John Ryle, Con 57411

At 5 p.m. a seven-man police patrol on Watercourse Road, Cork, was attacked by members of one of the Cork city battalions with a bomb being thrown into their midst by two men who had been hiding in a doorway. The blast blew off Constable Carolan's legs and he was taken to the North Infirmary. He was later moved to Cork Military Hospital but died from his wounds.

Constables Ryle, Hayes and Rothwell were also wounded, suffering severe lacerations. They too were taken to the North Infirmary and subsequently transferred to Cork Military Hospital. Constable Ryle died on 15 May and Constable Hayes on 23 May.

Before the attack the streets had been crowded, but on hearing the explosions people fled in all directions, which enabled the two attackers to escape in the confusion. Sentries guarding Victoria Barracks, which was built on an elevation overlooking the scene, observed a number of young men running from the scene into a field. The sentries opened fire on them and two were seen to fall but were carried away by their companions.

Constable Carolan, a thirty-five-year-old single man from Co. Cavan, was buried on 18 May in Killarney. He had fourteen years' service and was a farmer before joining the RIC.

Constable Ryle, a forty-six-year-old single man, was from Co. Kerry and was interred at Tralee. He had twenty-five years' police service, having been a farmer before joining the RIC.

Constable Hayes, forty-nine, single and from Co. Cork had twenty-five years' police service, having been a servant before joining the RIC.

14 MAY 1921, DRUMCOLLOGHER, CO. LIMERICK
Thomas Bridges, Con 69992

Three constables had gone to the village of Drumcollogher to purchase groceries when they were attacked by IRA men from the Third Battalion, West Limerick Brigade. Constable Bridges, a single man from Co. Roscommon, was shot dead. He would have been twenty-two years of age on 23 May. He had one year's police service, having been a farmer before joining the RIC.

14 MAY 1921, TRALEE, CO. KERRY
Francis Benson, H/Con 59293

Head Constable Benson had just left his home in Pembroke Street, Tralee, when members of Kerry No. 1 Brigade IRA shot and killed him a short distance away.

Benson, a forty-two-year-old married man with five children, was from Co. Sligo. He had twenty-one years' service, having been a farmer before joining the RIC.

14 MAY 1921, COOLBOREEN, CO. TIPPERARY
Harry Biggs, DI 76116

The DI and a military officer, along with three ladies, were travelling in a private motor car from Killorcully to Newport, Co. Tipperary, when they were ambushed at Coolboreen. The DI and Miss Barrington, the daughter of Sir Charles Barrington of Glenstal Castle, Murroe, Co.

Limerick, were killed. The other two ladies and the military officer escaped unhurt.

DI Biggs, a twenty-six-year-old single man, was from Hampshire. He joined the Auxiliary Division of the RIC on 3 August 1920, receiving the Auxiliary number 133 and the RIC number 72325. On 19 November 1920 he transferred to the RIC as a DI and was then given the new RIC number of 76116. During the First World War he had been a lieutenant with the Thirteenth Hussars. His body was later taken to England for burial.

Background

The DI and the military officer met a Mr Gabbett and the ladies at Newport. The party then went fishing at Newport river. In the evening they were returning in the DI's car when, as they reached Coolboreen Bridge, they were ambushed from both sides of the bridge and from behind. The DI was wounded in the throat but managed to get out of the car and run ten yards before he fell, whilst Miss Barrington, who was also wounded, fell from the car.

The army officer got through a hedge and returned the attackers' fire. He then made his way to the DI and turned him over. As he did so he was slightly wounded. By this stage he had expended his ammunition so he made his way across country to fetch help.

On seeing that there was a woman in the car, an IRA man called out that the attack was to stop. At this, twelve men came out from the area of the bridge and asked who was lying on the road. When told it was the DI, the leader of this group and several men made their way to him and fired at him ten to twelve times with rifles before all the IRA men left the scene. However, as one of them left he told the other lady, who had been slightly wounded, that he was sorry the women had been injured.

On 18 May the DI's body was taken from the Military Barracks, Limerick, to the railway station for the midday express to Dublin.

The band of the Royal Welch Fusiliers led the funeral to the railway station.

15 May 1921, near Skibbereen, Co. Cork
Hugh McLean, Con 74660

Constable McLean was a motor mechanic attached to the RIC. He was attacked by members of the IRA's Skibbereen Battalion two miles outside the town earlier in the day. He died from his wounds later in Skibbereen workhouse. When the constable was first found he said, 'I'm done.' He had resigned from the RIC and was to have left the force on 31 May.

The constable's mother, who lived at Lossie Wynd, Elgin, Scotland, and whose husband and another son were also in the RIC, received an envelope with an Edinburgh postmark. This envelope contained Sinn Féin literature and a threatening letter.[32] The constable's brother had also resigned from the RIC and was to have left the force with his brother on 31 May. The dead constable, a twenty-one-year-old single man, was from Moray, Scotland. He would have had six months' service on 20 May, having been a motor mechanic and a soldier before joining the RIC.

15 May 1921, Bansha, Co. Tipperary
John Nutley, Con 71087

A group of police officers were attacked as they left the church in Bansha. Constable Nutley was killed, while a sergeant was seriously wounded and another constable slightly wounded in the attack. Constable Nutley, a twenty-two-year-old single man, was from Co. Galway. He had one year's service on 22 April, having been a labourer and a soldier before joining the RIC.

15 May 1921,
Ballyturin House, Gort, Co. Galway
Cecil Arthur Maurice Blake, DI 76106
John Kearney, Con 62450

The DI, his wife, two army officers and another woman had been attending a tennis party at Ballyturin House, Gort, Co. Galway. On leaving the house, the car driven by the DI was ambushed. Twenty IRA men from Co. Galway were involved in the ambush.

When the DI arrived at the front gates to the house he found that they were closed. He got out of the vehicle to open them and was fired on from nearby shrubbery, falling dead. Armed and disguised men then appeared from their hiding places and ordered the ladies to leave the area. Mrs Blake called out that she would never leave her husband, saying that if she were to die she would die by his side. The other lady then left the scene and as she did so she heard more shots. Mrs Blake and the two army officers were all killed.[33]

Police and military rushed to the scene from Gort along with a doctor and a nurse. When they arrived a shot rang out and Constable Kearney fell from the lorry. He was taken to St Brigid's Home, Galway, where he died. The constable's coffin was later removed from the home by Auxiliaries and soldiers from the Seventh Lancers, and taken to the railway station for the journey to Dublin, where he was buried at Glasnevin Cemetery.

On arriving at the scene the police found Mrs Blake beside her husband; she had been shot five times. The DI's automatic pistol was missing. He was from Chelmsford and had served with distinction in the Royal Artillery during the First World War. He had once been an orderly for Brigadier General Crozier, who had recommended him for appointment to the RIC. Blake and his wife were buried at the New Cemetery, Galway, after a service in the Collegiate church of St Nicholas.

DI Blake was thirty-six years old and had six months' police service on 10 May, having been an army officer before joining the RIC.

Constable Kearney, thirty-seven and single, was from Co. Kerry. He had fourteen years' police service, having been a farmer prior to joining the RIC.

17 May 1921,
near Rathcline, Co. Longford
Edmund Kenyon, Con 74724

An RIC cycle patrol, which had left from Longford, was travelling between Lanesborough and Ballymahon through a wild and lonely part of the county. The patrol's progress had been impeded by trenched and barricaded roads. When the patrol reached Fortwilliam it was ambushed, which forced the police to take shelter in a nearby cottage.

Constable Kenyon, who had only recently returned to duty after his marriage, was killed and three other constables, one called Finneran, were badly wounded. Constable Kenyon's body was later taken to Dublin by train. A twenty-two-year-old married man from Co. Kildare, he would have had seven months' police service on 22 May, having been a stoker and a soldier before joining the RIC.

17 May 1921, Ballyseedy, Co. Kerry
Charles F. Mead, Con 77946

Constable Mead was stationed in Kerry and was reported missing on 17 May at Ballyseedy, Co. Kerry. His body was buried in a bog just off the Tralee to Castlemaine road, where it was discovered on 26 September 1926. (Reports received stated that a man wearing an RIC uniform was seen to be shot at by two men and that he fell. A quantity of blood was found where he fell and there were traces of blood from that spot for half a mile across country.)³⁴ Born on 13 November 1884, he was married on 16 April 1920 and came from Middlesex. Formerly a coppersmith and a soldier, he joined the RIC on 15 January 1921.

17 May 1921, Kinnity, King's County
Edward Doran, Con 69438
John Dunne, Con 69354

An RIC patrol which was serving juror summonses in the small village of Kinnity, seven miles from Birr, was fired on at Kilcormac Road as it passed the ruined police barracks. Constable Dunne was killed outright, with Constable Doran dying from his wounds on 19 May.

Constable Dunne, a twenty-two-year-old single man from Tuam, Co. Galway, was interred in Kilconly, Tuam, on 20 May. He had three years' police service, having been a farmer before joining the RIC. It was later reported that his grave had been desecrated on 21 May, when eight wreaths were removed from it and destroyed.

Constable Doran, a twenty-four-year-old single man, was from Co. Wexford. He would have had three years' police service on 4 June, having been a gardener prior to joining the RIC.

18 May 1921, Letterkenny, Co. Donegal
Albert Carter, Con 78015

A police patrol was ambushed in the town of Letterkenny. This resulted in the death of Constable Carter and the wounding of Sergeant Charles Maguire. As the assault on the patrol was taking place, the local RIC barracks was also attacked.

Constable Carter, a twenty-year-old single man, was from Co. Kildare. He would have had four months' police service on 19 May, having been a farmer before joining the RIC. After a service in the Protestant church at Letterkenny, the constable's remains were carried by his former comrades through the town as other RIC men marched alongside. The coffin was then placed into a motor hearse and taken to Co. Kildare. His brother travelled with it.

18 May 1921, Newport, Co. Mayo
Francis J. Butler, Sgt 59260

Sergeant Butler, a fifty-four-year-old married man from Co. Roscommon, was shot and wounded as he was making his way from his lodgings in Newport to his barracks. He died on 19 May in the County Infirmary, Castlebar. He had twenty-one years' service, having been a farmer prior to joining the RIC.

This attack was carried out by members of the West Mayo Brigade flying column, who shot the sergeant from across a river as he was making his way through the maze of barbed wire defences at the front of the barracks.

19 May 1921, Kilmeena, Co. Mayo
Harry Beckett, Con 80290

Constable Beckett was killed and Head Constable Potter seriously wounded when they and other police officers began to outflank an IRA ambush party which had earlier attacked their two-vehicle police patrol on the Westport to Newport road at Kilmeena village.

Beckett, a twenty-one-year-old single man, was from Lancashire. He had one month's police service, having been a cook and a Royal Marine before joining the RIC.

Background
After the attack on Sergeant Butler in Newport on 18 May, the

IRA's West Mayo Brigade flying column was led by its commander, Michael Kilroy, to the village of Ballincarrigan. Knowing that there would probably be security-force activity in the area as a result of the shooting, he again moved his column, this time to Kilmeena.

Once into the area, the IRA laid an ambush to the south of Knocknaboly crossroads for the police and military they expected to come in search of them. Later in the day two police lorries suddenly arrived at the ambush location, taking the IRA by surprise. The police were able to outflank the IRA and in the gun battle which followed, the constable and four IRA men were killed and several others wounded. Five IRA men were later captured. The remainder made their way to Lower Shirdagh, where they were billeted.

Another of the police officers involved in this counter-attack, Sergeant Creegan from Westport, was killed in an ambush on 2 June.

20 May 1921, Killeter, Co. Longford
Leonard Booth, Con 74959
William Stewart, Con 69853

The two unarmed constables were returning from leave and had left Longford to cycle back to their barracks at Ballinalee. When they reached Killeter, between the villages of Killoe and Ballinalee, they were ambushed.

Constable Stewart, a single man from Co. Tyrone who would have been twenty-one years of age on 23 May, was killed outright, while Constable Booth was shot and wounded in the shoulder. He managed to get away from the ambush scene but his attackers followed him and shot him again in the heart. Their bodies were found on 21 May after a civilian called at the RIC barracks at Longford and reported them lying on the roadway.

A young lady who had been friendly with one of the two constables attended their funeral. Later that night her parents' house at Edgeworthstown was fired into, fortunately without anyone being injured.³⁵ Tragedy was to strike the Stewart family again, when William's brother, Thomas, a member of the Ulster Special Constabulary, was accidentally shot dead in October 1923. Thomas had gone to shoot pigeons with a shotgun and as he was crossing a fence, the weapon accidentally discharged.

William Stewart had two years' police service, having been a draper before joining the RIC. Booth was to have resigned from the police but he withdrew his request on 18 February 1921. A married man, he was from Lancashire and would have been thirty-three on 21 May. He would have had six months' service on 29 May, having been a soldier prior to joining the RIC.

21 May 1921, Balbriggan, Co. Dublin
Joseph Anderson, Sgt 49436

Sergeant Anderson, a fifty-nine-year-old single man, was from Co. Donegal. A veteran RIC bandmaster from Gormanston, Co. Dublin, he was shot and killed at Hampton, Balbriggan, Dublin, by four men. He would have had thirty-nine years' service on 13 June, having been a farmer before joining the RIC.

21 May 1921, Mountfield, Co. Tyrone
Peter Joseph McDonagh, Sgt 64858

An RIC cycle patrol attached to Mountfield Barracks was returning from Greencastle when it was ambushed. Sergeant McDonagh, a thirty-one-year-old single man from Co. Fermanagh, was killed as a result of this attack. He was buried at St Mary's churchyard, Brookeborough, Co. Fermanagh. He had eleven years' police service, having been a shop assistant before joining the RIC. He had been promoted to temporary sergeant on 1 April 1921.

23 May 1921, Lower Shirdagh, Co. Mayo
Joseph Maguire, Con 66577

DI Munroe was in charge of an eighteen-man police patrol which was on duty in the Mayo Hills at Lower Shirdagh, four miles northeast of Newport. At 5 a.m. this patrol encountered thirty IRA men and a gun battle developed. DI Munroe was wounded and Constable Maguire was killed. At 7 a.m. a member of the police patrol was able to catch a farmer's horse, which he rode bareback under fire to fetch reinforcements. At 10 a.m., with police beginning to outflank them, the IRA broke off its attack and was pursued across country.

Constable Maguire, twenty-eight and single, was from Co. Fermanagh. He first joined the RIC on 15 May 1912, but was discharged as medically unfit by the surgeon on 17 May. He rejoined on 28 August 1912. He had been a farmer prior to joining the RIC.

Background
After the IRA's failed ambush at Kilmeena on 19 May, the West Mayo Brigade flying column had gone to the village of Lower Shirdagh. However, the police became aware of this fact and an operation to surround the IRA unit was mounted. It was during this operation that Constable Maguire was shot and killed.

26 May 1921, Cooga, Co. Clare
Edgar Budd, Con 72348

Two unarmed constables were ambushed at Cooga, Co. Clare, and Constable Budd was killed. They had been returning from leave to their barracks at Kildysart. Constable Irvine, who was wounded during the attack, was pursued by some of his attackers for two miles across country before escaping.

Constable Budd was a twenty-three-year-old single man from

Hampshire. He had nine months' police service, having been a gardener and a soldier before joining the RIC.

29 May 1921,
Mullaghfad Cross, Co. Fermanagh
Robert Coulter, S/Con
James Hall, S/Con

At 12.30 a.m. a twelve-man foot patrol of the Ulster Special Constabulary was on duty in the mountainous area between Fivemiletown and the border with Co. Monaghan. As the patrol, which was moving in two groups with eight men in the main party and four in the rear one, passed Mullaghfad Cross, the rear element was ambushed by forty IRA men at close range from behind a ditch.

Special Constable Coulter was killed instantly, while Special Constable Hall was seriously wounded. He dragged himself to a nearby house owned by a Sinn Féin member, who refused him assistance and, as a result, he was found dead outside the farmhouse.

30 May 1921, Kilrooskey, Co. Roscommon
George Redding, Con 72550

A police patrol from Roscommon encountered a party of armed IRA men digging a trench in the roadway at Kilrooskey, five miles from Roscommon. The police were fired on and Constable Redding was killed. At the scene the police recovered a rifle which had belonged to Constable Clarke, 64977, who had been killed on 14 July 1920 between Lanesborough and Roscommon. A number of IRA men were captured at the scene.

Constable Redding, a twenty-one-year-old single man, was from Buckinghamshire. He had nine months' police service, having been a hatter and a soldier before joining the RIC.

30 May 1921, Tullyvarragh, Co. Monaghan
Walter P. Perkins, Con 77306

A police cycle patrol was making its way from Carrickmacross to Castleblayney, Co. Monaghan, when it was ambushed at Tullyvarragh. Constable Perkins, a twenty-seven-year-old single man from the Isle of Wight, was killed. He would have had five months' police service on 4 June, having been a car driver and a soldier before joining the RIC.

1 June 1921, Kilworth, Co. Cork
Joseph C. Holman, Con 74002

Constable Holman was walking with a female friend along a road near Kilworth, a few hundred yards from his barracks, when he was fired on from behind a fence at a plantation and killed.

The constable, twenty-one and single, was from Sussex and lived at 14 Warrior Square, St Leonard's-on-Sea, Sussex. He would have had eight months' police service on 8 June, having been a Royal Marine before joining the RIC.

1 June 1921, near Castlemaine, Co. Kerry
Michael F. McCaughey, DI 67290
James Collery, Sgt 58355
Joseph Cooney, Con 69529
John S. McCormack, Con 71678
John Quirk, Con 63249

A police cycle patrol left during that morning from their barracks at Killorglin for Tralee. The IRA's Kerry No. 1 Brigade flying column under the command of Tadhg Brosnan was informed and set an ambush for the returning RIC patrol between Castlemaine and Milltown.

The ambush was on the Milltown side of Castlemaine railway bridge, with the IRA taking up a number of locations along a half-mile length of ditch. They hoped to be able to attack the whole police patrol, which had been observed in extended formation earlier in the day. As the patrol entered the ambush area at approximately 5 p.m. it came under heavy fire, and four officers were killed outright, with four other constables being wounded as they returned fire.

One IRA man was wounded during this attack and he was removed from the scene on a door used as a stretcher and placed into a horse-drawn car. The dead and wounded police were taken to Tralee by special train on the evening of 2 June and then to the military barracks.[36]

Constable McCormack was twenty and single, and came from Co. Leitrim. He died on 7 June. He would have had one year's police service on 17 June, having been a rigger and a soldier before joining the RIC.

DI McCaughey was from Co. Down. On 6 August 1915 he had joined the Irish Guards and in the latter part of 1918 was commissioned into the Indian Army. He rejoined the RIC on 3 March 1920, having previously enlisted on 15 March 1913 as a constable. He was a twenty-eight-year-old single man and had been a draper's assistant before joining the RIC.

Sergeant Collery, a forty-five-year-old married man with nine children was from Co. Sligo. He had twenty-two years' police service.

Constable Cooney, twenty-five and single, was from Co. Roscommon. He had two years' police service.

Constable Quirk, thirty-three and also single, was from Co. Cork. He had thirteen years' police service. All three had been farmers before joining the RIC.

2 JUNE 1921, KYLEBEG CROSS, CO. TIPPERARY

James Briggs, DCM, MM, Con 70463
John Cantlon, Con 52669
Martin Feeney, Con 65453
William Walsh, Con 55430

A twelve-man RIC cycle patrol was making its way from Borrisokane to Cloughjordan, where the men were due for court duty, while another sixteen-man patrol in cars was making its way in the same direction. The two patrols were ambushed at Kylebeg Cross, midway between the two locations.

Constable Briggs, DCM, MM, attached to Borrisokane Barracks, was killed outright, and four other constables were seriously wounded. A sergeant and three constables were also wounded during the attack but not as seriously. Of the four seriously wounded men, three died the next day. Constables Cantlon and Walsh were attached to Roscrea RIC Barracks, whilst Constable Feeney had been attached to Borrisokane.

Constable Briggs, a single man from Wigtown, would have been twenty-nine years of age on 11 June. He had one year's police service, having been a cheese-maker and a soldier prior to joining the RIC.

Constable Cantlon, a fifty-three-year-old married man, was from Co. Carlow. He had thirty-three years' police service, having been a farmer before joining the RIC.

Constable Feeney, thirty-two and single, was from Co. Roscommon. He had ten years' police service. Constable Walsh, a fifty-two-year-old married man, was from Queen's County. He had twenty-eight years' service. Both had been labourers before joining the RIC.

Background
The North Tipperary flying column was joined by eight IRA men

from the Cloughjordan Company, who were armed with shotguns. They laid an ambush between a double bend in the road for the police as they made their way from Borrisokane to Cloughjordan. As the IRA ambush party was settling down it was seen by a youth. The IRA man in charge of the shotgun party at the edge of the road questioned the youth, telling him to go and fetch his father. When his father arrived he was recognised as an ex-soldier and the IRA decided to shoot him as a spy after they had ambushed the police.

When the police patrol had almost reached the second bend, Seán Gaynor, the North Tipperary Brigade commandant, began the ambush by blowing a whistle, with the IRA's shotgun men opening fire on the first police vehicle, in which one of the policemen was singing loudly, 'I'm Forever Blowing Bubbles'. However, the vehicle at the rear of the patrol was able to turn around before it entered the ambush area and set off to get reinforcements.

After the ambush the IRA removed the arms and ammunition from the dead RIC, but in the excitement they had forgotten about their prisoner, who had managed to hide under some straw.[37]

2 JUNE 1921,
CARROWKENNEDY, CO. MAYO
Edward James Stevenson, DI 72024
Francis Creegan, Sgt 59658
Sydney Blythe, Con 78576
James Brown, Con 79746
John Doherty, Con 57416
Thomas Dowling, Con 60016
William French, Con 75811

At 7 p.m. a seventeen-man patrol was ambushed at Carrowkennedy on the main Westpoint to Leenane road, Co. Mayo. The attack by 70–100 men lasted for three and a half hours and resulted in the deaths of five police officers and the serious wounding of six others. Of the seriously wounded men, Sergeant Creegan died on 3 June and Constable Dowling died on 7 June in a Dublin hospital.

DI Stevenson, the son of James Verdier Stevenson, a former DI in the RIC who transferred to Scotland to be the chief constable of Glasgow (1902–22), was buried on 9 June at Ardnaree church, Ballina, in the family vault of the Littles (the late DI's mother was a family member). He was a twenty-two-year-old single man from Co. Down. During the First World War he had served with the Black Watch and the Royal Highlanders. He would have had one year's service on 22 July. He was promoted to DI on 1 October 1920.

Sergeant Creegan, a forty-three-year-old married man from Co. Fermanagh, lived at John's Row, Westport. He would have had twenty-one years' police service on 16 July, having previously been a farmer.

Constable Blythe, a twenty-six-year-old married man, was from Norfolk. He had four months' police service on 2 June, having been a groom and a soldier before joining the RIC.

Constable Brown, twenty-three, married, from Roxborough, Scotland, would have had three months' police service on 16 June 1921, having been a tweed mill worker and a soldier prior to joining the RIC.

Constable Doherty was a forty-seven-year-old married man from Co. Roscommon. He had twenty-five years' police service, having been a farmer before joining the RIC.

Constable Dowling was a forty-six-year-old married man from Queen's County. He had twenty years' police service, having been a farmer before joining the RIC.

Constable French was twenty-five and single. From Gloucester, he had six months' police service, having been a warehouseman and a soldier prior to joining the RIC.

Background

The IRA's West Mayo flying column, under the leadership of Michael Kilroy, was told that an RIC patrol of two lorries and a car was stopped by a trench dug in the Leenane road. When the trench was filled in the patrol moved off, but Kilroy knew it would probably have to return by the same road as the bridge at Delphin had been destroyed, so he planned to ambush it on its return.

The column, along with IRA men from the Westport Battalion, were placed into three ambush positions. The first, under the command of Brodie Malone, commandant of the Westport Battalion, was on rising ground behind a wall of boulders 150 yards from the roadway. Their task was to attack the first police lorry. The second position was approximately 150 yards from the first on the same side of the road. It was near the site of an old police hut that the Aghagower IRA Company had burned at Easter 1920. The IRA men at this second location were under the command of Tom Kitterick, the brigade's quartermaster, and they were to attack the second police lorry.

The third IRA unit of ten riflemen was placed on the other side of the roadway on ground behind a cottage. This position had good banks that screened the ambush party from the roadway. Their task was to attack the third police vehicle, a car, as well as the second police lorry.

As the ambush was about to take place, an old man who had been working in a potato plot below the IRA's first location became aware of the men's presence and began to call on them to stop destroying his wall.

As the first police lorry approached, the DI turned his head towards the ambush location as if he noticed something, but was shot dead by a bullet through the forehead. Another police officer in the lorry was also killed in the first volley of gunfire, with the other members taking cover and returning fire. The second police lorry driver, on hearing the gunfire, had stopped and the crew members, under heavy IRA gunfire, were able to make their way into the cottage below the third ambush location from which they prepared to fight. However, they had been unable to bring their spare ammunition with them from the lorry.

The police in the car also took cover on hearing the gunfire, with Constable French taking up a position on the right-hand side of the roadway below the IRA's second ambush party. Using the broken ground he moved towards the IRA party, directing his comrades to do likewise. When approximately seventy yards from the IRA he was shot by an IRA man, Jimmy Flaherty, who for nine years had been a member of the First Battalion, Connaught Rangers.

The battle had raged for over two hours when a police officer at the first lorry, who was about to throw a grenade, was shot. The grenade exploded in the vehicle, which resulted in the fatal wounding of another police officer. The IRA moved forward and captured the lorry, finding a senior constable leaning against a wall dead, with Sergeant Creegan lying in the lorry severely wounded from the grenade explosion, splinters of a rifle butt in his stomach and groin. All the police in this vehicle, with the exception of one officer, were either dead or wounded.

The IRA then turned their full attention on the police party in the cottage, bringing a Lewis machine gun captured in the first police lorry into play. As the police officers' ammunition was exhausted they were forced to surrender.[38] After this incident the IRA took all the weapons and remaining ammunition belonging to the police, which included a small revolver taken from the body of DI Stevenson, on which it was alleged there was an inscription from Sir Edward Carson to the DI's father.

5 June 1921, Swatragh, Co. Londonderry
Michael Burke, Sgt 66998

As a police patrol made its way through Swatragh, it drew near to a bridge on the outskirts of the village. A candle left burning in a cottage window showed the movement of the patrol as it passed. Twenty IRA men, who were behind a wall opposite, opened fire as the police passed the light. The police fought back, with Constable Anderson returning fire from the roadway beside the body of the dead sergeant.

This attack resulted in the death of Sergeant Burke and the wounding of Special Constable Kennedy. He was shot in the neck with pellets which damaged his vocal chords. As a result of his wound Kennedy was unable to speak properly again and became known in the area as 'Hoarse Johnny'.

Burke, a twenty-eight-year-old single man, was from Ballinrobe, Co. Mayo. He had eight years' police service, having been a farmer before joining the RIC.

5 June 1921, Abbeyfeale, Co. Limerick
Robert W. Jolly, Con 75228

The constable was part of a police patrol in Abbeyfeale engaged in removing seditious posters in the town when it was ambushed. Constable Jolly was killed outright and a sergeant and four constables were wounded.

Background
A large number of IRA men from the West and North Limerick Brigade flying columns under the command of Paddy O'Brien had set up an ambush on a steep road about a half-mile from the town, which was frequently patrolled by the RIC. A number of notices telling the Black and Tans to leave the country immediately were posted on gateways and in the vicinity of the ambush's previously prepared positions, which the IRA had taken up at dawn. However, the police did not patrol the road as expected, so eight sections of the

IRA took over houses overlooking the town square and posted more notices in the general area.

At 6.30 a.m. a police patrol left the barracks and had begun tearing down the posters when it was attacked. Constable Jolly, a thirty-seven-year-old married man, was from Kent. He had exactly seven months' police service, having been an upholsterer and a soldier before joining the RIC.

8 June 1921, near Newry, Co. Down
George Lyness, S/Con

Shortly before 8 p.m. a party of Ulster Special Constabulary patrolling on bicycles in the townland of Corrogs overlooking the Warrenpoint road, one-fifth of a mile from Newry, saw a number of men acting suspiciously on a hill nearby. The patrol, anticipating an ambush, dismounted and a gun battle followed, with one officer being wounded.

Police reinforcements were sent to help search the area, arriving at 8.45 p.m. When searching a house the police came under attack again and the special constable, who had been on guard outside, was shot dead. Two IRA men were killed and one was wounded during this incident.

Special Constable Lyness was twenty-five and engaged to be married. He lived with his parents at Riverside Covenanting church in Newry and had served with the Royal Irish Rifles in the First World War and later in the Machine Gun Corps.

9 June 1921, Carrigbeg, Co. Waterford
Denis O'Leary, Con 60374

The constable was cycling to his lodgings at Carrigbeg when he was shot dead. He had just reached the village when he was attacked.

Constable O'Leary, a forty-three-year-old married man, was from Rathmore, Co. Kerry. He had nineteen years' police service, having been a farmer prior to joining the RIC.

10 JUNE 1921, FALLS ROAD, BELFAST CITY
James Glover, Con 64889

A police foot patrol was making its way along the Falls Road and had just reached the Diamond Picture House at the corner of Cupar Street when they were attacked. Constable Glover and two other constables were wounded and taken to the Royal Victoria Hospital, but Glover died on 7 July.

During the First World War Glover had volunteered for active service, being one of the first 200 RIC men to go to France from Belfast, joining the Irish Guards on 13 January 1915. In the latter part of 1917 he became a machine gunner in the Guards. He received a gunshot wound to the back on 31 July 1917 and was discharged as unfit from the army, rejoining the RIC on 21 February 1919. Three of his brothers had also joined the British Army, whilst another three had joined the American Army. On the evening the constable was killed, his brother, a tramway inspector living at the Ardoyne Fire Station, was expecting him for a meal, which he postponed when he failed to turn up.

The constable's coffin, draped in a Union Jack, was borne by his comrades and civilian friends from his brother's home for a considerable distance, with between 25,000 and 30,000 mourners watching the funeral. The funeral then became mobile and left for Antrim, where Constable Glover's remains were buried in the New Cemetery.

Constable Glover, thirty-one and single, was from Co. Antrim. He had eleven years' police service, having been a gardener before joining the RIC.

12 June 1921, Kilbeggan, Co. Westmeath
James McElhill, H/Con 53480

McElhill and other police officers were making their way to Kilbeggan church when they were attacked and the head constable was killed. He was a fifty-three-year-old single man from Co. Tyrone. He had thirty-two years' police service, having been a farmer before joining the RIC.

12 June 1921, York Street, Belfast city
Thomas Sturdy, S/Con

Early on Sunday evening sporadic gunfire broke out in the York Street/Dock Street area of Belfast. Sniping was taking place in the northern end of York Street, which was deserted except for police and army touring the area in Crossley tenders and armoured lorries as they tried to quell the shooting.

At 9.30 p.m. Special Constable Sturdy was shot and fatally wounded as he sat in an armoured lorry at Dock Street/North Thomas Street, which came under gunfire from the upstairs window of a house. On 14 June his funeral left the Royal Victoria Hospital for Castlederg, but as it got under way it was jeered and attacked.

12 June 1921, Rainsford Street, Dublin city
Michael Brannan, Con 81087
John Frederick Smith, Con 81097

Between 8 and 9 p.m. the two constables were standing in Rainsford Street, Dublin, when three men came up to them and fired a number of shots. One constable was killed instantly, while the other died a short time after he had been admitted to Steeven's Hospital. Both men had only twenty-three days' police service, having joined the RIC on 20 May.

Constable Brannan, a twenty-six-year-old married man, was from Durham. He had been a seaman and a soldier before joining the RIC.

Constable Smith, twenty-five and single, was from Middlesex. He had been a carman and a soldier prior to joining the RIC.

16 June 1921, Newmarket, Co. Cork
William A. H. Boyd, Cadet 79144
Frederick E. Shorter, Cadet 79823

Twenty-five Auxiliary cadets attached to Millstreet were returning with stores from Banteer in four lorries when they were ambushed on the road between Lough and Rathcoole in the Newmarket area of Cork. Three mines exploded, blowing up two lorries, resulting in the deaths of these two cadets and the wounding of four others.

Background
A large combined force of 140 men from Cork's No. 2 Brigade, from the flying columns attached to the Millstreet, Kanturk, Newmarket, Charleville and Mallow battalions, under Paddy O'Brien, attacked the four police lorries. Four mines placed in the roadway were used, one each being detonated under the lead and rear vehicles, which trapped the other two vehicles. The third and fourth mines in the middle of the convoy were detonated but only one of them went off.[39]

Cadet Boyd was attached to C Company, having joined on 19 November 1920. His Auxiliary number was 774. During the First World War he had been a second lieutenant in the Royal Sussex Regiment. He was a twenty-one-year-old single man from Sussex, who would have had seven months' police service three days later.

Cadet Shorter, same age and status, was from Middlesex. He had joined the RIC on 30 November 1920, and was attached to C Company. His Auxiliary number was 1115.

17 June 1921, near Dundalk, Co. Louth
William Campbell, Con 76250

At 10.30 p.m. the off-duty constable had left his barracks at Bridge Street to cycle a short distance along the main Newry road to Newbridge Barracks. At the 11 p.m. roll-call it was found that the constable was missing. At 12.30 a.m. information was received that there was a body of a man in police uniform lying on the roadway one mile from the town. Police went to the scene in a Crossley and a Ford car, finding the dead constable along the kerb at New Inn, face down. He had been shot twice in the chest and once in the back, and his revolver was found to be missing. Thirty-five yards away his bicycle was found; it had a bullet mark on the top bar of the frame and its handlebars were twisted.

The constable's coffin was taken from Louth County Hospital and placed on a gun carriage, drawn by black chargers with outriders and flanked on either side by six of his comrades. The funeral was headed by a firing party from the Royal Field Artillery, with a further detachment of the Royal Field Artillery in the procession, along with a party of RIC with rifles reversed. A detachment of Auxiliaries brought up the rear of the funeral. The constable was buried with full military honours at St Patrick's Cemetery.

Constable Campbell, a twenty-one-year-old single man, was from Dumbarton. He had six months' service on 8 June, having been a casker and a soldier before joining the RIC.

18 June 1921, Fiddown, Co. Kilkenny
Albert Bradford, Con 72721

An RIC patrol was ambushed at Fiddown in the Thomastown district of Co. Kilkenny, resulting in the death of Constable Bradford and the serious wounding of Sergeant Sweatman. At 7.15 p.m. on 19 June, as the army was escorting the coffin of the constable, they were ambushed near Newbridge, Carrick-on-Suir, by a large party of armed men who were concealed on both sides of the roadway. Private Smith of the First Devons was killed as a result of this ambush.

Constable Bradford, a twenty-one-year-old single man, was from Essex. He would have had ten months' police service on 31 June, having been a labourer and a soldier before joining the RIC.

24 June 1921, Grafton Street, Dublin city
Leonard George Appleford, Cadet 73555
George Gerald Wames, Cadet 80208

The two Auxiliary cadets stationed at Dublin Castle had been out shopping and had gone into a restaurant for tea. On leaving, they were shot by three men near the junction with Chatham Street. These gunmen had been led up to the two officers by a girl dressed in a dark-blue sailor costume. When she approached she pointed at them and shouted, 'Here they are', before disappearing. The two men were then shot eighteen to twenty times by the gunmen.

Cadet Appleford, a twenty-seven-year-old single man, joined the RIC on 8 September 1920 and was attached to F Company, having the Auxiliary number 589. On 21 December 1920 he was made section leader. He was from Essex and his home was at 3 Globe Cottage, Haroldwood. During the First World War he held a commission in the Machine Gun Corps.

Cadet Wames, twenty-nine and single, had joined the RIC on 21 December 1920 and was also attached to F Company, having the Auxiliary number 1214. He was from Suffolk, with his home being at Cranley Grange Eye. During the First World War he had been a captain with the Fifth Suffolk Regiment. Before joining the RIC he was at Cambridge University.

Background
The Second Battalion of the IRA's Dublin Brigade planned to send eight groups of gunmen into Grafton Street at 6 p.m. from different side streets. They hoped to hem in all the members of the security forces on Grafton Street and then attack them. Another IRA unit, whose arms included a Thompson sub-machine gun, was in the general area in a captured military van so that it could also attack any police or military reinforcements despatched to the area and allow the IRA groups involved time to escape. At 6.05 p.m. on 24 June, when the attack took place, only two IRA units had been able to make it into the area because of military patrols, and it was one of these groups that attacked the two cadets.

26 June 1921,
Lower Baggot Street, Dublin city
William Frederick Hunt, Cadet 72296

Auxiliary cadets were staying in the Mayfair Hotel, 30 Lower Baggot Street, Dublin, with their wives. The party was seated in the dining-room taking tea when they were attacked. Cadet Hunt, who lived at Watford and was stationed with Q Company at the London and North-Western Railway Hotel, Dublin, was killed, while section leader White was wounded in the attack.

Hunt had served in the Royal Engineers before taking a commission in 1916 with the Royal Inniskilling Fusiliers. A thirty-five-year-old married man from Hertfordshire with a small daughter, he had ten months' police service and his Auxiliary number was 104.

On 27 June, his body, with those of Appleford and Wames, was placed on the mail boat at Kingstown for their return to England.

26 June 1921, Kildorrery, Co. Cork
Thomas Shanley, Con 65937

Constable Shanley, a thirty-year-old single man, and Sergeant Ryan were returning from the church at Kildorrery when they were attacked, with Constable Shanley being shot dead. From Co. Leitrim, he had ten years' police service, having been a farmer prior to joining the RIC.

27 June 1921, Cliffoney, Co. Sligo
Patrick Clarke, Con 61068

Constable Clarke, a forty-three-year-old single man from Co. Mayo, was stationed at Cliffoney and he had left his barracks to make his way to a lock-up shop at Creerykeel Cross, one mile north-east of Cliffoney, to buy cigarettes. As he approached the shop he was shot and killed by men concealed nearby. He had eighteen years' police service, having been a farmer before joining the RIC.

27 June 1921, near Milltown, Co. Galway
James Murren, Sgt 57292
Edgar Ernest Day, Con 77676

An RIC patrol on the Tuam to Milltown road was ambushed about 200 yards from their barracks in Milltown. Sergeant Murren was to have retired a week before his death on pension, but, owing to some delay, his papers had not arrived.[40] Both men were stationed in Milltown.

Sergeant Murren, a forty-seven-year-old single man, was from Sligo. He had twenty-five years' service, having been a farmer before joining the RIC. Constable Day, twenty-three and single, was from Nottingham. He had five months' police service on 13 June, having been a labourer and a soldier before joining the RIC.

Both men were buried in their native places on 29 June.

28 June 1921, St James's Walk, Dublin city
Owen Hoey, Con 78183

Constable Hoey, a twenty-three-year-old single man from Co. Monaghan, was in plain clothes and had just left his house in Dolphin's Barn on his way to Kingsbridge Station to catch a train. As he entered St James's Walk near the Grand Canal Harbour he was shot and killed. He had five months' police service on 25 June, having been a stoker/sailor and a member of the DMP before joining the RIC.

29 June 1921, Kilraine, Co. Donegal
Thomas Devine, Con 74477

A police patrol was ambushed at Kilraine, Glenties, Co. Donegal. Constable Devine was the only one injured during the attack. He died from his wounds on 15 July at Lifford Hospital. A thirty-five-year-old single man from Lancashire, he had eight months' police service on 15 June, having been a miner and a soldier before joining the RIC.

29 June 1921, Ballyduff, King's County
Thomas Hannon, ex-Con 61547

The body of a man was found on this date in a bog at Ballyduff near Philipstown, King's County. It was later identified as that of ex-Constable Hannon. He had been shot in the right temple and his hands were tied together with a rope. There was also a sack tied around his neck. He had been kidnapped at Clonbullogue nearly twelve months before his body was discovered in the bog near a place called Walshe Island.

The ex-constable had joined the RIC on 15 December 1905.

He resigned on 31 March 1913 to take over the management of the family farm from his brother. Ex-Constable Hannon was a thirty-eight-year-old single man from King's County. He had been stationed in Co. Meath during his police service.

30 June 1921,
Templemore RIC Barracks, Co. Tipperary
Joseph Bourke, Con 71315

Constable Bourke, a twenty-one-year-old single man from Co. Cork, was shot as he stood at the front door of Templemore Barracks. He had been recommended for appointment in the RIC by DI Swanzy, who was also killed by the IRA. He had one year's police service, having been a soldier prior to joining the RIC.

30 June 1921, Newry, Co. Down
Hugh Gabbie, S/Con

The special constable was walking in plain clothes along the footpath outside the market in John Mitchel Place when two gunmen emerged from the crowd and fired at him. He was taken to Newry General Hospital but died shortly after his arrival as he was being put to bed.

1 July 1921, near Dromore, Co. Sligo
Thomas Higgins, Con 62730
John King, Con 63068

A cycle patrol of seven constables from Ballina Barracks was ambushed six miles south-west of Dromore by two different parties of ambushers. Two constables were taken prisoner by the IRA and removed by them towards the Glenesk Mountains. As these men were being pursued by other police and military, the IRA killed both constables.

Constable Higgins, a thirty-seven-year-old single man, was from Co. Galway. He had exactly fourteen years' police service on 1 July, having been a farmer before joining the RIC.

Constable King, thirty-six and married, was from Co. Galway. He had thirteen years' police service having previously been a farmer.

1 JULY 1921,
NEAR BANSHA, CO. TIPPERARY
Joseph Shelsher, Con 70853

Constable Shelsher, a twenty-three-year-old single man from Camden town, London, was stationed at Bansha, Co. Tipperary. He was shot dead one and a half miles from the village at Barnlough. He had left the village alone and his body was found on the roadway, shot in the head. He had one year's police service, having been a packer and a soldier before joining the RIC.

2 JULY 1921, OOLA, CO. LIMERICK
Andrew Johnstone, Sgt 65864
William E. Hill, Con 74942

An RIC patrol had been sent to investigate the burning of a number of goods on the railway line at Oola in the New Pallas district of Co. Limerick when they came under heavy fire. Two members of the patrol were killed, with five other constables being wounded. After the attack the dead and wounded were brought back to Limerick.

Sergeant Johnstone, whose home was at Mountmellick, was twenty-eight, single and from Dublin. He had ten years' police service, having had no other employment prior to joining the RIC.

Constable Hill, a twenty-year-old married man, came from 56

Cardia Street, Liverpool. He had eight months' police service, having been a labourer and a Royal Marine before joining the RIC.

2 July 1921,
near Tallow, Co. Waterford
Francis Creedon, Con 60464

Ten RIC men were ambushed with a machine gun near Tallow. Constable Creedon, a forty-one-year-old married man from Macroom, Co. Cork, was killed. He had twenty years' police service, having been a farmer before joining the RIC.

3 July 1921, near Wicklow town
John Fitzgerald, Con 76431

Two off-duty constables were fired on by five men half a mile from the town of Wicklow. Constable Fitzgerald, a single man, died from his wounds on 4 July. During the attack he had put his hands up and told his attackers he was unarmed, but he was still shot. From Co. Westmeath, he would have been nineteen years old on 9 July. He would also have had seven months' police service on the same day, and had no other employment before joining the RIC.

5 July 1921, Hospital, Co. Limerick
Cyril F. H. Brewer, Con 75841

Constable Brewer, a twenty-six-year-old married man from London, was on his way to his lodgings in Hospital, accompanied by his wife and child, when he was attacked and wounded. He was taken to Kilmallock Military Hospital but died from his wounds on 7 July. He had six months' police service, having been a steward and a soldier prior to joining the RIC.

6 July 1921,
Union Street, Belfast city
Timothy Joseph Galvin, Con 67244

At 9.20 a.m. two constables were at the corner of Union Street and Little Donegall Street controlling traffic. A small group of men came out of Library Street and attacked them, and both were wounded. Constable Conway was taken to the Military Hospital and Constable Galvin to the Mater Infirmorum Hospital. Both were stationed at Glenravel Street. One officer's revolver was removed by his attackers.

Constable Galvin, a twenty-six-year-old single man from Co. Limerick, had eight years' police service, having been a scholar before joining the RIC. He died on 8 July.

7 July 1921, Ballinhassig, Co. Cork
James Connor, Con 75570

Constable Connor, who was stationed in Ballinhassig, had gone for a walk. While he was away from his barracks it was attacked by the IRA. The attack was repulsed by the police, who, after the incident went in search of their missing comrade and found his body riddled with bullets at the side of the road.

Connor, twenty-four and married with two children, was from Tipperary. He would have had eight months' police service on 16 July, having been a labourer and a soldier before joining the RIC.

7 July 1921, Carralavin, Co. Mayo
Anthony Foody, ex-Sgt 56773

The retired sergeant arrived home on 7 July. He had been stationed in Co. Fermanagh but was working in Co. Tipperary in the village of Bouladuff, which was known as the Ragg. When he was stationed there two brothers called Dwyer were shot dead and the IRA believed that the police were responsible for their deaths.

The retired sergeant's body was found by a postman at Carralavin, a small village midway between Ballina and Bonniconlon. There was a label around his neck bearing the inscription 'Revenge for Dwyer and the Ragg'.

Background
Edward Dwyer had been the adjutant for G Company, First Battalion, Third Tipperary Brigade IRA, while his brother Francis was captain of F Company. Both had been shot and killed by masked men at their home on 18 October 1920.

Sergeant Foody had retired only a few days before his death, having been pensioned from the force on 19 June. Contemporary reports stating that this man was still a serving officer highlight the difficulties involved in compiling this police casualty list.

7 July 1921, near Doolin, Co. Clare
James R. Hewitt, Con 76486

A party of police from Lisdoonvarna were bathing on the coast of Clare near Doolin when they were attacked. One constable was killed and another was seriously wounded. Both were removed to Ennistymon Hospital.

Constable Hewitt, a twenty-year-old single man, was from Dublin. He would have had seven months' police service on 10 July, having been a tram driver and a police officer (with the Manchester force) prior to joining the RIC.

8 July 1921, Rathdrum, Co. Wicklow
Frederick Cormer, Con 75845

Three constables had been shopping and were on the Fair Green, Rathdrum, Co. Wicklow when they were attacked by three armed men. They were taken to the barracks at Market Square but Constable Cormer died from his wounds.

Cormer, a single man, was from Middlesex and had just turned twenty on 6 July. He had six months' police service, having been a footman before joining the RIC.

10 July 1921,
Ross Street, Belfast city
Thomas Conlon, Con 64016

A police patrol in a Crossley tender was fired on in Ross Street (now a redeveloped area off Albert Street) in the Falls area of Belfast. Constable Conlon, who was attached to Springfield Road Barracks, was killed, while the driver, a special constable and another constable in the patrol were seriously wounded. Constable Conlon had no relations in Ireland as his sister had left for the USA two weeks before his death. He was buried in Newtownbreda.

A great deal of sniping also commenced on Sunday afternoon in Ashmore Street and Conway Street, spreading later to Townsend Street. Although it was first reported that fourteen people died in this rioting and gunfire, with a further eighty-four wounded, it was later revealed that eight of the wounded also died.

In a follow-up search of the area, police found 1,000 rounds of mark VII ammunition and a German rifle in premises known as 'The Club' in Ross Street. As a result of this and other incidents in the city, serious rioting developed, which continued intermittently for over a week.

Constable Conlon, a thirty-three-year-old single man, was from Co. Roscommon. He had thirteen years' police service on 3 July, having previously been a farmer.

10 July 1921, Ennis, Co. Clare
Alfred G. Needham, Con 76629

Constable Needham, a twenty-year-old man from London, was standing in O'Connell Street, Ennis, talking to a girl who, according to some sources, was his new wife (although his RIC file reports that he was single), when they were attacked.[41] Both were removed to the infirmary. The constable was seriously wounded in the neck and body and later died from his wounds. After the attack there was considerable military and police activity in the town, with notices posted throughout it fixing the curfew in the area to eight o'clock. Needham would have had seven months' service on 14 July. He had been a wireless telegrapher and a soldier before joining the RIC.

11 July 1921, Castlerea, Co. Roscommon
James King, Sgt 58121

Sergeant King, a forty-four-year-old married man with four children, was cycling to his barracks at Castlerea from his home when he was shot by two men in Patrick Street, Castlerea. He died from his wounds half an hour later. The sergeant had been stationed in Castlerea for eight years and was from Co. Clare. He had twenty-three years' police service, having had no other employment prior to joining the RIC.

11 July 1921, Edenderry, King's County
George Adam, Con 75633

Just minutes before the Truce was due to take effect, this officer was shot and wounded. He was pensioned from the RIC on 3 November 1921 and died from his wounds in Glasgow on 14 September 1922.

Constable Adam, a former soldier and native of Forfar, was twenty-six years of age. He would have had eighteen months' police service on 17 July 1921.

11 July 1921, Skibbereen, Co. Cork
Alexander Clarke, Con 52442

Constable Clarke, a fifty-two-year-old married man with a grown-up family, was shot dead by four men when he was going to his lodgings in Townsend Street, Skibbereen. He was from Co. Tipperary and had thirty-four years' police service, having had no other employment before joining the RIC.

Police Duty during the Truce

At noon on 11 July 1921 a truce between the government and the IRA came into force so that negotiations could take place. This Truce had been signed on 9 July in the Mansion House, Dublin, by General Sir Nevil Macready, the commander of all British forces in Ireland, and Commandant Robert Barton, acting for the IRA. At 2.30 a.m. on 6 December 1921 these negotiations finally led to the signing of a treaty between the British Government and Irish representatives, which included Michael Collins, in London. From a Republican point of view this treaty had two main stumbling blocks:

1. The acceptance of an Irish Free State within the British Commonwealth instead of a Republic.
2. Continuation of the partition of the island, with the six north-eastern counties making up Northern Ireland.

On 8 January 1922 the Dáil voted on the Treaty. Its acceptance was ratified by 64 to 57 votes and this caused the Republicans to split into two different factions, eventually leading to the Civil War. The first shots in this war were fired at 4.30 a.m. on 28 June 1922.

On 8 July 1921 members of the police and military were informed that a truce was to come into force and as a result they were ordered to scale down their operations. A number of orders about the coming Truce were issued to the police, the following one in Co. Armagh:

Co. Insprs Office
Armagh 10/7/21

Sergt Markethill

From 12 noon tomorrow Monday 11th July police will confine themselves to civil police duties on which they will go unarmed except otherwise specially ordered by the Co. Inspr. Police leaving barracks off duty must also be unarmed and Sergts will be held strictly responsible that these orders are complied with. Class B patrols are suspended from same time. Any infringement of the truce terms on part of any one must be immediately reported. The police are expected to loyally carry out these terms.

A.M.R. Dobby Co. Inspr[42]

The IRA was instructed by Richard Mulcahy, the minister for defence in Dáil Éireann, on 9 July that 'active operations by our troops will be suspended as from noon, Monday 11 July'. Republicans continued their campaign to within minutes of the noon deadline, killing two police officers on 11 July.

As a result of the Truce, guidance was circulated to the RIC for duty during its operation. The main points were as follows:

1. Levies. Not allowed but voluntary contributions could be made, provided that no intimidation was used.
2. Funerals. The restriction that in some areas only forty persons

were allowed to attend a funeral was removed. But neither arms nor uniforms were to be used or displayed at funerals. This rule about uniforms and arms also applied to IRA church parades.

3. Movement Crown Forces. Police and Military had to inform Sinn Féin (SF) Liaison Officer of any changes of quarters of troops or police. The movements of Auxiliary police in uniform was also to be notified to SF in order that these movements were not seen as being made in contemplation of offensive measures.
4. Commandeering of Premises. The commandeering of premises by SF was a breach of the truce and was to be notified to the local SF Liaison Officer. If police were not satisfied that the premises had not been placed voluntarily at the disposal of SF and could not be arranged locally for evacuation, then the police were to report the matter to their Headquarters.
5. Sinn Féin Police. RIC to tolerate them looking after IRA personnel only and were to restrict their operations to maintaining the Truce among the IRA. The RIC were informed that they (the RIC) were not to submit to any interference in the carrying out of their duties.
6. Drilling and Camps. If considered provocative by RIC, they were to be reported to local SF Liaison Officer and if not satisfactorily settled locally, were to be reported to Chief of Police for action with the Chief Liaison Official.
7. Sinn Féin Courts. If the holding of such a court came to the notice of the RIC the matter was to be taken up with the local SF Liaison Officer and immediately reported to higher authority for instructions. Arbitration courts, where no intimidation had been used against any of the parties or witnesses, were viewed by the authorities to be legal, but courts that attempted to deal with crime or to inflict or to enforce penalties were not.[43]

The government recognised that the situation during the Truce was difficult, calling for the exercise of great forbearance and self-control by everyone.

The RIC were informed that they were to utilise the local liaison arrangements to the fullest possible extent and any difficulties that could not be adjusted locally were to be referred at once to a higher authority. The government informed the RIC and the DMP that during the Truce they were to continue by every means in their power to secure the enforcement of the law and the protection of life and property.

There can be little doubt that police officers performing their duty during this period were tried to the very limits on numerous occasions and only with tremendous self-control and professionalism were they able to avoid any incident which might have been considered a breach of the Truce on their part.

When the draft terms of the Truce were published, the reaction in Northern Ireland was far from favourable, causing rioting in Belfast which claimed the lives of sixteen people.

Early Casualties in the New Northern Police

On 1 June 1922 the Royal Ulster Constabulary officially came into being. However, before this, the new northern police force had already buried forty of its officers who had been killed as a result of the ongoing political violence.

How were policemen who had not yet joined the RUC being killed prior to that force officially coming into being? In 1921 a separate parliament and executive was formed in Northern Ireland by the government under the Government of Ireland Act 1920, which partitioned Ireland. In that interim period, police officers serving in the Royal Irish Constabulary in the six counties which were to form Northern Ireland, before the RUC's official birth, came under its operational control and were to all intents and purposes (albeit not in name) RUC officers.

This situation was explained by the following circular:

P3/2674 A

DIG RIC

Commandant Auxiliary Division RIC   DC Belfast

1. It has been decided that all Irish Services (as defined in the Government of Ireland Act) in connection with the maintenance of law and order and the administration of justice are to be transferred to the Government of Northern Ireland on the 22nd November. On that date the Northern Government will take over all responsibilities of the Irish Government in connection with these matters as respects the six counties.
2. The Special Constables will be handed over completely and will become for all purposes the servants of the new Government.
3. The force of Royal Irish Constabulary stationed in the six counties will not be handed over at present but will be placed as from 22nd November at the disposal of the Northern Government for the maintenance of order and the suppression of crime and all directions given by the Ministry of Home Affairs through the responsible head of the Royal Irish Constabulary in Belfast are to be carried out with the same promptitude and regard for authority as have been displayed in the execution of Government orders heretofore.
4. After 2nd November no order will be issued by the Irish Government or by the police authorities in Dublin as respects the work of the police in the six counties.
5. On the other hand in matters relating to the internal administration of the Force, including questions of pay, promotion, discipline, transfer and pension, the Divisional Commissioner in Belfast will continue to be responsible for the Deputy Inspector General and the Chief of Police. He will of course consult in

these matters with the appropriate authorities of the Northern Government so far as may be necessary to ensure smooth and efficient working.

6. A circular giving the necessary instructions as to the steps to be taken in preparation for the transfer of the police in the six counties in the manner contemplated in Section 60 of the Government of Ireland Act 1920 is now being printed and will be issued to the entire force. Copies will be sent to you in a few days.

7. Until the transfer takes place all matters referred to in paragraph 5 above will be dealt with as heretofore with respect to the permanent Force. The County Inspectors and the Divisional Commissioner will deal with cases of discipline under the existing orders and cases which cannot be decided by them should be submitted to Headquarters. Recommendations for promotion, transfer from one county to another, pension, etc., will continue to be dealt with at Headquarters.

18 November 1921 (Sgd) H. H. Tudor
The Castle Dublin Major General Chief of Police[44]

It could be said that technically the first member of the northern force to be killed was Constable Michael Gorman, 59169, who lost his life on 2 December 1921 during an attempted escape from Londonderry gaol.

25 November 1921,
Milewater Road, Belfast city
John McHenry, Harbour Constable

At a quarter to four, Constable McHenry, an officer who was very popular both with his colleagues and the public, left the Harbour Offices to commence his beat, which included Milewater Road and the Duncrue Street area. At 6 p.m. shots were heard in the vicinity and some minutes later the constable's body was discovered with six bullet wounds near a place known locally as Milewater Gate. It was never ascertained whether the constable had been followed to this quiet location or whether he was shot whilst attempting to arrest someone.

After the attack the officer's revolver had been taken. The weapons' lanyard had been cut at the shoulder, but its holder had been left on the body, which was discovered to have eleven bullet wounds.

On 28 November his funeral left his residence at 15 Slate Street for burial at Milltown Cemetery. The street was packed, with the crowds extending to Cullingtree Road and Springfield Road. A detachment of harbour police and a guard of honour of RIC followed immediately behind the chief mourners. Constable McHenry had thirty years' service with the harbour police.

2 December 1921, Londonderry gaol
Michael Gorman, Con 59169
William Lyttle, S/Con

Three IRA prisoners arrested before the Truce were due to be hanged in February 1922. The IRA's GHQ ordered that an attempt be made to free them. On 2 December 1921, in the early hours, these prisoners attempted to break out of Londonderry gaol with the aid of outside accomplices. The escape bid was foiled by a police patrol outside the gaol, which fired on the men who had thrown a rope over the gaol wall.

Inside, Special Constable Lyttle and Constable Gorman were found lying dead in a cell block. Their deaths had been caused by a blow to the head and asphyxiation brought about by the administration of chloroform. Fifteen prisoners stood trial for their deaths and three were sentenced to hang.

Constable Gorman, a forty-five-year-old single man, was from Co. Donegal. He had twenty-two years' police service, having been a farmer before joining the RIC. Owing to the records of the Ulster Special Constabulary having been destroyed, no police records for Special Constable Lyttle are available.

12 December 1921,
Ballybunion, Co. Kerry
John Maher, Sgt 69137

Sergeant Maher, a twenty-four-year-old single man from Co. Carlow, and Constable Gallagher were standing on the Castle Green, Ballybunion, when they were attacked by four armed men. The sergeant was killed outright, whilst Constable Gallagher was seriously wounded. It was stated locally that the sergeant had been a marked man from 23 November 1920, when it was alleged he had shot a man in Ballylongford.[45] He had four years' police service, having been a shop assistant prior to joining the RIC.

14 December 1921,
Kilmallock, Co. Limerick
Thomas Enright, Con 71187

Constable Enright and Constable Timoney were travelling from Thurles to Kilmallock, to go to a coursing meeting in which the constable had two dogs entered, when they were attacked.

Constable Enright had held a commission in the army during the First World War and on 7 August 1920 had become a defence of barracks sergeant, reverting to the rank of constable on 16 February 1921. On 16 December his remains were taken to Listowel for burial. A thirty-one-year-old married man, the constable was from Listowel, Co. Kerry. He had one year's police service, having been a farmer and a lieutenant in the army before joining the RIC.

Constable Enright had served in the Canadian Army during the First World War and had met and married his wife, a nurse, in Canada. At the time of his death he had a six-month-old child.

27 December 1921, Oldpark Road, Belfast city
Francis Hill, Con 65425

At 7 a.m. a patrol of special constables under the command of Constable Hill set off from Antrim Road Specials Station. They were going up Oldpark Road when they saw a suspicious group of men at the corner of Gracehill Street. During the confrontation one civilian was killed and another wounded, as was the constable, who later died from his wounds in the Belfast Military Hospital.

Constable Hill, a thirty-two-year-old married man, was from Co. Leitrim. He had eleven years' police service, having been a shop assistant prior to joining the RIC. Six months before his death the constable's young twin daughters had died. The dead constable's wife lived at Dargle Street, Belfast.

Conclusion for 1921

Prior to the Truce coming into effect on 11 July 1921, a total of 241 police officers had lost their lives during the year, with the worst single month for casualties during the whole campaign being May, when fifty-eight policemen died. With the signing of the Truce the IRA campaign ended. However, by the end of the year the killings had resumed and after the signing of the Treaty on 6 December the number of attacks began to increase, especially in Northern Ireland, where the storm of political violence was about to break out again. The total number of police officers killed for the whole of 1921 was 247.

By the end of the year the morale of the police was low, primarily because of the continuing campaign of persecution and intimidation against both serving officers and their families and relations, as well as against former policemen. Sporadic attacks after the Truce had claimed officers' lives. Police officers watched men, whom they had actively been seeking during the campaign, freely and openly, and on many occasions flauntingly, return from hiding.

Police officers had deep concerns over their disbandment arrangements, including the financial implications, with many being suspicious of the government's future intentions. It was in this state of uncertainty that the RIC, and especially those officers stationed in the area that was to become Northern Ireland, faced the prospect of renewed violence in the coming year.

5

1922

The Coming Storm

In 1919 the government, under the leadership of Prime Minister David Lloyd George, introduced the 'Better Government of Ireland Bill', which replaced the Home Rule Act of 1914. It proposed partition for the island. After a long debate this bill, as the Government of Ireland Act, received the royal assent on 23 December 1920, and established two separate parliaments.

Although things were very serious in Ireland when this debate was taking place, the government was reluctant to introduce martial law, relying on the mobility of armoured cars to control areas in which trouble was prevalent. However, on 20 February 1920 a curfew was imposed for the Dublin Metropolitan District, coming into effect on 23 February, and it curtailed movement in the area between the hours of 12 midnight and 5 a.m. Curfews were later introduced in other parts of Ireland, with the army ordering one in Belfast that became effective from 30 August 1920 and remained in force until 1924.

As the violence spread in Ireland and the threat of industrial trouble in England grew, the government, in August 1920, had to withdraw troops from Ireland, which seriously hindered military operations against the IRA.

During this period, tensions in the six north-eastern counties that were to become Northern Ireland increased when the IRA's campaign claimed the life of a member of the security forces who was from the area. Such incidents caused reactions that triggered serious disturbances and lawlessness that spanned both the political and religious divides.

One such incident was the alleged drowning of Captain Lendrum, a resident magistrate for Kilrush, Co. Clare. From Trillick, Co. Tyrone, he had served in the Royal Inniskilling Fusiliers during the First World War. On 22 September 1920 he was ambushed, shot and killed between Ennistymon and Ennis, Co. Clare. However, a story was later disseminated that he had been buried to his neck in sand on a nearby beach by his attackers. On their return they supposedly found that they had buried their victim above the high tide line, so they then buried him below it and as a result he drowned.

As the violence in Ireland increased, the government, on 9 August 1920, introduced the 'Restoration of Order in Ireland Act', which provided for a wider range of offences to be tried by court martial than the Defence of the Realm Act had previously included. This new act gave military courts the power to carry out enquiries instead of inquests and also made it easier for the military to impose curfews, restrict traffic and imprison terrorists on suspicion. The number of IRA men arrested, tried and convicted by court martial dramatically increased.

However, as the situation further deteriorated, the government, on 9 December 1920, introduced martial law in Counties Cork, Kerry, Limerick and Tipperary, and it was extended to Counties Clare, Kilkenny, Waterford and Wexford on 4 January 1921. It was not until the signing of the Anglo-Irish Treaty on 6 December 1921 that the government started to relax these measures. The release of IRA prisoners from internment camps began on 9 December. This was followed on 13 January 1922 with the amnesty and release of 1,000 prisoners convicted of political crimes.

On 3 May 1921 the new Government of Ireland Act had become law, and King George V opened the northern parliament on 22 June 1921. This act caused some division of functions between the Northern Ireland Government and Dublin Castle with regards to the policing of Northern Ireland. On 22 November 1921 the government of Northern Ireland took over imperial control of the RIC under Section 60 of the Government of Ireland Act, with responsibility for law and order coming under the control of Minister for Home Affairs Richard Dawson Bates. At the time the general situation in Northern Ireland was serious, with twenty-seven people being killed in Belfast over the period 19–25 November.

On 1 February 1922 Minister Bates formed a committee to advise on police matters in Northern Ireland, which reported its findings on 31 March 1922. It recommended that the new police force should be 3,000 in number with one-third of the places being reserved for Roman Catholic members. It was also recommended that the prefix Royal be retained.

On 24 May 1922 the Constabulary Bill (Northern Ireland) was introduced, giving effect to the recommendations of the committee, and on 1 June 1922 the RUC was formed, with the large nucleus of this new force being former RIC officers. It had been laid down, in January 1922, that the establishment of 'B' Class special constables would be ten times the combined number of RIC and 'A' Class special constables in a county. This would have required 30,000 men for the region, but this figure was never reached.

After the government of the Irish Free State had formally been handed over to the Sinn Féin Provisional Government on 16 January 1922, it continued to supply various IRA units and to train northern units, while the IRA began to carry out more attacks against the police in Northern Ireland. On 18 April 1922 an IRA order stated that the aim was to make the six counties part of the Free State. This order was followed on 26 April 1922 by the Provisional Government virtually breaking off relations with Northern Ireland.

During elections in Northern Ireland in May 1922, Sinn Féin declared that they were 'out to smash the Ulster Parliament and if it cannot be smashed in this election, it will have to be smashed otherwise'. The situation in Northern Ireland remained volatile, with violence of the worst excesses and ferocity not previously seen there about to be unleashed.

2 FEBRUARY 1922, KILLARNEY, CO. KERRY
Charles F. Ednie, Con 75392

On 27 January 1922 the town of Killarney had been handed over to the IRA by the competent authorities. IRA men were patrolling the town on the evening of 2 February 1922 when, it is alleged, a group of RIC men fired on them and in the battle that followed the constable was killed.

Constable Ednie, a single man, was from Edinburgh and would have been twenty-six on 6 February 1922. He had one year's service, having been a journeyman and a soldier before joining the RIC.

3 FEBRUARY 1922, LISDOONVARNA, CO. CLARE
William Gourlay, Con 82097
Frank Kershaw, Con 73968

The two constables were leaving a public house at Lisdoonvarna, north Clare, when they were shot dead.

Constable Gourlay, thirty-two and married, was from Lanark. He would have had eight months' police service on 21 February 1922, having been a brass merchant and a soldier before joining the RIC. Constable Kershaw, a twenty-three-year-old married man, was from Lancashire. He had one year of police service, having been a steeplejack and a soldier before joining the RIC.

10 FEBRUARY 1922, CLADY, CO. TYRONE
Charles McFadden, S/Con

At 11.30 p.m. on 9 February 1922 an Ulster Special Constabulary patrol left Strabane to investigate a report of IRA activity in the village of Clady. The patrol left their Crossley tender on the outskirts of the village and walked the remainder of the way. At 12.30 a.m. a number of IRA men fired on the patrol from behind cover and a gun battle followed. The IRA fled and the police patrol withdrew to their vehicle, but one man was not accounted for.

The Specials returned to the scene of the ambush and found Special Constable McFadden lying fatally wounded on the footpath. He was an ex-soldier from Upperlands, Maghera, and was married with five children.

11 February 1922, Clones, Co. Monaghan
William Dougherty, S/Sgt
James Lewis, S/Con
William McFarland, S/Con
Robert McMahon, S/Con

An eighteen-man detachment of the Ulster Special Constabulary left Newtownards Camp en route for Enniskillen, to strengthen the force of 'A' Specials in Co. Fermanagh. They travelled by train and had to change trains at Clones for a connection to Enniskillen.

The IRA was alerted that the police were on the train and, led by Matt Fitzpatrick, the Clones Company captain, armed with a Thompson sub-machine gun, they made their way to the railway station. Once in the station Fitzpatrick began to question some of the police, most of whom were unarmed, and then opened fire on one carriage containing police officers, killing Special Constable McMahon. The passengers scattered in all directions.

Another officer further along the train, who was armed, shot Fitzpatrick and a gun battle broke out. At the battle's end, three other members of the detachment had been killed and eight more wounded. Carriage 85, in which the police had been travelling, was riddled with bullets. A few Special Constabulary members were able to escape along the railway line back to Newtownbutler; another few took refuge in local houses and the RIC barracks. The remainder were captured by the IRA, who held them prisoner.

At first the police prisoners were held in the IRA's headquarters in Clones, which was at the workhouse, but they were then moved to different locations. The last of the prisoners was eventually released on 10 April 1922.

After the attack the IRA extinguished the street lamps in the town and ordered that lights in local shops and houses be put out. Other IRA units from Monaghan, Fermanagh and Cavan made their way to the town, placing it under their control. The IRA later telephoned the RIC at Enniskillen and informed them that they intended leaving the bodies and the wounded special constables near the town.

This incident led to the temporary suspension of the evacuation of British troops from the Free State. It also led to rioting in Belfast which caused the death of twenty-seven people between 12 and 15 February 1922.

Special Sergeant Dougherty's funeral took place on 14 February from his mother's residence at 8 Florence Street, Londonderry, to the city cemetery, his remains having been brought from Enniskillen that morning by Crossley tender. A large number of Special Constabulary and RIC, approximately 500, took part in the funeral procession, with the route being lined with large crowds of mourners. Dougherty was twenty-three, having served in the Tenth Battalion of the Royal Inniskilling Fusiliers (Derry Regiment), Ulster Division, during the First World War.

Special Constable Lewis' funeral also took place on 14 February from his parents' residence at Lisnagirr, Mountjoy, Omagh, to the Presbyterian church at Mountjoy. Later a party of special constables, with arms reversed, led the cortège to the adjoining graveyard.

11 February 1922, Clonakilty, Co. Cork
Michael Keany, DI 53643

The district inspector was walking with his nineteen-year-old son when he was attacked and killed. His son was wounded during the incident. DI Keany would have had thirty-three years' service and would have been fifty-five years of age on 21 February. He was a married man from Co. Leitrim. Before joining the RIC he had been a labourer. A year earlier, to the day, the DI had been awarded a first-class favourable record and a grant of £10 for his actions during an ambush at Rosscarbery Barracks, where he got his men safely through the attack without any fatalities. It was also stated that six IRA men were killed and others wounded during this action.

16 February 1922, Edlingham Street, Belfast city
Hector Stewart, S/Con

From Saturday 11 February, Belfast had witnessed almost continuous gun and bomb attacks, which had resulted in the death of over thirty people and the wounding of nearly 100 others. However, from 14 February scarcely a shot had been fired until the morning of 16 February, when a twenty-four-year-old apprentice manager was shot dead in the New Northern Spinning Company's offices at Northumberland Street.

This attack triggered heavy gunfire throughout Belfast. Special Constable Stewart was shot and wounded in the jugular vein while at the corner of Edlingham Street and the New Lodge Road. The wounded twenty-one-year-old was removed to the Royal Victoria Hospital but died from his wounds.

17 February 1922, Garryowen, Co. Limerick
Lauchlin McEdward, Con 81157

The deceased and another constable were out walking late on the evening of 17 February in Garryowen when three or four armed men stepped out of a dark entry and fired point blank at Constable McEdward who received terrible wounds to his head. His colleague escaped uninjured.

Constable McEdward, a twenty-one-year-old married man, was from Edinburgh. He had eight months' police service, having been a motor mechanic and a member of the Royal Naval Reserve before joining the RIC.

2 March 1922, Phibsborough, Dublin city
John Cotter, Sgt 61742

Sergeant Cotter, a thirty-seven-year-old married man from Co. Clare was stationed at the depot, Phoenix Park, Dublin. He had been involved in the defence of Roskeen Barracks, North Tipperary, about two years beforehand, when a number of attackers, possibly three, were killed. At 3 p.m. he was shot and wounded at Phibsborough, Dublin, and died at 7.20 p.m. from his wounds in the Mater Misericordiae Hospital. He had been followed by three men along a laneway that connected Cabra Park, where he lived, and St Peter's Road, and when he reached the corner he was shot three times.

He would have had sixteen years' police service on 15 March 1922, having been a farmer before joining the RIC.

3 March 1922, Tipperary town
Christopher Davis, H/Con 59253
William Cummings, Con 74240

A police party in a Crossley tender and another vehicle was leaving Tipperary town for Dublin when they were ambushed from St Michael's Street and Bank Place. Head Constable Davis was killed. He had been in charge of Dundrum Barracks, Co. Tipperary. Two constables were seriously wounded and taken to hospital, with one of them, Constable Cummings, dying from his wounds on 7 March 1922 in Steeven's Hospital, Dublin.

Davis, a forty-two-year-old married man, was from Co. Galway. He had twenty-one years' police service, having had no other employment before joining the RIC. Cummings was twenty-five, single and from Hampshire. He had eighteen months' police service, having been a labourer and a soldier before joining the RIC.

It was later reported that the military in Dublin had arrested RIC men who were charged with complicity in this incident.[1]

9 March 1922, Hanover Street, Cork city
Dudley L. O'Sullivan, Con 82505

Two constables were walking in Hanover Street when they were attacked. Constable O'Sullivan, a twenty-seven-year-old single man from Dublin, was killed, but the other constable made good his escape and reached Tuckey Street Barracks. Constable O'Sullivan had one year's service on 9 February 1922, having been an army officer before joining the RIC.

10 March 1922, Falls Road, Belfast city
James Cullen, Con 80470
Patrick O'Connor, Con 63157

The two constables had been relieved from duty from their post at the corner of Argyle Street and Cupar Street around curfew hour and were returning to their barracks at Springfield Road. They had reached the junction of Dunlewey Street and the Falls Road when they were shot. Constable O'Connor was killed outright, whilst Constable Cullen was seriously wounded in the stomach. He later died in hospital.

Constable O'Connor, a thirty-five-year-old single man from Co. Clare, was the son of a police sergeant. He had joined the Royal Irish Regiment on 5 August 1914 and was captured after the battle of Mons. Rejoining the RIC on 16 March 1919, he completed fourteen years' police service, having been a cabinet-maker beforehand.

Constable Cullen, twenty-three and single, was from Wexford. He would have had eleven months' police service on 12 March but had been stationed in Belfast only since 14 January 1922. He had been a porter and a soldier before joining the RIC.

On 13 March 1922 the two constables were buried in adjoining graves in Milltown Cemetery.

13 March 1922,
Falls Road, Belfast city
Christopher Clarke, Sgt 59764

The sergeant was returning, with a constable, from the funeral of Constables O'Connor and Cullen. As they were walking they heard footsteps behind them. Seven or eight men called on the two officers to put up their hands. Both men were fired on, each being wounded. The constable fired six times at their attackers, who ran off towards Broadway. Sergeant Clarke knew that his life was in danger and at the time of his death he was wearing a bulletproof jacket.

Some days before his death he had arrested a man on whom was found a list of twelve policemen who had expressed their willingness to take service under the Northern Ireland Government. His name was not on the list.

Sergeant Clarke, a forty-two-year-old married man, was from

King's County. He lived at Forth River Gardens and had twenty-one years' police service, having previously been a clerk.

15 March 1922, Galway city
Tobias Gibbons, Sgt 60748
John Gilmartin, Sgt 55730

The two sergeants were shot dead as they lay in their hospital beds at St Brigid's Home, Galway, by four masked men. A constable was also wounded during this attack. The men were unable to offer any resistance as each of them was ill.

Sergeant Gibbons, a forty-four-year-old single man from Co. Mayo, was attached to the RIC at Fair Green, Westport, and had been admitted to the home on 24 February 1922. He would have completed twenty years' service on 16 March, having been a farmer before joining the RIC.

Sergeant Gilmartin, a fifty-year-old married man with two children, was from Co. Leitrim and was attached to the RIC at Oughterard. He had been admitted on 9 March. He had twenty-eight years' police service, having previously been a farmer.

17 March 1922, Upperlands, Co. Londonderry
Alexander Kirkpatrick, S/Con

The special constable was cycling towards Tobermore when he was challenged by a number of IRA men who were standing on the Moyola Bridge. They called on him to halt, then five shots were fired at him and he fell, fatally wounded.

Background
A large number of IRA men, with their faces blackened, were

working at the bridge with picks and shovels to prepare for its destruction by explosives. They had posted guards to challenge anyone who approached the bridge.

At 8 p.m. an evangelist meeting had ended in Tobermore and three special constables were stopped at the bridge by the IRA before the arrival of Special Constable Kirkpatrick. Special Constable Phillips, who was by himself, had been stopped first, with Special Constables Millar and Bradley being stopped later.

The IRA men were unaware of these men's identities and they released Phillips, who later raised the alarm. As the other two special constables were being moved over the bridge on to the Maghera side they heard gunfire. Later the bridge was partly severed, but four unexploded bombs were found in the partially destroyed structure.

The body of Special Constable Sandy Kirkpatrick was found lying astride his bicycle. It was thought that he had attempted to escape to warn of the attack on the bridge. This attack was to delay the arrival of police reinforcements travelling from Magherafelt to Maghera, where the IRA attacked the local barracks.

21 March 1922, Trillick, Co. Tyrone
Samuel Laird, S/Con

Under cover of darkness the IRA attacked the home of a veterinary surgeon at Glengeen Lodge, Trillick. The owner returned fire and after the attack he checked his grounds. During the search he found his employee, Special Constable Samuel Laird, lying in the yard with gunshot wounds from which he later died.

22 March 1922, Trillick, Co. Tyrone
George Chittick, S/Con

The IRA attacked the home of Special Constable Chittick near

Carrs Mountain, Trillick. His brother and sister noticed the IRA approaching the house and were able to barricade the door and prevent their entry. The attackers then fired at the house before they withdrew. On checking the area after the IRA had left, the family found their brother lying fatally wounded where he had been tending livestock.

23 March 1922, May Street, Belfast city
William Chermside, S/Con
Thomas Cunningham, S/Con

At 12.15 p.m. the two special constables were on foot patrol in Great Victoria Street and had just turned into May Street when IRA men came up beside them and fired a number of shots at them from revolvers. Both died shortly after the attack from their wounds.

Special Constable Chermside, twenty-one, had one year's service. He was from Portaferry, Co. Down.

Special Constable Cunningham, from Co. Cavan, lived in the Ormeau Road district of the city. He was buried on 25 March 1922 at Newtownbreda.

29 March 1922, Cullaville, Co. Armagh
Patrick Joseph Early, Sgt 66350
James Harper, S/Con

At 11.15 a.m. a police patrol was ambushed by the IRA at Ballincarrig Bridge, Cullaville. The IRA men involved in this attack were wearing uniforms belonging to special constables who had been captured at Clones Railway Station on 11 February 1922. The uniforms helped make the ambush and their movements easier. The sergeant and special constable were killed outright during the attack.

Sergeant Early was stationed at Crossmaglen. On 24 January

1916 he had joined the Army Service Corps, rejoining the RIC on 29 April 1919. He was a thirty-year-old married man from Co. Roscommon. He had ten years' police service, having been a farmer before joining the RIC.

Special Constable Harper was from Milltown, Co. Londonderry.

31 March 1922, Newry, Co. Down
David Allen, S/Con

A foot patrol of Ulster Special Constabulary was returning to its barracks when it was challenged by a number of IRA men near St Mary's Protestant church in John Mitchel Place. The police halted, thinking it was another patrol of specials, but then the IRA opened fire, fatally wounding Allen and also wounding Special Constable Warning. A bomb was thrown at the patrol but failed to go off. After an exchange of fire, the IRA escaped.

Background
At 11 p.m. the patrol of one sergeant and six constables left the military barracks and was making its way down Kilmorey Street in extended formation. The sergeant, Allen, and a Constable Maynes were in front. When they were in line with St Mary's they saw fifteen to twenty men in trench coats wearing bandoliers and carrying rifles in Hyde Market. Believing these men to be a patrol of 'B' Specials the police called out 'Friend' but at once came under a volley of rifle and revolver fire from approximately twenty to twenty-five yards away. Allen fell and was picked up and moved out of the line of fire by one of his colleagues. A gun battle then developed, with the patrol's ammunition being exhausted.

Another patrol in William Street was able to repel the attackers, but as they ran to the aid of the ambushed patrol they came under what appeared to be machine-gun fire.

Special Constable Allen was twenty and from Loughbrickland; he had joined the police in June 1921.

31 March 1922,
Short Strand, Belfast city
Thomas Hall, S/Con

At 11 p.m. two special constables in plain clothes were making their way back to their barracks at Ballymacarrett. They had just got off a tram and were walking along the road when they were assaulted by a number of men who then shot and wounded both of them.

The two men were taken to hospital, but Hall died from his wounds later that day in the Royal Victoria Hospital. He had spent seventeen years in the army, having served with the Royal Irish Rifles. On 2 April his funeral left from his parents' home at 28 Brownlow Terrace, Lurgan, to the New Cemetery in the town.

Two of Special Constable Hall's brothers had been killed during the First World War, and during one battle he had carried one of his brothers a mile and a half to safety.

3 April 1922,
Old Lodge Road, Belfast city
George Turner, Con 61297

The constable was on duty with a number of special constables on the Old Lodge Road. When they reached the corner of Lime Street, the patrol came under fire from an empty house at the corner of Stanhope Street and Constable Turner was shot in the head.

A forty-one-year-old married man from Mountcharles, Co. Donegal, he had nineteen years' police service, having previously been a factory clerk. He had served in the Irish Guards during the First World War and intended to join the RUC.

6 April 1922,
Garrison, Co. Fermanagh
James Edward Plumb, S/Con

At 9.30 a.m. a patrol of Ulster Special Constabulary was ambushed by a large number of IRA men near Garrison at the County Bridge. Four special constables were wounded before the remainder of the police patrol withdrew, leaving one of their number dead at the scene. The police returned with reinforcements and found that the IRA had taken the body of the constable. After an appeal by local religious leaders, his body was returned a few days later.

When the body was recovered it was found that it had been savaged after death. The officer's head had been battered in with rifle butts until it was almost unrecognisable. The buttons and all marks of identification had been cut off his tunic. The body was found just over the border by two clergymen who had been told where it was by the IRA.

At a military enquiry held at Enniskillen on 10 April 1922 it was stated that the constable's two jaw bones had been broken and that bone splinters were sticking through the skin. The skull had been beaten into one contiguous fracture and the other injuries were too horrible to be published. A Free State soldier stated that the IRA had lined up at Kiltyclogher and that each man had been permitted one blow at the remains with his rifle butt.[2]

Plumb had been a Royal Marine and a military policeman during the First World War, and was a POW for two years. He had only been stationed in Co. Fermanagh for a week, having just come from the training depot at Newtownards. His remains were removed to his Belfast home at 10 Stoneyford Street, Albertbridge Road. His funeral later took place to Dundonald Cemetery and was attended by a large crowd.

6 April 1922, near Keady, Co. Armagh
Alexander Compton, MC, S/HCon

The special head constable had been part of a mobile patrol of Ulster Special Constabulary on the main Keady to Monaghan road which was ambushed as it reached Roughan's Crossroads. As a result of this attack the vehicle in which the special head constable was travelling suddenly stopped. The officer lost his balance and he was thrown out of the vehicle onto the roadway. This fall broke his neck. He was taken to hospital but died later from his injuries.

8 April 1922, Templemore, Co. Tipperary
Edward McConnell, Sgt 71243

The body of the sergeant was found in the Old Demesne outside Templemore. He had been stationed at Castlefogarty and had been at a dance at the military barracks in Templemore but had not returned to his barracks after it had finished.

His body was found with six bullet wounds. He was twenty-six and was to have been married after Easter. He had been a sergeant major in the Irish Fusiliers during the First World War and was from Co. Tyrone. He had joined the RIC on 23 April 1920, being promoted to sergeant on 1 April 1921.

13 April 1922, York Street, Belfast city
John Bruin, Sgt 62929

The sergeant was making enquiries at Cosgroves public house, York Street, when he was shot in the chest. He was taken to the Mater Hospital but died from his wounds on 20 April. A thirty-seven-year-old single man from Co. Leitrim, he had fourteen years' police service, having been a farmer before joining the RIC.

13 April 1922,
Joy Street, Belfast city
Nathaniel McCoo, S/Con

At 11.30 p.m., Special Constable McCoo was part of a patrol travelling in a Lancia armoured car along Joy Street towards Ormeau Avenue when he was shot and wounded by a gunman. He was taken to hospital but died from his wounds on 5 May. The patrol had been involved in a follow-up operation after an earlier shooting incident which had occurred in May Street. The dead officer was from Scotch Street, Portadown, Co. Armagh.

18 April 1922,
Walton Place, Belfast city
William Robert Johnston, S/Con

Fierce firing took place in the network of small streets that comprised the Marrowbone district of Belfast. The trouble commenced early in the morning with intense rifle and revolver firing. This gunfire was accompanied by the attempted burning of houses and shops in the area. The officer in charge of the military on duty in the area had been wounded, and the Ulster Special Constabulary was called upon to assist the army. Special Constable Johnston, twenty-seven years old, of 100 Louisa Street, Belfast, along with several other men, volunteered to locate snipers in the area for the army. He had just taken up duty when he was shot four times as he stood at the corner of Walton Place at 4 p.m. He died from his wounds four hours later in the Royal Victoria Hospital. Military evidence proved that the deceased was shot when on duty by five or six men who had been armed with rifles and revolvers. These men had fired from behind a wrecked public house, before running off along Glenpark Street.

30 April 1922, near Drogheda, Co. Louth
Benjamin Bentley, Con 75312

Constable Bentley, a twenty-one-year-old single man, who was attached to the transport section at Gormanston Camp, was ambushed at Staneen near Drogheda. He was making his way to Drogheda to collect a clergyman to conduct divine service. From London, he had one year's service, having been a motor driver and a soldier before joining the RIC. Later the constable's RIC records were amended to show his name as Archibald Charles Bentley.

2 May 1922, Bellaghy RIC Barracks, Co. Londonderry
John Harvey, Con 62703

The RIC barracks at Bellaghy was attacked by a large number of IRA men. The constable was killed, whilst a Sergeant Kerr was seriously wounded.

Background
The attack on Bellaghy RIC Barracks was part of the IRA's ongoing attacks in the South Derry area. The IRA, on bursting into the barracks by the back door, shot the constable dead and seriously wounded the sergeant as they sat in the dayroom. An IRA man was wounded in the attack.

'B' Specials hurried to the scene after the attack and captured three of the raiders, who were taken to Magherafelt RIC Barracks. The seriously wounded sergeant was taken by Crossley tender to the Royal Victoria Hospital, Belfast.

During attacks in the area, an eyewitness who was on a hilltop stated that he saw signals exchanged all along the Sperrins between IRA units, who also put up Very lights to draw police patrols in the wrong directions. He also said that the countryside was lit up with the flames from burning houses and mills, and that he had seen nothing like it since the First World War.

Constable Harvey, a thirty-seven-year-old married man from Co. Monaghan, had fifteen years' service. He had first joined the RIC on 26 June 1907, but had been discharged as unfit by the police surgeon two days later. However, on 1 November 1907 he had rejoined the force. Before joining the RIC he had been a farmer. He had been stationed in Bellaghy for seven months.

3 May 1922, near Cookstown, Co. Tyrone
William T. McKnight, MM, S/Con

A mobile Ulster Special Constabulary patrol was ambushed by IRA men at Corbanaghan, six miles from Cookstown. The patrol came under fire when it stopped at a blown-up bridge. Special Constable McKnight was wounded in the abdomen and died from his wounds the next day in the Royal Victoria Hospital, Belfast. He had served in the army during the First World War, being awarded the Military Medal. He was buried in Portadown, Co. Armagh on 5 May and the RIC band accompanied the funeral.

3 May 1922, Annaghmore, Co. Armagh
Robert Cardwell, S/Con

At 3.30 a.m. a number of IRA men attacked the home of a special constable at Ballynacadly, Portadown. The shooting alerted an Ulster Special Constabulary patrol in the area, which rushed to the scene but was ambushed at Annaghmore. In the gun battle between the patrol and the IRA, Special Constable Cardwell was shot and fatally wounded.

3 May 1922, Ballyronan, Co. Londonderry
Frederick Frizelle, Sgt 59994
Edward Hegarty, S/Con
Thomas J. Hunter, S/Con

The three officers returning from patrol were approached by three men just outside Ballyronan. The men bid the policemen 'Good night', but as the patrol passed they drew revolvers and fired on the police. Hunter was killed instantly and the other two seriously wounded. Frizelle and Hegarty both died on 4 May from their wounds.

Sergeant Frizelle, a forty-one-year-old married man, was from Co. Mayo. He had twenty-one years' police service, having been a draper's assistant before joining the RIC.

8 May 1922, Castlecaulfield, Co. Tyrone
Samuel Milligan, S/Con

At 3 a.m. the IRA attacked three houses belonging to unionists at Clonaneese Glebe, Castlecaulfield. All three houses were defended by their families and Special Constable Milligan, eighteen years old, was shot and wounded in the leg as he defended his father's home. He bled to death before receiving medical treatment.

18 May 1922, Musgrave Street RIC Barracks, Belfast city
John Collins, Con 57485

In May 1922 the IRA planned to carry out a general attack against the security forces in Northern Ireland, with units from the five

Northern and Midland divisions being involved. However, this action was postponed for a short period as the IRA believed it could capture Musgrave Street RIC Barracks by a ruse, which it hoped would lead to the capture of two armoured cars that would be invaluable assets in its general attack.

On 18 May men dressed as police attempted to take the barracks. Constable Collins, a forty-nine-year-old single man from Co. Cork, was killed and a special constable was wounded during this confused attack. Collins had twenty-six years' police service, having been a farmer before joining the RIC and was to have resigned in a few weeks.

19 May 1922,
Millfield, Belfast city
William Heaslip, Con 68430

IRA men had raided an electric shop in Berry Street, Belfast, looking for equipment, but took very little. The shop assistant followed them and saw the men enter a lodging house in Millfield. The constable and a colleague from the Brickfields Barracks arrived on the scene and arrested two men, but then Constable Heaslip was shot and killed. Heaslip, a twenty-one-year-old single man, was from Co. Cavan. He had seven years' police service, having been a farmer before joining the RIC.

25 May 1922,
Springfield Road, Belfast city
James Murphy S/Con

At 5.45 a.m. the special constable and a colleague went to the aid of local police during a gun battle with IRA gunmen in the Springfield Road area of Belfast. The two special constables were coming to the Falls Road end of Conway Street when an IRA sniper shot and fatally wounded Special Constable Murphy. He was from Ballymena, Co. Antrim.

25 May 1922,
McAuley Street, Belfast city
George Connor, S/Con

A group of men was seen acting suspiciously during a curfew in McAuley Street, just off Cromac Street, Belfast. It appeared that these men set fire to a building to draw the police into an ambush. A police patrol went to the area and Connor was helping to evacuate the adjoining houses when he was shot by an IRA sniper and wounded. He died from his wounds the next day and was later buried in Lisburn Cemetery, Co. Antrim. During the First World War he had served with the Royal Irish Rifles.

27 May 1922,
Jonesborough, Co. Armagh
Herbert Martin, S/Con

Over a period of two days, 26 and 27 May, the IRA in the South Armagh area carried out a number of attacks on police vehicles, as well as attacks on local barracks. During one of these attacks in the Jonesborough–Forkhill area on 27 May, Special Constable Martin was shot dead.

28 May 1922,
Westland Row Railway Station, Dublin city
William Leech, Sgt 65034

At 10.45 p.m. Sergeant Leech, a thirty-two-year-old single man stationed in Limerick, had just left the railway station at Westland

Row, Dublin. He was followed by two men who shot and wounded him in the head. He died in the Mercer's Hospital half an hour later.

The sergeant, who was on temporary duty at Dublin Castle, was from Co. Galway. He had twelve years' police service, having been a shop assistant before joining the RIC. He had been promoted to sergeant on 1 November 1920.

28 May 1922,
Garrison, Co. Fermanagh
Albert Thomas Rickerby, S/Con

The special constable was the driver of a Lancia tender which was the first vehicle in a four-vehicle patrol leading three Crossley tenders in the Belleek–Garrison area of Co. Fermanagh. The patrol had reached a crossroads on the border at Belleek and had just turned on to the Enniskillen to Bundoran road when it was ambushed by a large number of Provisional Government (Free State) troops operating from an old fort overlooking the crossroads on high ground, who fired on the patrol with machine guns and rifles.

The special constable was killed and his vehicle crashed into the ditch, blocking the road. The remaining vehicles had to be abandoned and a gun battle began that lasted for several hours, until darkness fell and the patrol was able to get away.

Special Constable Rickerby had lived at 6 Springdale Gardens, Belfast.

29 May 1922,
McDonnell Street, Belfast city
John Megarity, S/Con

At 2.30 p.m. a police mobile patrol of ten men was ambushed in McDonnell Street in the Falls Road area of Belfast. As the Lancia armoured car came under fire, Megarity was shot and fatally wounded in the head. He was twenty years of age and stationed at Court Street Barracks, Belfast.

Background
The IRA changed tactics on 29 May 1922 and instead of burning buildings as they had been doing during the weekend, they began sniping operations in the Falls area. As a result of a number of attacks of this kind in the Grosvenor Road area, the police began to search it. Whilst these searches were being carried out, the IRA fired at the police from carefully concealed vantage points. It was at this point that police reinforcements from the mobile platoon at Court Street were sent to McDonnell Street.

29 May 1922, Cullingtree Road, Belfast city
Henry O'Brien, Con 69991

Constable O'Brien and a colleague were engaged in conversation with a civilian near their barracks in Cullingtree Road when they were fired on by a number of men from a range of fifteen to twenty yards. Constable O'Brien, a twenty-three-year-old single man from Co. Leitrim, was seriously wounded in the abdomen and left side, but the other constable was able to return fire on their attackers, possibly wounding one of them.

During this attack gunfire was also directed at the RIC barracks, resulting in a window being broken. After these attacks the gunmen escaped along Lady Street. The wounded constable was moved to the Mater Hospital, but died from his wounds the next day. He had two and a half years' police service, having been a labourer before joining the RIC.

31 May 1922,
Millfield, Belfast city
Andrew Roulston, S/Con
William Campbell, S/Con

At 5 p.m. two special constables were on beat duty in the Millfield area of Belfast when they were fired at. Both fell to the ground wounded and their IRA attackers then shot them again before running off. The officers were taken to hospital but Roulston, who was attached to Smithfield Barracks, died from his wounds in the Royal Victoria Hospital. He was buried at Strabane New Cemetery, Co. Tyrone, on 3 June. The Rifle Brigade band played the 'Dead March' while a large number of special constables marched with the hearse. After the funeral, the Last Post was sounded and volleys of shots were fired over the grave.

The other special constable wounded in this attack was William Campbell, who died at his home in Ahoghill from his wounds on 14 June 1924. He had been confined to bed since the date of the attack and left a wife and a large family.

Disbandment of the RIC

On 27 March 1922 a circular (D 806/1922) was sent to RIC barracks that informed all members that the disbandment of the RIC was to commence immediately, except in the six counties of Northern Ireland, and that it was to be completed not later than 31 May.

Members of the RIC who wished to join the RUC were informed that they could not join until they had been disbanded, and that they would be permitted to resign from the RIC giving one month's notice.

A second circular was then issued as follows:

D 810
1922

Royal Irish Constabulary Office
Dublin Castle
29 March 1922

Disbandment of the RIC

Paragraph 4 of circular D 806 issued herewith, is hereby cancelled and the following circular is to be substituted:

Free Travelling Warrants: A free travelling warrant to his home will be issued to each member of the Force. Where, however, any member of the Force considers that he would be in danger if he were to return to, or remain at, his home after dispersal, a free travelling warrant will be issued to enable him to remove himself and his family to a place in Great Britain and Ireland. Such warrants will be issuable only in respect of the member of the Force, his wife and children or other dependant normally supported by him as a member of his household. Where a member of the Force is moving his family and friends and finds it inadvisable to actually accompany them, a separate warrant will be issued for their use.

Travelling warrants will be issued on application prior to dispersal.

The following addition is to be made to Paragraph 9 of circular D 806:

'but an advance may be drawn by those requiring it on the following scale: Head Constables £15, lower ranks £10'.

With reference to Paragraph 11 of circular D 806, applicants for enrolment in the Northern Police Force will not be disbanded until their applications have been considered. The terms of the service in the Northern Force have not yet been definitely fixed but I am assured that, when the final announcement is made, the conditions for disbanded members of the RIC will be found to be acceptable and

that the future of the men, regardless of religion, will be safeguarded,
C. A. Walsh, Deputy Inspector General[3]

As members of the RIC started to disperse, they began increasingly to come under attack, with reports of members who had just been disbanded being killed when they returned to their homes.

On 27 March 1922 Colonel Ashley asked in the House of Commons what help was being given to ex-RIC members who were in danger or threatened with massacre if they returned home on disbandment. On 28 April it was reported that two ex-RIC men had been dragged from the Holyhead steamer at Dublin's North Wall as it was about to sail for England. These two men were reported as being killed and Winston Churchill raised the question of attacks on ex-members of the RIC in the House of Commons again.

Without doubt a number of disbanded or retired members of the RIC were killed just prior to, or shortly after, 31 May, when the Royal Ulster Constabulary was formed in Northern Ireland. The Civic Guard was formed in the South on 21 February 1922 and was the police force for the new Irish Government. The Civic Guard was reconstituted and renamed An Garda Síochána on 8 August 1923.

Due to the general turmoil prevailing at this period, a number of the incidents were either never reported or reported some time after their occurrence, which makes it very difficult now to try and associate men killed during this period with their former employment as police officers.

The following short list of incidents, however, graphically outlines the actions carried out against former policemen who remained in Ireland:

02.03.1921: Retired Constable Patrick Roche was taken from his home at Causeway, Listowel, Co. Kerry at 5 a.m. by armed men and shot. His body was found in a field a short distance away.

Pinned to his body was a card with the words 'Convicted Spy. All informers beware IRA'. The local RIC barracks was attacked at the same time as this incident was taking place.

03.04.1921: Retired RIC officer Thomas Morris was taken from his home near Kinvarra, Co. Galway. His body was found the next day at a crossroads.

06.04.1921: Retired Constable John Wymes, 49792, was taken from his home at Loughglynn in the Castlerea district of Co. Mayo by a number of armed men and shot.

15.04.1921: Retired Head Constable Jeremiah Looney, 49102, who had been pensioned from the RIC on 1 March 1920, was killed at Bandon, Co. Cork.

26.03.1922: Ex-Constable Patrick John Poland was seriously wounded near Patrick's Bridge in Cork.

27.03.1922: Ex-RIC Sergeant Arthur Gloster, 51756, was shot dead in Barrack Street, Cork. He had been retired from the force for two years, having been in charge of College Road Barracks prior to his retirement. As an inspector under the food and drugs act he had been extremely vigilant in the execution of his duty. The ex-sergeant was from Farranfore, Co. Kerry. He was married with a family.

06.04.1922: Two recently disbanded members of the RIC were shot in their homes in the town of Ballyhaunis, Co. Mayo. Ex-Constable Thomas Cranny, 76985, was in bed when he was shot and killed, whilst ex-Constable Butler was seriously wounded as he was sitting in the kitchen of his home. He was taken to a Dublin hospital.

07.04.1922: Five recently retired members of the RIC were shot and killed with another six being seriously wounded. Three of those killed came from Co. Clare, while the others killed were attacked in Tralee, Co. Kerry.

23.04.1922: Ex-Sergeant John Gunn, 52404, was killed in Ennis,

Co. Clare. He had been disbanded on 20 April 1922, having completed thirty-three years' police service.

04.05.1922: An ex-RIC constable was seized by armed men at Clonmel, Co. Tipperary, and taken away.

08.05.1922: An ex-policeman who had recently been disbanded from the RIC was shot and wounded in a field near Clarenbridge, Co. Galway.

11.05.1922: An-ex RIC man was injured in the arm when his house was taken over by ten armed men at Killymure, Convoy, Co. Donegal. The injured man was later taken to Derry City Hospital.

22.05.1922: Ex-Head Constable Joseph Ballantine was shot dead when he entered his home in Raphoe, Co. Donegal. He had just been disbanded and had returned to Raphoe where he had been formerly stationed to remove his furniture to Co. Armagh. He was a fifty-year-old married man.

23.05.1922: Ex-RIC Sergeant Walshe was on a visit to his wife and child in Newport, Co. Mayo, when he was shot dead. His body was removed to Abbeydorney, Co. Kerry, his native place.

23.05.1922: Ex-Constable Timothy O'Leary and his aunt were travelling by pony and trap from Kinsale when they were stopped by two armed men. He was removed from the trap and his body was later found on the roadway. He had only been disbanded recently and was making his way to Kilbrittain, Co. Cork, to visit his mother.

27.05.1922: An RIC pensioner (Sergeant James Greer, 49202) who had retired a couple of years before was taken from his home at Cootehall near Boyle, Co. Roscommon and shot dead. His killers then made their way to the home of his son, Thomas, also an ex-RIC member, 69446, and shot him too.

03.06.1922: All the ex-members of the RIC in Ballinasloe, Co. Galway, were visited and ex-Constables Taplye and Scanlon, father and son-in-law, were shot in the legs.

28.06.1922: An Ex-RIC man at one time stationed at Mallow, Co. Cork, was believed to have returned to the town on Saturday 24 June. He was kidnapped on Monday morning, 26 June, and taken away in a motor car. His body was found in the afternoon in a field at Killavullen, Mallow, shot in the head.

26.08.1922: Retired RIC member John Cullen of Ballymote, Co. Sligo, was brought to hospital in a motor car suffering from gunshot wounds from which he died at 8.30 p.m. the following day. At 2 a.m. on that day a raid was made on his residence for bicycles by a number of armed men. On being refused admission these men forced open the door and shot Mr Cullen. They then left, firing as they went.

13.10.1922: Retired Constable Patrick Clancy, who had only recently married, was shot in Leitrim Street, Cork, by three men who were armed with revolvers. These men lay in waiting near the tram standard. The former officer, a native of Clare who had twelve years' police service, was wounded in the back. He died shortly after admission to hospital.

Disbandment

The disbandment of the RIC commenced on 7 January 1922 and terminated on 31 August, by which time a total of 13,502 officers and men, which included 1,158 members of the Auxiliary Division, had left the force.

At the request of the northern authorities, disbandment did not begin in earnest in the six counties which were to form Northern Ireland until May, with the vast majority remaining until 31 May. The first members of the RIC to be disbanded were attached to the Auxiliary Division, with the last members being attached to the Dublin Castle Guard squads and clerical staff.

RIC officers were disbanded in batches of 200–300 from disbandment centres, many of which had previously been used to hold prisoners, an irony that did not escape the officers. On disbandment, each police officer received a remuneration calculated on his total length of service, and, irrespective of previous service, each of them was given an extra twelve years, which was used during these calculations. Many also received assistance in their resettlements both in Ireland and in other places as far away as China, Egypt and America.

As well as the 13,502 shown as having been disbanded, the General Personnel Register for the RIC from October 1870 to 31 August 1922 has a total of 2,952 entries which do not state the specific manner in which men left the force. A large proportion of these records are of men who joined the RIC from 1920 onwards. The general influx of recruits, transfers between the Auxiliary Division, and the RIC or its Transport Division, plus the running down of the police's administration ensured that the greater part of these missing records can probably be accounted for as clerical errors or oversights, a problem which undoubtedly worsened, especially as disenchantment and despondency began to spread within the RIC.

However, not all the discrepancies can be explained as merely being clerical problems, as there is evidence that some men simply 'walked away', while others felt compelled to leave due to the situation in the country, and a number left (without giving a reason) to assist the IRA. This fact is borne out as 1,136 former RIC members made applications for state pensions to the committee of inquiry which had been convened by the Irish Government, under the Free State Superannuation and Pensions Act of 1923.[4] By 1927, 631 of these applications had been approved by this committee, with a number of the successful awards being made to men whose RIC general records were incomplete.

Despite the fact that some RIC members helped the Republican movement, the majority distinguished themselves by their steadiness and loyalty whilst performing their duties under extreme physical and psychological pressures.

RUC Fatalities

After the formation of the Royal Ulster Constabulary in Northern Ireland, the IRA continued their attacks on police officers there. At first these attacks were carried out with the same vigour and ruthlessness as those before the signing of the Truce in July 1921. However, as the Civil War between the different Republican factions caused by the acceptance of the Treaty began to gather momentum, the intensity of the attacks on the police began to decrease, before eventually petering out.

Before the complete cessation of violence, the following incidents resulted in the deaths of police officers.

4 June 1922, near Pettigo, Co. Fermanagh
Thomas W. Dobson, S/Con

Special Constable Dobson was shot and killed by the IRA as he was driving a Crossley tender for the military from Enniskillen to Pettigo. The vehicle was ambushed half a mile from the village as it was being deployed in a military offensive to retake Pettigo from the IRA, who had control of the village at the time.

6 June 1922, Annaghroe, Co. Armagh
Thomas Sheridan, S/Con

At 11.45 p.m. Special Constable Sheridan had just arrived by bicycle at a vehicle checkpoint operating in the vicinity of Annaghroe, Caledon, Co. Armagh. He was about to commence duty at the checkpoint and was talking to the head constable when a single shot was fired. This sniper's bullet fatally wounded the special constable.

At the time of the attack the vehicle checkpoint had been approximately fifty yards from the border with the Irish Free State.

The dead officer had been stationed at Caledon. He was thirty-five and single, from Bawnboy, Co. Cavan.

17 June 1922, Drumintee, Co. Armagh
Thomas Russell, S/Con

At 12.45 p.m. an Ulster Special Constabulary patrol was ambushed by the IRA at Drumintee near Forkhill, Co. Armagh. The ambushers had been on both sides of the road and their gunfire fatally wounded Special Constable Russell, who was from Belfast.

19 June 1922, near Keady, Co. Armagh
William Mitchell, S/Con
Samuel Young, S/Con

The two special constables were cycling to join the remainder of their patrol when they were ambushed near the village of Keady, Co. Armagh. They had left the village at 8 p.m. and had just reached Drumalane when they were ambushed. Both men died from their wounds on 20 June. Their attackers made off towards the border after the ambush.

5 August 1922, Newtownards Road, Belfast city
Samuel Hayes, S/Con

The special constable was home on leave and was in a public house on the Newtownards Road. A crowd was pursuing a man, who took refuge in the same public house. Two gunmen fired into the bar after him, wounding two customers, one of whom was Special Constable Hayes. He later died from his wounds, being the last police officer to die as a result of political violence in Ireland during the period 1919–1922.

Conclusion for 1922

By 1 June 1922, when partition came into being, a total of fifty-five policemen had lost their lives during the year, with a further six officers being killed before the violence was finally to end. During the earlier part of the year the IRA continued to attack police officers and retired police officers in the south and west of Ireland. Many of those killed were attacked when they could offer little or no resistance. This was highlighted, as I have already noted, with one of the last attacks to cause a fatality of a serving officer in the south of Ireland, which was carried out on 15 March 1922. Then three police officers were attacked in their sick beds at St Brigid's Home, Galway, resulting in the death of two of them.

In Northern Ireland the attacks on police drastically increased and began to reach levels that had only been seen in the rest of Ireland before the Truce, as the IRA concentrated their members and weapons along the border in order to carry out concerted attacks. However, due to the split in their ranks, this campaign began to falter and eventually petered out as the two opposing Republican factions intensified their Civil War.

With the death of Special Constable Samuel Hayes on 5 August 1922, a total of 502 policemen had lost their lives from the first attack on a police patrol at Soloheadbeg on 21 January 1919, with another officer dying from his wounds later. This study contains as comprehensive a list as possible of all police casualties in Ireland during that period as a direct result of political violence. It may be assumed that it is not a definitive list, as even RIC microfilm records on occasion showed men as having been dismissed or resigned from the force when in reality they had been killed. Other sources studied also indicated that officers had died as a result of wounds received from an assassin, but these were later attributed to an accident or tragic mistake by a comrade.

These problems were compounded by the inaccurate reporting of some officers' deaths, while others reported as having been slightly wounded had not survived. Another major difficulty encountered during the research for this book was the unique problem that so many ex-service personnel who had joined either the RIC or its Auxiliary Division were, when killed, still referred to as soldiers or ex-soldiers and not as police officers. This meant that no report of casualties as a result of any kind of incident could be relied upon completely.

Alphabetical List of Men Killed

All these problems aside, the following is an alphabetical list of those serving police officers who paid the ultimate price during a period of unparalleled difficulty and disorder in Ireland:

Name	Rank	Date attacked
Adam, George	Constable	11.07.1921
Adams, Samuel	Constable	03.02.1921
Agar, William	Constable	31.10.1919
Allen, David	S/Constable	31.03.1922
Anderson, Joseph	Sergeant	21.05.1921
Appleford, Leonard George	Cadet	24.06.1921
Armstrong, Thomas Robert	Sergeant	21.07.1920
Bales, John Beets	Cadet	23.04.1921
Balls, Hedley A.	Cadet	05.12.1920
Barnes, William	Cadet	28.11.1920
Barney, Robert J. W.	Constable	26.01.1921
Barton, John	D/Sgt (DMP)	29.11.1919
Bayley, Cecil James W.	Cadet	28.11.1920
Beard, Bernard J. L.	Cadet	14.03.1921
Beasant, James R.	Constable	04.03.1921
Beckett, Harry	Constable	19.05.1921
Bell, George William	Constable	03.02.1921
Benson, Francis	H/Constable	14.05.1921
Bentley, Benjamin	Constable	30.04.1922

Name	Rank	Date
Biggs, Harry	Constable	23.10.1920
Biggs, Harry	DI	14.05.1921
Blake, Cecil Arthur Maurice	DI	15.05.1921
Bloxham, Henry J.	Sergeant	21.01.1921
Blythe, Sydney	Constable	02.06.1921
Bolam, Ernest Baran	Cadet	23.04.1921
Bolger, Edward	Constable	14.12.1919
Booth, Leonard	Constable	20.05.1921
Bourke, John Joseph	Constable	03.02.1921
Bourke, Joseph	Constable	30.06.1921
Bowles, Charles H.	Constable	31.03.1921
Boyd, Robert A. E.	Constable	17.01.1921
Boyd, William A. H.	Cadet	16.06.1921
Boylan, John	Constable	23.04.1921
Boynes, Joseph	Constable	10.04.1921
Bradford, Albert	Constable	18.06.1921
Bradshaw, Leonard	Cadet	28.11.1920
Brady, James Joseph	DI	30.09.1920
Brady, John Edward	Sergeant	29.04.1920
Brady, Philip	Sergeant	02.09.1919
Brannan, Michael	Constable	12.06.1921
Brennan, Smyth Thomas	Constable	21.08.1920
Brett, James	Constable	21.06.1920
Brewer, Cyril F. H.	Constable	05.07.1921
Brick, William	Constable	10.05.1920
Bridges, Thomas	Constable	14.05.1921
Briggs, James	Constable	02.06.1921
Brock, Alfred V. G.	Constable	28.02.1921
Brogan, Michael	Constable	25.09.1920
Brown, James	Constable	02.06.1921
Brown, Walter Thomas	Constable	04.05.1921
Bruin, John	Sergeant	13.04.1922
Budd, Edgar	Constable	26.05.1921
Buntrock, Charles	Constable	13.11.1920
Burke, James	Constable	19.07.1920
Burke, Michael	Sergeant	05.06.1921
Burke, Peter	H/Constable	20.09.1920
Bush, George	Cadet	02.02.1921
Butler, Francis J.	Sergeant	18.05.1921
Butler, James	Sergeant	08.05.1921
Campbell, William	Constable	20.03.1921

Campbell, William	Constable	17.06.1921
Campbell, William	S/Constable	31.05.1922
Cane, Arthur William	Constable	25.02.1921
Cantlon, John	Constable	02.06.1921
Cardwell, Robert	S/Constable	03.05.1922
Carey, Patrick	Constable	19.07.1920
Carolan, Peter	Constable	14.05.1921
Carroll, John	Constable	14.02.1921
Carroll, John J.	Constable	11.06.1920
Carroll, Patrick J.	Sergeant	18.04.1920
Carter, Albert	Constable	18.05.1921
Carter, Edward	Constable	03.02.1921
Carty, Stephen	Sergeant	13.01.1921
Caseley, Albert	Constable	31.10.1920
Chapman, Spencer R.	Cadet	11.12.1920
Chave, Clarence Victor	Constable	03.10.1920
Chermside, William	S/Constable	23.03.1922
Chittick, George	S/Constable	22.03.1922
Clapp, William	Constable	04.05.1921
Clark, Alexander Thomas	Constable	10.05.1921
Clarke, Alexander	Constable	11.07.1921
Clarke, Christopher	Sergeant	13.03.1922
Clarke, Martin	Constable	14.07.1920
Clarke, Patrick	Constable	27.06.1921
Clarke, Sydney George	Constable	22.01.1921
Clarke, William	DI	20.01.1921
Clayton, Harold	Cadet	02.02.1921
Clifford, Martin	Constable	17.04.1920
Coleman, Joseph E.	Sergeant	14.05.1921
Collery, James	Sergeant	01.06.1921
Collins, John	Constable	18.05.1922
Compston, Robert William	S/Constable	13.01.1921
Compton, Alexander	S/H/Constable	06.04.1922
Conlon, Thomas	Constable	10.07.1921
Connor, George	S/Constable	25.05.1922
Connor, James	Constable	07.07.1921
Cooney, Joseph	Constable	01.06.1921
Cooney, Peter	Constable	01.11.1920
Cooper, Walter H.	Constable	11.03.1921
Cormer, Frederick	Constable	08.07.1921
Cornyn, Thomas	Constable	14.05.1921

Cotter, John	Sergeant	02.03.1922
Coughlan, John	Sergeant	22.03.1921
Coulter, Robert	S/Constable	29.05.1921
Craddock, Thomas M.	Sergeant	22.08.1920
Craig, Alfred	S/Harbour Con	11.05.1921
Crake, Francis William	DI	28.11.1920
Craven, Francis Worthington	DI	02.02.1921
Crawford, John	Constable	12.10.1920
Crean, Cornelius	Sergeant	25.04.1920
Creedon, Francis	Constable	02.07.1921
Creegan, Francis	Sergeant	02.06.1921
Cronin, Henry	Sergeant	31.10.1920
Crook, Robert	Constable	11.03.1921
Cullen, James	Constable	03.05.1921
Cullen, James	Constable	10.03.1922
Cummings, John	S/Constable	06.02.1921
Cummings, William	Constable	03.03.1922
Cunningham, Thomas	S/Constable	23.03.1922
Curtin, Jeremiah	Sergeant	13.01.1921
Cuthbertson, George	Constable	01.05.1921
Dalton, Laurence	D/Constable (DMP)	20.04.1920
Davis, Christopher	H/Constable	03.03.1922
Day, Edgar Ernest	Constable	27.06.1921
Delaney, Timothy	Constable	08.09.1920
Depree, Frederick H.	Constable	07.05.1921
Devereux, William	Constable	22.03.1921
Devine, Thomas	Constable	29.06.1921
Dillon, Thomas	Constable	24.11.1920
Dobson, Thomas W.	S/Constable	04.06.1922
Doherty, Francis	Sergeant	07.10.1920
Doherty, John	Constable	02.06.1921
Donoghue, James	Sergeant	17.11.1920
Donohoe, James	Constable	19.09.1920
Doogue, John	Constable	20.01.1921
Doogue, Pierce	Constable	15.06.1920
Doran, Edward	Constable	17.05.1921
Dougherty, William	S/Sergeant	11.02.1922
Dowling, Michael James	Constable	22.03.1921
Dowling, Thomas	Constable	02.06.1921
Downey, John	Constable	29.09.1920
Downing, Michael	Constable (DMP)	19.10.1919

Doyle, Michael	Constable	03.02.1921
Dray, Ernest	Constable	29.12.1920
Duddy, Joseph	Constable	03.03.1921
Duffy, James	Constable	03.04.1921
Dunne, Edward	Constable	10.05.1920
Dunne, John	Constable	17.05.1921
Dunphy, Kyran	Sergeant	19.05.1920
Dyne, Robert	Constable	04.05.1921
Early, Patrick Joseph	Sergeant	29.03.1922
Ednie, Charles F.	Constable	02.02.1922
Elton, William	Constable	18.03.1921
Enright, Michael	Constable	13.05.1919
Enright, Thomas	Constable	14.12.1921
Evans, John Herbert	Constable	31.10.1920
Fahy, Patrick	Constable	14.07.1920
Falkiner, Walter	Cadet	12.03.1921
Fallon, Martin	Constable	03.05.1921
Fallon, Patrick	Sergeant	03.11.1920
Farrell, Francis Joseph	Cadet	14.03.1921
Feeney, Martin	Constable	02.06.1921
Finnegan, Luke	Constable	20.01.1920
Finn, William	Constable	09.04.1920
Finnerty, Patrick	Sergeant	14.04.1920
Fitzgerald, John	Constable	03.07.1921
Fitzgerald, John	Sergeant	21.11.1920
Flaherty, John	Constable	06.10.1920
Flood, Terence	Constable	29.09.1920
Fluke, John	S/Constable	10.04.1921
Flynn, John	Sergeant	10.05.1920
Foley, Martin	Constable	21.08.1920
Foley, Patrick	Constable	23.04.1920
Foody, Patrick	Constable	03.02.1921
French, William	Constable	02.06.1921
Frizelle, Frederick	Sergeant	03.05.1922
Gabbie, Hugh	S/Constable	30.06.1921
Gallagher, Francis	Constable	12.10.1920
Galvin, Timothy Joseph	Constable	06.07.1921
Garniss, Frank	Cadet	21.11.1920
Garvey, Denis	Sergeant	11.05.1920
Gaughan, John	Constable	08.09.1920
Gibbons, Tobias	Sergeant	15.03.1922

Gilmartin, John	Sergeant	15.03.1922
Gleave, James C.	Cadet	28.11.1920
Glover, James	Constable	10.06.1921
Gorbey, Robert	Constable	31.10.1920
Gordon, William	S/Sergeant	22.03.1921
Gorman, Michael	Constable	02.12.1921
Gourlay, William	Constable	03.02.1922
Graham, George	S/Constable	26.04.1921
Graham, Philip Noel	Cadet	28.11.1920
Grant, John	Constable	17.03.1921
Green, Samuel	Constable	02.02.1921
Greer, Martin John	Constable	23.02.1921
Guthrie, Cecil J.	Cadet	28.11.1920
Halford, Patrick J.	Constable	16.12.1920
Hall, James	S/Constable	29.05.1921
Hall, Thomas	S/Constable	31.03.1922
Hallissy, Michael	Sergeant	30.03.1921
Hanlon, John	D/Constable	21.08.1920
Harden, Ernest F.	Constable	16.12.1920
Hardman, Reginald	Constable	22.09.1920
Harper, James	S/Constable	29.03.1922
Harrington, Daniel	Constable	11.05.1920
Harte, Michael	Constable	22.09.1920
Harvey, John	Constable	02.05.1922
Haugh, Matthew	Constable	25.08.1920
Haverty, Patrick	Constable	21.08.1920
Hayes, Patrick	Constable	14.05.1921
Hayes, Samuel	S/Constable	05.08.1922
Hayton, William	Constable	03.02.1921
Healy, Charles	Constable	17.03.1920
Heanue, John Martin	Constable	04.03.1920
Hearty, Patrick	Sergeant	19.05.1920
Heaslip, William	Constable	19.05.1922
Heffron, Thomas	Constable	26.01.1921
Hegarty, Edward	S/Constable	03.05.1922
Hegerty, Robert Henry	Constable	22.01.1921
Hetherington, James	Constable	19.04.1921
Hewitt, James R.	Constable	07.07.1921
Hickey, Michael Joseph	Sergeant	19.03.1921
Higgins, John	Sergeant	01.04.1921
Higgins, Thomas	Constable	01.07.1921

Hill, Francis	Constable	27.12.1921
Hill, William E.	Constable	02.07.1921
Hillyer, Alfred	Constable	04.05.1921
Hodgsden, Alfred C.	Constable	27.12.1920
Hodnett, John	Constable	22.09.1921
Hoey, Daniel	D/Constable (DMP)	12.09.1919
Hoey, Daniel	Constable	23.02.1921
Hoey, Owen	Constable	28.06.1921
Holland, Timothy	Sergeant	06.06.1920
Holman, Joseph C.	Constable	01.06.1921
Holmes, Philip Armstrong	Div. Com.	28.01.1921
Hopkins, Thomas	Constable	07.05.1921
Horan, Michael	Constable	25.06.1920
Horan, Timothy	Constable	30.10.1920
Houghton, John A.	Cadet	02.02.1921
Howlett, George Horace	Constable	22.02.1921
Hugh-Jones, Stanley	Cadet	28.11.1920
Hughes, John William	Constable	22.02.1921
Hughes, Joseph	Sergeant	21.02.1921
Hugo, Frederick	Cadet	28.11.1920
Hunt, Michael	DI	23.06.1919
Hunt, William Frederick	Cadet	26.06.1921
Hunter, Thomas J.	S/Constable	03.05.1922
Hynes, Michael J.	Sergeant	22.09.1920
Jays, Harry Clement	Constable	21.11.1920
Johnston, Thomas R.	Constable	01.01.1921
Johnston, William Robert	S/Constable	18.04.1922
Johnstone, Andrew	Sergeant	02.07.1921
Jolly, Robert W.	Constable	05.06.1921
Jones, Albert G.	Cadet	28.11.1920
Jones, Wilfred	Constable	15.04.1921
Jones, William	Constable	22.12.1920
Kane, Thomas	Sergeant	28.05.1920
Keany, Michael	DI	11.02.1922
Kearney, John	Constable	15.05.1921
Kearney, John	H/Constable	21.11.1920
Keeffe, John Thomas	Constable	29.09.1920
Kelleher, Philip St John	DI	31.10.1920
Kells, Henry	D/Constable (DMP)	14.04.1920
Kelly, Michael	Constable	22.09.1920
Kelly, Thomas	Constable	19.04.1921

Kemp, John J.	Sergeant	14.01.1921
Kenna, John	Constable	14.05.1921
Kenny, Michael	Constable	12.10.1920
Kenny, Michael	Constable	01.04.1921
Kenward, Arthur Frederick	Constable	19.03.1921
Kenyon, Edmund	Constable	17.05.1921
Keown, Patrick	Constable	25.10.1920
Kershaw, Frank	Constable	03.02.1922
King, James	Sergeant	11.07.1921
King, John	Constable	01.07.1921
King, Thomas	Constable	12.06.1920
Kingston, James	Sergeant	06.05.1921
Kingston, William	Constable	03.02.1921
Kirkpatrick, Alexander	S/Constable	17.03.1922
Kirwan, Stephen	Sergeant	19.04.1921
Krumm, Edward	Constable	08.09.1920
Laffey, Patrick	Constable	25.10.1920
Laird, Samuel	S/Constable	21.03.1922
Larking, Sydney G.	Constable	02.11.1920
Lea-Wilson, Percival	DI	15.06.1920
Leary, Jeremiah	Constable	13.11.1920
Leech, William	Sergeant	28.05.1922
Lenihan, Michael	Constable	13.07.1920
Leonard, Thomas	Constable	25.09.1920
Leslie, Edward L.	Constable	23.03.1921
Lewis, James	S/Constable	11.02.1922
Longhead, John	Constable	18.10.1920
Lord, Frederick H.	Constable	08.04.1921
Lucas, Ernest William H.	Cadet	28.11.1920
Lucas, Samuel Wilfred	Sergeant	25.10.1920
Lynch, John P. (Jack)	Constable	13.02.1921
Lynch, Patrick	Constable	25.10.1920
Lyness, George	S/Constable	08.06.1921
Lyttle, William	S/Constable	02.12.1921
MacDonald, John Cyril	Constable	17.04.1921
Mackessy, Patrick	Constable	13.11.1920
Mackinnon, John Alister	Commander	15.04.1921
Madden, William	Constable	31.10.1920
Maguire, James	Sergeant	06.03.1921
Maguire, Joseph	Constable	23.05.1921
Maher, John	Sergeant	12.12.1921

Mahony, John	Constable	19.09.1920
Malone, Michael Francis	Constable	01.01.1921
Malynn, James Joseph	Constable	24.01.1920
Martin, Herbert	S/Constable	27.05.1922
Masterson, James F.	Constable	17.07.1920
Maunsell, Daniel	Sergeant	21.08.1920
Maxwell, William M.	Constable	02.11.1920
McArdle, Peter J.	Sergeant	12.10.1920
McCarthy, Daniel	Constable	09.04.1920
McCarthy, Martin	Constable	01.09.1920
McCarthy, Michael	Constable (DMP)	23.04.1920
McCaughey, Michael F.	DI	01.06.1921
McConnell, Edward	Sergeant	08.04.1922
McCoo, Nathaniel	S/Constable	14.04.1992
McCormack, John S.	Constable	01.06.1921
McCormack, Thomas	Sergeant	04.05.1921
McDonagh, Edward	Constable	23.02.1921
McDonagh, Peter Joseph	Sergeant	21.05.1921
McDonnell, James	Constable	21.01.1919
McDonnell, Patrick	Sergeant	10.05.1920
McEdward, Lauchlin	Constable	17.02.1922
McElhill, James	H/Constable	12.06.1921
McFadden, Charles	S/Constable	10.02.1922
McFadden, John	Sergeant	24.04.1921
McFarland, William	S/Constable	11.02.1922
McGoldrick, Patrick	Constable	25.04.1920
McGrath, Thomas James	DI	07.01.1921
McGuire, Denis P.	Sergeant	21.09.1920
McGuire, John	Constable	22.09.1920
McHenry, John	Harbour Constable	25.11.1921
McIntosh, John	Constable	11.03.1921
McKenna, Francis	Sergeant	03.05.1920
McKenna, James	Constable	20.03.1921
McKnight, William T.	S/Constable	03.05.1922
McLean, Hugh	Constable	15.05.1921
McMahon, Robert	S/Constable	11.02.1922
McNamara, John	Constable	24.08.1920
Mead, Charles F.	Constable	17.05.1921
Megarity, John	S/Constable	29.05.1922
Miller, John	Constable	13.11.1920
Milligan, Samuel	S/Constable	08.05.1922

Millin, Sidney	Constable	03.02.1921
Mitchell, William	S/Constable	19.06.1922
Mollaghan, Bernard	Constable	03.02.1921
Moore, Stanley L.	Constable	31.03.1921
Moran, Michael	Constable	20.01.1921
Morgan, George	Constable	31.10.1920
Morgan, Martin	Sergeant	03.09.1920
Moroney, Denis	D/Sergeant	15.05.1920
Moroney, Jeremiah	Sergeant	28.04.1921
Morris, Cecil A.	Cadet	21.11.1920
Morris, Frank E.	Constable	20.01.1921
Morton, Joseph	Constable	28.05.1920
Moyles, Thomas	Constable	28.01.1921
Mulherin, William	D/Sergeant	25.07.1920
Mullan, John	Constable	27.08.1920
Mullany, Patrick	Constable	02.02.1921
Mullen, Martin	Constable	29.12.1920
Mulloy, Michael	Sergeant	20.01.1921
Mulrooney, Edward	H/Constable	30.03.1921
Munnelly, James	Constable	26.08.1920
Murphy, Daniel Anthony	Constable	12.03.1921
Murphy, Edward	Constable	01.09.1920
Murphy, James	S/Constable	25.05.1922
Murphy, Michael James	Constable	04.08.1919
Murray	Sergeant	07.05.1921
Murray, James	Constable	27.07.1920
Murren, James	Sergeant	27.06.1921
Murtagh, Joseph	Constable	19.03.1920
Nathan, Cyril Henry	Constable	15.08.1920
Neazer, George	Sergeant	10.03.1920
Needham, Alfred G.	Constable	10.07.1921
Neenan, Michael	Constable	12.02.1920
Nixon, Samuel	S/Sergeant	22.03.1921
Noonan, Edward A.	Constable	29.09.1920
Nutley, John	Constable	15.05.1921
O'Brien, Henry	Constable	29.05.1922
O'Brien, James	Constable	16.03.1921
O'Brien, Martin	Constable	06.04.1919
O'Connell, Patrick	Constable	21.01.1919
O'Connor, Martin G.	Sergeant	12.10.1920
O'Connor, Patrick	Constable	10.03.1922

O'Connor, Patrick James	Constable	01.02.1921
O'Leary, Denis	Constable	09.06.1921
O'Loughlin, Denis	Constable	21.04.1921
O'Regan, Christopher Patrick	Constable	03.05.1921
O'Sullivan, Dudley L.	Constable	09.03.1922
O'Sullivan, Philip John	DI	17.12.1920
O'Sullivan, Tobias	DI	20.01.1921
Oakes, Herbert	Constable	03.05.1921
Oakley, Walter	Constable	24.07.1920
Pallester, William	Cadet	28.11.1920
Palmer, Albert H.	Constable	16.12.1920
Pearce, Arthur	Constable	03.02.1921
Pearson, Horace	Cadet	28.11.1920
Pearson, William H.	Constable	06.04.1921
Perkins, Walter P.	Constable	30.05.1921
Perrier, Frederick W.	Constable	23.02.1921
Perry, Patrick	Sergeant	25.10.1920
Phelan, James	Constable	04.05.1921
Plumb, James Edward	S/Constable	06.04.1922
Poole, Arthur F.	Constable	28.11.1920
Potter, Gilbert Norman	DI	27.04.1921
Potter, William J.	Constable	26.08.1920
Power, William	Constable	03.05.1921
Prendiville, Maurice	Constable	03.12.1920
Quinn, Michael	Constable	26.01.1921
Quinn, Timothy J.	Constable	27.11.1920
Quirk, John	Constable	01.06.1921
Quirk, Maurice	Constable	27.11.1920
Rea, Isaac James	Constable	21.11.1920
Redding, George	Constable	30.05.1921
Redman, Sydney R.	Constable	19.03.1921
Redmond, Robert	Constable	14.05.1921
Redmond, William C. F.	Sec. Asst Com. (DMP)	21.01.1920
Regan, John	Sergeant	03.05.1921
Reid, John	Constable	27.12.1920
Reilly, Patrick	Sergeant	21.08.1920
Reynolds, Charles O'M.	Constable	16.03.1921
Rickerby, Albert Thomas	S/Constable	28.05.1922
Riley, Ernest J.	Constable	12.03.1921
Riordan, John	Sergeant	04.08.1919

Rippingale, Bertie	Constable	21.10.1920
Roche, Daniel	Sergeant	17.10.1920
Roche, George	Constable	13.07.1920
Rocke, James	Constable	17.03.1920
Rogers, George Henry	Constable	13.04.1921
Roulston, Andrew	S/Constable	31.05.1922
Rundle, Albert	Constable	21.10.1920
Russell, Thomas	S/Constable	17.06.1922
Ryan, Thomas	Constable	08.03.1920
Ryle, John	Constable	14.05.1921
Satchwell, Thomas	Constable	22.02.1921
Seafield-Grant, James	Commandant	25.02.1921
Scully, Timothy	Constable	11.03.1920
Shanley, Thomas	Constable	26.06.1921
Shannon, Peter	Constable	17.12.1920
Shaw, Walter	Constable	01.05.1921
Shea, Ambrose	Sergeant	31.03.1921
Shelsher, Joseph	Constable	01.07.1921
Sheridan, Thomas	S/Constable	06.06.1922
Shortall, Francis	Constable	01.01.1921
Shorter, Frederick E.	Cadet	16.06.1921
Skeats, Albert Edward	Constable	13.05.1921
Smith, Arthur	Constable	16.12.1920
Smith, Henry	Constable	03.02.1921
Smith, John Frederick	Constable	12.06.1921
Smith, William Albert	Constable	30.04.1921
Smith, William J.	Constable	20.01.1921
Smyth, G. Brice Ferguson	Div. Com	17.07.1920
Smyth, Patrick	D/Sergeant (DMP)	30.07.1919
Soady, Clevel L.	Cadet	25.02.1921
Somers, Nicholas	Constable	08.03.1921
Stanley, William	Constable	07.10.1920
Steadman, William	Constable (DMP)	21.04.1921
Stephens, William H.	Constable	29.03.1921
Sterland, Frederick	Constable	08.05.1921
Stevenson, Edward James	DI	02.06.1921
Stewart, Hector	S/Constable	16.02.1922
Stewart, William	Constable	20.05.1921
Stokes, John	Sergeant	12.07.1920
Storey, William K.	H/Constable	08.05.1921
Sturdy, Thomas	S/Constable	12.06.1921

Swanzy, Oswald Ross	DI	22.08.1920
Sweeney, Thomas	Constable	16.03.1921
Taylor, Frank	Cadet	28.11.1920
Taylor, Frederick	Constable	13.12.1920
Taylor, Frederick	Constable	22.01.1921
Taylor, William H.	Constable	03.02.1921
Thompson, Harold	Constable	14.05.1921
Thorp, Arthur	Constable	29.12.1920
Tobin, Robert	Sergeant	02.07.1920
Turner, Archibald	Constable	09.11.1920
Turner, George	Constable	03.04.1922
Vanston, William	Constable	02.02.1921
Wadkins, Samuel H.	Constable	04.05.1921
Wainwright, Christopher	Cadet	28.11.1921
Wallace, Peter	Sergeant	13.05.1919
Walsh, John	Constable (DMP)	20.02.1920
Walsh, Patrick Joseph	Constable	12.02.1921
Walsh, Thomas	Sergeant	20.12.1920
Walsh, William	Constable	02.06.1921
Wames, George Gerald	Cadet	24.06.1921
Watkins, Ernest S.	Constable	07.08.1920
Webb, John F.	Constable	30.04.1921
Webster, Benjamin D.	Cadet	28.11.1920
Wheatly, Terence Patrick	Constable	15.09.1920
Wiggins, Hubert J.	Constable	08.04.1921
Will, Alexander	Constable	11.07.1920
Wilson, William Harding	DI	16.08.1920
Woodcock, Hedley D.	Constable	04.05.1921
Woods, James Thomas	Constable	09.11.1920
Woodward, George	Constable	10.04.1921
Young, Samuel	S/Constable	19.06.1922

6

MISSING MEN

After the Truce on 11 July 1921 newspapers began to carry reports about persons who had been kidnapped by the IRA and who had not been accounted for. On 22 August 1921 the *Irish Times* stated that on 1 July 1921 nineteen RIC and Auxiliary policemen had not yet been accounted for, whilst the *Irish Independent* on 17 February 1922 said that the number of persons kidnapped between August 1920 and 11 July 1921 was as follows: thirty-four policemen, five military and 131 civilians.

The paper further stated that seventeen police officers and all the military personnel had been released, as well as 115 of the civilians. Of the remaining police officers it was believed that fifteen had been killed, with the remaining two being forced to leave the country. Eight of the civilians were also believed to have been killed, with the fate of the other eight being unknown.

As can be seen, it is difficult to ascertain the exact numbers involved as officers reported missing or kidnapped were later shown as casualties and vice versa, or even reported as having been dismissed from the RIC.

This, therefore, is as complete a list of police officers reported missing or kidnapped (and presumed killed) as can be drawn up at this time:

1. 72842 Agnew, Bertram, Cadet. Born 14.01.1896, single, from Lancashire. Lieutenant in the Royal Naval Reserve, he joined the RIC on 18.08.1920. He was stationed in Cork West Riding and was reported missing on 06.11.1920 at Macroom, Co. Cork.

His Auxiliary number was 370. (Another constable was also reported missing during this incident.) Both were intelligence officers who were travelling from Macroom to Cork when they were kidnapped, interrogated and killed. The bodies were secretly buried by the IRA.

2. 71848 Bright, Ernest, Constable. Born 23.05.1886, single, from London. Formerly a presser and a soldier, he joined the RIC on 09.07.1920. He was stationed in Kerry and was reported missing on 31.10.1920 at Hillville, Tralee, Co. Kerry. (During this incident two other police officers were killed and another constable was also reported missing. Notices were later posted in prominent places in the town of Tralee, Co. Kerry. These notices stated the following, 'Take notice – warning – unless the two Tralee policemen in Sinn Féin custody are returned before 10 a.m. on the 2nd inst, reprisals of a nature not yet heard of in Ireland will take place in Tralee and surroundings.'[1] It was later reported that the two missing constables had been thrown alive into the furnace of the Tralee Gas Works.)

3. 73835 Buchanan, Robert, Constable. Born 18.05.1900, single, from London. Formerly a motor fitter and a soldier, he joined the RIC on 05.10.1920. He was stationed in Roscommon and was reported missing on 23.03.1921 at Frenchpark, Co. Roscommon. (One other constable was also reported missing in this incident. See pp. 272–3.)

4. 75769 Daly, Joseph, Constable. Born 20.09.1900, single, from Meath. An ex-labourer, he joined the RIC on 23.11.1920. He was stationed in Tipperary North Riding and was reported missing on 15.05.1921 at Nenagh, Co. Tipperary. Another constable was also reported missing in this incident. Both constables had been out cycling unarmed and in plain clothes from their barracks at Silvermines.

5. 68608 Dennehy, Michael, Constable. Born 18.03.1894, single,

from Kerry. An ex-farmer, he joined the RIC on 06.04.1915 and was stationed in Roscommon. He was reported missing on 23.05.1921 at Frenchpark, Co. Roscommon.

6. 73329 Duckham, George H., Constable. Born 06.05.1900, married, from London. An ex-milkman, he joined the RIC on 24.09.1920. He was stationed in Cork West Riding and was reported missing on 22.06.1921 at Bandon, Co. Cork, after his return from wedding leave in England. His father later received a number of documents which had been in the possession of his son when he had been kidnapped, along with a letter from Macroom which stated that the constable had been tried and executed by the IRA on the day after he had been kidnapped.

7. 70336 Evans, James, Constable. Born 29.06.1898, single, from King's County. Formerly a farmer and a soldier, he joined the RIC on 16.02.1920 and was stationed in Roscommon. He was reported missing on 23.03.1921 at Frenchpark, Co. Roscommon. He had left his barracks at Frenchpark to meet a girl, but was never seen again. (See pp. 272–3.)

8. 82537 French, Leonard J., Cadet. Born 17.01.1895, single, from Staffordshire. Formerly a second lieutenant in the RAF, he joined the RIC on 17.02.1921 and was stationed in Kilkenny. He was reported missing on 10.06.1921 at Woodstock, Co. Kilkenny. Two members of 'A' Company of the RIC's Auxiliary Division stationed at Woodstock had been ambushed near the village of Rower. One cadet escaped, but Cadet French was captured and never seen again.

9. 70812 Gallivan, Thomas, Constable. Born 16.02.1901, single, from Kerry. Formerly a labourer and a soldier, he joined the RIC on 22.03.1920 and was stationed in Tipperary North Riding. He was reported missing on 15.02.1921 at Nenagh, Co. Tipperary.

10. 73342 Harrison, Arthur, Constable. Born 22.02.1892, married, from Lancashire. Formerly a labourer and a soldier, he joined the

RIC on 24.09.1920. He had left Carrigadrohid for Coachford Railway Station, Co. Cork, on 30.04.1921 but never reached his home. He had completed his service with the RIC and it was reported that he was kidnapped at Coachford and afterwards shot. He had resigned on the day he was kidnapped because of his wife's ill health. 'It is believed he was taken from the train by the IRA and killed near Dripsey. He had left for the railway station at 2 p.m. travelling in a bread van.

11. 75635 McDonald, Alex, Constable. Born 09.07.1895, single, from Caithness. Formerly a motor man and a soldier he joined the RIC on 17.11.1920. He was stationed in Louth and was reported missing on 26.06.1921 at Dundalk, Co. Louth. (He had a favourable record dated 02.02.1921.) According to Stephen O'Donnell in *The RIC & Black and Tans in County Louth 1919–1922* he was shot by John McLoughlin, an IRA man from the Monaghan and North Louth area. McLoughlin and another IRA member met McDonald in the Dundalk area and challenged the officer as being one of the police involved in the killing of two Watters brothers in Dundalk on 18 June 1921.

12. 72848 Mitchell, Lionel R., Cadet. Born 08.01.1897, single, from Somerset. Formerly a lieutenant in the Royal Berkshire Regiment, he joined the RIC on 18.08.1920. He was stationed in Cork West Riding and was reported missing on 06.11.1920 at Macroom, Co. Cork. During the First World War he had been awarded a DCM. His Auxiliary number was 298.

13. 73788 Murdock, Charles, Constable. Born 14.11.1894. He was married on 06.01.1920 and came from Dublin. Formerly a checker and a soldier, he joined the RIC on 05.10.1920. He was stationed in Donegal and was reported missing on 10.05.1921 at Buncrana, Co. Donegal. (See p. 296.)

14. 73469 Round, Harold, Constable. Born 10.02.1898. He was married on 13.03.1919 and came from Lancashire. Formerly a

collier and a soldier, he joined the RIC on 28.09.1920. He was stationed in Roscommon and was reported missing on 16.06.1921 at Frenchpark, Co. Roscommon.
15. 69906 Walsh, Thomas Joseph, Constable. Born 10.02.1893, single, from Dublin. Formerly a mechanic and a soldier, he joined the RIC on 04.11.1919. He was stationed in Cork East Riding and was reported missing on 06.11.1920. (His RIC record stated that he was dismissed on that date.)
16. 69079 Waters, Patrick, Constable. Born 15.05.1896, single, from Galway. An ex-farmer, he joined the RIC on 17.04.1917. He was stationed in Kerry and was reported missing on 31.10.1920 at Tralee, Co. Kerry. In the probate court in Dublin on 16 May 1922, Mr Justice Dodd granted an application by his father, Patrick Waters of Loughenbeg, Spiddal, Co. Galway, to have his son officially stated as dead.

The following newspaper reports illustrate the problems facing a person investigating the question of kidnapped or missing police officers.

In September 1990 the *Irish Independent* and *The Irish Times* carried reports that a body exhumed from a shallow, isolated grave in a wooded hillside at Turaheen outside Rossmore, Co. Tipperary, was understood to have been a member of the RIC. The corpse was believed to be that of a forty-year-old man named Thomas Kirby, from the Glen of Aherlow, Co. Tipperary, who had served in the British Army in the First World War and was reported to have only just joined the RIC before his abduction and death. When the body was exhumed it was found that the turf bog in which it had been buried had preserved it, as the man's clothes were completely intact. It was reported that the deceased had been dressed in a British Army uniform and had a cap with the Lincolnshire Regiment badge. This cap and his army tunic and great coat were all well preserved.

Research by the Clonoulty Community Council suggests that he was kidnapped in January or February 1921 by the IRA, that he was shot dead at the spot where his body was found and that the site of the grave was said to have been well known among elderly local people. The council added that, according to local recollection, Thomas Kirby was held for approximately three weeks before being shot.

It is more than likely that this man was not a member of the RIC as no record of the name Thomas Kirby can be found on the force's microfilm records for the dates stated. The fact that his cap had a British Army regiment badge as opposed to the RIC harp and crown, which all Black and Tans wore irrespective of what uniform they had, coupled with the fact that by the end of 1920 the deficiency of police uniforms had been made up and all members of the RIC had been issued with police uniform, tends to suggest that this man may not have been a member of the RIC but rather of the British Army.

However, the newspaper reports also stated that it was not known if the deceased had worn the uniform he was found in when on duty as an Auxiliary or Black and Tan police officer and seized by the IRA, or if he was dressed in the uniform by his captors before he was killed.

This report graphically illustrates the difficulty in authenticating a man's membership of either the RIC or the British Army during this period.

7

OTHER CASUALTIES

Whilst researching this book I discovered that a number of other police officers had died as the result of tragic accidents or mistakes. Originally some of these incidents were reported as having been caused by hostile actions perpetrated against the police as a direct consequence of the ongoing political campaign of violence, only for me to discover that this was not the case. The following list outlines the names of men who lost their lives in such manner. It excludes those police officers who it can be verified died from natural causes:

54757 Ahern, Eugene, Constable, 18.02.1922. Accidentally shot.

73033 Anderson, William James, Cadet, 10.10.1920. Accidentally shot at Beggars Bush Barracks, Dublin. His Auxiliary number was 463 and he had been a second lieutenant in the Manchester Regiment.

Armstrong, Robert, Special Constable, 01.06.1921. At 5.20 p.m. the officer was in the kitchen of Gortin RIC Barracks, Co. Tyrone as he was about to come off duty. Another officer in the room pulled up his gun belt with a jerk causing his gun to go off. The bullet struck Special Constable Armstrong, who died from his wounds.

Black, Richard, Special Constable, 05.06.1922. A 'B' Special patrol noticed suspicious movement in a field at Molenan, Co. Londonderry. At the same time a whistle was also heard. Two Specials were sent to investigate and one was accidentally shot.

70900 Binion, Charles E., Constable, 26.02.1921. Died as a result of an accident on duty.

5506 Boyd, John, Head Constable, 17.03.1921. Shot by an ex-soldier named John Gordon who was carrying out a burglary at Newtownards. The head constable died on 23 March in the Union Hospital. (Gordon was subsequently charged with the murder, but the outcome of the charge is unknown.)

63555 Brandshaw, Thomas, Constable, 19.02.1921. Committed suicide in the stables at the rear of Monasteraden Barracks.

79386 Bunce, John E., Constable, 30.04.1921. Accidentally shot at Bandon Barracks, Co. Cork. He died from his wounds on 29.05.1921.

72022 Cahill, Michael Joseph, DI, 23.04.1921. Accidentally shot. Two cars travelling to Gormanston from Dublin were on the road leading to Swords when they were challenged by the military at Cloughran. The police did not hear the challenge and DI Cahill was killed outright in the gunfire which ensued.

59524 Campion, John J., Sergeant, 17.06.1920. He was accidentally shot in Granard Barracks, Co. Longford, while pumping his bicycle tyre in the hallway. His revolver fell out of his breast pocket and hit the floor, which caused it to go off.

Cochrane Thomas, Special Constable, 09.07.1922. At 9.45 a.m. he was accidentally shot by a comrade's rifle in Katesbridge Barracks, Co. Down. He succumbed to his wounds following an operation in the Banbridge Infirmary on 11 July. He was a married man with five young children.

75687 Cosnette, Ralph V., Constable, 11.04.1921. Found shot and believed to have committed suicide.

79339 Cowie, Henry, Constable, 30.04.1921. He accidentally shot himself with his own revolver in Newbliss Barracks, Co. Monaghan. He was admitted to hospital but died from his wounds on 01.05.1921.

72222 Denham, John A., Constable, 20.09.1920. Accidentally shot.

74307 Doherty, James, Constable, 27.05.1921. Accidentally shot by a comrade.

65954 Driscoll, Patrick, Constable, 22.11.1920. As a result of a motor accident three constables were killed and five others hurt. The accident occurred at Dromoland, Co. Clare. The vehicle had been travelling from Ennis to Limerick when it crashed into the front gateway leading into Dromoland Castle.

69645 Duffy, James, Constable, 19.08.1920. A police patrol in a vehicle was challenged by a foot patrol of six constables who had noticed the patrol vehicle approaching without lights. Once the challenge was issued, a shot was fired killing Constable Duffy, who was in the vehicle. This incident occurred near Boston, Co. Clare.

76234 Duncan, William J., Constable, 17.04.1921. Accidentally shot at Dungarvan Barracks, Co. Waterford.

67060 Fennessey, William, Constable, 23.02.1921. Accidentally shot.

70213 Fleming, Michael, Constable, 22.11.1920. Traffic accident (see Driscoll above).

71433 Foster, Thomas W., Constable, 07.07.1920. Committed suicide by shooting himself.

French, Hugh, Special Sergeant, 16.02.1922, Old Lodge Road Belfast. Shortly before 5 p.m. the special sergeant, who was a draper by trade, was sitting at the counter of his shop at 62 Old Lodge Road Belfast, reading the evening paper. Although there was no rioting in the area at the time, a disorderly crowd had looted a public house at 117 Old Lodge Road. At the same time, 4–5 men carrying weapons came down Stanhope Street and on reaching the corner of Sherbrook Street they fired a number of shots. It is believed that a few of these bullets passed through the window of Mr French's shop, wounding him in the head. He was taken to the Royal Victoria Hospital but died shortly after admission.

Friars, David E., Special Constable, 27.02.1922, Thompson Street, Belfast. The officer had been in the area of Thompson Street and was returning to his home at 69 McClure Street when he was waylaid by a number of armed men as he approached the Albertbridge Road. Shots were heard and he was seen by police half running half staggering, holding his hand to his side, before he collapsed on the roadway. He died from bullet wounds to the abdomen in the Royal Victoria Hospital. His funeral took place on 2 March from his residence to Dundonald Cemetery.

63877 Gaffney, William, Constable, 23.12.1920. Traffic accident at Mullaghslin near Carrickmore, Co. Tyrone. His vehicle left the road after crashing into another vehicle.

68927 Gilleece, Patrick, Constable, 31.05.1919. Drowned.

57367 Graham, Orr, Constable, 02.02.1921. Suicide (shot himself with a rifle at Bessbrook Barracks, Co. Armagh).

Graham, William, Special Constable, 08.03.1921. At 11.30 p.m. a special sergeant and a special constable were making their way on duty to Grogey Cross, where they were to be joined by Special Constable Graham. As they made their way along the road the two officers heard running footsteps behind them. The night was very dark and the person approaching, Graham, was not recognised, so he was called on to halt before being fired on by the sergeant. The wounded officer was removed to the Country Infirmary, where he died on 3 April.

55256 Greene, John, Sergeant, 12.09.1921. Suicide (shot himself with a revolver).

Greenfield, Thomas, Special Constable, 15.08.1922. The deceased and Constable Collins were on duty patrolling the railway lines near Randalstown, Co. Antrim, when a train travelling from Cookstown Junction struck the officer. He was a native of Gilford, Co. Down.

72340 Griffiths, John L., Cadet, 31.03.1921. Accidentally shot. He failed to answer a challenge to halt and was shot by a sentry when returning to his barracks in Dublin. He died later from his wounds in the Military Hospital. He had been a constable but had later become a defence of barrack sergeant.

79229 Hall, Philip, Constable. Accidentally killed.

Hamilton, Alexander, Special Constable, 11.08.1922. Died as a result of a gunshot wound at Greencastle, Kilkeel, Co. Down.

76166 Hardie, Arthur, Constable, 03.02.1921. Suicide.

73868 Harte, Leonard, Constable, 16.05.1921. Accidentally shot at Carrick-on-Shannon Barracks. (He had served in the RAF during the First World War.)

74332 Hayward, Francis, Constable, 11.07.1921. Drowned.

57781 Hughes, William Joel, Sergeant, 17.04.1921. Accidentally shot. The sergeant and other RIC officers were in plain clothes in the Shannon View Hotel at Castleconnell, Co. Limerick. The building was searched by a party of Auxiliary police from Killaloe who challenged the RIC members. A mistake took place resulting in a gun battle and the death of the sergeant, one Auxiliary police officer and the hotel owner. This incident was raised in the House of Commons. (The sergeant received a Constabulary Medal on 06.06.1921.)

Hume, Thomas, Special Constable, 11.06.1922. From 34 Chamberlain Street, Belfast, Hume was on duty at Magherafelt Workhouse when he was accidentally shot.

76402 Ikin, Thomas F., Constable, 08.08.1921. Suicide.

Johnston, George, Special Constable, 18.05.1922. Shortly after 2 p.m. the officer was part of a Crossley tender patrol on the Keady/Newtownhamilton road, Co. Armagh when the vehicle skidded out of control. Three officers were thrown from the vehicle and Special Constable Johnston died from his injuries the next day.

68857 Jones, George, Constable, 17.06.1921. Drowned whilst bathing.

65193 Keane, Timothy, Constable, 25.02.1921. Accidentally shot at Bandon, Co. Cork.

63613 Kearns, Hugh, Constable, 06.11.1920. Accidentally shot. Two constables were shot by the military in Foyle Street, Londonderry. Both were critically wounded, and Constable Kearns later died.

Background

During the evening of 6 November there had been a number of reports of gunfire in Foyle Street, Londonderry. Three constables from Victoria Station were sent out in plain clothes armed with revolvers to investigate. As they were making their way along Foyle Street they were accidentally fired on by the military. Two of the constables were wounded, with Constable Kearns being shot in the abdomen. He was taken to hospital but died from his wounds at 4.30 a.m. on 8 November.

60977 Keighary, Thomas, Sergeant, 01.12.1920. He was accidentally shot dead on a bridge over the River Boyne at Kilcarne, one mile outside Navan, Co. Meath. The sergeant had been cycling from Navan when he reached the narrow bridge, where he ordered a military lorry to stop. Due to a misunderstanding he was shot by the military from the lorry.

80859 Kelly, Matthias, Constable, 10.07.1921. Suicide.

64005 Keough, Maurice, 31.12.1919. Accidentally shot by a revolver.

Kidd, George Victor, Special Constable, 24.05.1922, New Lodge Road, Belfast. The officer worked in the building trade and on the evening of 24 May was making his way whilst off duty to a building yard, when he was shot and wounded on the New Lodge Road. He died shortly after admission to the Royal Victoria Hospital. His funeral took place on 27 May from his late residence at 44 Brookvale Avenue to Friends Burying Ground Balmoral.

59924 Lavin, Patrick, Sergeant, 14.04.1920. Suicide. The sergeant shot himself whilst in his room at the RIC depot where he was an instructor. During the First World War he had served with the Irish Guards, being wounded once.

Leggett, William, Special Constable, 20.06.1922. An accident took place near Garrison, Co. Fermanagh, when a Crossley tender driven by the officer overturned due to a burst tyre. Special Constable Leggett from Belfast was killed instantly.

MacGeagh, Foster, Special Constable, 20.03.1922. Died in the Royal Victoria Hospital from gunshot wounds accidentally received in Antrim Road Barracks, Belfast.

77809 Mason, Cyril Robert, DI, 16.06.1921. Accidentally shot. The DI was changing his revolver from his right pocket to the inside left breast pocket of his coat outside Wexford Barracks when it went off, killing him.

70598 McCann, Patrick, Constable, 26.12.1920. Accidentally shot by a comrade's revolver at Cappamore Barracks, Co. Limerick.

70694 McDonald, Patrick, Constable, 03.06.1921. Accidentally shot at Edenderry RIC Barracks, King's County, when the barracks was under attack.

56763 McDonnell, Thomas, Constable, 25.08.1921. Drowned whilst bathing.

McDowell, Robert, Special Constable 22.06.1922. The officer was on holiday at Windgates near Greystones, Co. Wicklow, as he was suffering from ill health. At 2.30 a.m. the household, which included relatives of the deceased, were awakened by 6–8 masked men, armed with rifles and revolvers. Having searched the house for arms, these men took the special constable outside to a lane, where they shot him dead.

McInnes, James, Special Constable, 20.02.1922. Accidentally shot. A Crossley tender crew of four 'A' Specials from Enniskillen was making its way to Kinawley. It was challenged by a patrol of 'B' Specials at the Spawell. The driver did not hear the challenge and the constable was killed.

62477 McKenna, Patrick, Constable, 17.06.1920. Drowned.

McNeill, Thomas, Special Constable, 20.05.1922. Accidently shot during an IRA attack on Martinstown RIC Barracks, Co. Antrim.

77437 Moore, Albert, Constable, 18.06.1921. Accidentally shot by a revolver at Kilnaleck Barracks, Co. Cavan. He died from his wounds in Steeven's Hospital, Dublin.

69962 Morgan, Henry Patrick, Constable, 13.10.1921. Committed suicide by shooting himself.

71418 Morley, Edward George, Constable, 09.09.1920. Suicide. Shot himself at Clonbullogue Barracks, Co. Offaly (King's County). He was an English recruit who had been in the Royal Navy during the First World War.

79475 Moscrop, Harry G., Constable, 16.04.1921. Suicide.

68857 Mugan, Thomas, Constable, 18.04.1921. Accidentally shot by his own rifle in Ballinamore Barracks, Co. Leitrim.

73036 Muir, William, Cadet, 27.12.1920. Suicide. The officer was found with his throat cut at Ballylongford Barracks, Co. Kerry. He had committed suicide with a razor. Prior to this incident he had been kidnapped and held for three days by the IRA.

Background

In November 1920 Constables Muir and Coughlan were captured by the Ballylongford Company of the IRA in Ballylongford. Constable Muir was taken to Moyvane, where the local company guarded him. The military in the area issued an ultimatum that Ballylongford would be razed to the ground if the two policemen were not released within forty-eight hours, forcing the local IRA brigade headquarters to order their release.[1]

61695 Mulholland, Edward J., Constable, 07.02.1920. Accidentally shot at Moyne, Co. Tipperary by his lifelong friend, Constable Danaher, as he loaded his revolver. Constable Mulholland was lacing his boots when he was wounded. He died on 8 February in Steeven's Hospital, Dublin.

61121 Mulvey, James, Constable, 31.10.1920. Accidental death. At first it was reported that he had been shot dead at Bruff, Co. Limerick, with his half naked body being found in a drain. Press reports recorded that 'Having finished his duty as guard he divested himself of his tunic and went for a stroll to the town before retiring for the night. To reach the town by a shortcut it was necessary to cross a pool of about three feet deep. It is surmised that in jumping this dyke he missed his footing and fell into it. He then grasped at some grass on one side of the pool but it came away in his hands, as when the body was discovered a tuft of grass was found in each hand.' A post-mortem examination revealed the fact that death was due to heart failure and exposure.

64361 Murphy, Timothy, Constable, 22.08.1919. Died from bullet wound, circumstances not known.

Murray, James, Special Constable, 03.06.1922. He and other police were guarding a bridge near Kinawley, Co. Fermanagh when the rifle of a comrade was accidentally discharged, killing him instantaneously. Special Constable Murray was one of the specials who survived the attack by the IRA at Clones Railway Station on 11 February 1922.

68983 Murtagh, William James, Constable, 24.12.1919. Accidentally shot. Constable Thomey's rifle went off by accident in Clonoulty police hut, Co. Tipperary, killing Murtagh.

64718 Nixon, James, Constable, 02.03.1920. Died from rifle wound, circumstances not known.

65199 O'Brien, Daniel, Constable, 12.11.1920. Traffic accident. The constable was attached to Tuckey Street Barracks, Cork, when he was killed in a collision between a lorry and a cart.

54065 Perrott, Samuel, Head Constable, 27.06.1920. Police were carrying out a search of a spirit grocer in Belfast's Sandy Row area when a mob attacked them. The head constable received a blow from a stone which left him in a serious condition. He died in hospital on 03.07.1920.

73889 Pimm, Frederick, Constable, 17.06.1921. Cycle accident in London.

79056 Pringle, Donald, Cadet, 17.04.1921. Accidentally shot (see Hughes above). His Auxiliary number was 707 and he had been a lieutenant in the East Lancashire Regiment.

61140 Richmond, A. H. R., DI, 18.01.1921. Suicide. Shot himself in a hotel room at New Ross, Co. Wexford. He had been stationed at Banagher. In 1914 he had joined the Sixth Battalion, Royal Irish Rifles, seeing service in Gallipoli and obtaining the rank of major.

71496 Roper, Edward G., Constable, 22.11.1920. Traffic accident (see Driscoll above).

Russell, John, Special Constable, 09.05.1921. Accidental death. When on guard duty he fell off a wall, having tripped on some sandbags which surrounded the post. He died later in Newry Hospital. He was an ex-member of the Royal North Downs who served in the Boer War. During the First World War he had served with the Royal Irish Rifles.

67575 Shevlin, Thomas, Constable, 17.09.1921. Suicide. Shot himself with a revolver.

71895 Smith, Albert W., Constable, 09.04.1921. Accidentally shot.

70426 Smyth, Frederick Gordon, Constable, 09.01.1921. Accidental death. He had been attached to RIC Grove Hill, Rathdrum but was killed at Gormanston in a traffic accident.

58634 Smyth, Patrick, Sergeant. Died from burns as a result of an accident with a signal rocket.

73276 Southgate, George, Constable, 06.06.1921. Accidentally shot. He had been on sentry duty at Ballaghaderreen Barracks, Co. Roscommon. He had come off duty and was unloading his rifle when it went off. He died from his wounds on 10 June.

72620 Stiff, Harold, Constable, 07.03.1921. Suicide.

74590 Stockdale, George E. A., Constable, 18.06.1921. Drowned.

Sugenor, David, Special Constable, 27.07.1922. At 8 a.m. he was accidentally shot in Smithfield Barracks, Belfast. He and another officer had just returned to barracks having completed their duties. Both were in the day room when the other officer lifted a revolver from a table which he believed was unloaded.

76552 Sweeney, Terrence G., Constable, 30.01.1921. Accidentally shot.

79658 Tasker, Thomas, Constable, 20.05.1921. Accidentally shot by a comrade but had first been reported as killed by Sinn Féin. Tasker joined using an alias of his brother's name; he was, in fact, Frederick Samuel Tasker.

Torrens, David, Special Constable, 09.06.1921. Accidentally shot at Castlerock Barracks, Co. Londonderry.

Vokes, Charles, Special Constable, 12.03.1922. Accidentally shot in Belfast by the military.

77983 Walls, Ernest Guy, Constable, 05.05.21. Traffic accident.

8

DATABASES AND DETECTIVE WORK

In order to produce a comprehensive and accurate list of police casualties, the collection and verification of information had to be drawn from the widest possible variety of sources.

The collection of this information took place in a number of phases, the first and most obvious being a detailed analysis of the RIC General Personnel Register contained on microfilm (PRO HO 184/1–48). To ensure that no omissions or oversights occurred, I began my search with officers who had joined the RIC from January 1870 onwards. This starting point was selected for two important reasons. Firstly, the RIC standing rules and regulations published on 1 May 1860, which, under the heading 'Recruiting General Qualifications', stated that a recruit's age was not to exceed twenty-seven years. This rule was subsequently amended so that recruits had to be between the ages of nineteen and twenty-seven years.

Secondly, before the issue of new RIC retirement regulations on 10 August 1866, an officer could not retire unless he exceeded sixty years of age, or as a result of a medical inspection was 'found to be unable, from mental or bodily infirmity, to perform his duty'.

Taking these two regulations into account it was, in theory, feasible that a nineteen-year-old man, who joined the RIC in 1870, could still have been a serving officer in 1919, being sixty-eight years of age, and having forty-nine years' service. However, I concluded that this was unlikely, and this was subsequently borne out by the discovery that the longest serving police officer killed was found to have been a sixty-four-year-old, who had thirty-eight years' police service.

In perusing the RIC register, those records which did not list a specific manner for men leaving the force were placed on a list of possible casualties, whilst those with one of a variety of entries ranging from the words 'dead' and 'murdered' to statements affirming that the member had been assassinated by 'Sinn Féiners', 'rebels' or 'unknown persons', were placed onto a list of probable casualties. This process was then repeated using the officers' lists as the source material. These lists were then consolidated by cross-referencing with the RIC's Constabulary Lists, a half-yearly publication printed in January and July which contained a wide range of information pertaining to policing and the judiciary in Ireland.

The next step was the inspection of the RUC's memorial book, which was found to be a very fruitful source for early Ulster Special Constabulary casualties, and these were added to the probable casualties list. Other police documents checked included the monthly reports of the inspector general and county inspectors of the RIC (PRO CO 904/102–16). Although these reports were not set out in any standardised format, as each individual author had a different style of reporting, and were not complete (especially for the spring of 1920), they nevertheless proved worthwhile contemporary reports recording a reasonably comprehensive list of police casualties. The RIC weekly summaries of actions, which commenced in August 1920 and ended in 1921 (CO 904/148–50), were found to establish a reasonably authoritative account of many of the incidents that claimed police officers' lives.

The second phase was a complete daily survey of the newspapers from 1 January 1919 to 31 August 1922. *The Irish Times*, a national newspaper, provided the bulk of the statistics obtained from newspapers, but was cross-referenced with *The Cork Examiner* and the *Belfast Telegraph*, which provided regional inputs, as well as confirming information previously collated elsewhere. A surprisingly comprehensive and accurate source of incidents throughout Ireland was the *Northern Whig and Belfast Post*. This paper reported three casualties (which occurred in Belfast) that no other publication, including local papers, did. During the survey of newspapers, two lists were again compiled, one containing the names of officers reported as having either died at the scene of any incident or subsequently died from their wounds, and the second containing names of officers who were reported as having been wounded. All other corroborating material from inquest reports and claims for compensation either from deceased officers' families or from wounded officers was also noted, as this was found to be an accurate means of confirming the details of policemen killed.

The third phase was a repetition of phase two, with the source material being a wide and varied range of books and other publications which dealt with all aspects of the conflict, from the autobiographies and reminiscences of participants on both sides to those that covered all shades of political opinion and government assessments of the situation. No one source was found to give a full or unbiased account of events, with many variations of incidents being uncovered. There were also numerous spellings for the names of officers and conflicting information as to their force numbers.

Therefore, to produce an accurate account of events, only confirmed casualties have been included, with the spelling of RIC officers' names having been obtained from the force's General Personnel Register. As no such register now exists for the Ulster Special Constabulary, I relied on the spelling of officers' names as they were found in the RUC's memorial book (with the exception of three names). These names were found to have been spelt consistently in the same manner in both newspaper articles and on the officers' birth and death certificates, and so I chose the spelling for their names as set out in these documents.

Having completed my research I began a computer-assisted process which consolidated the information into a list of confirmed casualties. This analysis procedure soon exhausted the probable casualty lists obtained from the research carried out on the RIC General Personnel Register but did not completely exhaust the other probable casualty lists gleaned from different sources. It was at this stage that mistakes in the RIC personnel register came to light. These included officers not being issued with force numbers and as a consequence not appearing in the register at all, and other entries which stated that officers had resigned from the force that were subsequently found to be inaccurate. The final comprehensive list of confirmed casualties was checked against the death certificates held by the Church of Jesus Christ and Latter-Day Saints, Belfast, to ensure accuracy.

Having completed all these stages, there remained several names which had all been obtained from the one source which could not be accounted for. Having checked both the RIC and church records again using a variety of different spellings for the names, I still could not locate them. In view of this and the fact that previous information from the same source was found to be inaccurate, these names were discarded.

Before the final casualty list was printed it was sent to the National Memorial Arboretum in Wiltshire, England, for verification. They were unable to add any further names to it. A survey of all memorials in RUC stations also failed to produce any further information.

In view of the methods employed, safety precautions used, and the verification procedures utilised, I am confident that the final list produced is a comprehensive and accurate police casualty list. The only additions that could possibly be made to it would be officers who died from their wounds after 31 August 1922.

NOTES

1 Introduction

1. Curtis, Robert, *The History of the Royal Irish Constabulary* (McGlashan & Gill, London, 1871), pp. 186–94.
2. Fedorowich, Edward Kent, 'The Problems of Disbandment: The Royal Irish Constabulary and Imperial Migration, 1919–1929', *Irish Historical Studies* Vol. XXX, No. 117 (May 1996), pp. 88–110.
3. *Ibid.* See also Annual Civil Service Report for RIC, PRO 165/49, pp. 22–3.
4. O'Halpin, Eunan, *The Decline of the Union: British Government in Ireland 1892–1920* (Gill & Macmillan, Dublin, 1987), p. 64.
5. *Ibid.*, p. 103.
6. O'Donoghue, Florence, *No Other Law* (Anvil Books, Dublin, 1986), p. 65.
7. Bennett, Richard, *The Black and Tans* (Barnes and Noble Inc., New York, 1995), p. 18.
8. Gaughan, Anthony J., *Memoirs of Constable Jeremiah Mee, RIC* (Mercier Press, Cork, 2012), p. 401.
9. Coogan, Tim Pat, *Michael Collins* (Arrow Books, London, 1990), p. 78.
10. Younger, Calton, *Arthur Griffith* (Dublin, 1981), p. 17.
11. O'Donoghue (1986), p. 186.
12. Younger (1981), p. 41.
13. Martin, F.X. (ed.), *The Irish Volunteers 1913–1915: Recollections and Documents* (James Duffy & Co., Dublin, 1963), p. 17.
14. Dalton, Charles, *With the Dublin Brigade: Espionage and Assassination with Michael Collins' Intelligence Unit* (Mercier Press, Cork, 2014), p. 27.
15. Coogan (1990), p. 36.
16. Gleeson, James, *Bloody Sunday* (Four Square, London, 1962), p. 13.
17. Coogan (1990), p. 36.
18. *Ibid.*, p. 16.
19. *Ibid.*, p. 54.
20. *Ibid.*, pp. 72–3.
21. *Ibid.*, p. 115.
22. Martin (1963), p. 111.
23. *Ibid.*, p. 81.
24. *Ibid.*, pp. 44–5.
25. *Ibid.*, p. 148.
26. O'Donoghue (1986), p. 162.
27. *Ibid.*, p. 30.
28. *Ibid.*, p. 43.
29. Martin (1963), p. 171.

30 Ó Conchubhair, Brian (ed.), *Limerick's Fighting Story 1916–1921* (Mercier Press, Cork, 2009), pp. 165–73.
31 O'Donoghue (1986), p. 165.
32 Ó Conchubhair, Brian (ed.), *Rebel Cork's Fighting Story 1916–1921* (Mercier Press, Cork, 2009), p. 29.
33 Ó Conchubhair, Brian (ed.), *Dublin's Fighting Story 1916–1921*, (Mercier Press, Cork, 2009), p. 229.
34 O'Halpin (1987), p. 161.
35 Breen, Dan, *My Fight for Irish Freedom* (Anvil Books, 1981), p. 31.

2 1919

1 Ryan, Desmond, *Seán Treacy and the Third Tipperary Brigade* (The Kerryman, Tralee, 1945), pp. 60–75.
2 Gleeson (1962), p. 39.
3 Breen (1981), pp. 35–53.
4 Ó Conchubhair, Brian (ed.), *Limerick's Fighting Story*, pp. 318–19.
5 *Ibid.*, pp. 103–7.
6 *Ibid.*, pp. 108–11. For Dan Breen's account of the Knocklong rescue see Breen (1981), pp. 35–53.
7 Ó Conchubhair, Brian (ed.), *Limerick's Fighting Story*, pp. 111–17. See also Ryan (1945), pp. 90–107.
8 Ó Conchubhair, Brian (ed.), *Limerick's Fighting Story*, pp. 117–20.
9 RIC statement (copy in the Police Museum, Belfast).
10 MacEoin, Uinseánn, *Survivors: The Story of Ireland's Struggle as Told through Some of Her Outstanding Living People* (Argenta Publications, Dublin, 1980), p. 262.
11 MC circular dated 10 November 1919, McAllister Collection.
12 *The Irish Times*, 19 May 1919.
13 RIC circular, McAllister Collection, dated 5 February 1920.
14 Ó Conchubhair, Brian (ed.), *Dublin's Fighting Story*, p. 378.
15 Coogan (1990), p. 107.
16 *Ibid.*, p. 116.
17 Gleeson (1962), p. 110.
18 *The Belfast Telegraph*, 8 May 1920.
19 Lowe, W. J. and Malcolm, E. L., 'The Domestication of the RIC' in *Irish Economic and Social History*, Vol. XIX (University of Liverpool, 1992), p. 46.
20 Fedorowich, The Problems of Disbandment', pp. 88–110. (See also note on Irish Situation 25 July 1920, PRO Anderson Papers Co. 904/188/1.)
21 O'Halpin (1987), p. 168.
22 *Ibid.*, p. 185.
23 *Ibid.*, p. 178.

3 1920

1. *Belfast Telegraph*, 23 January 1920
2. Bennett (1995), p. 28.
3. Neligan, David, *The Spy in the Castle* (MacGibbon & Kee, London, 1968), p. 64.
4. Coogan (1990), pp. 128–31.
5. Street, C. J. C., *The Administration of Ireland 1920* (London, 1921), p. 93.
6. RIC circular dated 1 April 1920, McAllister Collection.
7. RIC circular dated 4 February 1920, McAllister Collection.
8. RIC circular dated 18 June 1920, McAllister Collection.
9. RIC Constabulary Lists (Police Museum, Belfast).
10. Gaughan (2012), p. 70.
11. Kee, Robert, *The Green Flag Volume III: Ourselves Alone* (Penguin, London, 1989), p. 95.
12. Bennett (1995). p. 36.
13. Hogan, David, *The Four Glorious Years* (Irish Press, Dublin, 1953), pp. 158–9.
14. Neligan (1968), p. 68.
15. *The Irish Times*, 26 April 1920.
16. Gaughan, Anthony J., *Listowel and Its Vicinity* (Mercier Press, Cork, 1973) p. 368.
17. Ó Conchubhair, Brian (ed.), *Limerick's Fighting Story*, p. 326.
18. Ryan (1945), pp. 127–8.
19. Details of the plan and attack taken from Ó Conchubhair, Brian (ed.), *Limerick's Fighting Story*, pp. 149–59.
20. *The Belfast Telegraph*, 29 May 1920.
21. *Ibid.*, 6 October 1920.
22. RIC circulars dated 23 June 1920, McAllister Collection.
23. RIC circulars dated 31 May 1920, McAllister Collection.
24. Gleeson (1962), p. 30.
25. Ó Conchubhair, Brian (ed.), *Kerry's Fighting Story*, p. 294.
26. Ryan (1945), pp. 137–9.
27. O'Malley, Ernie, *Raids and Rallies* (Mercier Press, Cork, 2011), pp. 26, 83.
28. MacEoin (1980), pp. 227–9.
29. O'Malley (2011), pp. 61–93.
30. *The Irish Times*, 17 July 1920.
31. Gaughan (2012), p. 143.
32. *Ibid.*, pp. 97–101.
33. *Ibid.*, pp. 245–51.
34. Gleeson (1962), p. 107.
35. Ó Conchubhair, Brian (ed.), *Dublin's Fighting Story*, pp. 271–7.
36. Ó Conchubhair, Brian (ed.), *Limerick's Fighting Story*, pp. 323–4.

37 Barry, Tom, *Guerilla Days in Ireland* (Mercier Press, Cork, 2013), pp. 37–8.
38 Bennett (1995), p. 44.
39 Gleeson (1962), p. 82.
40 RIC circular dated 9 August 1920, McAllister Collection.
41 Gleeson (1962), p. 55.
42 *Ibid.*, p. 58.
43 Bennett (1995), p. 110.
44 *The Irish Times*, 16 March 1922.
45 Breen (1981), pp. 167–8.
46 O'Donoghue (1986), pp. 108–10.
47 *Belfast Telegraph*, 4 February 1921.
48 *Ibid.*, 23 August 1920.
49 *Ibid.*, 8 September 1920.
50 *Ibid.*, 12 February 1921.
51 Gleeson (1962), pp. 82–3.
52 Street (1921), p. 302.
53 O'Malley (2011), pp. 95–107.
54 Street (1921), p. 215.
55 Younger (1981), p. 80.
56 General order of the IRA dated 4 June 1920, McAllister Collection.
57 *Belfast Telegraph*, 6 May 1921.
58 RIC circular dated 7 October 1920, McAllister Collection.
59 RIC circular dated September 1920, McAllister Collection.
60 Neligan (1968), p. 131.
61 Gaughan (2012), pp. 242–4.
62 *Belfast Telegraph*, 23 November 1920.
63 *Ibid.*, 3 March 1921.
64 *Ibid.*, 1 July 1921. (At court martial, Victoria Barracks, Belfast.)
65 Ó Conchubhair, Brian (ed.), *Kerry's Fighting Story*, p. 242.
66 Ryan (1945), pp. 190–1.
67 Hart, Peter, *The IRA and Its Enemies: Violence and Community in Cork 1916–1923* (Oxford University Press, Oxford, 1998), pp. 3–18.
68 Gleeson (1962), p. 134.
69 Bennett (1995), p. 121.
70 Gleeson (1962), p. 137.
71 Coogan (1990), p. 159.
72 Gleeson (1962), p. 70.
73 Hart (1998), p. 35.
74 Barry (2013), pp. 74–82.
75 *Ibid.*, pp. 83–7.
76 Street (1921), p. 158.
77 Kee (1989), p. 121.

78 Ó Conchubhair, Brian (ed.), *Rebel Cork's Fighting Story*, p. 103.
79 *The Irish Times*, 8 February 1922.
80 Ó Conchubhair, Brian (ed.), *Limerick's Fighting Stories*, pp. 198–9.
81 Ó Conchubhair, Brian (ed.), *Rebel Cork's Fighting Story*, p. 231.
82 Kee (1989), p. 101.
83 Fedorowich, *Irish Historical Studies*, pp. 88–110.
84 O'Halpin (1987), pp. 198–9.
85 Winter, Sir Ormonde, *Winter's Tale* (Richards Press, London, 1955), p. 294.
86 O'Halpin (1987), p. 212.

4 1921

1 RIC circular dated 28 September 1920, McAllister Collection.
2 Bennett (1995), p. 100 (Greenwood speech).
3 Hansard, House of Commons Debate, 20 October 1920, vol. 133 c925. Available at https://api.parliament.uk/historic-hansard/commons/1920/oct/20/vote-of-censure-proposed.
4 *Ibid.*, vol. 133 cc946–948.
5 Bennett (1995), p. 151.
6 RIC circulars dated 12 November 1920 and 6 December 1920, McAllister Collection.
7 Bennett (1995), p. 115.
8 Gaughan (1973), p. 380.
9 *Ibid.*, p. 393 (Mr Kane's last letter reproduced on p. 457).
10 Information contained in Colonial Office Papers (hereafter CO) 904/114, The National Archives, Kew (hereafter NAK).
11 Ó Conchubhair, Brian (ed.), *Rebel Cork's Fighting Story*, pp. 192–3.
12 Police survivor to his son. Sourced from private letter from son to author dated 13/1/1996.
13 Ó Conchubhair, Brian (ed.), *Dublin's Fighting Story*, p. 328.
14 Ó Conchubhair, Brian (ed.), *Limerick's Fighting Story*, pp. 203–10.
15 NAK, CO 914/114.
16 Ó Conchubhair, Brian (ed.), *Kerry's Fighting Story*, pp. 271–4.
17 Neligan (1968), p. 73.
18 Ó Conchubhair, Brian (ed.), *Rebel Cork's Fighting Story*, pp. 142–5.
19 Ó Conchubhair, Brian (ed.), *Dublin's Fighting Story*, pp. 305–8.
20 Barry (2013), pp. 240–5.
21 Ó Conchubhair, Brian (ed.), *Limerick's Fighting Story*, pp. 335–6.
22 Ó Conchubhair, Brian (ed.), *Kerry's Fighting Story*, p. 249.
23 *Ibid.*, p. 250.
24 MacEoin (1980), p. 357.
25 NAK, CO 904/115.

26 Breen (1981), pp. 160–1.
27 *The Irish Times*, 10 May 1921.
28 Breen (1981), p. 162.
29 MacEoin (1980), p. 285.
30 O'Malley (2011), pp. 161–72.
31 RIC circular dated 10 May 1921, McAllister Collection.
32 *Belfast Telegraph*, 25 May 1921.
33 Winter (1955), pp. 312–5.
34 Dwyer, T. Ryle, *Tans, Terror and Troubles: Kerry's Real Fighting Story 1913–23* (Mercier Press, Cork, 2001), p. 304.
35 NAK, CO 904/115.
36 Ó Conchubhair, Brian (ed.), *Kerry's Fighting Story*, pp. 261–3.
37 O'Malley (2011), pp. 191–209.
38 *Ibid.*, pp. 248–52, 256–65.
39 Ó Conchubhair, Brian (ed.), *Rebel Cork's Fighting Story*, pp. 199–201.
40 *The Irish Times*, 28 June 1921.
41 The fact that Needham is with his new wife at the time of the attack is mentioned in http://www.policerollofhonour.org.uk/forces/ireland_to_1922/ric/ric_roll.htm and in http://www.policememorial.org.uk/rollofhonour.php#.
42 RIC circular dated 10 July 1921, McAllister Collection.
43 RIC circular dated 30 October 1921, McAllister Collection.
44 RIC circular dated 18 November 1921, McAllister Collection.
45 Gaughan (1973), p. 402.

5 1922

1 *The Irish Times*, 7 March 1922.
2 *Belfast Telegraph*, 11 April 1922.
3 RIC circular dated 29 March 1922, McAllister Collection.
4 Lowe, W. J., 'The Old RIC in the New Free State: Disbandment and After'. Presented at the American Conference for Irish Studies annual meeting, Queen's University, Belfast, June 1995.

6 Missing Men

1 *The Irish Times*, 3 November 1920.

7 Other Casualties

1 Gaughan (1973), p. 378.

BIBLIOGRAPHY

Andrews, C. S., *Dublin Made Me* (Dufour Editions, Dublin, 1979)

Barry, Tom, *Guerilla Days in Ireland* (Mercier Press, Cork, 2013)

Barry, Tom, *The Reality of the Anglo-Irish War 1920–21 in West Cork: Refutations, corrections and comments to Liam Deasy's Towards Ireland Free* (Anvil Books, Dublin, 1974)

Bennett, Richard, *The Black and Tans* (Barnes and Noble Inc, New York, 1995)

Breen, Dan, *My Fight for Irish Freedom* (Anvil Books, Tralee, 1981)

Bretherton, C. H. E., *The Real Ireland* (London, 1925)

Brewer, John D., *The Royal Irish Constabulary: An Oral History* (The Institute of Irish Studies, Belfast, 1990)

Clark, Wallace, *Guns in Ulster* (Constabulary Gazette, Belfast, 1967)

Coogan, Tim Pat, *Michael Collins* (Arrow Books, London, 1990)

Crozier, Brigadier General F. P., *Impressions and Recollections* (T. Werner Laurie, London, 1930)

Crozier, Brigadier General F. P., *Ireland Forever* (Jonathan Cape, London, 1932)

Curtis, Robert, *The History of the Royal Irish Constabulary* (McGlashan & Gill, London, 1869)

Dalton, Charles, *With the Dublin Brigade: Espionage and Assassination with Michael Collins' Intelligence Unit* (Mercier Press, Cork, 2014)

Deasy, Liam, *Towards Ireland Free* (Mercier Press, Cork and Dublin, 1973)

Deasy, Liam, *Brother Against Brother* (Mercier Press, Dublin and Cork, 1982)

Doherty, J. E. and Hickey, D. J. A., *Chronology of Irish History since 1500* (Gill & Macmillan, Dublin, 1989)

Fedorowich, Edward Kent, 'The Problems of Disbandment: The Royal Irish Constabulary and Imperial Migration, 1919–1929', *Irish Historical Studies* Vol. XXX, No. 117 (May 1996)

Figgis, Darrell, *Recollection of the Irish War* (Ernest Benn Ltd, London, 1927)

Gaughan, J. Anthony, *Listowel and Its Vicinity* (Mercier Press, Cork, 1973)

Gaughan, J. Anthony, *Memoirs of Constable Jeremiah Mee, RIC* (Mercier Press, Cork, 2012)

Gleeson, James, *Bloody Sunday* (Four Square, London, 1962)

Harnden, Toby, *'Bandit country': the IRA and South Armagh* (Coronet, London, 2000)

Hart, Peter, *The IRA and Its Enemies: Violence and Community in Cork 1916–1923* (Oxford University Press, Oxford, 1998)

Hezlet, Arthur, *The 'B' Specials: A History of the Ulster Special Constabulary* (Tom Stacey Ltd, London, 1972)

'Hogan, David' (Frank Gallagher), *The Four Glorious Years* (Irish Press, Dublin, 1953)

Kee, Robert, *The Green Flag. Volume III: Ourselves Alone* (Penguin, London, 1989)

Lowe, W. J. and Malcolm, E. L., 'The Domestication of the RIC', *Irish Economic & Social History*, Vol. XIX (University of Liverpool, Liverpool, 1992)

Lowe, W. J., 'The Old RIC in the New Free State: Disbandment and After'. Presented at the American Conference for Irish Studies annual meeting, Queen's University, Belfast, June 1995

MacEoin, Uinseánn, *Survivors* (Argenta Books, Dublin, 1980)

McDonnell, Kathleen Keyes, *There is a Bridge at Bandon* (Mercier Press, Cork, 1972)

Martin, F. X. (ed.), *The Irish Volunteers 1913–1915: Recollections and Documents* (James Duffy & Co., Dublin, 1963)

Neligan, David, *The Spy in the Castle* (MacGibbon & Kee, London, 1968)

O'Connor, Frank, *The Big Fellow* (Poolbeg Press, London, 1979)

O'Donoghue, Florence, *No Other Law* (Argenta Books, Dublin, 1986)

O'Halpin, Eunan, *The Decline of the Union: British Government in Ireland 1892–1920* (Gill & Macmillan, Dublin, 1987)

O'Malley, Ernie, *On Another Man's Wound* (Anvil Books, Dublin, 1979)

O'Malley, Ernie, *Raids and Rallies* (Mercier Press, Cork, 2011)

Phillips, W. Alison, *The Revolution in Ireland 1906–1923* (Longmans, London, 1926)

Ryan, Desmond, *Seán Treacy and the Third Tipperary Brigade* (The Kerryman, Tralee, 1945)

Sheills, Derek, 'The Politics of Policing Ireland 1919–1923' in Emsley, C. and Weinberger, B. (eds), *Policing Western Europe: Politics, Professionalism, and Public Order, 1850-1940* (Greenwood Press, New York & London, 1991)

Street, C. J. C., *The Administration of Ireland 1920* (London, 1921)

Ó Conchubhair, Brian (ed.), *Dublin's Fighting Story* 1916–1921 (Mercier Press, Cork, 2009)

Ó Conchubhair, Brian (ed.), *Kerry's Fighting Story* 1916–1921 (Mercier Press, Cork, 2009)

Ó Conchubhair, Brian (ed.), *Limerick's Fighting Story* 1916–1921 (Mercier Press, Cork, 2009)

Ó Conchubhair, Brian (ed.), *Rebel Cork's Fighting Story* 1916–1921 (Mercier Press, Cork, 2009)

Winter, Sir Ormonde, *Winter's Tale* (Richards Press, London, 1955)

Younger, Calton, *Arthur Griffith* (Gill & Macmillan, Dublin, 1981)

Other Sources

Central Library, Belfast
Linen Hall Library, Belfast
National Library of Ireland, Dublin
Public Record Office Kew, Richmond, Surrey
Registrar General's Offices, Belfast & Dublin
RIC Constabulary Lists
RIC Inspector General and County Inspector Monthly Reports (PRO CO 904/102–16)
RIC Micro Films (PRO HO 184/1–48)
RIC Weekly Summaries (CO 904/148–50)
The Church of Jesus Christ of Latter-Day Saints, Belfast

INDEX

A

A Specials 180, 181, 353, 409
Active Service Units (ASUs) 33, 34, 195
Adam, Const. George 338, 339, 384
Adams, Const. Samuel 247–250, 384
Agar, Const. William 57, 58, 384
Agnew, Cadet Bertram 397, 398
Ahern, Const. Eugene 403
Aherne, Michael 92
Allen, S/Const. David 362, 363, 384
Anderson, Const. 322
Anderson, Sir John 185
Anderson, Sgt Joseph 312, 384
Anderson, Cadet William James 403
Andrews, Const. John H. 242
Anglo-Irish Treaty 213, 339, 347, 350, 381
Antrim County
 Lisburn 80, 143, 144, 145, 183, 286, 371
 Martinstown Barracks 410
 Randalstown 406
Appleford, Cadet Leonard George 328, 329, 384
Armagh County
 Annaghmore 368, 369
 Annaghroe 381
 Armagh City 48, 232, 233
 Bessbrook Barracks 406
 Creggan 280
 Crossmaglen 98, 108, 231, 232, 280, 361
 Cullaville 361
 Cullyhanna 108, 231
 Drumintee 382
 Forkhill 371, 382
 Jonesborough 371
 Keady 174, 365, 382, 407
Armstrong, S/Const. Robert 403
Armstrong, Sgt Thomas Robert 131, 384
Army Service Corps 260, 272, 362
Ashe, Thomas 41
Ashley, Col 13, 376
Auxiliary Division 14, 15, 133–138, 154, 155, 185, 193, 194, 196, 198, 200–208, 218, 227, 228, 234, 237, 244–247, 255, 258, 259, 263–265, 281, 284, 285, 299, 302, 305, 307, 326–329, 341, 343, 379, 380, 384, 397, 399, 400, 402, 403, 407, 412

B

B Specials 181, 182, 184, 271, 351, 362, 367, 403, 409
Bainbridge, Major-Gen. E.G.T. 145
Bales, Cadet John Beets 284, 384
Ballantine, Ex-Head Const. Joseph 378
Balls, Cadet Hedley A. 207, 384
Bannon, Const. 172
Barnes, Cadet William 197–204, 384
Barney, Const. Robert J. W. 240, 384
Barrett, William 131
Barrington, Miss 304, 305
Barry, Dr Thomas 49
Barry, Tom 139, 199–202, 257, 258, 267, 268, 275
Barton, D/Sgt John 58, 59, 384
Barton, Robert 339
Bates, Richard Dawson 351
Bayley, Cadet Cecil James W. 197–204, 384
Baynham, DI Hubert L. 263
B Division, DMP 20, 89, 284
Beard, Cadet Bernard J. L. 264, 265, 384

Beasant, Const. James R. 261, 384
Beckett, Const. Harry 310, 311, 384
Belfast 15, 66, 67, 70, 103, 121, 143–145, 178, 179, 181–183, 185, 239, 240, 245, 262, 274, 299, 324, 325, 342, 343, 349, 351, 354, 355, 358, 364, 366, 382, 409, 413, 416, 417
  Albertbridge Road 364, 406
  Antrim Road 347, 409
  Berry Street 370
  Brickfields Barracks 279, 370
  Brown Square 245
  Chamberlain Street 407
  Court Street Barracks 373
  Cromac Street 371
  Cullingtree Road 345, 373
  Dargle Street 347
  Donegall Place 284
  Edlingham Street 355
  Elmgrove Street 260
  Falls Road 159, 324, 357, 358, 370, 372
  Great Victoria Street 109, 144, 361
  Grosvenor Road 373
  Joy Street 366
  Kingswood Street 300
  Little Donegall Street 335
  Louisa Street 366
  Mater Hospital 174, 335, 365, 373
  May Street 361, 366
  McAuley Street 371
  McClure Street 406
  McDonnell Street 372, 373
  Milewater Road 344
  Military Hospital 240, 335, 347
  Millfield 370, 374
  Milltown Cemetery 109, 345, 358
  Musgrave Street Barracks 67, 369, 370
  New Lodge Road 355, 408
  Newtownards Road 382
  Northumberland Street 355
  Old Lodge Road 363, 405
  Oldpark Road 252, 347
  Ross Street 337
  Royal Victoria Hospital 159, 173, 262, 284, 324, 325, 355, 363, 366–368, 374, 405, 406, 408, 409
  Sandy Row 411
  Ship Street 299
  Short Strand 363
  Smithfield Barracks 374, 413
  Springdale Gardens 372
  Springfield Road 58, 159, 337, 345, 358, 370
  Thompson Street 405
  Townhall Street 239
  Union Street 335
  Victoria Barracks 175, 188, 228
  Victoria Square 262
  Walton Place 366
  York Street 325, 365
Bell, Alan 215
Bell, Const. George William 247–250, 384
Benson, H/Const. Francis 106, 304, 384
Bentley, Const. Benjamin (Archibald Charles) 367, 384
Biggs, Const. Harry 171, 172, 385
Biggs, DI Harry 304, 305, 385
Binion, Const. Charles E. 403
Bird, William Robert 83
Black and Tans 12, 15, 69, 81, 83, 84, 114, 158, 160, 185, 322, 402
Black, S/Const. Richard 403
Black Watch 206, 208, 319
Blake, DI Cecil Arthur Maurice 307, 308, 385
Blake, Michael 132
Blake, Mrs 307
Blake, Patrick 132
Bloxham, Sgt Henry J. 106, 238, 385
Blythe, Const. Sydney 106, 318, 319, 385
Boer War 24, 25, 143, 412
Bolam, Cadet Ernest Baran 284, 285, 385
Bolger, Const. Edward 59, 385
Booth, Const. Leonard 311, 312, 385

Bourke, Const. John Joseph 247–250, 385
Bourke, Const. Joseph 332, 385
Bowles, Const. Charles H. 275, 276, 385
Boyd, H/Const. John 403
Boyd, Const. Robert A. E. 106, 233, 234, 385
Boyd, Cadet William A. H. 326, 385
Boylan, Const. 231
Boylan, Const. John 76, 285, 385
Boynes, Const. Joseph 280, 385
Bradford, Const. Albert 327, 328, 385
Bradley, Sgt 148
Bradshaw, Cadet Leonard 197–204, 385
Brady, Const. 113
Brady, DI James Joseph 161–163, 220, 385
Brady, Sgt John Edward 92, 106, 385
Brady, Sgt Philip 54–56, 106, 385
Brandshaw, Const. Thomas 404
Brannan, Const. Michael 325, 326, 385
Breen, Const. 175
Breen, Dan 11, 35, 37, 38, 42, 43, 45, 47, 58, 118, 128–130, 170, 287
Breen, John 88
Breen, Philip 172, 173
Brennan, Const. 159
Brennan, Michael 99
Brennan, Const. Smyth Thomas 142, 385
Brett, Const. James 112, 385
Brewer, Const. Cyril F. H. 334, 385
Brick, Const. William 94, 385
Bridges, Const. Thomas 106, 304, 385
Briggs, Const. James 317, 318, 385
Bright, Const. Ernest 398
British Secret Service 65–68, 215, 216
Brock, Const. Alfred V. G. 260, 385
Brogan, Const. 149
Brogan, Const. Michael 106, 159, 385

Brooke, Basil 185
Brosnan, Tadhg 119, 315
Brown, Const. James 318–321, 385
Brown, Const. Walter Thomas 106, 147, 292, 293, 385
Brugha, Cathal 30, 34
Bruin, Sgt John 365, 385
Buchanan, Const. Robert 273, 398
Budd, Const. Edgar 313, 314, 385
Bunce, Const. John E. 289, 404
Buntrock, Const. Charles 189, 190, 385
Burke, Const. James 130, 385
Burke, Michael 113
Burke, Sgt Michael 106, 321, 322, 385
Burke, M. J. 72
Burke, H/Const. Peter 76, 154, 155, 220–222, 385
Bush, Cadet George 245–247, 385
Butler, ex-Const. 377
Butler, Sgt Francis J. 310, 385
Butler, Sgt James 295, 385
Byrne, Brigadier General Sir Joseph 50, 60
Byrne, Constable 85
Byrne, Robert 41–43, 99
Byrnes, John Charles 66–68

C

C Specials 182, 183
Cahill, DI Michael Joseph 404
Calder, Const. Francis D. 242
Callery, Const. Francis 242
Cameron Highlanders 268
Campbell, Const. William (62454) 269, 270, 385
Campbell, Const. William (76250) 327, 386
Campbell, S/Const. William 374, 386
Campion, Sgt John J. 404
Cane, Const. Arthur William 258, 259, 386

Cantlon, Const. John 317, 318, 386
Cardwell, S/Const. Robert 368, 369, 386
Carew, Tom 40, 41
Carey, Const. Patrick 130, 131, 386
Carlow County
  Rathrilly 58
  The Mall 278
  Tullow 58, 151
Carney, Frank 172
Carolan, Const. Peter 303, 386
Carolan, Prof. John 128
Carroll, Const. John 252, 253, 386
Carroll, Const. John J. 110, 386
Carroll, James 55
Carroll, Sgt Patrick J. 76, 88, 106, 386
Carter, Const. Albert 309, 310, 386
Carter, Const. Edward 251, 386
Carty, Sgt Stephen 230, 231, 386
Caseley, Const. Albert 178, 386
Casement, Sir Roger 25, 93
Cavan County
  Arva 289
  Bawnboy 382
  Cootehill 93
  Kilnaleck 410
  Redhills 56
  Swanlinbar 210
Chamberlain, Austen 13
Chapman, Cadet Spencer R. 207, 208, 386
Charman, Sgt Arthur E. 242
Chave, Const. Clarence Victor 163, 386
Chermside, S/Const. William 361, 386
Chittick, S/Const. George 360, 361, 386
Churchill, Winston 133, 185, 376
Clan na Gael 24
Clancy, Const. Patrick (rtd) 379
Clancy, Peadar 86, 129, 195
Clapp, Const. William 292, 293, 386
Clare County
  Boston 171, 405

Broadford 159, 236, 262
Cooga 313
Cratloe 230
Crusheen 146
Doolin 336
Dromoland 405
Ennis 158, 170, 230, 338, 350, 377, 405
Ennistymon 54, 156–158, 336, 350
Feakle 164
Glenwood 236
Kildysart 94
Kilmihil 88
Kilrush 141, 285, 350
Lahinch 156, 157
Lisdoonvarna 336, 352
Meelick 43
Miltown Malbay 156, 157, 169, 276
Moyona police hut 154
O'Brien's Bridge 160, 161
Rineen 156, 220
Ruan 170, 171, 231
Sixmilebridge 236, 237, 262
Tulla 96
Clark, Const. Alexander Thomas 296, 386
Clarke, Const. Alexander 339, 386
Clarke, Const. Martin 120, 314, 386
Clarke, Const. Patrick 330, 386
Clarke, Const. Sidney George 238, 239, 386
Clarke, DI William 236, 237, 386
Clarke, Sgt Christopher 76, 106, 358, 386
Clarke, Tom 23, 111
Clayton, Cadet Harold 245–247, 386
Clayton, DI 81
Cleary, Const. Patrick 146
Clifford, Const. Martin 88, 386
Clune, Conor 195
Cochrane, S/Const. Thomas 404
Coleman, Sgt Joseph E. 302, 386
Colgan, Const. 92
Collery, Sgt James 315, 316, 386
Collins, Const. 88

Collins, Const. John 369, 370, 386
Collins, Michael 11, 25, 26, 33–35, 52, 53, 56, 58, 65–67, 80, 83, 86, 111, 118, 143, 170, 183, 194, 195, 339
Compston, S/Const. Robert William 231, 232, 386
Compton, S/HConst. Alexander 365, 386
Conlon, Const. Thomas 337, 386
Connolly, James 24
Connor, DI 94
Connor, S/Const. George 371, 386
Connor, Const. James 335, 386
Connor, Thomas 92
Conway, Bernard 172–175
Conway, Const. 335
Conway, Martin 212
Cooney, Const. Joseph 315, 316, 386
Cooney, Const. Peter 179, 386
Cooper, Const. Walter H. 262, 386
Cork City
  Barrack Street 282, 377
  Cook Street 295
  County Club 120–122
  Cove Street 282
  Dillons Cross 207, 227
  Hanover Street 357
  Leitrim Street 379
  Lower Glanmire Road 95
  Parnell Bridge 229
  Patrick's Bridge 377
  Patrick Street 163
  Pope's Quay 80
  Watercourse Road 303
  White Street 190, 191
Cork County
  Allihies 75
  Ballinhassig 251, 335
  Ballinspittal 91
  Ballyvourney 258
  Bandon 59, 91, 94, 132, 133, 198, 201, 202, 257, 267, 289, 377, 399, 404, 407
  Bantry 57, 95, 110, 112, 147, 192
  Castlemartyr 197, 288
  Castletownbere 57
  Castletownroche 139, 267
  Charleville 252, 326
  Clonakilty 90, 91, 133, 291, 293, 355
  Clonee Wood 112
  Coachford 11, 39, 41, 400
  Crossbarry 268
  Drimoleague 243
  Enniskeane 103
  Glandore 171
  Glanmire 79
  Glengarriff 80, 110, 146
  Innishannon 91, 301
  Kilbrittain 59, 378
  Kildorrery 138, 280, 330
  Killavullen 379
  Kilmichael 197–207, 257
  Kilworth 315
  Kinsale 210, 267, 268, 378
  Leap 171, 192
  Lissagroom 267
  Macroom 54, 140, 178, 198–201, 203, 205, 206, 258, 259, 278, 279, 334, 397–400
  Mallow 326, 379
  Midleton 213, 214, 217, 302
  Newmarket 241, 326
  Rosscarbery 260, 275, 355
  Scart 280
  Shronebeha 261
  Skibbereen 79, 131, 154, 171, 209, 243, 306, 339
  Timoleague 94, 95
  Upton 91, 94, 267
  Waterfall 238
  Youghal 207
Cormer, Const. Frederick 336, 337, 386
Cornyn, Const. Thomas 302, 386
Corridan, Patrick 92
Cosnette, Const. Ralph V. 404
Costello, Const 187
Cotter, Sgt John 356, 387
Coughlan, Const 410
Coughlan, Sgt John 270, 271, 387
Coulter, S/Const. Robert 314, 387

Cowie, Const. Henry 404
Craddock, Sgt Thomas M. 142, 143, 387
Craig, County Inspector 121
Craig, James 185–187
Craig, S/Harbour Const. Alfred 299, 300, 387
Crake, DI Francis William 197–204, 387
Cranny, Ex-Constable Thomas 377
Craven, DI Francis Worthington 245–247, 387
Crawford, Const. John 169, 387
Crean, Sgt Cornelius 91, 387
Creedon, Const. Francis 334, 387
Creegan, Sgt Francis 106, 311, 318, 319, 321, 387
Cromwell, Const. 228
Cronin, Sgt Henry 177, 387
Crook, Const. Robert 262, 387
Crowe, Tadhg 38, 39
Crowley, Const. 267
Crowley, Tim 99
Crozier, Frank Percy 136, 307
Cruise, Const. 110
Culhane, Seán (Jack) 121, 122, 143, 144
Cullen, Const. James (79391) 291, 292, 387
Cullen, Const. James (80470) 357, 358, 387
Cullen, John (rtd) 379
Cullen, Tom 195
Cumann na mBan 35
Cummings, S/Const. John 251, 252, 387
Cummings, Const. William 356, 357, 387
Cunningham, S/Const. Thomas 361, 387
Curtin, Sgt Jeremiah 76, 106, 230, 231, 387
Cuthbertson, Const. George 289, 387

D

Dáil Éireann 30, 34, 35, 47, 56, 165, 215, 339, 340
Dalton, D/Const. Laurence 89, 90, 387
Daly, Const. Joseph 398
Daly, Ned 111
Daly, Paddy 65, 67, 86
Danaher, Const. 410
Darragh, Detective Constable 96
Davis, H/Const. Christopher 356, 357, 387
Davis, George Charles Peel 72
Day, Const. Edgar Ernest 330, 387
de Valera, Éamon 26, 29, 34, 166
Dease, DI 163
Deasy, Pat 202
Dee, Sgt 243
Defence of the Realm Act (DORA) 44, 62, 350
Delaney, Const. Timothy 151, 387
Denham, Const. John A. 404
Dennehy, Const. Michael 398, 399
Depree, Const. Frederick H. 147, 294, 387
Devereux, Const. William 270, 387
Devine, Const. Thomas 106, 331, 387
Devoy, John 24
Dillon, Const. Thomas 196, 387
Dixon, Capt. 201
Dobson, S/Const. Thomas W. 381, 387
Doherty, Sgt Francis 106, 164, 387
Doherty, Const. James 404
Doherty, Const. John 318, 319, 387
Dolan, Joe 170
Dolan, Sergeant 294
Donegal County
  Binnion 296
  Buncrana 400
  Convoy 378
  Donegal Town 254
  Dunfanaghy 166

Falcarragh 269
Kilraine 331
Letterkenny 309, 310
Mountcharles 254, 255, 363
Raphoe 378
Donegan, Maurice 112
Donnelly, Jack 264
Donoghue, Sgt James 190, 191, 387
Donohoe, Const. James 153, 387
Donovan, Daniel 121
Doogue, Const. John 236, 237, 387
Doogue, Const. Pierce 112, 387
Doran, Const. Edward 309, 387
Dougherty, S/Sgt William 353, 354, 387
Dowling, J. 119
Dowling, Joe 67
Dowling, Const. Michael James 270, 387
Dowling, Const. Thomas 318, 319, 387
Down County
  Ballynahinch 187
  Banbridge 121, 128, 233, 234, 404
  Dromore 121
  Gilford 406
  Holywood 274
  Katesbridge 404
  Kilkeel 407
  Newry 117, 191, 286, 323, 332, 362, 412
  Newtownards 168, 181, 243, 353, 364, 404
  Portaferry 361
  Warrenpoint 251
Downey, Const. John 160, 161, 387
Downing, Const. Michael 57, 319, 387
Doyle, Const. 95
Doyle, Const. F. R. 49
Doyle, Const. Garret 78
Doyle, Const. Michael 247–250, 388
Doyle, Const. Richard 49
Dray, Const. Ernest 76, 213, 214, 388

Driscoll, Const. Patrick 405
Driscoll, Sgt 112
Dublin City
  Ballymun 67
  Beggars Bush Barracks 193, 194, 403
  Brunswick Street 20, 52, 56, 66, 264, 287
  Capel Street 170
  College Street 58
  Croke Park 195
  Dawson Street 50
  Drumcondra 26, 51–53, 128, 129
  Dublin Castle 17, 20, 24, 61, 62, 65, 73, 74, 104, 105, 135, 140, 167, 170, 185, 186, 195, 209, 216, 219, 220, 224–226, 256, 301, 328, 344, 350, 372, 375, 379
  Earlsfort Terrace 192
  Essex Street 256
  General Post Office (GPO) 29, 178, 276
  Glasnevin 67, 102, 163, 193, 210, 234, 302, 303, 307
  Grafton Street 77, 328, 329
  Green Street Courthouse 55
  Harcourt Street 56, 65
  Henry Street 209
  High Street 57
  Jervis Street Hospital 209
  King George V Hospital 196, 265, 283
  Leeson Park 207
  Liberty Hall 25
  Lower Baggot Street 329
  Lower Camden Street 86
  Lower Mount Street 193, 194
  Mansion House 29, 35, 339
  Mary Street 283
  Mater Misericordiae Hospital 53, 68, 87, 89, 129, 130, 302, 356
  Mercer's Hospital 57, 58, 68, 244, 372
  Mountjoy gaol 41, 264
  Mountjoy Street 89
  Northumberland Street 193, 194
  Ormond Quay 170
  Parliament Street 256
  Parnell Square 52

Phibsborough 356
Phoenix Park 16, 50, 103, 154, 196, 219, 220, 239, 244, 356
Pleasants Street 86
Rainsford Street 325
Rotunda Hall 27
Rotunda Hospital 111
Sallymount Avenue 207
Steeven's Hospital 63, 92, 141, 244, 246, 254, 274, 300, 325, 357, 410, 411
St James's Walk 331
Suffolk Street 77
Townsend Street 56, 337
Trinity Street 244
Westland Row 371
Wynn's Hotel 27
Dublin County
Balbriggan 87, 154, 155, 220–223, 244, 252, 312
Ballough 252
Ballyboghil 283
Ballyfermot 274
Cabinteely 300
Rush 92
Dublin Metropolitan Police (DMP) 13, 14, 18–22, 35, 51–53, 56–59, 61, 65, 73, 77, 83, 86, 89, 90, 121, 170, 185, 195, 196, 215, 234, 235, 244, 283, 331, 342, 384, 387, 390, 392, 394–396
Duckham, Const. George H. 399
Duffy, Const. James (69645) 405
Duffy, Const. James (77133) 278, 388
Duddy, Const. Joseph 260, 388
Duncan, Const. William J. 405
Dunleavy, Sgt 77
Dunne, Const. Edward 76, 94, 95, 106, 388
Dunne, Const. John 309, 388
Dunphy, Sgt Kyran 97, 98, 106, 388
Dwyer, Edward 336
Dwyer, Francis 336
Dwyer, Paddy 116
Dyne, Const. Robert 292, 293, 388

E

Early, Sgt Patrick Joseph 361, 362, 388
Eastwood, Major General F. R. 204, 212
Ednie, Const. Charles F. 147, 352, 388
Egan, Sergeant 237
Elton, Const. William 267, 388
Enright, Const. Michael 43, 46, 48, 388
Enright, Const. Thomas 106, 346, 347, 388
Essex Regiment 257
Evans, Const. James 273, 399
Evans, Const. John Herbert 178, 388

F

Fahy, Const. Patrick 119, 120, 388
Falkiner, Cadet Walter 263, 264, 388
Fallon, Const. Martin 76, 106, 291, 292, 388
Fallon, DI 119
Fallon, Sgt Patrick 187, 188, 240, 388
Farrell, Cadet Francis Joseph 264, 265, 388
Feeney, Const. Martin 317, 318, 388
Fennessey, Const. William 405
Fermanagh County
Brookeborough 312
Enniskillen 55, 210, 353, 354, 364, 381, 409
Garrison 364, 372, 409
Kinawley 409, 411
Lisbellaw 183
Mullaghfad Cross 314
Pettigo 381
Rosslea 271, 272
Tempo 172, 173, 175
Ferris, Const. 160
Fifth Suffolk Regiment 329
Finn, Séan 119
Finn, Const. William 85, 388

INDEX 435

Finnegan, Const. Luke 63, 64, 218, 388
Finnerty, Sgt Patrick 87, 88, 388
First Devons 328
FitzAlan, Lord 230
Fitzgerald, Const. John 334, 388
Fitzgerald, Sgt John 192, 193, 388
Fitzgerald, Ned 121, 122
Fitzpatrick, Const. 42
Fitzpatrick, Matt 353
Flaherty, Const. John 164, 388
Flaherty, Jimmy 321
Fleming, Const. Michael 405
Fleming, Major, DI 83, 114, 135
Flood, Const. Terence 160, 388
Fluke, S/Const. John 280, 388
Flynn, Sgt John 76, 94, 95, 388
Flynn, Patrick 38, 39
Foley, Const. 55
Foley, Const. Martin 142, 388
Foley, Const. Patrick 90, 388
Foley, Edmund 48
Foley, Edward 45
Foody, Const. Patrick 106, 247–250, 388
Foody, Ex-Sgt Anthony 335, 336
Forde, Const. H. F. 199
Foster, Const. Thomas W. 405
French, Cadet Leonard J. 399
French, Const. William 318–321, 388
French, Lord 80
French, S/Sgt Hugh 405
Friars, S/Const. David E. 405
Frizelle, Sgt Frederick 369, 388
Frongoch 25
Fuller, Const. 251

G

Gabbie, S/Const. Hugh 332, 388
Gaelic Athletic Association (GAA) 23, 26
Gaelic League 23, 27, 35

Gaffney, Const. William 406
Gallagher, Const. 346
Gallagher, Const. Francis 107, 169, 388
Gallagher, Head Const. 152, 153
Gallivan, Const. Thomas 399
Galvin, Const. Timothy Joseph 335, 388
Galvin, John 92
Galway City 359
   New Cemetery 307
   Railway Station 151
   St Brigid's Home 307, 359, 383
Galway County
   Ballinasloe 90, 141, 143, 171, 378
   Castledaly 176
   Clarenbridge 378
   Clifden 77, 266, 270
   Glenamaddy 154
   Gort 307
   Killimor 80
   Kilmilkin 285
   Kinvarra 171, 377
   Maam 278, 285
   Milltown 330
   Oranmore 142
   Oughterard 278, 285, 359
   Rosmuck 252
   Roundstone 110
   Spiddal 401
   Tuam 64, 130, 257, 309, 330
   Williamstown 64
Garniss, Cadet Frank 193, 194, 388
Garvey, Sgt Denis 95, 388
Gaughan, Const. John 151, 388
Gaynor, Seán 318
Gibbons, Sgt Tobias 359, 388
Gilleece, Const. Patrick 406
Gilligan, John 55
Gilmartin, Const. 240
Gilmartin, Sgt John 76, 359, 389
Gleave, Cadet James C. 197–204, 389
Gloster, ex-RIC Sergeant Arthur 377
Glover, Const. James 324, 389
G Men/Division 20, 52, 61, 65, 66, 83, 89, 170, 215

Godfrey, Edward 38
Gorbey, Const. Robert 76, 107, 178, 179, 389
Gordon, John 404
Gordon, S/Sgt William 271, 272, 389
Gorman, Jim 116, 118
Gorman, Const. Michael 147, 344–346, 389
Goulden, Sergeant 42
Gourlay, Const. William 147, 352, 389
Government of Ireland Act 180, 342–344, 349–351
Graham, S/Const. George 286, 389
Graham, Const. Orr 406
Graham, Cadet Philip Noel 197–205, 389
Graham, S/Const. William 406
Grant, Const. John 147, 266, 389
Green, Const. Samuel 244, 389
Greene, Sgt John 406
Greenfield, S/Const. Thomas 406
Greenwood, Sir Hamar 13, 186, 216, 219, 221–223
Greer, Sgt James (rtd) 378
Greer, Const. Martin John 256, 389
Greer, Const. Thomas (rtd) 378
Griffin, Constable 243
Griffiths, Cadet John L. 406
Grimsdale, Const. 94
Grove, Sgt Joseph 48, 49
Gunn, Ex-Sergeant John 377
Guthrie, Cadet Cecil J. 197, 199, 205, 389

H

Halford, Const. Patrick J. 208, 209, 389
Hall, S/Const. James 314, 389
Hall, Const. Philip 407
Hall, Capt. Reginald 25
Hall, S/Const. Thomas 363, 389

Hallissy, Sgt Michael 107, 274, 389
Hamilton, S/Const. Alexander 407
Hamilton, Sgt 93
Hampshire Regiment 204
Hanlon, D/Const. John 107, 141, 389
Hannon, Ex-Const. Thomas 331, 332
Harden, Const. Ernest F. 208, 209, 389
Hardie, Const. Arthur 407
Hardman, Const. Reginald 156–158, 389
Hargaden, Const. 175
Hargrove, Const. William 245
Harper, S/Const. James 361, 362, 389
Harrington, Const. Daniel 95, 389
Harrison, Const. Arthur 399
Harte, Const. Leonard 407
Harte, Const. Michael 156–158, 389
Hartney, Michael 97
Harvey, Const. John 367, 368, 389
Haugh, Const. Matthew 147, 389
Haverty, Const. Patrick 141, 389
Hayes, Const. 93
Hayes, Const. Patrick 303, 304, 389
Hayes, S/Const. Samuel 382, 383, 389
Hayton, Const. William 248–250, 389
Hayward, Const. Francis 407
Healy, Const. Charles 79, 80, 107, 389
Healy, Daniel 121
Heanue, Const. John Martin 77, 389
Hearty, Sgt Patrick 97, 98, 389
Heaslip, Const. William 107, 370, 389
Heffron, Const. Thomas 76, 107, 239, 240, 389
Hegarty, S/Const. Edward 369, 389
Hegerty, Const. Robert Henry 238, 239, 389
Heggert, DI 295
Henderson, Arthur 220
Henderson, Leo 129
Hennessy, Dr 47

Hennessy, Jack 202
Hennessy, Seamus 158
Hetherington, Const. James 282, 283, 389
Hewitt, Const. James R. 336, 389
Hickey, Constable 292
Hickey, Sgt Michael Joseph 268, 269, 389
Higgins, Sgt John 107, 277, 389
Higgins, Const. Thomas 332, 333, 389
Higginson, Brigadier General 217
Hill, Const. Francis 347, 390
Hill, Const. William E. 333, 334, 390
Hillyer, Const. Alfred 292, 293, 390
Hoare, Const. James 242
Hobson, Bulmer 27
Hodgsden, Const. Alfred C. 211–213, 390
Hodnett, Const. John 156, 158, 390
Hoey, Const. Daniel 256, 257, 390
Hoey, D/Const. Daniel 56, 57, 390
Hoey, Const. Owen 331, 390
Hogan, Michael 55
Hogan, Seán (John Joseph) 38, 42–47, 58, 78
Holland, Sgt Timothy 108, 109, 390
Holman, Const. Joseph C. 315, 390
Holmes, Divisional Commissioner Philip Armstrong 236, 240–243, 390
Home Rule 24, 27, 28, 349
Hooey, Const. Arthur 101
Hopkins, Const. Thomas 294, 390
Horan, Const. Michael 113, 390
Horan, Const. Timothy 176, 177, 390
Houghton, Cadet John A. 245–247, 390
Howlett, Const. George Horace 255, 256, 390
Hugh-Jones, Cadet Stanley 197–205, 390
Hughes, Const. John William 254, 255, 390

Hughes, Sgt. Joseph 107, 253, 254, 390
Hughes, Sgt William Joel 407
Hugo, Cadet Frederick 197–205, 390
Hume, S/Const. Thomas 407
Hunt, DI Michael 48–50, 107, 140, 390
Hunt, Cadet William Frederick 329, 390
Hunter, S/Const. Thomas J. 369, 390
Hurley, Charlie 94, 268
Hurley, Jim 260
Hyde, Douglas 27
Hynes, Sgt Michael J. 156, 158, 390

I

Igoe, Const. Eugene 97
Ikin, Const. Thomas F. 407
Irish Citizen Army 24
Irish Guards 90, 113, 133, 157, 161, 187, 229, 266, 316, 324, 363, 409
Irish Parliamentary Party 28
Irish Republican Brotherhood (IRB) 14, 22–29, 66
Irish Volunteers 23, 24, 26–31, 34–36, 41, 51, 56, 165, 221
Irvine, Const. 313

J

James, Henry 278
Jays, Const. Harry Clement 192, 390
Jeffers, Dan 119
Johnston, Const. Thomas R. 229, 390
Johnston, S/Const. George 407
Johnston, S/Const. William Robert 366, 390
Johnstone, Sgt Andrew 333, 390
Jolly, Const. Robert W. 322, 323, 390
Jones, Albert 131
Jones, Cadet Albert G. 198–205, 390
Jones, Const. George 407
Jones, Const. Wilfred 282, 390
Jones, Const. William 211, 390

K

Kane, James 236
Kane, CI John 236
Kane, Sgt Thomas 76, 98, 101, 102, 104, 390
Keane, Const. 177
Keane, Const. Timothy 407
Keany, DI Michael 107, 355, 390
Kearney, Const. John 307, 308, 390
Kearney, H/Const. John 191, 390
Kearns, Const. 257
Kearns, Const. Hugh 408
Keeffe, Const. John Thomas 160, 161, 390
Keighary, Sgt Thomas 408
Kelleher, DI Philip St John 177, 178, 390
Kells, D/Const. Henry 86, 390
Kelly, Const. Matthias 408
Kelly, Const. Michael 107, 156, 158, 390
Kelly, Det. Const. Patrick 96
Kelly, Patrick 64
Kelly, Const. Thomas 282, 283, 390
Kemp, Sgt John J. 232, 233, 391
Kenna, Const. John 301, 391
Kennedy, S/Constable 322
Kenny, Const. Michael (63217) 169, 170, 391
Kenny, Const. Michael (65275) 107, 276, 277, 391
Kenward, Const. Arthur Frederick 267, 268, 391
Kenyon, Const. Edmund 107, 308, 391
Keogh, Tom 170
Keough, Maurice 408
Keown, Const. Patrick 175, 176, 391
Kerr, Sergeant 367
Kerry County
   Abbeydorney 266, 378
   Annascaul 90, 91
   Ballybrack 188
   Ballybunion 255, 256, 346
   Ballyduff 78, 178
   Ballylongford 92, 255, 346, 410
   Ballymacelligott 59, 188, 281
   Ballyseedy 308
   Banna Strand 25
   Cahirciveen 191
   Castleisland 241, 242, 295
   Castlemaine 315, 316
   Cloghane 119
   Deelis 90
   Dingle 118, 119
   Farranfore 188, 377
   Gale Bridge 92
   Hillville 178
   Inchigeela 140, 199, 205
   Killarney 60, 259, 303, 352
   Killorglin 178, 315
   Listowel 92, 101, 122, 234–236, 241, 263, 346, 376
   Rathmore 114, 292, 324
   Toureengarriv 236, 240, 241
   Tralee 78, 93, 94, 119, 140, 188, 241, 242, 263, 281, 284, 303, 304, 308, 315, 316, 377, 398, 401
   Tubrid 263
   Tullacremin 266
   Waterville 85, 88
Kershaw, Const. Frank 147, 352, 391
Kidd, S/Const. George Victor 408
Kildare County
   Greenhills 141
   Maynooth 253
Kilkenny County
   Callan 210, 263
   Fiddown 327, 328
   Hugginstown 77
   Woodstock 399
Kilroy, Michael 271, 311, 320
King, Const. 149
King, Const. John 332, 333, 391
King, Const. Thomas 110, 391
King, Sgt James 338, 391
King's Own Scottish Borderers 121, 259
King's Royal Rifles 272

Kingston, Sgt James 76, 107, 293, 391
Kingston, Const. William 248, 250, 391
Kinsella, Constable 275
Kirby, Thomas 401, 402
Kirkpatrick, S/Const. Alexander 359, 360, 391
Kirwan, Sgt Stephen 283, 391
Kitterick, Tom 320
Krumm, Const. Edward 151, 152, 391

L

Lacey, Dinny 190, 286
Laffey, Const. Patrick 175, 176, 391
Laird, S/Const. Samuel 360, 391
Laois [Queen's] County
    Maryborough 95, 245
Larkin, Head Const. 238
Larking, Const. Sydney G. 187, 391
Lavin, Sgt Patrick 408
Lea-Wilson, DI Percival 111, 391
Leary, Const. Jeremiah 189, 391
Leech, Sgt William 371, 372, 391
Leggett, S/Const. William 406
Leitrim County
    Augharaso Cemetery 54
    Ballinamore 282, 410
    Drumsna 160
    Mohill 164
Lemass, Seán 195
Lendrum, Capt. 350
Lenihan, Const. Michael 118, 119, 391
Leonard, Denis A. 174, 175
Leonard, Const. Thomas 159, 160, 391
Leslie, Const. Edward L. 272, 273, 391
Lewis, S/Const. James 353, 354, 391
Limerick City 41, 99, 119, 128, 212, 230, 231, 237, 279, 288, 305, 405
    Edward Street 139
    Henry Street 131
    John Street 279
    Mallow Street 97
    Parkbridge 288
    Railway Hotel 110
    Union Hospital 41
Limerick County
    Abbeyfeale 153, 322
    Adare 119
    Ballylanders 47, 98
    Bruff 211, 212, 411
    Castleconnell 407
    Dromkeen 247, 248
    Drumcollogher 47, 304
    Fedamore 248, 249, 280, 281
    Foynes 119
    Galbally 45, 189
    Garryowen 356
    Hospital 334
    Kilmallock 47, 48, 98, 99, 102–104, 234, 235, 261, 334, 346
    Knocklong 43–45, 47, 50
    Mountmahon 153
    Newcastle West 47, 66, 89, 120
    Oola 132, 333
    Pallaskenry 78
    Rathkeale 78
Lincolnshire Regiment 401
Lloyd George, David 64, 80, 185, 216, 226, 349
Londonderry/Derry City 95, 183, 208, 287, 354
    Bishop Street 164
    Bridge Street 96
    Creggan Road 277
    Fountain Street 96
    Foyle Street 96, 408
    Lecky Road 276, 277
    Londonderry Gaol 344, 345
Londonderry County
    Ballyronan 369
    Bellaghy 367, 368
    Castlerock 413
    Maghera 353, 360
    Magherafelt 360, 367, 407
    Milltown 362
    Molenan 403

Swatragh 321
Upperlands 353, 359
London Regiment 208
Long, Walter 18, 19
Longford County
  Ballinalee 179, 208, 229, 230, 245, 246, 311
  Graigue 149
  Granard 177, 179, 230, 245, 404
  Killeter 311
  Lanesborough 120, 308, 314
  Longford town 245, 246, 273, 308, 311
  Rathcline 308
Longhead, Const. John 170, 171, 391
Looney, Head/Constable Jeremiah (rtd) 377
Lord, Const. Frederick H. 278, 279, 391
Lordan, John 201
Loughran, Patrick 174
Louth County
  Drogheda 367
  Dundalk 109, 142, 152, 153, 228, 327, 400
Luby, Thomas Clarke 22
Lucas, Cadet Ernest William H. 198, 202, 205, 391
Lucas, Sgt Samuel Wilfred 107, 172, 173, 175, 391
Lynch, Const. John P. (Jack) 252, 391
Lynch, Const. Patrick 175, 176, 391
Lynch, Seán 45, 46
Lynch, Sgt 53
Lyness, S/Const. George 323, 391
Lyttle, S/Const. William 345, 346, 391

M

MacBride, John 25
MacCarthy, J. 99
MacCarthy, Sgt Matt 67
MacCurtain, Tomás 80, 95, 143
Mac Diarmada, Seán 56
MacDonald, Const. John Cyril 107, 147, 282, 391
MacEoin, Seán 230, 245–247
MacGeagh, S/Const. Foster 409
Machine Gun Corps 194, 207, 323, 328
Macken, Const. 120
Mackessy, Const. Patrick 189, 190, 391
Mackinnon, Major John Alister 281, 391
MacNeill, Eoin 23–25, 27–29
MacPherson, Ian 80
Macready, Gen. Sir Nevil 185, 186, 216, 339
Madden, John 55
Madden, Patrick 272, 273
Madden, Const. William 178, 179, 391
Maguire, Sgt Charles 309
Maguire, Const. 270
Maguire, Sgt James 107, 261, 391
Maguire, Const. Joseph 107, 313, 391
Maguire, Sam 25
Maguire, Tom 290, 291
Maher, Sgt John 346, 391
Maher, Paddy 48
Mahoney, Warder 42
Mahony, Const. John 107, 153, 154, 392
Malone, Brodie 320
Malone, Const. Michael Francis 76, 147, 228, 229, 392
Malone, Thomas (aka Seán Forde) 98, 99
Maloney, Const. 113
Maloney, May 44
Malynn, Const. James Joseph 68, 392
Martin, S/Const. Herbert 371, 392
Martyn, Constable 88
Mason, DI Cyril Robert 409
Masterson, Const. James F. 120, 392

INDEX 441

Maunsell, Sgt Daniel 107, 140, 141, 392
Maxwell, Const. William M. 187, 392
Maynes, Const. 362
Mayo County
  Ballina 131, 336
  Ballinrobe 96, 290, 322
  Ballycastle 149, 240
  Ballyhaunis 274, 377
  Belmullet 11, 39, 112
  Carralavin 335, 336
  Carrowkennedy 318
  Castlerea 377
  Drummin 270
  Kilmeena 310, 311, 313
  Lefane 294
  Lower Shirdagh 311, 313
  Newport 271, 310, 313, 378
  Tourmakeady 265, 289, 290
  Westport 51, 270, 271, 310, 311, 319, 320, 359
May, Paddy 290, 291
McArdle, Sgt Peter J. 169, 392
McCann, Const. Patrick 409
McCarthy, Const. Daniel 85, 392
McCarthy, Jim 213
McCarthy, Const. Martin 150, 392
McCarthy, Sgt Matt 143
McCarthy, Const. Michael 90, 392
McCarthy, Michael 199, 202
McCaughey, DI Michael F. 315, 316, 392
McConnell, Sgt Edward 365, 392
McCoo, S/Con. Nathaniel 366, 392
McCorley, Roger 143, 144
McCormack, Const. John S. 315, 316, 392
McCormack, Patrick 38
McCormack, Sgt Thomas 292, 392
McDonagh, Const. Edward 256, 257, 392
McDonagh, Sgt Peter Joseph 107, 312, 392
McDonald, Const. Alex 400
McDonald, Patrick 409
McDonnell, Const. James 11, 37–39, 41, 392
McDonnell, Sgt Patrick 93, 107, 392
McDonnell, Const. Thomas 409
McDowell, S/Const. Robert 409
McEdward, Const. Lauchlin 356, 392
McElhill, H/Const. James 325, 392
McFadden, S/Const. Charles 352, 353, 392
McFadden, Sgt John 76, 107, 285, 392
McFarland, S/Const. William 353, 392
McFarland, Sgt John 49
McGirr, Const. Patrick 63
McGoldrick, Const. Patrick 11, 91, 392
McGrath, DI Thomas James 229, 230, 246, 392
McGuire, Sgt Denis P. 155, 392
McGuire, Const. John 156, 158, 392
McHenry, Har/Const. John 344, 345, 392
McInnes, S/Const. James 409
McIntosh, Const. John 262, 392
McKee, Dick 129, 195
McKenna, Sgt Francis 92, 93, 392
McKenna, Const. James 269, 392
McKenna, Const. Patrick 410
McKnight, S/Const. William T. 368, 392
McLean, Const. Hugh 306, 392
McLoughlin, John 400
McMahon, S/Const. Robert 353, 392
McNamara, Const. John 76, 107, 146, 392
McNeill, S/Const. Thomas 410
Mead, Const. Charles F. 308, 309, 392
Meaney, Sgt 187
Meardy, Sgt Joseph 49
Meath County
  Ballivor 57, 176
  Gormanston 84, 154, 155, 171, 244, 262, 312, 367, 404, 412

Navan 58, 408
Trim 57, 89, 240
Mee, Const. Jeremiah 122
Megarity, S/Const. John 372, 373, 392
Miller, Const. John 189, 190, 392
Milligan, S/Const. Samuel 369, 392
Millin, Const. Sidney 248, 250, 393
Milling, DI John Charles 51
Millings, Sub-Insp. 103
Mitchell, Cadet Lionel R. 400
Mitchell, S/Const. William 382, 393
Mollaghan, Const. Bernard 248, 250, 393
Moloney, Sgt 213
Monaghan County
   Ballybay 228
   Clones 272, 353, 354, 361, 411
   Newbliss 404
   Stranooden 238, 239
   Tullyvarragh 315
Monahan, Peter 268
Moore, Const. Albert 410
Moore, Const. Stanley L. 147, 276, 393
Moran, Const. Michael 236, 237, 393
Morgan, Const. George 178, 179, 393
Morgan, Const. Henry Patrick 410
Morgan, Sgt Martin 150, 393
Morley, Const. Edward George 410
Moroney, D/Sgt Denis 95, 96, 393
Moroney, Sgt Jeremiah 288, 393
Morris, Cadet Cecil A. 193, 194, 393
Morris, Const. Frank E. 236, 237, 393
Morris, Thomas (rtd) 377
Morton, Const. Joseph 76, 98, 101–104, 107, 393
Moscrop, Const. Harry G. 410
Moylan, Seán 241
Moyles, Const. Thomas 240–243, 393
Mugan, Const. Thomas 410
Muir, Const. William 410
Mulcahy, Richard 340
Mulhearn, Sgt 142
Mulherin, D/Sgt William 107, 132, 133, 393
Mulholland, Const. Edward J. 410
Mullan, Const. John 76, 107, 149, 393
Mullany, Const. Patrick 107, 244, 393
Mullen, Const. Martin 213, 214, 393
Mulloy, Sgt Michael 76, 107, 236, 237, 393
Mulrooney, H/Const. Edward 107, 274, 393
Mulvey, Const. James 411
Munnelly, Const. James 148, 149, 393
Munroe, DI 313
Murdock, Const. Charles 296, 400
Murphy, Const. Daniel Anthony 262, 263, 393
Murphy, Const. Edward 150, 393
Murphy, S/Const. James 370, 371, 393
Murphy, Michael 48
Murphy, Const. Michael James 54, 393
Murphy, Const. Patrick 48
Murphy, Const. Timothy 411
Murray, Const. James 133, 393
Murray, S/Const. James 411
Murray, Sgt 294, 393
Murren, Sgt James 330, 393
Murtagh, Const. Joseph 80, 393
Murtagh, Const. William James 411

N

Nathan, Const. Cyril Henry 139, 393
National Volunteers 28, 29
Neary, Const. 57
Neazer, Sgt George 78, 108, 393
Needham, Const. Alfred G. 338, 393
Neenan, Const. Michael 75, 76, 393
Neligan, David 83, 170, 195
Nineteenth Durham Light Infantry 264

Ninth Lancers 272, 273
Nixon, Const. James 411
Nixon, S/Sgt Samuel 271, 272, 393
Noonan, Const. Edward A. 160, 393
Norfolk Yeomanry 284
Northumberland Fusiliers 205
Nutley, Const. John 306, 393

O

Oakes, Const. Herbert 289–291, 394
Oakley, Const. Walter 131, 132, 394
O'Boyle, Const. 175
O'Brien, Art 66
O'Brien, Charlie 191
O'Brien, Const. Daniel 411
O'Brien, Éamon 45–47
O'Brien, Const. Henry 373, 393
O'Brien, Const. James 265, 393
O'Brien, John Joe 45, 46
O'Brien, Const. Martin 41–43, 393
O'Brien, Michael 290, 291
O'Brien, Paddy 252, 322, 326
O'Brien, William 191
O'Connell, John J. 121
O'Connell, Const. Patrick 11, 37–41, 393
O'Connor, Const. Patrick 357, 358, 393
O'Connor, Const. Patrick James 243, 394
O'Connor, Justin 191
O'Connor, Sgt Martin G. 169, 393
O'Donnell, Const. Hugh 172
O'Donoghue, Paddy 212
O'Donoghue, Séan 121
O'Donoghue, Tom 212
O'Driscoll, Daniel 244
O'Dwyer, Patrick 38, 39
Offaly [King's] County
  Ballyduff 331
  Birr 43, 55, 130, 309
  Clonbullogue 331, 410
  Edenderry 57, 338, 409
  Ferbane 155
  Kinnity 309
  Parkwood 171
  Tullamore 155, 177
official reprisals policy 64, 214, 217, 226, 227, 287
O'Hannigan, Donnchadh 99, 139, 249
O'Hara, Head Const. 161–163
O'Hegarty, Seán 122, 258
O'Keeffe, Brigid 43, 44
O'Leary, Const. Denis 323, 324, 394
O'Leary, Ex-Const. Timothy 378
O'Loughlin, Const. Denis 284, 394
O'Mahoney, Jim 91, 301
O'Mahony, Jeremiah 103
O'Mahony, John 22
O'Malley, Ernie 98, 116–118
O'Malley, Patrick 285
O'Meara, Seán 38
O'Neill, H/Const. Henry 174
O'Neill, Ignatius 157, 158
O'Neill, James 132
O'Neill, Stephen 201
O'Regan, Const. Christopher Patrick 108, 289–291, 394
O'Shaughnessy, Paddy 78
O'Shea, T. P. 92
O'Sullivan, Cornelius 121
O'Sullivan, Const. Dudley L. 357, 394
O'Sullivan, Jim 202
O'Sullivan, DI Philip John 209, 210, 394
O'Sullivan, Ted 110
O'Sullivan, DI Tobias 76, 108, 234–236, 241, 394
O'Sullivan, Sgt Tobias 101, 102

P

Pallester, Cadet William 198–205, 394
Palmer, Const. Albert H. 208, 209, 394

Pearce, Const. Arthur 248–250, 394
Pearse, Patrick H. 29
Pearson, Cadet Horace 198–205, 394
Pearson, Const. William H. 278, 394
Pearsons, Harold C. 136
Peek, Capt. Sir Wilfred 273
Peel, Robert 15
Perkins, Const. Walter P. 76, 315, 394
Perrier, Const. Frederick W. 108, 257, 258, 394
Perrott, H/Const. Samuel 411
Perry, Sgt Patrick 175, 176, 394
Phelan, Const. James 292, 293, 394
Phillips, S/Const. 360
Pilkington, William 176
Pimm, Const. Frederick 412
Plumb, S/Const. James Edward 364, 394
Plunkett, Joseph 24, 58
Poe, Lt Col Sir Hutcheson 50
Poland, Ex-Const. Patrick John 377
Poole, Const. Arthur F. 198–206, 394
Potter, DI Gilbert Norman 286, 287, 394
Potter, Head Const. 310
Potter, Mrs 286, 287
Potter, Const. William J. 149, 394
Power, Const. William 289–291, 394
Prendiville, Const. Maurice 207, 394
Pringle, Cadet Donald 412
Purcell, John 248

Q

Quille, Denis 255
Quinn, Const. Michael 76, 108, 239, 240, 394
Quinn, Const. Timothy J. 197, 394
Quirk, Const. John 315, 316, 394
Quirk, Const. Maurice 197, 394

R

Rabbett, Constable 92
Raisdale, Const. 109
Rea, Const. Isaac James 192, 394
Redding, Const. George 314, 394
Redman, Const. Sydney R. 268, 269, 394
Redmond, John 28
Redmond, Const. Robert 302, 394
Redmond, Ass. Com. William Charles Forbes 65–68, 215, 394
Regan, Const. 131
Regan, Sgt John 289–291, 394
Reid, Const. John 211–213, 394
Reidy, Const. 149
Reidy, Seán 78
Reilly, Const. 44, 46, 47
Reilly, Sgt 270
Reilly, Sgt Patrick 141, 270, 394
Rennie, Const. 267
Reynolds, Const. Charles O'M. 266, 394
Richmond, DI A. H. R 412
Rickerby, S/Const. Albert Thomas 372, 394
Riley, Const. Ernest J. 263, 394
Ring, Const. 44, 46
Riordan, Sgt John 54, 108, 394
Rippingale, Const. Bertie 171, 395
Robinson, Dr 65
Robinson, Séamus 37, 38, 43, 45, 47, 58
Roche, Sgt Daniel 170, 395
Roche, Const. George 118, 119, 395
Roche, James 78
Roche, Paddy 78
Roche, Const. Patrick [rtd] 236, 376
Rocke, Const. James 79, 80, 395
Rogers, Const. George Henry 280, 281, 395
Roper, Const. Edward G. 412
Roscommon County
    Ballaghaderreen 150, 169, 412
    Ballinderry 169
    Blackwood 270

Boyle 176, 188, 378
Castlerea 85, 142, 254, 338
Cootehall 256, 378
Frenchpark 150, 398, 399, 401
Kilrooskey 314
Knockcroghery 149, 160
Rathmacross 150
Scramogue 272
Rothwell, Const. 303
Roulston, S/Const. Andrew 374, 395
Round, Const. Harold 400
Royal Air Force (RAF) 137, 178, 204–206, 297, 399, 407
Royal Artillery 158, 307
Royal Berkshire Regiment 400
Royal Dublin Fusiliers 206, 265
Royal Engineers 121, 205, 245, 260, 275, 329
Royal Field Artillery 109, 128, 204, 247, 327
Royal Highlanders 319
Royal Inniskilling Fusiliers 300, 329, 350, 354
Royal Irish Fusiliers 208, 233, 242
Royal Irish Regiment 111, 178, 230, 242, 358
Royal Irish Rifles 68, 206, 237, 243, 323, 363, 371, 412
Royal Marines 132, 159, 310, 315, 334, 364
Royal Naval Reserve 210, 259, 356, 397
Royal Navy 83, 110, 210, 213, 243, 246, 258, 410
Royal Sussex Regiment 205, 247, 326
Royal Ulster Constabulary (RUC) 101, 342, 351, 363, 374, 376, 381, 415–417
Runane, Sgt 141
Rundle, Const. Albert 171, 395
Russell, DI 163
Russell, S/Const. John 412
Russell, S/Const. Thomas 382, 395
Ryan, John 43

Ryan, Michael 38
Ryan, Const. Thomas 77, 78, 395
Ryle, Const. John 303, 395

S

Sampson, DI 249
Satchwell, Const. Thomas 108, 254, 395
Scanlon, Ex-Const. 378
Scanlon, Jim 45, 47
Scully, Liam 101, 103, 235
Scully, Const. Timothy 79, 395
Seafield-Grant, Comdt James 258, 259, 395
Selve, Const. 237
Seventh Lancers 307
Shanahan, Michael 47
Shanahan, Thomas 44–46
Shanley, Const. Thomas 330, 395
Shannon, Const. Peter 76, 210, 395
Shannon, Sgt Thomas 211
Shateford, Const. E. 208
Shaw, Const. Walter 289, 395
Shaw Kennedy, Col 15
Shea, Sgt Ambrose 275, 276, 395
Shelsher, Const. Joseph 77, 333, 395
Sheridan, S/Const. Thomas 236, 237, 381, 382, 395
Shevlin, Const. Thomas 412
Shortall, Const. Francis 229, 395
Shorter, Cadet Frederick E. 326, 327, 395
Shropshire Regiment 205
Sinn Féin 14, 19, 20, 34, 35, 49, 52, 56, 63, 64, 81, 87, 90, 97, 107, 122, 123, 126–128, 134, 144, 155, 165, 166, 169, 174, 176, 182, 186, 215, 217–219, 222, 224, 226, 227, 301, 306, 314, 341, 351, 398, 413
Sixth Cavalry Division 265
Skeats, Const. Albert Edward 300, 395
Slattery, Jim 170

Sligo County
  Ballisodare 282, 283
  Ballymote 162, 187, 188, 240, 265, 379
  Chaffpool 161, 220
  Cliffoney 173, 176, 330
  Dromore 332
  Moneygold 175, 176
  Tubbercurry 142, 161–163
Smith, Const. Albert W. 412
Smith, Const. Arthur 208, 209, 395
Smith, Col Barton 206
Smith, Const. Henry 248–250, 395
Smith, Const. John Frederick 325, 326, 395
Smith, Pte 328
Smith, Insp. Gen. T. J. 73, 74, 80, 104, 106, 135, 167, 168
Smith, Const. William Albert 288, 289, 395
Smith, Const. William J. 238, 395
Smyth, Const. Frederick Gordon 412
Smyth, Major George Osbert Stirling DSO MC 128, 129
Smyth, Lt Col Gerald Brice Ferguson, DSO 120–122, 124, 125, 127, 128, 241, 395
Smyth, D/Sgt Patrick 51–53, 395
Smyth, Sgt Patrick 412
Soady, Cadet Clevel L. 258, 259, 395
Somers, Const. Nicholas 261, 395
Southgate, Const. George 412
Spencer, Const. 89
Spillane, Const. 42
Spindler, Capt. Karl 25
Squad, the 33, 34, 52, 53, 56, 58, 65, 67, 68, 86, 129, 170, 192, 195, 215
Stack, Michael 'Batty' 42
Stagg, Frank 290
Stanley, Const. William 164, 395
Stapleton, Jim 50, 140
Steadman, Const. William 283, 284, 395

Stephens, James 22
Stephens, Const. William H. 274, 395
Sterland, Const. Frederick 147, 295, 296, 395
Stevenson, DI Edward James 318–321, 395
Stewart, S/Const. Hector 355, 395
Stewart, Const. William 311, 312, 395
Stiff, Const. Harold 413
Stockdale, Const. George E. A 413
Stokes, Sgt John 116, 117, 395
Storey, H/Const. William K. 108, 295, 395
Strickland, Major-Gen. E. P. 301
Sturdy, S/Const. Thomas 325, 395
Sugenor, S/Const. David 413
Sullivan, Thomas 292
Swanzy, DI Oswald Ross 81, 143–146, 263, 332, 396
Sweatman, Sgt 328
Sweeney, Const. Terrence G. 413
Sweeney, Const. Thomas 266, 396

T

Taplye, Ex-Const. 378
Tasker, Const. Thomas (Frederick Samuel) 413
Taylor, Cadet Frank 198, 206, 396
Taylor, Const. Frederick (74612) 108, 208, 396
Taylor, Const. Frederick (75307) 238, 239, 396
Taylor, Const. William H. 251, 396
Teeling, Frank 194
Thirteenth Hussars 305
Thompson, Sir Basil 66, 215
Thompson, Const. Harold 302, 396
Thornton, Frank 67, 194, 195
Thorp, Const. Arthur 213, 214, 396
Tierney, Const. 42
Timoney, Const. 346

Tipperary County
  Ballinure 113
  Ballyquirk 55
  Ballywilliam 252, 253
  Bansha 189, 306, 333
  Bouladuff 77, 336
  Cappawhite 233, 293
  Carrigahorig 54, 55
  Cashel 113, 261
  Clogheen 286
  Clonmel 287, 378
  Cloughjordan 187, 317, 318
  Coolboreen 304, 305
  Drumbane 40
  Dualla 113
  Dundrum 39, 40, 357
  Emly 44, 45, 100
  Glenbower 210
  Goold's Cross 93
  Inches Cross 189
  Kilcommon 208, 209
  Killoskehan 160
  Kylebeg Cross 317
  Lackamore Wood 85
  Limerick Junction 37, 100, 132
  Lorrha 54, 55
  Moyne 410
  Mullinahone 269
  Nenagh 79, 252, 253, 398, 399
  Newport 85, 304, 305
  Newtown 293
  Rearcross 85, 116–118
  Rosegreen 40
  Rossmore 401
  Soloheadbeg 11, 36–43, 62, 130, 287, 383
  Templemore 139, 140, 160, 332, 365
  Thurles 43–45, 48, 63, 64, 77, 103, 140, 209, 346
  Tipperary town 37, 39, 40, 190, 356, 357
  Toomevara 79
  Upper Church 81
Tobin, Liam 111, 194
Tobin, Sgt Robert 113, 396
Torrens, S/Const. David 413

Traynor, Tom 264, 287
Treacy, Seán 11, 35, 37, 38, 41, 43–48, 58, 118, 128–130, 170
Truce 14, 48, 83, 235, 264, 301, 338–342, 345, 347, 348, 381, 383, 397
Tudor, Maj.-Gen. H. H. 102, 121, 129, 134, 136, 185, 225, 226, 344
Turner, Const. Archibald 188, 189, 396
Turner, Const. George 363, 396
Tyrone County
  Carrickmore 406
  Castlecaulfield 369
  Clady 352, 353
  Cookstown 173–175, 368
  Dromore 93, 294
  Drumquin 148
  Dungannon 174
  Gortin 403
  Mountfield 113, 312
  Trillick 140, 350, 360, 361

U

Ulster Special Constabulary 14, 145, 179–187, 215, 232, 251, 271, 272, 280, 286, 312, 314, 322, 323, 325, 332, 337, 343, 345–347, 351, 353–355, 359–366, 368–372, 374, 381–383, 403–416
Ulster Volunteer Force (UVF) 27, 183, 186, 233

V

Van Best, Const. 228
Vanston, Const. William 245, 396
Vaughan, Johnny 249
Vaughan, Peter 158
Vize, Joe 129
Vokes, S/Const. Charles 413

W

Wadkins, Const. Samuel H. 292, 293, 396

Wainwright, Cadet Christopher 198–206, 396
Wallace, Sgt Peter 43–48, 396
Walls, Const. Ernest Guy 413
Walsh, Deputy Inspector General C. A. 220, 224, 226, 376
Walsh, J. J. 90
Walsh, Const. John 77, 396
Walsh, John 92
Walsh, Const. Patrick Joseph 252, 396
Walsh, Patrick 92
Walsh, Sgt Thomas 210, 211, 396
Walsh, Const. Thomas Joseph 401
Walsh, Const. William 49, 317, 396
Walshe, ex-RIC Sgt 378
Wames, Cadet George Gerald 328, 329, 396
Warning, Const. 362
Waterford County
  Cappoquin 192, 197, 260
  Carrigbeg 323
  Dungarvan 268, 269, 405
  Kilmacthomas 150
  Scartacrooks 260
  Tallow 334
  Waterford City 93, 150, 268
Waters, Const. Patrick 401
Watkins, Const. Ernest S. 138, 396
Webb, Const. John F. 288, 289, 396
Webster, Cadet Benjamin D. 198–206, 396
Westmeath County
  Athlone 142, 143, 149, 158, 187
  Auburn Glasson 187
  Ballynacargy 294
  Kilbeggan 172, 325
West Yorkshire Regiment 205, 230
Wexford County
  Enniscorthy 111, 284
  Galbally 77
  Gorey 111, 294
  Inch 294
  New Ross 412
  Newtownbarry 211
  Wexford Town 409
Wheatly, Const. Terence Patrick 152, 153, 396
White, Capt. 128
Wickham, Lt Col Sir Charles George 182, 183
Wicklow County
  Baltinglass 68
  Rathdrum 336, 337, 412
  Wicklow Town 334
Wiggins, Const. Hubert J. 279, 396
Wilkinson, Col 212
Will, Const. Alexander 77, 108, 114, 396
Wilmott, Const. 171
Wilson, DI William Harding 108, 139, 140, 261, 301, 396
Winter, Sir Ormonde de l'Épée 129, 216
Witherden, Const. 142
Woodcock, Const. Hedley D. 292, 293, 396
Woods, Const. James Thomas 108, 188, 189, 396
Woodward, Const. George 280, 396
Worth, Corp. 128
Wylie, Mr 185
Wymes, Const. John (rtd) 377

Y

Yorkshire Regiment 205
Young, S/Const. Samuel 382, 396